A CITY IN TURMOIL

Dublin 1919–21

The Author

Pádraig Yeates is a journalist, publicist and trade union activist. He is a distinguished social and labour historian and the author of *Lockout*, the standard work on the great 1913 labour dispute. He is also author of the acclaimed *A City in Wartime: Dublin 1914–18* and *A City in Civil War: Dublin 1921–4*.

Praise for Pádraig Yeates' 'Dublin at War' trilogy

'A powerful social history … reminds us that for all the headline grabbing events, putting bread on the table was still the most important priority for most'
Professor Diarmaid Ferriter, *The Irish Independent*

'Reminds the reader of how daily life went on side by side with the great events of history. In short, this is an excellent addition to the current literature'
Irish Literary Supplement

'Pádraig Yeates excels as a social historian and never loses sight of the ordinary citizen'
The Irish Times

'Absorbing and beautifully written'
Catriona Crowe, *The Irish Times*

'A fascinating study of the shifting political forces shaping Dublin'
Dermot Bolger

'Fascinating'
The Irish Times

Praise for *Lockout: Dublin 1913*, also by Pádraig Yeates

'Essential reading for anyone interested in Irish labour, the history of industrial relations and Dublin society in the early twentieth century'
The Irish Times

'A concentrated, authentic and definitive account of an event that had a major influence on the political, economic and social life of this country'
The Irish Independent

A CITY IN TURMOIL

Dublin 1919–21

PÁDRAIG YEATES

Gill & Macmillan

Gill & Macmillan
Hume Avenue, Park West, Dublin 12
www.gillmacmillanbooks.ie

© Pádraig Yeates 2012, 2015
978 07171 6727 2
First published in hard cover 2012
First published in this format 2015

Index compiled by Róisín Nic Cóil
Typography design by Make Communication
Print origination by Síofra Murphy
Printed and bound by CPI Group (UK) Ltd, CR0 4YY

The paper used in this book comes from the wood pulp of
managed forests. For every tree felled, at least one tree is
planted, thereby renewing natural resources.

A CIP catalogue record for this book is available from the
British Library.

5 4 3 2 1

For Simon and all young Dubliners, in the hope of better days

CONTENTS

ACKNOWLEDGMENTS

Like *A City in Wartime: Dublin, 1914–1918*, this book grew out of one written over a decade ago called *Lockout: Dublin, 1913*. It picks up the story from the end of the First World War to the Truce in July 1921. Aspects of this story have been told many times, particularly the military activities and the intelligence war, but no attempt has been made to tell the history of the city and its citizens as a whole. This is my attempt to do so. The military aspects of the story are not ignored, nor can they be, as some of the consequences, such as the imposition of the curfew and the munitions strike, affected every Dubliner. As in the period from 1914 to 1918, a revolutionary elite, now working with a popular mandate, set the agenda. Dublin was not, of course, Ireland: in fact it was very different from the rest of the island, but it remained a vital theatre of political and military struggle, which is why its story must be told and hopefully will receive the attention it deserves in the decade of centenaries now upon us.

This is not a centenary book, but it is written in the hope of influencing how the revolutionary decade is understood and remembered. I cannot claim that it is comprehensive: many aspects of life in the city are covered sparsely or not at all; but it does try to avoid adopting any one vision of the past or, worse still, blandly accepting all of them. That said, I owe my own preconceptions of events during those years in large part to the recollections of my parents and others who lived through them.

Many people assisted me during my research. I wish to make special mention of the Dublin Civic Archives—a wonderful resource for everyone interested in Dublin and its past. Mary Clark, Máire Kennedy and their colleagues facilitated my requests with unfailing courtesy. I also wish to thank the staff of the National Archives and Caitríona Crowe, who has helped revolutionise access to public records; to Commandant Victor Lang and his colleagues at the Bureau of Military History; Brendan Byrne and the Irish Labour History Society; Dan Loughrey and Michael O'Farrell for access to Bank of Ireland records; Jack McGinley of SIPTU and the staff of the Berkeley Library, Trinity College, Dublin; Gerry Kavanagh, Keith Murphy and their colleagues at the National Library of Ireland and the National Photographic Archives; Noelle Dowling of the Dublin Diocesan Archive; Seamus Helferty and his colleagues at the UCD Archives;

Éamon Devoy of the Technical, Engineering and Electrical Union for access to early records of the Irish Engineering, Shipbuilding and Foundry Trades Union; Miriam Moffitt for her assistance and advice regarding loyalist claims for compensation and the staff of the Public Records Office, Kew; Bill McCamley, Seán Redmond and Paddy Weston for information on their families in the War of Independence; Noel Gregory and Terry Fagan for information on the north inner city; Joe Mooney for East Wall; Ruth McManus, Theresa Moriarty, Eve Morrison, Ed Penrose, Ann Matthews, Margaret Ó hÓgartaigh and Tom Morrissey sj for their insights into the era; and Eunan O'Halpin for running his marathon series of seminars at TCD on contemporary Irish history, far too few of which I managed to attend. Special thanks to Diarmaid Ferriter for his very kind review of *A City in Wartime* in the *Irish Independent*, which encouraged me to write a sequel. I hope he and other readers will not be too disappointed with the result. Oonagh Walsh's ground-breaking *Anglican Women in Dublin* was also most helpful and provided useful pointers for the next book. Special thanks are due to Peter Rigney for not alone providing access to the files of the Irish Railway Records Society but reading the proofs of this book, and to Valerie Jones and the Vestry Committee of St Ann's Church in Dawson Street, Dublin, for access to its magnificent collection of stained-glass windows. Special thanks also to Paddy Moran's niece for supplying additional material on her uncle and for correcting errors in the hardback edition of this book. At Gill & Macmillan I wish to thank my editor, Séamas Ó Brógáin, for his meticulous work and background knowledge of the period, Deirdre Rennison Kunz for managing the manuscript through the production process, Jen Patton for obtaining pictures, Don O'Connor for another magnificent cover, Teresa Daly for spreading the word and Fergal Tobin for staying with the project. Finally, I have to thank Eddie Barrett for making his home mine in London, my son Simon for his support and Geraldine Regan for her encouragement over many years. As far as possible I have tried to recruit my prejudices and predilections constructively to the task of writing this and all my books.

ABBREVIATIONS

ASE	Amalgamated Society of Engineers
ASU	active-service unit
DMP	Dublin Metropolitan Police
DUTC	Dublin United Tramways Company
GHQ	General Headquarters
GSWR	Great Southern and Western Railway
IBOA	Irish Bank Officials' Association
IESFTU	Irish Engineering, Shipbuilding and Foundry Trades Union
IRB	Irish Republican Brotherhood
ITGWU	Irish Transport and General Workers' Union
ITUC&LP	Irish Trades Union Congress and Labour Party
LGB	Local Government Board
MRA	Municipal Reform Association
NEC	National Executive Committee
OC	officer commanding
PR	proportional representation
PUS	Public Utility Society
RAMC	Royal Army Medical Corps
RIC	Royal Irish Constabulary
TUC	[British] Trades Union Congress
VAD	Voluntary Aid Detachments

A note on money
The pound (£) was divided into twenty shillings (s) and the shilling into twelve pence (d). Intermediate amounts were written in a combination of denominations, e.g. £2 10s; 3s 6d. Some relatively small amounts in pounds might be written entirely in shillings, e.g. 42s (£2 2s).

Chapter 1 ～

A VICTORY BALL, 'A REGULAR LITTLE ARSENAL' AND A MIDNIGHT VISIT TO DETECTIVE HEADQUARTERS

A Victory Ball at Dublin Castle ushered in the new year for 1919 with a fanfare by the trumpeters of King Edward's Horse Regiment. 'Such a scene has not been enjoyed since 1914,' the *Weekly Irish Times* enthused. Nearly 1,200 guests attended the subscription dance for the British Red Cross, which was presided over by Isabelle Shortt, wife of the Chief Secretary for Ireland. While the main event was held in St Patrick's Hall, 'the more discriminating dancers' preferred the less crowded facilities of the Throne Room or the billiard room of the Red Cross hospital, which still occupied most of the State Apartments. Patients had decorated the rooms for the guests, and eight soldiers recovering from their wounds watched 'some distance away from the joys they were unable to share.'

Among the social luminaries to survive the trauma of the war years was the perennial Lady Fingall, who organised the 'state lancers' quadrilles for the older set. For the younger set there were foxtrots and the popular one-step and two-step tunes that occupied most of the programme, as well as numerous waltzes. After the singing of 'Auld Lang Syne' to the accompaniment of the combined military bands there was 'spirited cheering' and 'the taking of many flashlight photographs,' which 'set everyone laughing and chattering on their way to supper.' Subsequently the dancing was renewed 'with fresh vigour' and continued into the early hours.

The *Irish Times* paid its usual attention to the gowns of the ladies. Most of the women, such as Lady Emily Campbell, wife of the Lord Chancellor and former unionist MP for Dublin University (essentially Trinity College), wore black in memory of close relatives killed in the war. An exception was Mrs Shortt, 'to whose executive ability the success of the ball was largely due.' She wore 'a gown of mauve crepe de chine,' although she had lost her only son in the defence of the British Empire. One of many constant reminders of the toll exacted from ascendancy families was the seemingly endless 'Roll of Honour' column in the *Irish Times* each morning, listing those who had died of their wounds or who had been listed as missing in action and were now confirmed dead.

The other notable difference between the Victory Ball and similar social functions from the pre-war years was that there was no longer any flamboyant display of Irish fashions. If Irish gowns and accessories were worn at all, they were not flaunted.[1]

In the dark, wintry Dublin of January 1919 there was not even the pretence of a shared future or identity of interest between the celebrants in Dublin Castle and the hostile citizens outside, who, a fortnight earlier, had voted overwhelmingly for Sinn Féin and independence. Two days after the Victory Ball, Dublin Corporation (as the city council was then called) held a special meeting requisitioned by fifty-eight members to offer the honorary freedom of the city to the president of the United States, Woodrow Wilson. They called on him 'to use your mighty influence in urging the Peace Congress to give a just judgement of Ireland's cause and to arrive at a just settlement of her claim.'

The following Sunday there were rallies in Dublin and Kingstown (Dún Laoghaire) and throughout the country to protest against the continued detention of almost two-thirds of the new Sinn Féin MPs in various Irish and British prisons. In Dublin's own Mountjoy Prison, Sinn Féin and Irish Volunteer prisoners embarked on a hunger strike over being kept in the same appalling conditions as 'ordinary criminals'.

On 2 January 1919 Dublin Corporation met to strike the rate (local property tax) for the new year; but the debate consisted primarily of attacks on the composition of the government's new advisory committee for rebuilding the Irish economy. The councillors argued, with some justification, that the committee was dominated by members of the Kildare Street Club and leading lights of the unionist establishment, such as the Marquis of Londonderry, the Earl of Granard, Lord Dunraven, Sir Henry Robinson (vice-president of the Local Government Board) and Eddie Saunderson, son of a former leader of the Unionist Party, now private secretary to the Lord Lieutenant, Field-Marshal Sir John French.

The proposed rate was a record 18s in the pound, to meet the soaring costs of running the city. War inflation still drove the economy, with wages chasing prices. The earnings of white-collar workers had increased between July 1914 and January 1919 by 60 per cent, those of skilled workers by between 120 and 140 per cent and those of labourers by as much as 210 per cent. Unfortunately, retail prices had risen by 240 per cent. The corporation had no control over prices, and the business community felt strongly that further pay demands by city employees should be firmly resisted, including a novel claim for a shorter working week without any cut in wages.

When traditional champions of the business community, such as Alderman David Quaid and the Sheriff, John McAvin, protested that the corporation 'was going from bad to worse' they were told by nationalist colleagues that 'it was better to give the workers money for services rendered than endure a strike that would deprive the city of power and light.' The increase was provisionally agreed, by 33 votes to 10.

The threat to power supplies did not arise only from industrial militancy. For the first quarter of 1919 Dublin Corporation often had less than two weeks' reserves of coal. The January sales suffered from shops having to close early to conserve fuel and observe government restrictions on indoor lighting. The illusion that peacetime plenty was returning helped boost seasonal sales but was belied by shorter opening hours. Fanciful sketches of attractive women on the front pages of the newspapers, displaying fur coats with generous discounts of 25 per cent, could not hide the fact that the furs themselves were of seal and moleskin. On the other hand, in a salute to better times ahead, flexible corsets previously advertised as 'suitable for war work' were now promoted as 'suitable for dancing.'

On Tuesday 6 January thirty Sinn Féin MPs still at liberty met under the chairmanship of George Noble Plunkett (generally referred to as Count Plunkett after being made a Papal count in 1877), father of the executed 1916 leader Joseph Plunkett, in the Mansion House, Dublin, to demand the release of their colleagues. They agreed in principle to convene Dáil Éireann, the first national assembly in almost 120 years, and to invite all elected representatives of the Irish people to attend.

That evening there was a debate in the Abbey Theatre on the issue of 'Irish Federalism versus an Irish Republic' between Captain Stephen Gwynn, former Irish Party MP for Galway, and P. S. O'Hegarty, a leading propagandist of advanced nationalism and member of the Irish Republican Brotherhood.

Hopes were high that a still-embattled empire would have to concede independence quickly. Dublin Corporation's quandary over how to contain wage demands without provoking a strike was as nothing compared with the dilemmas facing the British government. That same week more than seven thousand soldiers left their camp in Shoreham, Kent, and marched to Brighton to protest at delays in demobilisation, and members of the Army Service Corps drove lorries up and down Whitehall in London to demand a speedy return to civilian life. Further protests followed on Tuesday in London, Aldershot and Bristol.

The government and military authorities held firm, not least because the armistice of 11 November 1918 would run out within the month if permanent peace terms could not be reached. The only consolation was that British soldiers were driving more or less peacefully through the capital rather than trading political differences with machine-gun bullets, as was now a regular occurrence in Berlin.[2]

Irish separatists taking comfort from Britain's difficulties failed to realise that the urgent need to address serious unrest on its doorstep meant that the government in London had little time to attend to their problems.

A Cabinet reshuffle the following week saw yet another Liberal home-rule lawyer, Ian Macpherson, replace Edward Shortt as Chief Secretary for Ireland, while Field-Marshal Lord French remained ensconced in the Viceregal Lodge. But the most fateful event of the month came on 21 January, when Dáil Éireann, or the 'Sinn Fein National Assembly', as the *Irish Times* preferred to call it, convened in the Mansion House. The Irish Volunteers provided stewards for controlling access to the event, admission to which was by ticket only. Well before the doors opened at 3 p.m. the queue stretched down Dawson Street and around the corner into Molesworth Street. The presence of large numbers of young Catholic priests was noted by the Chief Commissioner of the Dublin Metropolitan Police, Lieutenant-Colonel Sir Walter Edgeworth Johnstone, and the Inspector-General of the Royal Irish Constabulary, Sir James Byrne. Unlike the estimated hundred journalists admitted to record the proceedings, the police officials had to settle for watching the crowd discreetly from an upstairs window of the Royal Irish Automobile Club across the street.

As Sinn Féin activists waited patiently to enter the Mansion House they were treated to the spectacle of nearly four hundred members of the Royal Dublin Fusiliers marching behind the band of the Royal Hibernian Military School to attend a concert at the Theatre Royal in Hawkins Street. The men had just finished a welcome-home dinner in the Pillar Room, organised by the regiment's Prisoners of War Committee. The committee had shrunk over the years into an appendage of the Dublin Women's Unionist Club, out of whose premises it operated, but it made up in commitment for its dwindling numbers.

The dining tables had been draped in the Allied colours, and cigarettes were supplied by courtesy of Sir James Gallagher, the tobacco magnate and former Lord Mayor of Dublin. The Countess of Mayo, Lady Arnott and Mrs Gaisford St Lawrence, who had carried the burden of fund-raising in the war years, were among the dignitaries present. The soldiers, some of whom had spent more than four years in captivity, as their 1914 Mons badges testified, marched down Dawson Street past a bemused crowd of Sinn Féin supporters on one side and welcoming family and friends on the other. The contrast was so bizarre that 'the situation became humorous rather than serious,' as one newspaper reported. A city trader broke the ice when he declared: 'No city in Europe can beat Dublin after all.' Some harmless banter followed as the soldiers reached the safer environs of Grafton Street, ablaze with bunting; but no reporter appears to have asked the men themselves what they thought of their city, changed as it was since the heady days of their send-off.

At the Theatre Royal the former prisoners of war were joined by four hundred wounded soldiers from Dublin's hospitals and nursing homes to enjoy the entertainment. Father Crotty, who had been Catholic chaplain to the Limburg and Giessen prisoner-of-war camps, asked the men to lead the good lives they had promised to live when they returned home. 'I know that you have been what Irishmen and Irish Catholics should be: proud of and true to your faith and your country.'[3]

But a few streets away, the Sinn Féin MPs gathering in the Mansion House just vacated by the Fusiliers were redefining what being true to their country meant. That the business was mainly conducted in Irish did not add to its clarity or inclusiveness. The minority of thirty Sinn Féin MPs at liberty[4] adopted a Declaration of Independence that gave democratic ratification to the establishment of the Irish Republic, proclaimed in arms in the same city on 24 April 1916. They issued an Appeal to the Free Nations of the World to recognise Ireland's right to choose its own form of government and adopted a Provisional Constitution and a Democratic Programme.

The idea of the Democratic Programme, outlining the social and economic aspirations of the infant republic, had first been mooted by the Dublin Trades Council. The invitation to draft it came from the Sinn Féin leadership, in recognition of Labour's decision not to contest the general election. This helped ensure a Sinn Féin victory in at least three Dublin constituencies,[5] which Irish Party or unionist candidates might otherwise have won. The main author of the programme was Thomas Johnson, secretary of the Labour Party, assisted by William O'Brien, president of the Irish Trades Union Congress, and Cathal O'Shannon of the Irish Transport and General Workers' Union. It was amended by Seán T. Ó Ceallaigh, one of the new MPs who had served for many years on Dublin Corporation as a Sinn Féin councillor alongside Labour colleagues. He did so to meet objections from Michael Collins and other senior IRB men, who wanted the removal of explicit affirmations of socialist principles. Despite his concerns, Collins did not bother attending the discussions with the Labour men, leaving it to Harry Boland and Ó Ceallaigh to dilute the programme's social radicalism. The IRB most objected to such clauses as the right of the country 'to resume possession' of the nation's wealth 'whenever the trust is abused or the trustee fails to give faithful service.' Another excision was the clause encouraging 'the organisation of people into trade unions and co-operative societies.' Worst of all was the last clause of the Labour draft, effectually calling for the abolition of capitalism:

> Finally, the Republic will aim at the elimination of the class in society which lives upon the wealth produced by the workers of the nation but gives no useful service in return, and in the process of accomplishment will give freedom to all who have hitherto been caught in the toils of economic servitude.[6]

Nevertheless, the final draft reasserted the claim in the 1916 Proclamation that national sovereignty 'extends not only to all men and women of the Nation, but to all its material possessions, the Nation's soil and all its resources, all the wealth and all the wealth-producing processes within the Nation.' It further reaffirmed 'that all right to private property must be subordinated to the public right and welfare.'

'In return for willing service' every citizen had the right to 'an adequate share of the produce of the Nation's labour.' Furthermore:

> It shall be the first duty of the Government of the Republic to make provision for the physical, mental and spiritual well-being of the children, to secure that no child shall suffer hunger or cold from lack of food, clothing or shelter, but that all shall be provided with the means and facilities requisite for their proper education and training as Citizens of a Free and Gaelic Ireland.

For many on the left the programme, read into the Dáil record by the man known as 'the Alderman', Tom Kelly MP, was a promissory note that the Republic would see working people come into their own.[7]

Some elements of the Democratic Programme were still considered too 'communistic' by senior figures in Sinn Féin, such as Piaras Béaslaí and

Kevin O'Higgins. Yet Collins and Cosgrave, who had been among those most insistent on changes, were not averse to state involvement in the economy *per se*. Collins was a firm advocate of developing Ireland's natural resources and its manufacturing base by whatever means necessary, while Cosgrave advocated a state monopoly in the insurance industry. There was widespread acceptance of the co-operative ideal for promoting such enterprises as banking, farming, fisheries, and retailing. Éamon de Valera would espouse it during his forthcoming trip to America, and Arthur Griffith would write a pamphlet commissioned by the new Dáil cabinet extolling co-operatives.

General economic thinking was somewhat woolly. Collins, for instance, argued that county councils 'and other Public Bodies' should take over the exploitation of valuable mineral deposits, while the Department of Local Government should take the initiative in ensuring that 'in any negotiations with firms Labour should be consulted, as they [Dáil Éireann] could not support any firm which "sweated" its employees.' These initiatives contained within them the seeds of the future statist approach of successive Irish governments to economic and social development.[8]

The dilution of the Democratic Programme failed to impress the leader-writer of the *Irish Times*, who condemned the 'astonishing vagueness' with which it permitted the Dáil 'to be associated with any one of a hundred brands of modern Socialism, or with them all.' The writer drew attention to the fact that, a few hours before the Sinn Féin MPs invoked 'God's blessing' on their labours,

> two Irish policemen were murdered foully in the fulfilment of their duty ... It should compel the nominal leaders of the Republican Party to ask themselves a serious question. Can they control the developments of the movement which they profess to guide—a movement that is based on hatred of constituted authority in Ireland? ...
>
> There are two sets of Republicans in Ireland today. One set filled the public eye on Tuesday with its theatrical protests against British rule. It consists of a body of idealists who nurture themselves quite honestly on visions of an independent, but peaceful and pious Ireland. The other set has a very different ideal—the ideal which has submerged unhappy Russia in shame and ruin.[9]

It was a valid point. Earlier that Tuesday morning a group of Volunteers had ambushed and killed Constable James McDonnell and Constable Patrick O'Connell as they escorted a consignment of gelignite from the military magazine in Tipperary to Solloghodbeg quarry. They were certainly not acting on the orders of Dáil Éireann, which would not convene for several more hours. The Chief of Staff of their own organisation, Richard Mulcahy, condemned the Solloghodbeg killings; but Collins—the man who felt the Democratic Programme was too extreme—was already in touch with the perpetrators, including their ringleader, Seán Treacy, a senior IRB man. Treacy was a regular visitor to Dublin, with his boon companion Dan Breen. By July 1919 these Volunteers, in collaboration with members of the Dublin Brigade and acting under Collins's orders, would be shooting policemen on the streets of Dublin.

Meanwhile the New Ireland Assurance Society anticipated a different aspect of the struggle for independence, nor did its directors wait for Dáil Éireann to convene before claiming its endorsement for their products. Their prescience was understandable, given that all were close associates of Collins, soon to be the Republic's new Minister for Finance. The directors included the newly elected Sinn Féin MPs and senior Volunteer officers Michael Staines and Éamonn Duggan. Staines, who would be chairman and treasurer of the company, was Quartermaster-General of the Irish Volunteers; Duggan, a solicitor, was Director of Intelligence. The other company director was Liam Tobin, who would become Deputy Director of Intelligence when Collins took over as director from Duggan later that month.

There was one more political gathering of significance in Dublin in January 1919. This was a meeting of the Irish Unionist Alliance in the Freemasons' Hall, Molesworth Street, on 24 January, and it resulted in a split. The issue, appropriately enough, was partition. Lord Midleton, the long-established president of the alliance, proposed a motion that Ulster unionists should not have a vote in the association on any government proposals for new constitutional structures affecting the rest of the country. Midleton and his supporters were even more opposed to partition than to a weakening of the Union: they faced political extinction if the British government negotiated such a settlement with advanced nationalists. The strength of the unionist community rested with its 900,000 members in the north-east. Together with 250,000 Southern unionists they comprised a significant block. Unfortunately, it was becoming increasingly clear to Midleton that his Northern brethren preferred the certainty of partition, which guaranteed Protestant majority rule in the North, to a defence of the Union that might leave all unionists at the mercy of the Catholic majority in the South.

Surprisingly, Ulster unionists were able to persuade a majority of delegates at the conference of the Unionist Alliance in January to vote down Midleton's proposal, on the grounds that it would show divided counsels in their ranks. This proved to be the outcome anyway, as Midleton and his supporters withdrew to form the Anti-Partition League. The revolt by militant rank-and-file Southern unionists against their betters was not a new phenomenon in Dublin and before the war had proved fatal to election hopes in the city; but in this instance the effects would be more far-reaching. Having responded to the Ulster call for unity, they found themselves without any effective leadership in the South dependent on unreliable Northern allies in the British Parliament.

In turn, the leading figures in Southern Unionism who joined the Anti-Partition League found that they were a general staff without an army. Besides Lord Midleton they included the Earl of Donoughmore, grand master of the Grand Lodge of Free and Accepted Masons of Ireland, Lord Iveagh, head of the Guinness dynasty, and the Earls of Arran, Bandon, Kenmare, Kerry, Desart, Courtown, Mayo and Wicklow, not to mention most of the leading figures in Dublin's business community. These included Sir John Arnott, owner of the *Irish Times*, Sir William Goulding, chairman of the Great Southern and Western Railway, John Mooney, a leading city baker, John Good of the Dublin Master Builders, Edward Andrews, wine merchant and chairman of the Chamber of Commerce, Sir Maurice Dockrell, head of the main building suppliers' company in the city, and the hotelier Sir Thomas Robinson. Good, Robinson and Dockrell had all been unionist candidates in the 1918 general election and Dockrell had actually won Rathmines for the party—the only unionist victory outside Ulster and the Dublin University constituencies.

The new chairman of the rump Alliance was Lord Farnham. Among its more prominent members were William Morgan Jellett KC, one of the unsuccessful candidates in the 1918 election for a Dublin University seat, and J. Mackay Wilson, a brother of the Chief of the Imperial General Staff, Sir Henry Wilson. But its supporters generally came from the Protestant 'small farmers, the shopkeepers and rural clergymen.'[10]

There were few immediate consequences of the split in Southern Unionism. However, over time the Anti-Partition League developed into a think-tank. Colonel Walter Edward Guinness, eldest son of Lord Iveagh and unionist MP for Bury St Edmunds, told an early meeting that the Sinn Féin policy of abstention would reinforce the 'natural tendency to neglect Irish problems' in London unless the league actively engaged British political leaders in discussions on Ireland's future. He urged the extension of the new health legislation to Ireland, through an Irish ministry able to take account of local conditions as a means of doing so.

Andrews urged members of the league 'to support in every way possible the introduction of proportional representation' in local elections to protect the rights of minorities. While his immediate concern was to prevent the further erosion of unionist representation on Dublin Corporation, the advocacy of such measures sounded uncannily like Sinn Féin policy.

There would be little to show for these efforts in the chaotic months ahead as British policy veered between neglect and incompetent efforts at repression; but eventually the senior policy-makers in Whitehall and Dublin Castle came to realise that Lord Midleton's group offered alternative solutions to some of the most pressing problems they faced in Ireland. By then Midleton and his colleagues had concluded reluctantly that the rebel administration offered a better long-term prospect of stability and order in the South than the government to which they had so often pledged their allegiance.[11]

Of more immediate concern was the wave of industrial unrest that swept through the United Kingdom after the war. From November 1918 the British government had passed a series of Wage Regulation Acts aimed at maintaining pay at levels prevailing on Armistice Day. It continued to use the tripartite mediation system, involving employers, unions and the state, to avoid conflict. But once wartime restrictions were lifted there was a surge in militancy. Belfast's engineering workers took the lead in the private sector, demanding a reduction in the working week from 54 to 44 hours with the same basic pay scales.[12] The demand for a shorter working week grew not only out of a desire to escape the drudgery of working in jobs that could consume sixty or seventy hours a week of a man's waking life but out of concern to ensure that returning ex-servicemen were reabsorbed into the work force without displacing hundreds of thousands of other workers. Belfast employers, many of them committed to employing returning ex-servicemen, offered a 47-hour week, which was first accepted and then rejected by a militant rank and file who engaged in what proved to be a futile three-week general strike in the city.

Inevitably, the trouble spread to Dublin, where engineering and shipbuilding unions secured a reduction in the 50-hour basic week to 47 hours. As we have seen, a similar claim made on Dublin Corporation had been conceded for most of its manual employees at the beginning of January. However, the Town Clerk, Sir Henry Campbell, was reluctant to reduce hours for related occupations in the municipal power station and other areas. Consequently a week's notice of a general strike was served on Monday 27 January. Many workers were already operating the shorter working week, and the strike committee was barely allowing enough gas and electricity to be generated to keep the city's businesses operating on reduced hours. Only hospitals were provided with power for twenty-four hours a day. Campbell, a pillar of the old home-rule establishment in the city for more than twenty-five years, was outraged. His protests about breaches in procedures were overborne; councillors voted by 28 votes to 4 to concede the shorter week, now seen as the new norm. Simultaneously, the railway companies reduced their 60-hour week for employees to 48.

Yet pressure on living standards remained intense. The National Executive Committee of the Irish Trades Union Congress and Labour Party convened a special conference in Dublin to demand a 44-hour week nationally, an increase of at least 150 per cent on pre-war rates of pay for all workers and a minimum wage of 50s a week.[13] A proposal from the Dublin representatives for a 40-hour week was rejected as unrealistic, but it was agreed to call for the abolition of overtime, piecework and any other 'system of payment by results.' Thomas Farren of the Stonecutters' Union, who was vice-chairman of the ITUC&LP, explained the rationale behind a minimum wage of 50s a week as the amount a man with six dependants would receive on the dole. A working man deserved at least as much. At the same time the president of the ITGWU, Tom Foran, said that the government must control prices, because 'if things keep going as they have been going for the past four years, we will wind up having a minimum wage of £10 and being in a far worse position than we were when we had only 25s a week.'

The inflationary spiral appeared unstoppable. When lowly milkers and yardmen working for the Dublin Cowkeepers' and Dairymen's Association demanded an increase of 15s, to bring their weekly rate to 60s, the association was willing to pay up if a price increase was sanctioned.[14]

The formation of the Railway Clerical Workers' Union, the Irish Asylum Workers' Union and the Irish Bank Officials' Association were further manifestations of new-found confidence and militancy. There were nine hundred members in the Dublin Branch of the Railway Clerical Workers' Union, and they struck on Tuesday 4 February in pursuit of recognition. The action disrupted cattle trains, parcel deliveries and cross-channel traffic. The employers conceded recognition almost immediately. Workers in the Richmond Asylum demanded a reduction in their working week from 70 hours to 48. The management committee said it could not afford to take on the 115 extra employees that would be required to meet the new schedules and pay the £11,000 extra in wages; however, most committee members supported a proposal from Councillor P. T. Daly, leader of the Labour group in the corporation, to cut the working week to 56 hours, at a cost of £7,500. When Alderman William Dinnage, a unionist representative for Glasnevin, proposed that only a package costing £5,500 be conceded, he found little support. The Irish Bank Officials' Association secured recognition, a pay scale, agreed overtime rates, pensions, lunch breaks and holiday entitlements from their employers without having to go on strike.[15]

The pusillanimity of the city fathers reflected the state of political flux. Sinn Féin had almost swept the board in Dublin during the general election of December 1918, yet the discredited old Irish Party councillors remained in office, because local elections had been suspended for the duration of the war, and none were planned.

Major problems loomed as the Dublin labour market was flooded with demobilised soldiers and men returning from redundant British war industries. Hundreds of women munitions workers were also let go from the National Shell Factory in Parkgate Street and the Dublin Dockyard Company's shell plant. Thousands more were made redundant by other war contractors or demobilised from Queen Mary's Army Auxiliary Corps, the Royal Army Medical Corps (nurses), the Women's Legion (drivers), the Women's Forage Corps and Voluntary Aid Detachments.

How many of the 25,644 Dubliners who joined the colours in the Great War or the more than eight thousand labourers who worked in war industries in Britain came home is not clear. Approximately half the total of Irish soldiers who survived the war never returned to Ireland, or returned only to emigrate again by 1920. Many labourers who went to Britain failed to send money home, which suggests that they too lost contact with their families.

It is equally unclear how many of the women serving in the armed forces and Voluntary Aid Detachments abroad returned. Those who did were certainly better off than their civilian sisters laid off by war industries, because they received a lump sum of two months' pay and extra allowances on being honourably discharged. But both groups fared worse than male comparators. The scale of benefits applying to soldiers and civilians employed in war industries, demobilised from 12 December 1918 onwards, discriminated significantly between men and women. Men received 29s a week and women 25s; boys received 14s 6d a week and girls 12s 6d. However, soldiers, including female auxiliaries, were entitled to 26 weeks of 'war donations' (unemployment benefit) in the year following demobilisation; a civilian could claim only 13 weeks.

The ex-servicemen's associations that sprang up in Britain and other former belligerent countries were replicated in Ireland by the Irish Nationalist Veterans' Association, and British associations established Irish branches as well. As early as February 1919 steps were taken to set up a VAD Club for ex-servicewomen, including volunteers who served at home with the Red Cross Society and the St John Ambulance Brigade. The club was housed at 24 Molesworth Street, beside Buswell's Hotel, and had a dining-room, lounge, waiting-room, writing-room and library and a classroom for meetings and lectures. 'Bedrooms can be had in emergencies,' the promotional material announced, and the premises were open from 11 a.m. until 10 p.m. each day, except Sunday, when opening hours were 3 to 10 p.m. Individual membership was available for 2s 6d a year, and the prospectus added that 'an entire St John's Ambulance Division or Red Cross Detachment can join for a guinea [21s] a year.' St John Ambulance divisions from Clontarf, Rathgar, St Stephen's Green, Carrickmines, Earlsfort Terrace, Grafton Street, Harcourt Street and the Fitzwilliam district had taken up the offer by mid-February. The less socially prestigious Central Nursing Division for the Building Trades Corps and Inchicore railway works also joined.[16]

One voluntary body linked to the services that disbanded in early 1919 was the Women's Branch of the Royal Dublin Fusiliers' Association. During the first year of the war its leading lights, such as the Countess of Mayo, Lady Arnott and Mrs Marcus Goodbody, had financed activities themselves. Subsequently the Army Council provided a subsidy. Some activities were simple morale-boosting exercises, such as sending large consignments of shamrock to the regiment's battalions on St Patrick's Day each year; but the association's main work had been providing support for soldiers' families and sending supplies of food and clothing to members serving at the front or held as prisoners of war. Among the items despatched were 27,929 pairs of socks, 10,146 scarves, 12,093 mittens and 19,894 pairs of leather bootlaces. Other items included cardigans, shirts, underpants, vests, handkerchiefs, books, magazines and even helmets. Mrs W. E. Purser had single-handedly knitted three hundred scarves. Candles, soap, sweets, games, fifty thousand cigarettes and 215 pounds of tobacco were among the items sent to prisoners. A Soldiers' Wives' Workroom had provided training that enabled women to obtain regular well-paid employment, and at the end of the war the association outfitted six hundred returning prisoners.

At the final meeting of the branch Major-General Fry presented War Badges to members. He told them that

before the war a great many people were doubtful about the capacity of women in taking a large part in the affairs of the world, but one of the lessons that the war had taught was the enormous value of the work that women were capable of.

They had played an essential role in 'keeping up the spirit of the troops in the field and in relieving the anxiety of their dependants.' Thus encouraged, the men were made to feel that 'they had a grateful people behind them at home who were worth fighting for.'[17]

In reality the association had become an outpost of the Unionist Party in the city, as isolated and adrift from the prevailing sentiments of the wider community as many of the soldiers they had cared for over the years.

The changed political scene in Dublin was most apparent in the opening proceedings of Dáil Éireann and a subsequent session in April when Éamon de Valera was elected Príomh-Aire. He had been in Lincoln Prison when the Dáil convened in January. He escaped in February, with the assistance of Michael Collins and Harry Boland, the Dublin tailor and leading IRB member who had had a hand in redrafting the Democratic Programme. It was March before de Valera returned to Dublin, and when Collins announced that he would be greeted by the Lord Mayor, Laurence (Larry) O'Neill, and presented with the keys of the city at Mount Street Bridge, the General Officer Commanding in Ireland, Lieutenant-General Sir Frederick Shaw, issued a proclamation banning the ceremony, along with any other seditious meetings or demonstrations to welcome the escaper.

The greeting of de Valera at Mount Street Bridge would have been heavily symbolic. Not only had he been commandant of the area during this Irish Thermopylae, when a handful of Volunteers fought the enemy advance to a standstill in Easter Week, but the casualties had been among English soldiers rather than the Irish troops who made up half the British losses elsewhere in the city. Without the 234 dead and wounded Sherwood Foresters at Mount Street Bridge it would have been hard to portray the Rising in the simple 'them' and 'us' terms that now dominated political debate.

Far from having the keys of the city bestowed on him, de Valera had to hide in the gatekeeper's lodge of the Archbishop's Palace in Drumcondra. The arrangement was made by Boland with Father Michael Curran, the archbishop's private secretary, a virulent nationalist and friend of the late Patrick Pearse. Officially the presence of the fugitive rebel leader was 'not known' to the archbishop, Dr William Walsh, but in fact he knew of the presence of his guest and was reputed to have met him regularly for tea. It would have been odd if he did not, as they had worked closely together during the anti-conscription campaign of the previous year.[18]

De Valera's first executive act was to appoint a cabinet. Arthur Griffith, who had been Acting President during de Valera's incarceration, was appointed to Home Affairs, Cathal Brugha to Defence, W. T. Cosgrave to Local Government, Michael Collins to Finance, Count Plunkett to Foreign Affairs, Constance Markievicz to Labour and Eoin MacNeill to Industry. The ministries would later be extended to include Robert Barton as Minister for Agriculture, Seán Etchingham for Fisheries, Ernest Blythe for Trade and Commerce and J. J. O'Kelly for the Irish language. Austin Stack would take over Home Affairs when Griffith deputised again as President while de Valera was in America.

The failure to make Agriculture and Fisheries full cabinet posts from the beginning was evidence of the overwhelmingly urban composition of the separatist leadership, with no fewer than four members of the cabinet being native Dubliners and most of the rest living there.[19] Many members of the Dáil were also Dubliners or residents of the capital. Their election owed more to their being 'out' in 1916 than to their politics.

The new government placed great hopes on securing international recognition. The prospect of being able to put Ireland's case to the Paris Peace Conference had heightened Sinn Féin's electoral appeal in December 1918 and showed that it had an ambition beyond the modest, jaded demands of the Irish Party. That these hopes were misplaced would emerge only after the separatist cause was well ensconced. Dublin Corporation played its own modest role in the process when Seán T. Ó Ceallaigh was despatched to Paris, ostensibly to present the honorary freedom of the city to the president of the United States, Woodrow Wilson, but also in the hope that Wilson would secure his admission to the Peace Conference as emissary of the new Irish Republic. He failed, even after the socially more polished MP for South County Dublin and Francophile George Gavan Duffy was despatched to assist him.

Wilson did not ignore Dublin Corporation entirely. On 1 April 1919, after persistent lobbying in Dublin and London, the Lord Mayor of Dublin, Laurence O'Neill, was notified by the US consul, Edward Adams, that 'constant pressure of his engagements' in Paris prevented the president from accepting the invitation to receive the freedom of the city.[20]

Disappointment in Paris and the United States did not negate the useful political, financial and military aid generated during these international excursions. Similar trips to Australia and the wider Irish diaspora followed. Ó Ceallaigh described his experience as 'a forlorn hope, almost a concession, made by fiercer spirits among the Sinn Féin leaders to those of their comrades who urged that every possible instrument of peaceful negotiation should at least be tried.' It also honoured an election pledge: as Arthur Mitchell put it, 'it was something Sinn Féin had to go through with.'[21]

The only successful excursion into the international arena occurred when Thomas Johnson and Cathal O'Shannon attended the first gathering after the war of the Socialist (Second) International in Bern, Switzerland, where they secured separate representation for Ireland from the British contingent. Meanwhile another political pariah, the Bolshevik government in Russia, recognised its Irish revolutionary counterpart. Ironically, the relentless drive by Lenin to build the Communist (Third) International helped split the Socialist International, and Ireland once more slipped off the institutional socialist map as larger issues than Irish independence swamped the debate.

Parallel with the fitful public political life of the new republic was the emergence of a surreptitious administration, both military and civil. The military machine emerged first, partly because the Irish Volunteers provided a ready-made structure, partly because its violence made a rapid and indelible impact on the public consciousness, and above all because its activities were destructive and therefore more readily achieved than the construction of an alternative government.

The war party within the Volunteers was congregating around Michael Collins. Most of the General Headquarters staff moved quickly into the 'war' camp, committed to renewing the fight as soon as possible. Collins cultivated militant local leaders, such as Seán Treacy in Co. Tipperary and Tomás Mac Curtáin, head of the Volunteers in Cork. But even more crucial was the adherence of Dick McKee, former commandant of the 2nd Battalion in Dublin, who had become commandant of the Dublin Brigade after Richard Mulcahy was elected Chief of Staff. It was in Dublin that Collins meant the fight to dismantle the enemy state machine to begin. McKee was a tall, phlegmatic character. Taciturn, speaking with a slow drawl, he inspired a fierce loyalty among the city's Volunteers. A printer by trade with the publishing firm of M. H. Gill and Son, he constructed a firing range below the firm's premises in Sackville Street. His deputy, Peadar Clancy, ran an outfitters' shop in nearby Talbot Street. Not alone was Collins fortunate in having McKee and Clancy as senior commanders in Dublin but there were plenty of Volunteers willing to carry the fight to the enemy in ways not envisaged in 1916. Unfortunately, a shortage of arms posed a problem.

Although there were far fewer weapons in private hands in Dublin than in country districts, gun shops and private homes suspected of harbouring weapons were raided. In March 1919 the 2nd Battalion carried out systematic raids on all such premises in the north-east of the city. This had tragic results for Alfred Pearson, a foreman at Harrison's Monumental Works in Great Brunswick Street (Pearse Street). His son was a staff sergeant in the Royal Engineers, which was probably why he had a couple of ancient rifles, two or three pistols and two swords in the house. On Tuesday 11 March, shortly after 7 p.m., Pearson was entertaining his housekeeper, Agnes Martin, and her friend Katie Orr to tea in the kitchen of his home at 146 Richmond Road, Drumcondra, when there was a knock at the front door. He answered it to find no-one there. A second knock followed shortly afterwards, and he was confronted by three or four youths, two of them wearing what Orr later described as 'boy scouts uniforms'. There was a scuffle in the hallway and on the stairs as they forced Pearson to the upper floor. When one of the young men entered the kitchen brandishing a revolver, Orr declared, 'I am a Sinn Féiner, don't shoot me for mercy's sake.' The youth replied: 'They have arms above but won't give them [up].'

Pearson was badly beaten about the head and then shot in the chest. He staggered out of the house towards a milk bar opposite but collapsed on the road. In a response as interesting in its way as Katie Orr's, Constable Patrick Kennedy, on foot patrol nearby, did not attempt to intervene until the armed group had fled. The few weapons in the house had not been taken. The coroner's jury brought in a verdict of death from 'a rupture of the heart and haemorrhage caused by a bullet fired from a revolver by some person or persons unknown.' In all likelihood Pearson's was the first gunshot fatality of the War of Independence in Dublin.[22]

A far more successful arms raid took place at Collinstown Aerodrome in north Co. Dublin on the night of 20 March 1919. The construction of the new facility was one of the few untrammelled benefits the Great War bestowed on Dublin, although construction began only as the conflict ended. It was a major source of well-paid employment for local labour and provided the infrastructure for what would evolve into Ireland's largest international airport. A number of Irish Volunteers worked on the site, including Patrick Houlihan, who had fought in 1916. Working 'for the enemy ... but keeping my eyes open to see what I could do to help the Republic to which we had pledged our allegiance,' he soon discovered there was 'a regular little arsenal' on the site, and McKee organised a raid, with GHQ sanction.

Houlihan was put in charge and allowed to choose men from throughout the brigade. He deliberately picked single men, except for Pat Doyle, a carpenter who worked on the site; he had recently married but insisted on taking part or he would resign from the Volunteers. The men were supplied with khaki uniforms and masks. They fed poisoned meat to the guard dogs and quickly overpowered the RAF sentries. The Volunteers used sledge-hammers to wreck military vehicles and prevent pursuit before loading seventy-six rifles and five thousand rounds of ammunition into the motor transport provided by McKee. The raid was a success, despite serious mishaps: one vehicle had to be pushed the last three miles to the dump, and a taxi had to take thirteen passengers after a third vehicle failed to turn up.

The military authorities reacted angrily to what was to be the largest loss of weapons by the British army from a single operation during the War of Independence. Lieutenant-General Shaw not alone banned de Valera's proposed triumphal entry into Dublin the following weekend but sacked all eight hundred workers on the Collinstown site. They were replaced by military personnel, with the agreement of the contractor, John Good—one of the defeated unionist candidates in the 1918 general election. It was an act of collective punishment, recognised and resented as such.

Shaw then issued an order for sentries to fire on any civilian who failed to halt when challenged on approaching a military post. The first casualty of this order was 51-year-old Charles Church, a jeweller and watchmaker of Upper George's Street, Kingstown. Church was somewhat deaf and so failed to hear a sentry challenge him twice while he was walking along Crofton Road beside the Royal Mail Hotel, which was serving as a temporary barracks. The bullet shattered Church's hand and the walking-stick he was carrying.

Quite a few participants in the Collinstown raid would become part of the activist Volunteer core in the city. Two would be executed in Mountjoy and two shot dead by Crown forces in 1921. The oldest, at twenty-seven, was Patrick Doyle, the married man who refused to be left out. He was typical of the rank and file in Dublin. A craft worker from the inner city, he had attended O'Connell Schools, a regular breeding-ground for rebels. He was an active member of the Amalgamated Society of Carpenters, Cabinetmakers and Joiners and had played for the Seaview team that won the Leinster Junior Football League during the 1912/13 season. He married in 1916 and had a daughter, Constance (named after Constance Markievicz), in 1917. A son, Patrick, would be born in 1919 only to die of pneumonia.

The youngest participant, Barney Ryan, was executed with Doyle for his part in the same Drumcondra ambush in 1921. He was an apprentice tailor, still in his teens at the time of the Collinstown raid. He lived with his widowed mother and invalid sister in Royal Canal Terrace, Phibsborough, and was the family breadwinner. Like Doyle, he was a keen sportsman: he played Gaelic football and had won a number of medals for swimming. The other participants who failed to survive the War of Independence were Michael Magee, killed in the

Drumcondra ambush, and Seán Doyle, killed during the burning of the Custom House in May 1921.[23]

There was a further boost to the morale of the Volunteers almost immediately after the Collinstown raid when twenty prisoners escaped from Mountjoy Prison on Saturday 29 March by the simple ploy of overpowering the warders in the exercise yard when a rope ladder was thrown over the wall. By the time the military arrived to restore order only seven republican prisoners were left. This was the largest escape in Mountjoy's history, preceded by the humiliating escape two weeks earlier of Robert Barton from the infirmary. In a note to the governor Barton complained that 'owing to the discomfort of the place I felt compelled to leave.' He would send for his luggage later.[24] It was widely acknowledged that many prison officers were republican sympathisers. One bonus of these prison breaks was an increased attendance rate by TDs at Dáil sessions.

The prison break underlined one of the new facts of political life in Ireland to which the *Irish Times* had alluded in condemning the Solloghodbeg ambush. The motor of the revolution was not Sinn Féin but the Irish Volunteers, with the latter providing Dáil deputies as well as foot soldiers for the party. Even in Dublin, where British surveillance was greatest, the Volunteers functioned almost openly. The journalist and Sinn Féin propagandist Frank Gallagher, using the pseudonym David Hogan, wrote:

> Beneath a placid surface, there was an activity unbelievable in its intensity. Through their streets, with their sauntering couples, went a young lad here and there who, at some unpretentious doorway, melted away from the scene. That was usually around seven-thirty or eight in the evening and these young men did not come back on to the streets again until ten o'clock or after. Without hurry or apparent secretiveness, they rejoined the saunterers and went home on the late trams.

Volunteer companies often assembled at halls associated with the wider national movement, such as those of the Gaelic League and the Ancient Order of Hibernians, or, better still, union premises, such as Liberty Hall and the Dublin Typographical Society offices in Lower Gardiner Street, or the premises of such organisations as the Dublin Total Abstinence League and Workmen's Club in York Street, where Hogan's company sometimes met. The captain of κ Company, 3rd Battalion, was Tom Cullen, who would later be a leading figure in Michael Collins's assassination squad. Another member was a young Seán Lemass.

These were ideal venues within the city centre, where people came and went without attracting attention and with meeting-rooms set back from the street and escape routes at the rear.

Parades included elementary drill but were mostly given over to lectures and training. Lectures often dealt with the exploits of Boer commandos in South Africa against the British or, more usefully, lessons to be learnt nearer home from the Easter Rising, usually given by a revered veteran of the event. Arms and engineering classes—essentially how to manufacture mines and grenades—were the other main activity.

Volunteers were a cross-section of the skilled working class and lower middle classes. They did not generally include the unemployed or very poor, who could not afford the weekly subscription let alone turn out decently dressed or contribute to arms and equipment funds. Hogan stressed that,

> with most of these listeners in the ranks, it wasn't that they wanted to be soldiers as such, or yearned for a life in arms. It was that somehow they saw coming a struggle in which, if they trained, they could be of some use. That drilling had been declared illegal had something to do with it … The more the right to serve our own nation was condemned, the more we felt that right must be asserted.

Despite his avowed aversion to the military life, Hogan, like many a young man, could still 'remember the excitement of the first lesson in the workings of a rifle.'[25]

No-one had died during the Collinstown raid or the Mountjoy prison break, but these events did mark a serious stepping up of political violence in the city. In his memoir Hogan reflected that 'a careful watcher' of any venue where Volunteer parades took place would have noticed fifty or sixty men entering over perhaps half an hour. The 'careful watchers' included, of course, G Division, the intelligence branch of the Dublin Metropolitan Police; and on the night of 7/8 April 1919 the Volunteers' new Director of Intelligence, Michael Collins, paid them a visit. It followed a meeting the previous evening between Collins and Ned (Éamonn) Broy at the home in Cabra of Mícheál Ó Foghlú, a leading figure in the Gaelic League. Broy was a member of G Division, and when he told Collins he could give him access to the DMP intelligence archives in Great Brunswick Street the following night Collins accepted the invitation with alacrity, even though a special ard-fheis of Sinn Féin was to take place the following day to regularise the relationship between the party and Dáil Éireann.

At the ard-fheis de Valera would tell delegates that from now on they would be the 'civic army' of the Dáil, political activists who would put its policies into practice.

For the moment the Volunteers would retain their autonomy within the movement. Collins managed to combine seamlessly his roles as a member of the civilian administration of the Republic and a senior officer in its still-autonomous army. Broy would be an important intelligence asset: although a very junior member of G Division, he had the crucial job of typing the handwritten daily notes of detectives as well as confidential reports, such as the list of suspects to be arrested in the 'German Plot' round-up of May 1918. He had earlier sent notes to the Volunteers through Harry O'Hanrahan, a brother of a Citizen Army officer executed in 1916, but he appears to have been formally recruited to the Volunteers through Ó Foghlú's wife. By chance she worked as a bookkeeper in Findlater's shop, where Broy was regularly despatched by more senior colleagues to collect groceries.

Broy was often on night duty alone at Great Brunswick Street station, and this facilitated the visit by Collins. Collins brought Seán Nunan with him. Like Ó Foghlú, Nunan was a member of the IRB but was involved primarily in the civil administration of the infant republic. He would serve as secretary to Éamon de Valera in America and act as registrar for the Dáil Éireann bonds issued to finance the independence struggle. Collins probably wanted to maximise an unexpected opportunity to compile information by having the assistance of a highly competent apparatchik. The two men had to use candles to examine records, as switching on lights in the archive would have attracted attention.

Éamonn Broy was by no means the first policeman to switch sides. That honour went to Eugene Smith, who supplied information to the Irish Volunteers from before the Easter Rising until his retirement in 1918.

The only surprising aspect of the gradual disaffection of members of the police, which was occurring in the provinces as well as Dublin, was the failure of senior British administrators to anticipate it. Quite apart from the rapidly changing political climate that reached into almost every section of society, there had been disaffection within the DMP for many years over pay and conditions. In belated recognition of this, members received a pay increase of 1s a week at the outbreak of the Great War, their first increase since 1884. They received another 3s 6d weekly 'war bonus' from 1 July 1916, two months after the Rising. However, they demanded a 50 per cent increase, or another 12s a week, together with full retrospection from 1 September 1914. Like that of white-collar corporation staff, the demand was driven as much by comparative deprivation as by wartime inflation. DMP members were angered at the spectacle of manual workers in unions passing them out in the pay stakes.

Given the disturbed state of Ireland, the government had little choice but to give ground. It agreed an increase of 2s a week to men with less than three years' service and 3s a week for longer-serving members. The same increases were given to the Royal Irish Constabulary (the armed police force that operated throughout the country), and at the end of 1918 the wartime coalition government improved pensions for both the DMP and the RIC in one of the last pieces of legislation it passed.[26] Members of the Irish Party returned to London to vote for the measure before facing political extinction at the polls.

The financial gains made by DMP members came at a high price. The ringleaders of the revolt were dismissed, and about half, who had joined the Ancient Order of Hibernians to get around the ban on forming a police union, resented having to resign from the order under duress. One particular straw in the wind that the authorities missed was the fact that Éamonn Broy and an older member of G Division, Joe Kavanagh, had been among the activists in the abortive attempt to unionise the force. Kavanagh would become one of the first members of G Division to contact Collins, and he began passing information through a mutual acquaintance, the IRB member Thomas Gay, who worked in the corporation's Commercial Library in Capel Street. In May 1918 Kavanagh was one of at least three detectives to warn Collins of the 'German Plot' raids.

Personal factors also played a role in the disaffection of the DMP. Sergeant Moynihan, who was attached to the Bridewell, wrote to Laurence O'Neill to thank him for his intervention at the funeral of the veteran radical nationalist journalist Séamus O'Kelly when

> without any cause whatsoever one of the Ulster Covenanters [Superintendent Willoughby] gave us an order to cross the street and break up the innocent boys and girls returning home. Fortunately you arrived on the scene not a moment too soon and the prompt action you took prevented serious trouble and bloodshed. My three sons, who are only mere boys ... took part in the procession and in all probability would have run up against a truncheon.

Moynihan said he would have 'thrown off my uniform and pitched it in the face of the Orangeman who gave the uncalled for word of command' but for the fact that he had 'nearly 25 years service and I must try to restrain my passions a little longer.'

Men such as Moynihan became a valuable asset to the IRA intelligence network, and they were assured that they were of more value to the national cause by remaining at their posts. The hostility they felt towards senior officers such as Willoughby was fuelled by a long-standing resentment that these 'Orangemen' owed their promotion to their religion and their membership of the Orange Order or the Freemasons rather than merit. These feelings predated the Great War but were heightened by developments since, when faith and fatherland converged.[27]

While men such as Moynihan could provide the Volunteers with valuable operational information, such as tip-offs on impending raids, Collins's visit to the G Division archive on 7 April gave him a unique insight into the main enemy intelligence organisation in the city, including details of its informants. The enemy within was the one most feared, especially in a conflict where fundamental allegiances were contested. But first Collins had a more immediate task: to neutralise G Division. The commandant of the Dublin Brigade, Dick McKee, was given a list of detectives in each battalion area, and two nights later groups of Volunteers rounded them up to persuade them 'to take no further part in ... treacherous work against their country.' Not all were receptive. Detective-Sergeant Halley fired at Volunteers who called to his home on 9 April, and another veteran of the force, Detective-Sergeant Daniel Hoey, retaliated to threats by raiding a civic reception held at the Mansion House on 12 April, which Collins had to flee by climbing over a back wall.[28]

Collins realised that more forceful methods would be required, but a number of other things would have to happen before cold-blooded killings would become politically acceptable on the city's streets.

Of course death was commonplace in the Dublin slums, and mortality rates soared as a result of the influenza epidemic, which had affected the city since the previous summer. It returned in the winter of 1918/19, when such deaths far exceeded those due to political violence. Dr Kathleen Lynn, Sinn Féin's joint Director of Public Health, had been living on the run since the previous May and subsequently had to give up her medical practice. But,

> as doctors were so very badly wanted, I just decided that I would go home and I did. I was arrested immediately and brought to Oriel House [headquarters of G Division]. I was told I would be deported. Miss ffrench-Mullen, the Lord Mayor and everybody kicked up an awful "shine." Doctors were terribly wanted at that time. I was permitted to remain in practice if I did not leave the City of Dublin.

On her release she tested a flu vaccine on two hundred members of the Citizen Army at Liberty Hall. Once satisfied with the results, she used it on other patients.[29]

One of those who protested most vigorously at Lynn's arrest, and probably brought most influence to bear on Dublin Castle, was Sir Charles Cameron, Chief Medical Officer of Dublin. Yet it was only towards the end of February 1919 that the corporation decided to make the notification of all cases of influenza and pneumonia compulsory. At a conference of hospital doctors and the Public Health Department on 20 February it was suggested that schools, theatres, cinemas and public libraries be closed and that dances and other social functions be suspended, to limit the spread of infection. However, the corporation had no power to enforce such draconian measures. The Theatre Royal and the Gaiety, Queen's, Empire and Tivoli Theatres all continued to put on nightly performances, as did the city's cinemas. The Pillar Picture House, owned by J. J. Farrell, a member of the corporation, remained open all day.

Cameron could only appeal for co-operation; and efforts to heighten public awareness of the risks were undermined by his comment that the infection was now less virulent than in the autumn. There were only 19 deaths in the week ending 15 February, a small fraction of the 250 a week in November 1918. Unfortunately, the figure soared again the following week, when there were 376 deaths, a rate of 45 per thousand in the metropolitan area (the city plus the surrounding townships) and 50 in the city. The corporation introduced health measures, such as a requirement on drivers of public-service vehicles to disinfect them after carrying infectious cases to hospital. Meanwhile employees of the city's cemeteries were grossly overworked. Between forty and forty-five funerals a day were common at the city's main cemetery in Glasnevin, including Sundays.[30]

As usual, the death rate was highest in the poorer districts of the inner city, reaching 56 per thousand by the middle of March 1919. The total city mortality rate was 35 per thousand in the first quarter of 1919, or approximately 50 per cent higher than average for the time of year. Of 95 cases of influenza in the Dublin metropolitan area in the week ending 22 February, 80 were in the poorest districts.[31]

Yet even the catastrophe of an epidemic could not slow the momentum of the Sinn Féin cause. The so-called 'Spanish flu' raged through the prisons even more rampantly than outside. In December 1918 Richard Coleman, a veteran of the Battle of Ashbourne in 1916, had died in Usk Prison in Monmouthshire, and his remains were given a hero's welcome almost as great as that given to his commanding officer at Ashbourne, Thomas Ashe, when the latter died after forcible feeding on hunger strike in 1917. On 6 March 1919, as the epidemic reached its climax, another hunger-striker, Pierse McCann, MP for East Tipperary, died in Gloucester Prison. His death could not have been more politically opportune, for Sinn Féin had launched a campaign to demand the release of all political prisoners, citing their incarceration during an influenza epidemic as tantamount to a death sentence. After de Valera's escape in February, McCann's death depicted British policy as vindictive as well as ineffectual. Like many local authorities, Dublin Corporation condemned McCann's death unanimously, although unionist councillors and their allies made it clear that they did not agree with some of the sentiments expressed in the debate.[32]

Fear of infection had not prevented Dublin Chamber of Commerce from holding its annual general meeting in the Commercial Buildings, Dame Street, that January. The wine merchant E. H. Andrews was re-elected to the chair, and the annual battle cry for a reduction in the city's commercial rates was raised. A petition had been collected with four thousand signatures from property-owners with an aggregate rateable valuation of £270,000, and this would be presented to Lord French within the week. Despite this there was little support for a call by James Brady, a solicitor, for organising a rates strike. Nor did fear of influenza deter members who were shareholders in the Dublin United Tramways Company from attending its general meeting two weeks later, on 14 February, presided over by its legendary chairman, William Martin Murphy, who had defeated the Irish Transport and General Workers' Union in the 1913 Lockout.

As in every year since then, the company announced a healthy profit, despite wartime shortages and civil strife. The familiar practice of topping up the modest first half-yearly dividend with a more generous tranche for the second six months was maintained. The 4 per cent paid for the first six months of 1918 was increased to 6 per cent, making the annual dividend 5 per cent. In addition, shareholders received an extra 10s for every £10 they held in ordinary stock. Murphy felt that the extravagance was warranted, given the company's 'terminable existence'.

The exigencies of war had hampered services, and fuel shortages continued to do so. A constraint that exercised shareholders more was the tight municipal control of fares. Only 1d could be charged within 1½ miles of the city centre, and on long-established suburban routes the maximum fare was 2d. Higher fares could be charged on newer routes not subject to the corporation's fares regime, but 41 million out of 71 million fares in 1918 had been for 1d. The tramcars were crowded, because fuel shortages limited the number of vehicles on each route, and uniform tickets with no destination listed were issued because of paper and ink shortages. Despite all the difficulties, the trams had travelled 7 million miles in the last year of the Great War conveying passengers across the city.[33]

He did not know it at the time, but Murphy's own 'terminable existence' was nigh at hand. This was the last DUTC shareholders' meeting that he would attend. He died the following June, aged seventy-four. The son of a small west Cork builder, born when the Great Famine was at its height, Murphy had created a commercial empire based on light railways and tramway networks on three continents and had made the Independent group of newspapers the dominant force in Irish publishing. But he probably realised he would be associated for ever in the public mind with two issues. One was his generalship of Dublin's employers during the great Lockout of 1913, when a third of the city's population was starved back to work in an ultimately unsuccessful attempt to smash the ITGWU; the second was the editorial in the *Irish Independent* calling for the execution of Seán Mac Diarmada and James Connolly in May 1916.

Murphy opposed the union not alone because it sought better pay and conditions for its members but because its leaders, Jim Larkin and James Connolly, were advocates of socialism and threatened the conservative Catholic nationalist values he championed. The editorial in the *Irish Independent* had in fact been written by the editor, T. R. Harrington, who candidly admitted he had misjudged the public mood, but such was Murphy's reputation for cold vindictiveness that the legend persisted, despite the fact that in his latter years he took a strategic decision to abandon the Irish Party, for which he had once been an MP, representing the old St Patrick's division of Dublin. He despised John Redmond for capitulating to Carson on partition. His newspapers helped secure Sinn Féin's electoral landslide in 1918, but he was condemned to live in popular memory as the epitome of the sanctimonious, avaricious and conservative breed of businessman that would dominate modern Ireland for decades to come. A contemporary and sometime friend, P. A. Chance, memorably described him as a man 'who carried a copy of the Companies Act in one hand and *The Imitation of Christ* in the other.'[34]

A special meeting of Dublin Corporation on 23 February re-elected Laurence O'Neill to his third term as Lord Mayor. O'Neill was an unlikely revolutionary. An auctioneer by profession, he owned a considerable amount of land around his family home in Strand Road, Portmarnock, Co. Dublin. He had been a radical independent-nationalist member of the Corporation for many years and was first elected Lord Mayor in the aftermath of the Easter Rising. He had not participated in the fighting but had been arrested as a suspected sympathiser, which gave a timely boost to his political career. He had a gift for obfuscation that was outstanding even by Irish standards and could maintain a public stance of defiance to the British authorities while developing a working relationship with senior officials. In other words, he made an ideal chief magistrate in those troubled times, expressing the aspirations of a citizenry that had voted overwhelmingly for Sinn Féin in the general election of December 1918 and simultaneously reassuring the incumbent nationalist majority in the Corporation that some degree of stability and continuity would be maintained in the governance of the city. Until the government lifted its ban on local elections, O'Neill would hold the ring between the home-rule old guard and impatient young Sinn Féin contenders. Many of the former were so convinced of their imminent demise that they ceased attending meetings, making it hard to drum up a quorum, even for such important matters as striking the rate.

The ascendency of Sinn Féin was implicitly recognised the day before O'Neill's re-election when W. T. Cosgrave was co-opted to the corporation after a technical forfeiture of his seat for non-attendance because he was in prison. At the same meeting Seán McGarry was co-opted to replace William Reigh, a nationalist businessman who had died.[35] Ordinarily it was the party of a deceased councillor that nominated a replacement, and a fellow-nationalist, John P. Farrelly, was proposed to replace Reigh. However, Farrelly withdrew his nomination in favour of McGarry. The latter was an electrician from Fairview and, more pertinently, president of the IRB. The fact that he was on the run, having escaped with de Valera from Lincoln Prison in February, and that this might hamper him in discharging his duties as a public representative, does not appear to have been considered an impediment.[36]

The new mood of incipient revolution affected matters great and small, as the continuing debate over the rates showed. One of the first, and meanest, savings was the ending of payments to dependants of corporation staff serving in the British armed forces. It was proposed by William T. Cosgrave at his first meeting after being released from prison. He argued that families would not need the payments, as the men concerned would soon be demobbed and able to resume work. The only surviving unionist alderman, William Dinnage, voted with Cosgrave and the majority of his colleagues to abolish the payment, demonstrating that party loyalties rarely usurped the higher allegiance most councillors felt to the ratepayers who elected them. On this occasion the amount saved was minute: £300 out of a total budget of £893,450.

In 1918 the rates had reached a record figure of 15s 8d in the pound for the north side of the city and 14s 11d for the south side, but an even higher unified rate of

16s 10d or even 18s in the pound was now envisaged. There were three main reasons for the soaring costs. One was the continuing price-wage spiral, a legacy of the war; a second was the amalgamation of the North Dublin Union (workhouse) and South Dublin Union, which should have yielded savings but had the reverse effect; and the third was the corporation's defeat in a legal battle with Dublin Castle over whether the police rate should be levied on the basis of the city's much lower pre-war valuation.

War-fuelled inflation was the most powerful of these drivers. Prices for essentials such as food, coal and clothes remained particularly high. Some of this could be explained by the high freight charges resulting from a post-war shipping shortage. This further contributed indirectly to the cost of other items, such as the 50 per cent increase in the cost of public lighting, which was generated from imported coal and coke. Fuel prices also remained high because of the disarray of the British mining industry and protectionist measures that kept out cheap American coal. At the same time Britain boosted foreign earnings by subsidising coal exports to war-torn Europe.

Wages and salaries for corporation employees rose by £150,000 in 1918 and by another £80,000 in 1919. The spiralling costs of the Dublin Union were a particular problem. In late 1918 the British army had commandeered the North Dublin Union buildings as winter quarters for soldiers, and inmates were transferred to the South Dublin Union. A generous topping up of the pension fund for redundant workers at the North Dublin Union incurred significant extra costs. So did large pay increases for the remaining staff, ranging from 125 per cent for the Master on assuming responsibility for the amalgamated institution to between 30 and 60 per cent for the rest. But by far the biggest item of expenditure was the growing number of Dubliners claiming outdoor relief (unemployment assistance not involving residence in the workhouse). The number of applicants rose by 50 per cent between 1916 and 1919. Weekly entitlements also rose. The rates were set by the British government but paid by Dublin ratepayers, providing further cause for disaffection.

The new police rate, which was subsumed under the poor rate estimate for the Dublin Union, was even more bitterly resented. Unlike British cities, Dublin had no control over the DMP or the RIC (whose personnel sometimes operated in the city). Both forces were under the direct control of Dublin Castle. The city fathers had mounted a successful legal challenge to the grounds on which the police rate was levied, only to lose their case on appeal to the House of Lords. As a result the city had to pay not only the increased rate for 1919 but £4,590 in retrospection on funds withheld in 1918. Another legacy bill of £5,000 was due to the British army, the outstanding balance of a successful claim for malicious damage to cavalry fodder caused by an arson attack on its East Wall depot in August 1916. The total bill had been £11,200.

The only good news was that the amalgamation of the Poor Law unions meant that north-side ratepayers would no longer be bearing a disproportionate share of the burden of looking after the city's poor, who had been housed primarily in the area of the old North Dublin Union. The south-side ratepayer would now be taking up some of the slack.[37] However, this was as far as welfare reform went.

The new Dublin Union was as bedevilled by scandal and infighting as the old ones. No sooner was it established than it was mired in controversy over the manner in which goods valued at £19,744 from the old North Dublin Union were disposed of before the building was handed over to the military. An inquiry by the Local Government Board uncovered only one serious irregularity. The Assistant Master, Maurice Kavanagh, had bought twenty-six beds for 27s 6d each, along with fibre mattresses at 10s each and pillows for 2s 6d each, to establish a lodging-house in Edenderry, Co. Offaly. But as the complainants failed to attend and make good their allegations, and as the prices paid by Kavanagh were the market value of the goods involved, the inquiry absolved him of blame. The subsequent meeting of the Board of Guardians (governors) of the Dublin Union degenerated into a dogfight over who was responsible for incurring the costs of the LGB investigation. This was followed by a debate over who should fill a teaching post in the Cabra Auxiliary Schools, run by the Union. As usual it came down to a vote, which was won by John J. Colbert with 46 votes, to 35 for Ignatius Freyne, in a final run-off ballot after all other candidates had been eliminated.[38]

Not only jobbery but the bigger perennial issues facing the old corporation regime in its twilight year evoked the same responses that they had always done. The debate over sickness pay for the corporation's staff was a good example. John Ryan, a nationalist councillor representing the wealthy Clontarf ward, proposed cutting the estimate in 1919 by a third, from £1,500 to £1,000. P. T. Daly, leader of the Labour group, protested that there had been an influenza epidemic in the city, and 'some men had gone back to work before they were fit to do so, and died in consequence.' A chastened Ryan assured Daly that he was not suggesting that there had been any malingering, only for Alderman David Quaid, a solicitor representing the equally prosperous suburb of Drumcondra, to insist that there had indeed been 'a great deal of malingering.' The situation was defused when the City Secretary, Fred Allan, pointed out that the increase in sickness pay reflected pay increases rather than higher rates of absenteeism. The irony was that Ryan had been a member of Arthur Griffith's non-violent Sinn Féin movement in his youth, while Daly and Allan as young men had both served on the Supreme Council of the IRB. Indeed Allan had revived his interest in the IRB and now worked assiduously to promote its interests. The debate showed in miniature the complex realignments taking place in municipal politics.

The annual row over the workshop budget was another standard fixture of the debate on the estimates. At the same meeting a nationalist councillor, John Foley of Fairview, challenged Daly over the accounts. 'The Doges of Venice and their Council of Ten were never so absolute in their secrecy as the Workshop Committee,' he railed, to little effect. Daly, as ever, defended the employees.

The Lord Mayor could only appeal to that institutional champion of the ratepayers, the Citizens' Association, and its allies in the council to bear in mind that the main cause of the rising cost of running the city was something they had no control over: the war and its aftermath. He also reminded the trades council and the Labour councillors that high rates were bad for business and led ultimately to unemployment. Every member should 'diligently attend to their duties' and remember that, as 'they were not going to be there very long … they would leave a legacy to those who came after them.'

His appeal had little effect. In a burst of extravagance, £5,000 was committed to the Clontarf Promenade project, even though it could not proceed until Fairview Park and a new slobland dump were opened. It proved a short-lived gesture: when no supplementary funds were forthcoming from the Local Government Board, the project was abandoned.[39]

A far bigger challenge for the corporation was tackling the city's slums. The high incidence of influenza, pneumonia, TB, sexually transmitted and other diseases was due in large part to the abnormally large proportion of the population consigned to the tenements. Attempts at slum clearance before the Great War had been pitiful and collapsed during the conflict, when nearly 1,000 additional tenements were closed as unsafe and 3,563 of the 4,150 families living in them became homeless. By 1918 only 327 new houses had been built in a city that urgently needed to rehouse 50,000 of its poorest inhabitants. Much of the blame could be laid at the door of the Local Government Board for failing to take advantage of British government funds available to local authorities. The achievements of nearby Pembroke Urban District Council, which built 759 houses for £175,000 during the war, showed what could be achieved where the political will existed.

In the first quarter of 1919 Dublin Corporation engaged in yet another of its interminable debates about slum clearance in the certain knowledge that the problem would be resolved by others. The Local Government Board had dangled a carrot for the councillors at the end of 1918, informing them that British government funds were once more available. It requested information on any proposals the city might have for building schemes on sites designated before or during the war, such as Crabbe Lane, Spitalfields, Mary's Lane, Boyne Street, Church Street, North Lots and Newfoundland Street. The Housing Committee reluctantly agreed that five or six leading architectural firms in the city should be asked to undertake the task of designing suitable schemes.

When the Assistant City Architect, H. T. O'Rourke, protested that the work could be undertaken directly for half the £10,000 it was planned to pay to private firms, this led to further delays. Eventually the chairman of the committee, Alderman Tom Kelly of Sinn Féin, proposed that the best course would be to subcontract the work, because if the LGB finally sanctioned it the corporation would incur no expense, and if the board did not sanction the work the corporation would not be obliged to pay outside architects either, as their contracts would be subject to loan approval by the LGB.

'As to Mr O'Rourke, there is no question of his ability,' Kelly said, 'but it is absurd that he should carry out the work to a conclusion at the cost he has suggested.' As a sop, Kelly said the Housing Committee 'had it in mind to reserve the [proposed] Marino scheme for Mr O'Rourke where he had the full scope for the exercise of his abilities.' While Kelly conceded that the housing question in Dublin 'was a very urgent one,' it would require anything from £8 million to £12 million to resolve, 'and there was very little chance of getting it from the British government.' As for the Local Government Board, its ways were as dark and as full of tricks as 'the Heathen Chinese,' and no store could be put in its promises.[40]

In fact there were good grounds for scepticism by councillors over the intentions of the British government, whatever about the peculiar racial terms in which Kelly expressed it. The new Chief Secretary for Ireland, Ian Macpherson, told Irish local authorities airily that Irish banks would provide any capital required for housing. The banks thought differently and saw Dublin Corporation as a bad risk, given the disturbed state of the country.[41]

At least Dubliners could look forward to an improved fire service. The corporation decided after many years of prevarication to complete the motorisation of the Fire Brigade, begun in 1910. While the *Irish Times* agreed that, 'beyond question, the motor machine is speedier than the horse drawn apparatus,' it confessed that 'we shall regret the disappearance of the horse drawn engines from the streets. They represent a truly stirring sight as they dash through the thoroughfares.'[42]

Chapter 2 ～

'I HAD NO REVOLVER MYSELF AND I AM GLAD NOW … AS I MIGHT HAVE SHOT SOME OF THEM'

In May 1919 St Ultan's Hospital for Infants opened at 37 Charlemont Street. The prime mover was Dr Kathleen Lynn, Sinn Féin's joint Director of Public Health, and it arose directly out of propaganda work she had been engaged in with her fellow-director Dr Richard Hayes.

At the time of their appointment in 1918 both had been concerned at the potential effect of the mass demobilisation of soldiers once the war ended. They estimated that some fifteen thousand Irish soldiers returning home would have contracted syphilis and would therefore pose a serious threat to Irish women. With some justification, Lynn described the battlefields of Europe and the rear areas where troops were concentrated as a 'factory' for TB, influenza, venereal disease (as sexually transmitted disease was then called) and other infectious diseases. The spectre of a plague of STD was regarded as the vilest and most humiliating manifestation of Ireland's subjugation to the British Empire. Women active in the suffrage movement, Sinn Féin and Cumann na mBan, the women's auxiliary of the Volunteers, were all too ready to rise to the challenge, answering the rallying call by forming the Committee for the Protection of Ireland from Venereal Disease.

The Charlemont Street premises had been occupied for many years by Providence House, a Protestant charity that provided training for orphan girls 'of good character' so that they could find employment as domestic servants. Empty now and quite run down, it was purchased by Ethel Rhodes, a Quaker friend of Lynn, for use at a low rent 'until the committee were in a position to buy the house.'

The combination of fear and outrage that motivated the movement is evident in a letter that Lynn's life companion, Madeleine ffrench-Mullen, wrote to her fellow-activist Hanna Sheehy Skeffington, explaining that the house would serve

> as a small hospital for the treatment of infants suffering from syphilis ... We all realise that the number of such babies is alarmingly on the increase, especially in the case of boarded out babies. Such infants are a terrible danger to the families who receive them.

Even Lynn, who was usually measured in her language, told delegates to the 1918 Sinn Féin ard-fheis that

> the evil we prophesied has already fallen upon us. All over the country syphilis is showing itself, introduced by soldiers on leave and the huge British garrison quartered on our land.

Like ffrench-Mullen, she warned delegates against

> the increasing number of war babies sent over here from England to be boarded out. These babies have been known to infect whole households with syphilis.

Despite, or perhaps because of, the public revulsion aroused by this prospect, the Committee for the Protection of Ireland from Venereal Disease found it hard to raise funds until it amended its objective to 'a general hospital for infants, with a portion of the building to be set aside for the syphilitic infants.' Once the hospital was open, the emphasis quickly shifted to include the welfare of mothers as well as their babies.[1] There is no denying Lynn's contention that

> the lack of knowledge of the treatment of infants [in the city] ... was appalling and the attention given to them in general hospitals was very defective; only surgical cases being treated. No interest was taken in malnutrition or kindred complaints. We considered it high time this state of affairs should be remedied.

The women certainly brought an urgency and commitment to the project that was missing from the provision of statutory services. Like many of their

supporters, Lynn and ffrench-Mullen saw it as an extension of the struggle for
the social objectives of the Republic outlined in the 1916 Proclamation and
reaffirmed in the Democratic Programme of Dáil Éireann. Both women had
served in the Irish Citizen Army during the Easter Rising. Lynn had been drawn
to the organisation by her admiration for its commander, James Connolly, and
was recruited by her cousin Constance Markievicz. She knew that beyond the
theatrical costumes and dramatics Markievicz 'was full of sound sense and was
quite practical.' Although she was given the rank of captain, there is no evidence
that Lynn fought in the Rising or underwent military training. 'I never drilled.
I had no time for that sort of thing,' she said. But she certainly possessed tenacity
of purpose. A member of the City Hall garrison in 1916, she tended the wounded
even as the rebel garrison contested each floor with British infantry until driven
onto the roof and forced to surrender.

After her release from prison Lynn immersed herself in Sinn Féin rather
than the labour movement. While she retained her socialist principles, she felt,
like many activists, that more could be achieved in this way. Like most women
involved in the struggle for independence, Lynn would eventually be marginalised
by the new Free State regime, but she was a crucial figure in those years.

Her new premises in Charlemont Street were totally unfit for their purpose.

The women of the Citizen Army, of one accord on a Sunday came to that
derelict house and cleaned it up. The pigeons had got into one of the top
rooms which had been a dormitory and it was filthy dirty. The women
cleaned it and made it presentable as far as possible ... Countess Markievicz
helped and Countess Plunkett brought bedding. We got help from friends
around. It was a very scratch affair.

She added that 'before we had time to convert it into a children's hospital the
'flu epidemic had broken out.' Having successfully tested the flu vaccine on
Citizen Army men, Lynn proceeded to use it in Charlemont Street.

Not one patient that was admitted to the hospital died. We had some
patients that were very bad, among them Mrs. Cathal Brugha who, at the
time, was expecting a baby. We had Michael Staines there. His friends in the
I.R.A. were constantly trying to visit him, but I refused permission.

When the epidemic was over, we closed the hospital for the time being.
It was formally opened as St. Ultan's Infants' Hospital on Ascension
Thursday, May 29th, 1919. We had £70 in the bank, and there were two infants
in the hospital.

The choice of a holy day of the Catholic Church was intended as an ecumenical gesture by Lynn, who knew that most of her patients would be Catholic working-class women. She does not appear to have been drawn to Catholicism, as Constance Markievicz and a number of other republican activists from a Protestant background were, but she was alive to the danger of sectarianism undermining the work of the hospital. Crucial support came from the Catholic Archbishop of Dublin, Dr William Walsh, whom the committee visited during the planning phase of the hospital in 1918. It is not clear if a Church of Ireland endorsement was sought; if it was, the outcome of the meeting was not announced. Walsh, on the other hand, gave the project his very public blessing, and it was significant that Lynn thought it important that he should.

To consolidate support in the wider community Lynn organised an annual 'pilgrimage-cum-picnic' to Ardbraccan, Co. Meath, the reputed site of St Ultan's well. This social and fund-raising event was intended to be bilingual and multi-denominational. In 1921 de Valera agreed to support the outing, boosting its popularity and fund-raising capacity if not necessarily its ecumenical appeal. Lynn's efforts to build bridges across the sectarian divide with her co-religionists, such as Gaelicising the Church of Ireland liturgy, were less successful. She would be estranged from her father, a Church of Ireland minister in Cong, Co. Mayo, for most of these years.

Her work for St Ultan's did not end Dr Lynn's political career. She served on the Executive Committee of Sinn Féin, was elected to Rathmines Urban District Council and was a founder-member of the League of Women Delegates (later Cumann na dTeachtaí) within Sinn Féin. Her home provided a place of convalescence for republicans, such as Laurence Ginnell and Constance Markievicz, after terms of imprisonment. Ironically, it was never used by wounded Volunteers, because of the regularity with which it was raided.[2]

St Ultan's was the most important public-health initiative undertaken by the independence movement in Dublin. Whatever other factors influenced these pioneers, the vital imperative was to reduce the dreadful level of infant mortality in the city. Between 1911 and 1915 infant mortality was 91 per 1,000, compared with 50 per 1,000 in rural areas. Within the city there were sharp social differentials: mortality was 7 per 1,000 among the professional classes, 22 per 1,000 for the middle classes and 120 per 1,000 among the children of unskilled workers. Syphilis was indeed a significant factor in the high mortality rate, and was probably underestimated, as doctors were reluctant to record it as a cause of death.[3] Yet even more potent in their effects were poverty, overcrowding, malnourishment and lack of education in basic hygiene.

If St Ultan's differed from other voluntary hospitals in its objectives, it also differed in the nature and motivation of its founders. Voluntary hospitals had tended to be founded by nursing orders, most notably the Mater Misericordiae Hospital by the Sisters of Mercy and St Vincent's Hospital by the Sisters of Charity. St Ultan's was a creation of modern, lay female professionals. Some male medical specialists were employed as required, but St Ultan's pursued a policy of 'positive discrimination' when it came to recruitment, and almost all members of the staff were women. There seems to have been no difficulty filling vacancies. By 1920 women constituted 11 per cent of the medical profession in Dublin but they could not secure senior posts in the hospital system. Kathleen Lynn had herself been one of those excluded women. She had qualified in 1902, undertook postgraduate research in the United States and was awarded a Royal College of Surgeons fellowship; nevertheless she failed to secure a permanent position. After her involvement in the Easter Rising she had little choice but to set up in private practice. St Ultan's filled an important gap in the development of the profession for the first generation of Irish women doctors, while paediatrics, fortuitously, was a new discipline that even conservative male colleagues accepted as particularly suited to the skills and insights of women.

After a shaky start Lynn was able to tap into the sympathy of a broad range of people concerned about public health, not all of them feminists or republicans. In 1919 the barrister Louis Ely O'Carroll opened the grounds of his house, the Lawn, at Peter Place, off Adelaide Road, for a series of fund-raising events. Bridge parties were organised in other large houses, and the Abbey Theatre put on a fund-raising performance of Ibsen's *An Enemy of the People*, probably through the good offices of the actor, trade union activist and Citizen Army member Helena Moloney. The Catholic Young Men's Society organised a whist drive, with a £10 note and a ton of 'best coal' as the main prizes. The Royal College of Surgeons in Ireland presented lectures by leading English medical experts on paediatrics to raise public awareness and to help finance the project. The very fact that these events were taking place was an important acknowledgement of the breakthrough achieved by Lynn and her colleagues.[4]

The support group included intellectuals such as George Russell, the artist Jack Yeats and Professor Thomas Bodkin, governor of the National Gallery. The general secretary of the Irish Women Workers' Union, Louie Bennett, whose pacifism prevented her from becoming involved in militant republicanism, was another supporter of the hospital. So was Lady Carson, wife of the Ulster unionist leader. She donated a goat to the small herd that was kept to provide mothers and children with tuberculosis-free milk. (Inevitably it was christened 'Carson'.) But the core of the hospital was its doctors and nurses. Some of them, such as Dr Katherine Maguire, met Lynn through the suffrage movement before the war, and several were co-religionists, such Dr Dorothy Stopford Price and Dr Ella Webb, whose father was Dean of St Patrick's Cathedral. What united them was an interest not just in paediatrics but in the beneficial effect public-health reform could have on the wider community. Webb founded the Stillorgan Children's Sunshine Home, while the first chairman of the St Ultan's board, Lucy Griffin, was an inspector for children in the South Dublin and Rathdown Union.

If St Ultan's seems small by modern standards, with only thirty-five cots by the late 1920s, it did help reduce infant mortality to between 66 and 74 per 1,000—still higher than British urban rates but well below that of Belfast. The hospital concentrated on lower-income groups, where mortality was highest. In 1924, for instance, 44 per cent of its patients were from families in which the father was unemployed. Infant mortality remained persistently high for 'illegitimate' children, who accounted for 15 per cent of patients but had a 30 per cent mortality rate, more than four times the average figure.[5]

As Lynn had predicted, the demobilisation of millions of soldiers caused a sharp increase in infection rates from sexually transmitted diseases throughout Europe. In fact they rose more than twice as fast for men in Dublin than in England and Wales, and five times faster for women. The municipal authorities could not remain oblivious to such a serious threat to public health. Even before the war ended, in June 1918, Dublin Corporation moved to establish a special two-ward unit in Dr Steevens' Hospital to supplement the existing facilities at Sir Patrick Dun's Hospital and the Westmoreland Lock Hospital. The latter dealt exclusively with female patients, most of whom were prostitutes. Far more women depended on prostitution as a survival strategy in Dublin during the immediate post-war years than in British cities; yet so blinded were advanced nationalists by their own propaganda that even health professionals such as Dr Lynn failed to question why STD rates rose so much faster in Dublin than in Britain, where far more soldiers were demobilised in both relative and absolute terms.

The new facility at Dr Steevens' Hospital was proposed by P. T. Daly, chairman of the Public Health Committee of Dublin Corporation, who had been concerned about the problem since 1915. His corporation ward included some of the worst 'kips' or brothels in the city.[6] The venereal disease unit in Dr Steevens' Hospital opened in January 1919, and in its first three months it recorded 452 male attendances and 59 female attendances. By the first quarter of 1920 the figures were 2,298 and 529, respectively, a more than fivefold increase in male attendances and an almost tenfold increase in female attendances. The number of cases continued to increase long after the British army departed, reaching a peak in 1934, when attendances at outpatient clinics reached 40,086 and the number of inpatient days was 10,487.[7] As early as 1926 an interdepartmental committee on venereal disease proposed a register for prostitutes to regulate their trade, but the Catholic hierarchy vetoed it. The myth that the fight for independence had cleansed Dublin of the corrupting influence of Anglo-Saxon decadence was thus preserved.[8]

The achievement of Kathleen Lynn and her colleagues was all the more remarkable given the difficulties that hospitals in Dublin were experiencing as a result of cuts in government spending to restore the public finances after the most expensive war in history. The trio of 'House of Industry' hospitals were forced to close temporarily in 1919 after the newly established Department of Health, for which the Chief Secretary was responsible, refused to meet their shortfall in funding.

The Richmond, Whitworth and Hardwicke Hospitals formed a neat red-brick complex in North Brunswick Street, adjoining the grounds of the North Dublin Union recently taken over by the military. They were among the oldest hospitals in the city and, unlike the great voluntary institutions set up by religious orders, were almost totally dependent on public funding. They complemented each other, with the Richmond providing surgical services and the Whitworth providing medical services while the Hardwicke was a fever hospital. An auxiliary block served as an emergency unit and helped cater for epidemics and for military patients.

These hospitals primarily served the poor of north Dublin and the surrounding counties. Incredibly, they had managed to survive on an annual government grant of £7,600 a year, a sum set during the Crimean War era of the 1850s, with small subventions from Dublin Corporation. Wartime inflation made this level of funding unsustainable. The average cost of a bed rose from £64 per year in 1914 to £119 by 1919. During the war the number of beds rose from 250 to 300. The modest debit balance of £306 5s 8d in 1914 had been reduced to £39 9s 6d by 1916, and by May 1919 the three hospitals were running a deficit of £12,654. The board wrote to the Chief Secretary's Office in 1918 alerting him to the crisis, only to be told repeatedly that no funds were available and that there was no legal obligation to provide them, even though the hospital lands and buildings had been ceded to the Board of Works. The Lord Lieutenant, Sir John French, refused to accept the resignations of the Board of Governors, who felt they could no longer continue in office when porters, nurses and other employees had to be laid off because there was no money for wages. Suppliers had not been paid since February. When the senior medical personnel at the hospitals called on the new Chief Secretary, Sir Ian Macpherson, in April they received no satisfaction either. Subsequently the senior surgeon at the Richmond, Sir Thomas Myles, wrote to Macpherson, requesting instructions on what to do with the two hundred remaining patients, many of them soldiers. Macpherson replied that it was not his job 'to give instructions or advice.'

By May, Dublin Castle was embroiled in an acrimonious row with the citizenry of all political persuasions. At a meeting on 21 July the leader of the Sinn Féin group on the city council, Alderman Tom Kelly, proposed that the corporation take over the hospitals, with the proviso that admission 'be reserved for the citizens' and that rural referrals be excluded. But Dr James McWalter, a nationalist representative for the north inner city, pointed out that this was still beyond the financial resources of the city, and the council settled for sending a delegation to see Macpherson. It achieved no better results than the hospital management. By the beginning of August fewer than sixty beds were occupied in the complex, and it closed shortly afterwards.

While nationalist criticism of the cuts could be expected, and Sir Thomas Myles would be counted in this camp for his role before the Great War in helping arm the Irish Volunteers, the blatant abdication of responsibility by Dublin Castle enraged unionists as well. The two unionist MPs for Dublin University raised the issue in the House of Commons, and in an open letter to the new under-secretary responsible for health, James McMahon, the chairman of the hospitals' Board of Governors, Barrington Jellett, made no attempt to conceal his contempt for Macpherson. He wrote:

It is to be regretted that the Chief Secretary for Ireland did not personally visit these hospitals. I have no hesitation in asserting that, had he done so, he would have been satisfied that a discontinuance of the work done ... would be a cruel wrong to the poor of Dublin.[9]

Unfortunately, Macpherson, a Liberal member of the government, was one of many Chief Secretaries with a marked reluctance to visit Ireland, even allowing a unionist colleague, Walter Long, to undertake a fact-finding tour of the country on behalf of the Cabinet.

The problem of funding the 'House of Industry' hospitals had fallen victim to administrative infighting. They were the only hospitals in the United Kingdom to be financed directly by a parliamentary vote, and if the subvention was increased a government desperate to cut expenditure feared it would open the floodgates for every indigent hospital to petition Parliament. Dubliners were not impressed. As the *Irish Independent* remarked, not only was the complex 'famous as a school of clinical instruction' but the original House of Industry had been 'established by an Act of the Irish Parliament in 1772. On the passing of the Act of Union it was a Government Institution, and was so adopted by the Imperial Parliament.' The board was appointed by the Lord Lieutenant, and 787 soldiers had been among those treated during the war. The *Independent* pointed out that the government's own Board of Superintendence of the Dublin Hospitals, in its report for 1917/18, had made 'one of the clearest cases that can be made for an increased grant.' The fact that a bill of £1,808 for soldiers treated there had never been paid added grist to the mill.[10]

The *Irish Times* was equally scathing and praised the 'public spirit of the governors and medical staff' for averting 'a real calamity from the poor of Dublin' when it was announced in September that the complex would reopen without government funds. It did so on the strength of a small charge 'from such patients as can afford to make it' and an appeal to the generosity of Dubliners to supplement the 'utterly inadequate grant' from the state. The secretary of the governors, W. Webster Smith, thanked the newspaper for its support and informed readers that the hospitals would continue to provide 'the best medical and surgical care free from any suggestion of charity'; but 'the number of free beds at present will necessarily be comparatively small and can be increased only by revenue obtained from outside sources.'[11]

The main achievement of the government's parsimony had been to drive Dubliners deeper into the embrace of Sinn Féin, as is shown by a letter to the *Irish Independent* from Dr McWalter in September, before the House of Industry hospitals had announced their decision to reopen. McWalter used the issue to launch a general attack on the government's health policy for Ireland.

> I don't write to complain that only one third of the new Irish Public Health Council just started by the Government are Catholics.
>
> I don't simply wish to point out that the Chief Secretary has—metaphorically—spat in the faces of the 400 Irish Catholic officers who voluntarily joined the R.A.M.C. [Royal Army Medical Corps] by refusing to appoint a single one of them on his Public Health Council; I don't even ask you to note that even of the few Catholics now on the Council Mr. Macpherson has not directly appointed one—they are nominated by public bodies—but I do wish to demonstrate that the new Public Health Council can recommend the Chief Secretary, as Minister of Public Health, to contribute to the upkeep of the Richmond and Whitworth hospitals.

The irate McWalter went on to cite section 10 of the 1772 act, which gave Macpherson the power to take discretionary measures 'for the prevention and cure of diseases.' He ended by claiming that Dublin was treated less generously than Belfast or Derry in the provision of funds for health services. 'We know that any appeal from the South is treated with callous contempt whilst any threat from the North makes the Government tremble.'[12]

McWalter, a long-serving nationalist member of Dublin Corporation, was the only councillor to take a place on the reviewing platform alongside Lord French at the victory march through the city in July. He may well have been angry that this demonstration of loyalty had not been rewarded, and he was no doubt recalling with mixed feelings the day in June 1915 when he had entered the Dublin council chamber resplendent in the uniform of a lieutenant in the RAMC and announced his decision to volunteer, to the congratulations of his nationalist colleagues. None of them followed his example; McWalter was the only public representative from Dublin city or county to join the Colours in the First World War. By removing the ladder of patronage Dublin Castle was cutting one of its last slender links to middle-class Catholic professionals. The controversy also affected unionist attitudes in the city, reinforcing the belief among thoughtful members of that community, for whom social reform was an important concern, that reaching agreement on the structures required for the effective provision of essential services such as health was as important as constitutional frameworks.

The attitude to the House of Industry hospitals was seen by some as part of a general approach to Ireland, equally revealed by two new pieces of legislation that proposed a standard inferior to that of parallel measures for England and Wales. Both covered emotive issues: one was the health of children and the other was housing.

The Public Health (Medical Treatment of Children) (Ireland) Bill made provision for local authorities to carry out medical inspections and to treat children in elementary schools. Under its provisions, half the cost of the inspections would be met by central government and the other half locally, with some or all of the latter recouped from the parents. Unlike its British counterpart, the Irish bill was discretionary. In other words, there was no obligation on Irish local authorities to administer the scheme. The battle to have the bill amended fell entirely to the unionists and the rump of the Irish Party, mainly in Ulster, as Sinn Féin members abstained from the British House of Commons.

As traditional defenders of the Irish ratepaying classes, members of the Irish Party were happy to let things sit. The leader of the group, Joe Devlin, argued that as a new Irish Ministry of Health was being established under the Chief Secretary's remit it made sense to leave implementation of the scheme to that body—especially as 'the starting of a new system of rating and taxation for the purpose would create very serious trouble and irritation.' By contrast, unionist MPs were forthright in their criticism of double standards. Colonel Walter Guinness asked why the bill was 'in a weaker form than the English Act.' He concluded that 'it was surely inadvisable to leave the provisions optional in Ireland where public opinion was much more backward.' Sir Maurice Dockrell, the only unionist MP representing a Dublin constituency other than Dublin University, used the occasion to give his first speech in the House of Commons. He produced figures supplied by his fellow-unionist and fellow-Freemason Sir Charles Cameron, Dublin's Chief Medical Officer, demonstrating why mandatory medical inspections were 'absolutely necessary in the interests of public health.'[13]

The figures for 1918 showed that there had been 1,116 deaths among infants under the age of twelve months, 836 among one to five-year-olds and 470 among five to fifteen-year-olds. Dockrell said that

> I should be wanting in my duty if I failed to support the Bill, but at the same time it should ... be made mandatory, as that would make the results to the health of the children at once apparent.

The government accepted the unionist amendments.[14]

Despite the best efforts of Dockrell and his colleagues, they were less successful in their efforts to amend the Housing (Ireland) Bill. It was an inadvertent tribute to the effectiveness of the Irish Party in its heyday as a champion of rural Ireland. According to Ruth McManus, the historian of Dublin's housing policy, 'by 1914, Ireland's rural labourers were among the best housed of their class in Western Europe.'[15] Some 48,000 cottages had been built by 1921, at a cost of £8½ million, as opposed to only 10,000 houses in urban areas, at a cost of £2½ million. A new Housing Act was passed in 1914 to finance local authority projects during the war, but the Local Government Board did not submit Dublin's proposals in time. Attempts to raise a loan on the private investment market in America also fell through, although it had the endorsement of Dublin Chamber of Commerce and Archbishop William Walsh.

In 1917 the Chief Secretary, Henry Duke, had arranged for funds to be released for work on corporation schemes, following a visit to slum areas in April that left him appalled at conditions. It was also part of a policy for defusing unrest, but only one modest scheme, at Spitalfields in the south inner city, had been completed by the end of the war. It was in this context that the Housing (Ireland) Bill wended its way through the House of Commons, in tandem with a similar bill for England and Wales. While the British bill provided for the English Local Government Board to underwrite 75 per cent of local authority loans and to make up any shortfall between the cost of providing housing and the rental income from low-income families, its Irish counterpart provided for only half the rental shortfall to be met from the exchequer. It was not until July 1919 that one of Duke's successors, Macpherson, agreed to increase the government subvention from £1 for every £1 expended by the Irish local authorities in rent subsidies to 25s for every £1, or 27s 6d 'in exceptional cases.'

The political obstacles that even large Irish local authorities, such as Dublin Corporation, faced in raising funds for quite modest developments—the Spitalfields project added 5d in the pound to the rates—would have been significant in normal times. In the growing turmoil of 1919, slum clearance was a pipe dream.[16] Even the *Irish Times* was critical of the British government's stance, pointing out that no bank in Ireland was prepared to advance loans on the strength of the inadequate safeguards in the legislation.[17]

However, one piece of legislation was passed in Westminster that year that would have a profound effect on the nascent Irish state, and Sir Maurice Dockrell would be among its most fervent advocates. This was the introduction of proportional representation for Irish elections, which had so far been determined by the 'first past the post' system that prevailed in the rest of the United Kingdom. The government decision followed a pilot scheme in Sligo, where PR was used to conduct a special municipal election that denied Sinn Féin an outright majority. Ironically, Sinn Féin had long advocated PR, and de Valera welcomed the proposed change, even though it was being introduced to achieve 'a crooked object'.[18]

The main opposition came from the Unionist Party. It opposed the bill on principle, because it would differentiate between the way public representatives were elected in Ireland and Britain, and because it would ensure a voice for the nationalist minority in the North. Sir Maurice Dockrell had been formally admitted to the ranks of the Ulster Unionist group in the House of Commons in February 1919, along with the successful independent unionist candidate for Dublin University, Sir Robert Woods. This ensured that Dockrell had speaking as well as voting rights, and he did not allow the position of the group on PR to prevent him from voicing his support for the government measure. He said that he 'stands in the House today as the sole representative of 350,000 Unionists of the South of Ireland.' The bill 'would bring about a transfusion of blood in local representation.' If proportional representation had been used in the general election, he said, at least one other unionist MP would be with him representing Dublin. His position was strongly supported by the Proportional Representation Society of Ireland, of which a well-known Dublin social reformer, E. A. Aston, was secretary.[19]

The legislation for the provision of better child health services and local authority housing meant little in practice, because of the growing disorder in Ireland. A hiatus had developed between an old regime that had lost its mandate and a new one in the making.

In April 1919 Dáil Éireann set up its own Department of Local Government, under W. T. Cosgrave. Cosgrave had ten years' experience on Dublin Corporation to help him, but he suffered from ill-health and bouts of imprisonment over the next couple of years. Even with the assistance of a very able deputy, Kevin O'Higgins, the obstacles were formidable. The local authorities were still dominated by Irish Party councillors and, in the case of the Dublin authorities, there were significant numbers of unionists unwilling to co-operate with the new republic. The biggest handicap, however, was the lack of a thought-out programme of local authority reform. There was also evidence of complacency and, understandably, exhaustion after the frenetic events of 1918, culminating in the landslide general election victory.

Only 60 per cent of Sinn Féin cumainn had re-registered by mid-1919, and most of the funds collected locally appear to have been spent locally. There was a renewed membership drive later in the year, when a number of new organisers were appointed. These spent much of their time on educational work, trying to explain Sinn Féin policies to members. Metaphysics took precedence over ideology, and often there was a strong assertion of the traditional Catholic values that had become pronounced within the party following the death of Thomas Ashe in 1917.[20] Meetings were frequently held after Mass on Sundays, and the ideals espoused by Pearse, well on his way to secular sainthood, were emphasised for the guidance of members.

Contrary to the fears of Southern unionists articulated by the *Irish Times*, there was no question of Sinn Féin replicating the Bolsheviks in Russia and the party becoming a state within a state, as it not only lacked a coherent ideology but its ultra-democratic structures did not allow for democratic centralism. As the year progressed it was militant elements in the Irish Volunteers and in the cabinet grouping around Michael Collins who set the political pace.[21]

Meanwhile, in an effort to come to terms with this policy vacuum, Dáil Éireann established a commission in June 1919 to survey Ireland's natural resources. A Land Bank was established and a programme for the promotion of Irish. The process enabled Sinn Féin to create links with interest groups around the country and to promote its policy of economic self-sufficiency without a direct confrontation with Dublin Castle at a time when it was not organisationally ready to do so. Above all, the commission was well within Dáil Éireann's financial and organisational resources. Figures as varied as Colonel Maurice Moore, the former Inspector-General of the Redmondite National Volunteers, the Labour leaders Thomas Johnson and William O'Brien, and Professor Hugh Ryan, professor of chemistry at UCD, were among those recruited to the commission.

It went about its business methodically, if slowly. Its first public hearing, in November 1919 at the offices of Monaghan County Council, was suppressed by the RIC, but a subsequent meeting in Dublin was allowed to go ahead. Reports of the proceedings were heavily censored. Fortunately, the censorship regulations did not apply to British newspapers readily available in Ireland, making the exercise futile.[22] While there was some criticism in the Dáil of the slow pace of the commission's work, and its high cost, it did eventually produce eight reports by 1922, covering dairying, coal, the production of industrial alcohol, milk-processing, turf, fisheries, stock-breeding and hydro-electric power. At a cost of £6,000 it was, as Arthur Mitchell, historian of the revolutionary Dáil, put it, 'good value for money.'

Dáil Éireann itself conducted its business in a relatively low-key, methodical way. Sessions at the Mansion House were banned in June and it had to convene in secret. The main venue was 3 Mountjoy Square, home of the wholesale fruit merchant Walter Cole, a long-standing friend of Arthur Griffith and a former Sinn Féin alderman in Dublin. Sessions were also held around the corner at Fleming's Hotel. Secrecy was facilitated by the small number of MPs—or teachtaí Dála, as they now preferred to be called—who were able to attend meetings.

The newly constituted republic went on something of a property spree in the capital, purchasing four buildings, including 76 Harcourt Street, just up the road from the Sinn Féin premises at number 6, and renting nineteen others through various supporters and front organisations, generally in good locales, such as the city centre and upper-middle-class suburbs.[23] The *Irish Bulletin*, official propaganda organ of Dáil Éireann, had to move regularly but showed a similar penchant for salubrious venues, such as Molesworth Street, Upper Mount Street and Rathgar, where the *Bulletin* was produced in a large house surrounded by 'flowered gardens'. The Army Council and Dáil Éireann cabinet met regularly in two of the most exclusive addresses in the city, 36 Aylesbury Road, the home of Nell Humphreys, sister of the executed 1916 leader Michael O'Rahilly, and 40 Herbert Park, where O'Rahilly's widow, Nan, lived. The use of such venues could be rationalised as hiding in plain sight at addresses where the enemy were least likely to look, although that argument hardly applied to the last two. It also made life on the run far pleasanter than it would have been for the revolutionary elite in the Dublin slums and suggests a sense of entitlement that did not sit easily with the revolutionary rhetoric of the 1916 Proclamation or the Democratic Programme of Dáil Éireann.[24]

Vaughan's Hotel at 29 Parnell Square, the premises of George Moreland, cabinet-maker, at 10 Middle Abbey Street and the offices at 3 Crow Street served a different purpose. Vaughan's was a 'clearing house' for Collins, where he met Volunteer leaders from the country who shared his commitment to resuming the armed struggle. In 1920, when Vaughan's began to attract heavy British surveillance, much of the business was transferred to Kirwan's and Devlin's pubs around the corner in Parnell Street, which were owned by supporters. The Moreland premises in Middle Abbey Street would serve as a base for the 'Squad', the team of Volunteers that Collins assembled in late 1919 as the combat section of his intelligence organisation in the city. Moreland shared the premises with a trade union, the Stationary Engine Drivers' Association. The offices at Crow Street were over the printing firm of J. F. Fowler and constituted the national headquarters of Collins's intelligence department. Like many premises used by the Volunteers, they were acquired through connections in the Dublin craft unions, reflecting the traditional links between the latter and radical republicanism.[25]

The formation of the Squad and overtly violent paramilitary activity in the city were still months away when Dáil Éireann decided on 10 April 1919 to order a peaceful boycott of the RIC and DMP. The Irish Volunteer newspaper, An tÓglach, had already declared that every 'policeman, warder, judge or official must be made realise that it is not wise to distinguish himself by undue zeal in the service of England.' The declaration, which was adopted at one of the best-attended Dáil sessions during the War of Independence, was only slightly more restrained in its call and undoubtedly strengthened the growing public mood of hostility towards the police. Arthur Griffith in particular catalogued various incidents in which civilians had been beaten, shot or imprisoned by the authorities over the previous year. He added that the history of the police was 'a continuity of brutal treason against their own people,' from which 'the Irish people, as an organised society, have a right to defend themselves. The social ostracism which I propose … is a first step in exercising that right.' The same session approved the preparation of a prospectus for a national loan of £1 million by Collins in his role as Minister for Finance.[26] It would be September before the details were completed and the loan ready to be launched. In the meantime Collins had already taken drastic steps against individual members of the DMP's G Division that went far beyond a boycott.

As we have seen from his support for the Tipperary Volunteers who carried out the Solloghodbeg ambush in January, and by his cultivation of senior militants in the movement, such as Tomás Mac Curtáin in Cork and the new commandant of the Dublin Brigade, Dick McKee, Collins was building a consensus for resuming the armed struggle. The defection of Éamonn Broy and his colleagues in the DMP meant that he now had the inside information he needed to neutralise and if necessary kill key detectives of G Division in the city. The only question was whether the citizens of Dublin were ready to accept such drastic measures.

The shooting of Alfred Pearson and the raid on Collinstown Aerodrome in March had been condemned in official circles but had not provoked much hostility from ordinary Dubliners. In fact the success of the arms raid had the opposite effect. The next serious stepping up of violence came in June at a memorial concert in the Mansion House to celebrate the birthday of the 1916 signatory James Connolly. It was not formally banned, but the Lord Mayor and the leaders of Connolly's union, the ITGWU, were told it would not be tolerated. A strong force of DMP under that 'Ulster Covenanter' Superintendent George Willoughby[27] barred access by the public to Dawson Street. A large crowd gathered at the St Stephen's Green end of the street, and when the DMP tried to disperse it an automatic pistol was produced. The gunman was disarmed but managed to get away while the constable and sergeant who tried to arrest him were themselves attacked. In the subsequent scuffle two or three Citizen Army members drew pistols and fired, apparently to cover the retreat of their companion. A DMP sergeant, three constables and a young woman were wounded. As armed DMP members drew their weapons, the crowd, about two thousand strong, fled. The young woman, Margaret Hayes, was shot in the leg but managed to hop as far as the St Stephen's Green Club, where her wound was dressed before she was taken to St Vincent's Hospital around the corner. The wounded policemen were given first aid by the St John Ambulance Brigade at the Royal Irish Automobile Club in Dawson Street before being taken to St Vincent's as well. They were all from A Division, based in Great Brunswick Street.

Members of G Division retaliated with a series of raids in the city that weekend on small businesses run by known republicans. These included an

electrical fitting and bicycle shop run by Joe Lawless, son of the Sinn Féin TD
and 1916 veteran Frank Lawless. Young Lawless was arrested when a rifle part
was found in his workshop. The most active policeman in the raids was
Detective-Sergeant Daniel Hoey, the same one who almost caught Collins in
the raid on the Mansion House in April. Collins must have noted that the
shootings on the Green had barely raised a ripple of public concern. On the
other hand, the activities of detectives such as Hoey, armed with local
knowledge and determined to do their duty, threatened the cohesion of the
Dublin Brigade on which Collins relied in prosecuting his war in the capital.

Any doubts about the changed public mood were removed, ironically
enough, by the news on Saturday 28 June that the peace treaty formally ending
the Great War had been signed at Versailles. Allied flags were quickly flown from
leading businesses and private houses, especially in the middle-class suburbs
and townships to the south and north-east of the city, and 101-gun salutes were
fired at all the main barracks in Dublin. However, once it grew dark trouble
erupted in the city centre. Hostile crowds gathered in Sackville Street and
College Green, where soldiers were continuing to celebrate the peace. According
to the *Irish Times*, anyone wearing or carrying a miniature Union Jack had it
snatched and thrown away or set on fire, while the crowd countered the music-
hall favourites of the servicemen with renditions of 'The Soldier's Song' and
'The Red Flag'.

At the corner of Sackville Street and Henry Street groups of soldiers and
civilians exchanged blows until the DMP intervened. They took the soldiers down
to the quays and put them on board a tram back to their camp in the Phoenix
Park, only for fighting to erupt with civilians on the top deck. A midshipman
(cadet) of the Royal Naval Volunteer Reserve and an ex-soldier with a motorbike
and side car were attacked in Westmorland Street, and Major Martin Alexander,
mistaken for an RIC officer as he drove to the Sackville Street Club, was dragged
from his car and badly beaten. Things became noticeably worse just before
midnight when a Royal Air Force lorry passing through Sackville Street *en route*
to Gormanston backfired. The crowd thought they were being fired upon, but
instead of scattering they attacked the vehicle. Corporal Robert Gale was dragged
from the cab and beaten senseless. The lorry was set alight.

In the early hours of Sunday there was real gunfire when Constable William
Dawson was shot in the back as he tried to arrest two Australian soldiers in
Westmorland Street, one of whom was carrying a large 'Sinn Féin flag' and the
other acting as cheerleader for a crowd chanting 'Up Sinn Féin!' Fortunately
one bullet missed Dawson, and the heavy-duty uniform belt he was wearing
took most of the impact of the other, but still he was out on sickness leave for

five weeks as a result of his injuries. The two Australians were arrested after a violent scuffle and subsequently court-martialled. Both men claimed they were drunk at the time and that they thought they were participating in an Allied victory march. That one of the men had been decorated for gallantry and the other came from a family that owned a 7,000-acre farm in New South Wales, and that the court-martial was composed exclusively of Australian officers, may help explain their acquittal.

The most serious casualty of the night was the Dublin ratepayer. The corporation had to pay £150 to the RAF for the burnt-out lorry, and various soldiers and DMP members successfully claimed for malicious damage, including Major Alexander, who received £120, Corporal Gale, who received £25, and Constable Dawson, who received £100.[28]

The formal victory march in Dublin took place on Saturday 19 July, to coincide with that in London. The streets were once more ceded to the military and their supporters during the day, only to be contested by republicans at night. Some fifteen thousand soldiers and sailors, including units from the Dublin garrison and contingents from all the Irish regiments, supplemented by five thousand demobilised ex-servicemen, marched past Lord French on a reviewing platform outside the Bank of Ireland in College Green. Armoured cars and tanks brought up the rear, the first time most Dubliners had seen these tracked behemoths of the western front on their streets. The day was sunny and the mood in the immediate vicinity of College Green reminiscent of Armistice Day. 'A great Union Jack kept watch on Trinity's sombre pile,' the *Irish Times* reported, 'and many hued banners fluttered down Dame Street, spreading from house to house the fabulous message of peace, while roofs all around are a crawl with human bodies.'

But the *Irish Independent* noted that there were far smaller crowds in the rest of the city and that the few cheers raised were for the demobilised ex-servicemen. The latter's numbers were depleted by a decision of the Irish Nationalist Veterans' Association not to participate. At a mass meeting in the Mansion House the previous Wednesday, attended by three thousand members of the association, it was decided that they could not be involved 'in bolstering up the Government, whose first and great principle was the coercion of this country.' The motion was moved by Captain John Esmonde, a former Irish Party MP. Among the speakers was Mary Kettle, widow of another former Irish Party MP and British officer, Tom Kettle. She called 'for better treatment for the widows and orphans of the men who served.' The association used the opportunity to voice wider grievances at the coalition government's failure to provide ex-servicemen with either jobs or decent pensions.[29]

The only nationalist politician to share the saluting platform with Lord French was Surgeon-Captain James McWalter, still blissfully unaware of the snub that Irish Catholic RAMC officers would receive in the autumn, when not one of their number would be nominated to the new Irish Public Health Council. The Lord Mayor, Laurence O'Neill, declined an invitation to attend, although he was tactful enough to cite the short notice and lack of an opportunity to consult colleagues for their views on whether to accept.[30]

Mindful of the mood in the city, the military authorities organised evening entertainments in the main barracks. Inevitably some off-duty soldiers wandered onto the streets. At first there was just 'a little excitement … caused by individual altercations' between servicemen and civilians, but at 9:30 p.m. two soldiers were chased from Bachelor's Walk along the Liffey until finally caught by the mob at Ormond Quay. Sergeant Roche of the DMP intervened when their pursuers decided to throw one of the soldiers into the river. The sergeant was shot in the back with a revolver, the bullet narrowly missing his spine. DMP members reacted angrily to the news. They baton-charged a crowd of about three hundred people gathered in Beresford Place singing 'The Soldier's Song' and then another crowd that had gathered outside the GPO and booed a passing police patrol. One youth was badly injured and taken to Jervis Street Hospital, where Sergeant Roche was being treated. Another sixteen civilians were treated there for 'scalp wounds'.[31]

Serious disturbances in Limerick and Cork followed similar victory parades, and in Cork an RIC constable was shot in the thigh. Although a number of RIC members had been killed or wounded in encounters with the Volunteers in Co. Tipperary, these were the first shootings in an urban setting, and there was no public outcry.[32] It is probably more than coincidental that Collins convened an informal meeting of Volunteers to form the Squad and begin eliminating hostile detectives of G Division shortly afterwards.

At first some 1916 veterans approached to join the Squad refused: they had moral objections to what they regarded as nothing less than murder. This would be very different from the weekend soldiering excursions that preceded the Rising, or the conventional fighting of Easter Week itself: it would be more akin to Mafia-style killings, although it was the example of the 1916 veterans that an eager new generation of Volunteers, such as Charlie Dalton, sought to emulate.

The first target was Detective-Sergeant Patrick Smyth, who was shot on 30 July. He had twenty-eight years' service in the DMP. A native of Co. Cavan, he lived in Millmount Avenue, Drumcondra, with his wife and their seven children. Four members of what would become the Squad—Jim Slattery, Tom Keogh, Tom Ennis and Mick Kennedy—were involved. They had tracked Smyth home a week earlier but did not shoot him, because they were uncertain of his identity. On the second occasion they opened up at close range after he got off the tram at the bridge over the Tolka River. To their amazement, he was able to outrun them almost to his front door, despite a leg wound. Fortunately for them, Smyth was not armed. They abandoned their attack when his teenage son Francis and daughter Mary ran out into the street to find their father leaning against a wall, clutching his side. Smyth's youngest son, Eugene, came out as well, vowing 'to catch those who shot Dada.' Smyth did not die from his wounds until 8 September. In a statement to colleagues in hospital he said:

> In all about ten or twelve shots were fired at me. I shouted for assistance, but no-one came to me except my own son. I had no revolver myself, and I am glad now ... as I might have shot some of them when I turned around after the first shot, as I would not have liked to have done that.

His attackers, who would become the core of the Squad, had no regrets, and had learnt a number of valuable lessons. One was to trade in their .38 revolvers for the larger-calibre .45, which could stop a man in his tracks. Another was to refine their tactics. In future they tended to work in pairs. One man would fire at the victim's body to immobilise him while his partner would finish off the target with a shot to the head. Other members of the group would provide back-up and cover the assassins' retreat.[33]

As Collins expected, there was nothing like the level of public outrage that followed the Solloghodbeg killings in January. One reason was that Smyth was not killed outright; another was that the public were increasingly becoming inured to violence and hostile to all manifestations of British authority.

Attacks on members of the RIC were continuing around the country, resulting in two constables being killed in Co. Clare and another in Co. Tipperary. Then an arms raid on a military patrol attending a church parade in Fermoy, Co. Cork, on 7 September resulted in one soldier being shot dead and three wounded.[34] Taken with Detective-Sergeant Smyth's death the next day, this resulted in the Chief Secretary, Sir Ian Macpherson, finally getting his way. He had been pressing for tougher measures since May, against the advice of Sir Edward Carson and senior civil servants. On 10 September, Sinn Féin, the Irish Volunteers, Cumann na mBan and, for good measure, the Gaelic League were banned. Dáil Éireann followed on 12 September, and the same day the DMP raided the Sinn Féin offices at 6 Harcourt Street. No warning was given, and a number of senior officials were on the premises, one of whom, Ernest Blythe, was arrested after being found hiding in a store-room. Collins bluffed his way out by berating the officer in charge of the search of the upper floors, Detective-Inspector Ned McFeely. McFeely did not know Collins, whom he found in an office surrounded by female office staff. Collins had probably been the only armed man on the premises. 'I stuck Mick's revolver down my stocking,' Eibhlín Lawless, a secretary, recalled later, 'and anything else incriminating we girls took charge of it.' It was one of many incidents in which women would play the hero and give a hint of glamour, or even a frisson of sexual excitement, to these haphazard encounters. An important psychological advantage Collins enjoyed on this occasion was that he had been well briefed by Broy about McFeely. The detective-inspector was a home-ruler unhappy with the turn events were taking. When McFeely asked him for the documents he was holding, Collins poured forth a torrent of invective, telling McFeely he was bringing shame on himself and his family by 'spying on your countrymen.' McFeely withdrew, thoroughly embarrassed and cowed.

However, it was also luck that saved Collins, for at least one zealous policeman searching the lower offices knew him by sight. This was Detective-Sergeant Daniel Hoey. That evening the Squad, which had yet to be formally established, claimed its second victim. Hoey had gone to a milk bar in Tara Street for a break and was shot as he returned to Great Brunswick Street police station. Detectives later said the rapidity of the shots sounded like someone running a cane across the railings outside. On this occasion there were no mistakes. Three senior members of the Squad—Jim Slattery, Mick McDonnell and Tom Ennis—carried out the execution at point-blank range. Hoey was dead on arrival at Jervis Street Hospital.[35]

McDonnell, who had taken charge of the attacks on Hoey and Smyth, was quartermaster of the 2nd Battalion, which covered the north-east quadrant of Dublin. It was Dick McKee's old battalion, from which a high proportion of active Volunteers would be drawn in the War of Independence. Collins was now well on the way to building the organisational sinews for his campaign of terror in the capital.[36]

The Republic's Minister for Defence, Cathal Brugha, and the Chief of Staff of the Irish Volunteers, Richard Mulcahy, both regarded the ban on Dáil Éireann and the Volunteers as a declaration of war, and they sanctioned the formal establishment of the Squad at the end of September. Brugha wanted its first targets to be members of the British Cabinet, but this operation was called off as impractical.

There was a certain symmetry between British and Irish thinking at this stage. Macpherson explained the ban on Dáil Éireann to Carson by saying that it was one thing to allow 'these members [of the House of Commons] to sit in consultation if they wished,' but when they 'conspired by executive acts to overthrow the duly constituted authority, then we could act.'[37]

Looking back years later, Mulcahy believed that 'what turned passive resistance and defensive tactics into an offensive war was the suppression of the Dáil.' He argued that action against the DMP was necessary because

the authorities were apparently biding their time to have certain preparations made before the Dáil was suppressed. The work of men like Smyth, Hoey and Barton and the G Division generally, [was] being effectively snowballed to increase information regarding the persons who were particularly active and important both on the political and the volunteer side. To have allowed it to develop ... would have been disastrous.[38]

The last-mentioned, Detective-Sergeant John Barton, would be the third G Division member to be killed in the city. His execution on 29 November 1919 would expose weaknesses in Collins's organisation. Even before this the killing of another member of the DMP, Constable Michael Dowling, on 19 October showed that a state of war now existed on the streets of Dublin. Dowling was a young recruit from Collins's own west Cork with only three years' service. He was shot at about 1 a.m. on 19 October in High Street when he approached three men while on routine beat duty. Asked by a colleague who rushed to the scene if he had any information about them, he answered, 'Not the least, except that one of them wore leggings.' A passer-by said that the man who drew a revolver from his pocket wore a trench coat, reinforcing the impression that Volunteers were involved.[39]

The attack on Barton was planned, if not over-planned. Collins's impatience to counter the threat from the DMP had resulted in two *de facto* Squads emerging by November 1919. Some of the original members around Mick McDonnell and recruited primarily from the 2nd Battalion never really accepted the official structures subsequently established, with Paddy Daly in charge.[40] Daly had been in Mountjoy when the first attacks took place; however, he was present at the meeting in the offices of the Keating Branch of the Gaelic League at 46 Parnell Square on 19 September that marked the formal establishment of the unit, and he was appointed to command it, reporting directly to Collins. The only men who could issue orders to the Squad in the absence of Collins were Mulcahy and McKee, who had first suggested its formation. Collins made it clear to the men that they would operate on a tight rein and only carry out killings that were authorised. This applied especially to the DMP, whose indiscriminate shooting was forbidden. 'We [only] discovered afterwards how many of them were our friends,' Daly recalled.

That injunction did not apply to Detective-Sergeant Barton, who continued to harry the Volunteers and had just uncovered an arms dump. Vinnie Byrne, a McDonnell loyalist, was shadowing Barton with Tom Keogh and Jim Slattery in Grafton Street when Daly himself appeared, with Joe Leonard and Ben Barrett in tow on the same errand. 'Now it was a race to see whose party would get Barton first,' Byrne recalled later. 'As one party would pass out the other to have a go, people would come in between us and our quarry.' Barton almost made it back to his station when he was fatally wounded in College Green by members of yet another group, Seán Treacy and his comrades, who had been brought up from Co. Tipperary by Collins as a tried and tested back-up team to augment the activities of the Squad. As Barton lay dying he asked, 'Oh, God, what did I do to deserve this?' He managed to return fire as his attackers fled but failed to hit any of them. He died in Mercer's Hospital.[41]

While this degree of dual power within a unit as crucial to operations as the Squad was dangerous, it does not appear to have worried Collins unduly. As the military historian Michael Foy suggests, it probably 'suited Collins's distaste for clear chains of command and his obsessive need for control.'

Barton's death was presaged by the shooting of another G Division veteran, Detective-Sergeant Thomas Wharton, which illustrates defects in the British administration's own methods for prosecuting the war that were more serious than those confronting the enemy. Wharton was shot by Paddy Daly on 10 November in Cuffe Street. Daly pressed home the attack, although Wharton was in the company of three other detectives. Wharton's life was saved when Daly's gun jammed after the first shot. Nevertheless the bullet, which passed through the detective's right lung and slightly injured a female student passing by, incapacitated Wharton for life. In turn, Daly owed his own life to the fact that one of the detectives accompanying Wharton was working for Collins. He stepped into the line of fire of his companions while ostensibly trying to shoot the gunman himself.[42]

Events then took an unusual turn, for a member of the public not only pursued Daly and his accomplices but, failing to apprehend them, subsequently came forward to identify the gunman. This public-spirited citizen was Captain William Kearns Batchelor, who had been demobilised in September and was living on the South Circular Road, waiting to hear if he had been successful in his application for a post with the Colonial Service. Unfortunately the man he identified as the gunman was James Hurley, a newspaper vendor with a stand nearby, on which the titles for sale included the *Volunteer* and the *United Irishman*. Hurley had no involvement with Sinn Féin or the Irish Volunteers; indeed, like Batchelor, he was a veteran of the Great War. Nevertheless he was convicted on Batchelor's evidence and would have been hanged if Wharton had died. Instead he was sentenced to fifteen years' imprisonment. Released during the Truce, Hurley was killed during the Civil War helping a wounded soldier to Jervis Street Hospital.

Because of the increasing frequency and seriousness of the attacks on members of G Division, the authorities decided to offer a reward of £5,000 for information leading to the arrest and conviction of Wharton's assailant. Batchelor came forward before the reward was announced, and it seems that he never learnt of its existence. However, he did use his involvement in the incident to press his claim for a post with the Colonial Service. It took nearly two years to deal with his application, during which time he was subjected to death threats and had to move to London with his wife. He was not even reimbursed for his out-of-pocket expenses for the trial until early 1920. The Chief Commissioner of the DMP, Lieutenant-Colonel Johnstone, became his most ardent champion. He wrote to Macpherson's successor as Chief Secretary, Sir Hamar Greenwood, in February 1920:

> Captain Batchelor's conduct ... was courageous and praiseworthy in the extreme. I think that in justice he should be awarded the full £5,000 to which he would have been entitled had he delayed in coming forward until a reward was offered.

In a letter to the Assistant Secretary responsible for financial matters, Sir John Taylor, he pointed out that 'Captain Batchelor has well earned the full reward at the imminent risk to his life. Of all the witnesses of murders in the City he is the only one who has come forward.' Eventually it was agreed to pay Batchelor £1,000, provided it came out of the DMP budget, and he was appointed to the Colonial Service in June 1920. With classic British understatement, Johnstone told Taylor: 'The delay in doing something for this officer is a poor encouragement to others.'[43]

Captain Batchelor was undoubtedly right to use his zeal in the apprehension of a suspect in the Wharton shooting—albeit the wrong man—to press his claim for a colonial post. In 1919 Dublin was awash with discharged soldiers looking for work; and no group was more quickly forgotten in the 'land fit for heroes' than the heroes themselves. Average unemployment among ex-soldiers was 10 per cent in the United Kingdom but 46 per cent in Ireland.[44] A few were fortunate enough to return to such employers as Guinness and the Great Southern and Western Railway, which honoured commitments to keep their jobs open, provided the men were fit for work.

A plethora of organisations was established to assist demobilised soldiers and sailors—no fewer than nineteen in Dublin alone. Organisations also sprang up among ex-servicemen themselves, of which the two most significant were the local branches of the Discharged and Demobilised Sailors' and Soldiers' Federation and the Demobilised Sailors' and Soldiers' Protection Society. Both held meetings in August to protest at delays in payments to members and their families. Much of their ire was directed at the local war pensions committee. This was supposed to distribute benefits to demobilised men, particularly those who were disabled, and to the widows of war veterans. These were often in dire straits.

The secretary of the City of Dublin Pensions Committee, W. G. Fallon, explained to the Central Committee in London that many of the delays could be traced to the bureaucracy and inaccessibility of those with decision-making powers at the top. He instanced an application for a woman widowed in July 1918 for whom 'nothing had happened since.' The woman's separation allowance had been stopped twenty-six weeks after her husband's death, and there were a great many similar cases. While many of the complaints Fallon laid against the central bureaucracy echoed the concerns of local pension committees in Britain, his interrogators were shocked to hear of the hostility shown to ex-servicemen in Dublin, particularly the disabled. This hostility extended to trade unions, which made finding work for unemployed ex-servicemen difficult. When one member of the Central Committee, Sir John Butcher, protested incredulously that 'these men have been fighting in France for our country,' Fallon replied:

> These men went off amidst tremendous enthusiasm five years ago … When these men came back disabled and broken down they found their own relations had altered their views on public affairs, and things were exceedingly uncomfortable for these unfortunate men.

He added that during disturbances between civilians and servicemen, disabled ex-servicemen in the vicinity looking on appeared to attract the special ire of the mob. Fallon made a special plea for ex-servicemen so physically or mentally disabled as to require hospital treatment.

I contend that there should be separate institutions for these men ... 80 per cent ... require hospital and sanatorium treatment after their discharge. It would not be very expensive to carry on one of the Red Cross hospitals which were now closing down as a War Pensions Institution.

He further advised that if the government was going to implement the wartime promise of land for Irish veterans it should provide holdings in tandem with the allocation of land under existing schemes. To treat the veterans preferentially 'would lead to certain trouble.' Although there were public meetings and at least one protest march through Dublin by ex-servicemen, they were on a modest scale compared with those in Britain. The formation of the British Legion by Earl Haig effectually subsumed all these bodies into more constructive and politically innocuous activities.

The patience, or passivity, of Irish veterans served them ill. Ten years later many were still looking for land, or jobs. Those lucky enough to be given government employment often found themselves discriminated against or made redundant after the change of government in 1922.[45]

As the War of Independence developed, a few ex-servicemen in Dublin offered their services as 'touts' or informants to the British forces for money, but far more appear to have offered their services to the Volunteers. William Corrie from Ringsend had seen active service in Salonika, Belgium and France, and on demobilisation in 1919 he

immediately joined a Sinn Féin Club and attended a meeting at 144 Pearse Street. This address was used by the 3rd Battalion. I been [being] a fully trained soldier, I thought I should join the IRA.

He was proposed by a friend for B Company, but the company OC

objected on the grounds that I was an ex-serviceman and should not be trusted. However I succeeded in joining E Company, First Battalion [and] after a couple of weeks I was appointed a Section Leader. Shortly afterwards the Military made a general round up of the Battalion area and arrested my Company OC and Company Staff. I was then appointed by the Battalion OC, Commandant P. Holohan to reorganise the Company, which I did and carried out ambushes in my Company area.

He later served in the Free State army and said, 'During my service with the IRA I met *hundreds* of ex-servicemen' (emphasis in original).

William J. Walsh, from Shankill, Co. Dublin, was demobilised in late 1919 and joined F Company, 3rd Battalion, in early 1920. He was appointed training officer and served later in the same capacity with the 6th (South County) Battalion when it was established in 1921.

> I was later appointed Captain of D Company, 6th Battalion, Dublin Brigade. While in this Company I recruited some ex-servicemen who afterwards became very active volunteers, one of whom died of wounds received in action in Dun Laoghaire in June 1921.

A Free State army memorandum assessing the role of British ex-servicemen during the War of Independence, probably written by J. J. O'Connell, states:

> A factor, the importance of which should not be under-estimated, was the acquisition to the Volunteer ranks of a certain number of World War veterans in the last two years of the conflict, more particularly. These men contributed a valuable number of instructors and general 'stiffening' which proved very helpful. This influx of seasoned men corresponded in point of time with a corresponding loss of similar personnel on the enemy side. It must not be overlooked that—as far as the regular Army was concerned—the British fought their last war in Ireland with raw troops very largely. It should also be noted that ex-servicemen would have joined up in considerably greater numbers were it not that serious and quite natural difficulties arose in the matter of employing them.[46]

The truth probably lies somewhere between O'Connell's concern to acknowledge the role of ex-servicemen in the struggle for independence and the well-recorded incidents of public hostility. No doubt O'Connell was partially influenced by the fact that half the recruits to the Free State army in the Civil War were ex-servicemen.

It may well be that Dublin was a special case. The sheer number of ex-servicemen in Dublin, at twenty thousand, far exceeded the number of active Volunteers in the War of Independence, who probably numbered well under two thousand in reality.[47] It would have made little sense to antagonise such a large group, their relatives and friends in the working-class communities where they lived and worked. One indicator of levels of hostility to ex-servicemen may be found in the changed recruitment patterns to the British army from Ireland between January 1919 and December 1921, when Munster became the prime recruiting ground and such traditional areas as Dublin and Belfast ceased to be significant. This suggests that the environment for ex-servicemen was distinctly kinder in the latter cities than in Cos. Cork or Tipperary.

What is not disputed is that, although many offers of help were refused by suspicious local IRA commandants, when accepted the British army veterans played an important role and often rose to senior positions in the Volunteers, continuing to fight for the rights of small nations, in this case their own.

A very different process was taking place within the Crown forces, and by 1919 the RIC and DMP were increasingly debilitated. The DMP was visibly retreating from the streets. The number of arrests in 1914 was 10,181 but this had fallen to 4,394 by 1919. There was a similar drastic fall in summonses served, from 26,801 in 1914 to 16,261 in 1919.

One last effort was made by Lord French to revive the emasculated G Division of the DMP. He appointed District Inspector William Redmond of the RIC, 'a pugnacious outsider from Belfast,' as Assistant Commissioner. Redmond made the fatal error of selecting Detective-Sergeant Jim McNamara, one of Collins's moles, as his aide. On 21 January 1920, only three weeks into the job, Redmond was shot dead as he returned from Dublin Castle, unescorted, to his rooms at the Standard Hotel in Harcourt Street, not far from the Sinn Féin offices. Paddy Daly fired the fatal shot. He aimed at Redmond's head, as he knew his target would be wearing a bullet-proof vest. Passers-by carried the dying man to a nearby chemist's, still clasping his revolver. He never had a chance to use it.[48]

Collins had already set his sights higher. During the autumn of 1919 he made persistent attempts to assassinate the Lord Lieutenant, Field-Marshal French, who personified British repression in the minds of republicans. In truth it was the Cabinet's preoccupation with more pressing problems at home and abroad that prevented it from adopting a more constructive approach to Ireland than mere repression.

As with the Barton shooting, Collins contracted out some attempts on French to the Tipperary men, assisted as required by Dublin Volunteers. Usefulness to Collins did not, however, guarantee access to funds for Seán Treacy and his comrades: their own brigade in Co. Tipperary was expected to provide for them, and they often ran short. They sometimes found it easier to tap the General Treasurer of the ITGWU, William O'Brien, for a sub than to look for assistance from Volunteer headquarters, Sinn Féin or Dáil Éireann. Members of the Squad, on the other had, were paid a regular wage of £4 10s a week, equivalent to that of a skilled worker, which some of them had been before becoming full-time revolutionary artisans. It was certainly an attractive income for younger recruits, including those entering Collins's intelligence department and the Dublin Brigade's Active Service Unit (full-time section), which had been set up shortly after the Squad. Some of these youngsters, such as Charlie Dalton, were barely out of school.

Some of the Tipperary men—Treacy, Seán Hogan, Dan Breen and Séamus Robinson—worked closely enough with GHQ to be called to a briefing of Squad members with the Volunteers' Chief of Staff, Richard Mulcahy, at the end of September 1919. At the meeting the guerrilla tactics to be employed in the city were outlined. For the moment Volunteers on active service were told they had to avoid capture or detection at all costs in order to protect Dáil Éireann and its administrative staff. Mulcahy warned the men: 'There must not be even a laundry mark on your clothing to identify you.' It occurred to some of those present that they were being asked to do a lot to protect apparatchiks who took far fewer risks for far greater pay—between £7 and £10 a week.

Treacy and his group were deployed shortly afterwards, along with members of the Squad, to ambush Lord French on his way to an Armistice Day dinner in Trinity College, but he failed to take the expected route. Seán Hogan, who had prematurely removed the pins from two hand grenades, had to walk through the crowded streets clutching them until he reached a safe house and could obtain assistance in securing new pins. French's luck held all year, and the nearest the group ever came to killing him was on 18 December as he was returning via the Ashtown Gate to the Viceregal Lodge in the Phoenix Park. The car he was expected to be in was riddled with bullets and grenade shrapnel, but he had decided to travel in the first car of the convoy, which passed unmolested through the ambush party. The only fatality was Lieutenant Martin Savage of the 2nd Battalion, who had joined Treacy and his comrades at the last minute. Breen suffered a bad leg wound in the shoot-out with French's military escort but was helped to escape on a bicycle to fight another day. Thanks to the wonders of modern technology, the survivors were able to watch a newsreel of the attempt on French's life in a Dublin cinema a few days later.[49]

After the Ashtown ambush, Lord French attended very few public engagements in the capital. The Viceregal Lodge became his prison.

While fifteen members of the RIC and DMP had been killed by the end of 1919, the assassination attempt on the Lord Lieutenant was perceived as a challenge to the British state of an altogether different order. The *Irish Independent* compared it to the assassination of the Chief Secretary, Lord Henry Cavendish, and the Under-Secretary for Ireland, Thomas Burke, by the Invincibles in the

Phoenix Park in 1882. Normally supportive of Sinn Féin, the paper condemned the attack as 'wrong, criminal and absolutely reprehensible,' for which it paid with a raid on its premises by the Dublin Brigade, whose members smashed printing equipment.

Not surprisingly, the *Irish Times* declared that 'the attempt on the Lord Lieutenant's life has sent a thrill of horror through the whole Kingdom.' If the assassins had succeeded they 'would have blackened Ireland's name for generations in every quarter of the world.' However, it was spared a visit from the Volunteers. The *Irish Independent* was singled out because, in Dan Breen's words, it 'depended on the support of the people who had voted for the establishment of the Irish Republic.'[50]

More worrying from a separatist viewpoint were the condemnations from leading Catholic prelates, Cardinal Logue and Archbishop Walsh of Dublin. Logue's condemnation was to be expected, but Walsh was seen as the staunchest ally in the hierarchy of the advanced nationalist cause. Typically, his wording was, to quote his biographer, 'elusive'. He described the perpetrators as deluding themselves if they believed that 'such a method of seeking redress of the misgovernment of this country is likely to help the efforts of the righteous men who are working earnestly, with the single purpose of re-establishing ... the reign of liberty and justice.' Walsh made his statement in the wake of an interview by his secretary, Father Michael Curran, only three days before the attempt on Lord French, in which he told the *Morning Post* of London that all killing was wrong but that to condemn attacks on the Crown forces would appear to be taking sides with an oppressive government. He added that the archbishop regarded British rule as 'the source of all evil.'

Curran was typical of the younger generation of clergy, who were quite conservative on social and economic issues but had become convinced separatists. Not surprisingly, Curran had to go, and Walsh had to condemn the attack on Lord French.

Even more convoluted was the language of condemnation used by the Lord Mayor, Laurence O'Neill. When John Hollwey, a shipping broker and chairman of Dublin Port and Docks Board, proposed a motion at its December meeting congratulating the Lord Lieutenant on surviving the assassination attempt, O'Neill had little choice as a board member but to vote for it. He explained his decision by saying:

It does not matter whether the crime or murder was hatched in high or lowly places, or whether the attempt to murder was made on a peer or a peasant ... whether it was out of personal spite or political revenge, or whether it was committed by a Catholic or by a Protestant, by a Nationalist or by a Unionist, and no matter what organisation took part in it, let it be Sinn Féin, Hibernian or Freemasonry. The church to which I belong tells me, 'Thou shalt not kill' ... Consequently I have no hesitation in joining with the chairman and other members of the Board in supporting the motion.

In reality the attempt on Lord French had no effect on the lives of ordinary Dubliners beyond confirming their belief that society was sinking into a general morass of lawlessness. On the day after the Ashtown ambush the Chief Commissioner of the DMP, Lieutenant-Colonel Johnstone, appealed to citizens to become special constables. 'Owing to the necessity of grouping the police in strong patrols in substitution for the ordinary beat system, the city is at present insufficiently guarded by night for the protection of property, with the result that robberies and outrages are increasing.' There were few takers, and efforts to press civil servants into the role were vigorously resisted by those concerned, who had no wish to be boycotted by their neighbours.[51]

On the same day as the Commissioner's appeal there was a series of raids on the homes of prominent members of Sinn Féin and the Irish Volunteers in the city, including George Plunkett, Kathleen Clarke, widow of the executed 1916 leader Tom Clarke, and Alderman Thomas Kelly, leader of the Sinn Féin group on Dublin Corporation, who was deported to England. Such prominent security swoops failed to disguise the growing ineffectiveness of the DMP. Almost as confirmation of the impotence of his own force, Johnstone brought a company of infantry with him on a raid of the Mansion House, complete with four Lewis machine guns, when O'Neill refused to cancel a meeting. The Commissioner had so many troops that some had to be posted in the Royal Irish Automobile Club premises opposite until the search was completed, because they could not be accommodated in the Mansion House. The subversives turned out to be a committee planning Aonach na Nollag, the annual Christmas fair of Irish goods. The fair was promptly banned,[52] providing yet another seasonal political gift to the enemy. It was all the more welcome as the long-awaited local elections for urban areas were finally called for January 1920.[53]

Chapter 3 ~

'ONE HALF OF THE POPULATION IS WRONG AND THE OTHER ISN'T'

On Thursday 15 January 1920 local elections were held in Dublin and the surrounding urban districts or townships of Howth, Rathmines and Rathgar, Pembroke, Blackrock, Killiney and Ballybrack, Kingstown and Dalkey, as well as in every other Irish urban authority area. They were the first since 1914 and the first under proportional representation.

The *Irish Independent* published a series of articles explaining the new system, including encouragement for every voter 'to mark his ballot paper as fully as possible.'[1] The measure was welcomed by Southern unionists, who feared that their voice would be drowned under the old system, and by Sinn Féin, which had long campaigned for PR and was confident that it would confirm the party's new dominance. In a rare example of co-operation, all parties worked with the Local Government Board to ensure that the necessary training was undertaken by candidates and canvassers. Local authority officials were also inducted into the process, and, of course, the electorate.

The new electoral system did nothing to lift the spirits of the once-omnipotent constitutional nationalists of the Irish Party who had dominated Dublin Corporation for decades. Sinn Féin and its Labour allies expected to sweep to power in the capital and to poll well in the middle-class townships, where republicanism and social reform were becoming fashionable. The veteran Parnellite William Field, who had represented the St Patrick's division of the city for a quarter of a century in the House of Commons, now felt safe running as an independent nationalist candidate only in the predominantly unionist Blackrock Urban District. He was nominated by one of his old sponsors, the

Dublin Victuallers' Association, which urged members to put their vehicles at his disposal and that of a handful of other named Irish Party stalwarts who were running in the city.

A Municipal Reform Association had sprung up to fight some of the more prosperous city wards. It comprised former unionists and nationalists, with six candidates from each camp. The former unionists included Sir Andrew Beattie, a leading businessman in the city who had run successfully as an independent councillor in the past, and J. Hubbard Clark, a company director who had failed in a previous effort to secure a seat. The nationalists were all members of the outgoing corporation, such as Sir James Gallagher, Dr James McWalter and James Moran. Gallagher belonged to the tobacco-manufacturing dynasty and was a former Lord Mayor, knighted for his role in saving Grafton Street from looters during the 1916 Rising. McWalter had a large medical practice among the poor of the north inner city, and Moran was a hotelier in Clontarf, where he was dependent for a seat on transfers from the large middle-class unionist electorate.

It was this capacity to tap in to middle-class concerns across the political and sectarian divide that gave the MRA a relatively stable power base in a period of rapid change. However, some of its candidates suffered from an identity crisis. Sarah Harrison, a portrait artist and the first woman to be elected to Dublin Corporation, had built a reputation as an independent nationalist and social reformer. She had founded the highly successful allotments movement in the city during the war and had decided at the last minute to run once more as an independent.[2]

The unionists were severely depleted by defections to the MRA and in the north of the city decided to contest only Electoral Area 2, comprising the three wards of Clontarf, Drumcondra and Glasnevin, which had been the party's north-side heartland. In most southern townships they fielded a significant number of candidates: 15 in Rathmines, 12 in Kingstown, 7 in Pembroke and 6 in Blackrock, including Lady Dockrell, wife of the unionist MP for Rathmines, Sir Maurice Dockrell. This would be the party's Last Hurrah. Given the numbers put forward in Rathmines, Kingstown and Blackrock, it clearly hoped to reassert itself in traditional strongholds. In Pembroke the possibility of a coalition with the Ratepayers' Association beckoned. Unlike the MRA, the Ratepayers' Association had no central structure, although it relied on a similar electoral base. Its stronghold was Bray, where it ran ten candidates. Significantly, no unionists were running in the town, which they had once dominated.

The reduction in the Southern unionist political profile was even more dramatic outside Dublin city and county, where intangible relics of the past preserved a semblance of normality, such as the advertisements in the *Irish Times* for the January sales and for pantomimes such as *Old King Cole* at the Gaiety Theatre and *Jack and the Beanstalk* at the Queen's.

A chilling reminder of the changed realities had been provided on New Year's Day when the burial took place with military honours of Lieutenant Frederick Boast in the British army's Phoenix Park cemetery. He had been a victim of 'friendly fire' on Sunday 27 December, shot near the Viceregal Lodge by fellow-soldiers who thought the Irish Volunteers were mounting another attempt on Lord French. A farm labourer on his way home from work, Laurence Kennedy, was killed in the same incident. The coroner's jury treated the two shootings quite differently, finding that Boast's death was accidental while condemning the military for shooting Kennedy 'in a heartless way.' The jurors stopped short of using the word 'murder'.

On 2 January there was a joint raid by the DMP and military on the offices of the New Ireland Assurance Society at 56 Lower Sackville Street. Among those questioned was Michael Staines, treasurer of the society and a Sinn Féin MP. The Sinn Féin offices at 6 Harcourt Street, the Sinn Féin Bank in the same building and the Dáil Éireann offices at 76 Harcourt Street were all closed by the British authorities that afternoon. The Sinn Féin offices had already been closed 'permanently' on two occasions in 1919.[3]

In Cork it was the Volunteers who were on the offensive. RIC barracks at Carrigtohill, Carrignavar, Inchigeelagh, Kilmurry and Rathcormack were attacked on the night of Saturday 3 January. Telegraph wires were cut and trees felled to delay relief columns. The numbers in the attacking parties were estimated to be in their hundreds, which allowed police garrisons to cast themselves in a good light with their superiors, while the Volunteers did not contradict claims that projected an image of strength.

The only post captured was that at Carrigtohill, after a siege that lasted from 10:30 p.m. until 3 a.m. Up to 1,600 rounds were reportedly fired, but no-one was injured. The final phase of the attack came after the police garrison ran out of ammunition and the attackers were able to place a mine against the gable wall. A local veteran of the Great War described the ensuing charge through the debris of the explosion as 'for all the world ... like going over the top in Flanders for an attack on a pillbox.' Station-Sergeant Scott ordered his five constables to fix bayonets, but 'this weapon ... was unavailing against the revolvers of 50 men who rushed through the breach in the wall,' and he told his men to surrender. The leader of the attacking party purportedly told the policemen: 'Ye defended well. You are good Irishmen.' Having handcuffed their prisoners, who were reportedly 'most popular in the village,' the attackers broke into the school to eat their sandwiches 'before departing on a long march to the distant neighbourhood' from whence they came. In fact the attackers were from the local 4th Battalion of the East Cork Brigade, according to the recollection of one participant many years later, but the newspaper narrative suited all concerned. Perhaps the most accurate comment on events came from the correspondent of the *Cork Constitution*, who reported: 'The residents of Carrigtwohill did not sleep many hours on Saturday night.'[4]

Such elaborate operations were not possible in Dublin, but attacks on individual policemen could be more effective and less risky than barrack attacks, as the assassinations of G Division detectives had shown. Nor was the lesson lost on rural cousins. On the same night as the Carrigtohill attack a constable was left in a critical condition after being wounded by a shotgun at close range in Ballylongford, Co. Kerry. He was hit by 160 pellets in his neck and shoulder, but survived.[5]

The Volunteers who captured Carrigtohill barracks used a motor car to remove the RIC weapons and files. The growing use of cars by the rebels introduced a new aspect to the conflict in rural Ireland, but it also had an effect on the life of Dubliners. On 15 November 1919 Dublin Castle introduced motor permits, with personal details and a photograph. Drivers were required to stick a copy of the permit on their vehicles. This was intended to ensure that only loyal subjects of the Crown could use motorised transport. Members of craft and transport unions in the city reacted by refusing to service, repair or drive vehicles whose owners applied for them, a stance fully supported by the NEC of the ITUC&LP. The mood was well reflected at a meeting in the Dublin Trades Hall on Sunday 30 November 1919 when Éamonn McAlpine of the Irish Automobile Drivers' and Automobile Mechanics' Union said that no British government would turn his union into 'a semi-spy organisation' by coercing members to co-operate with the authorities.[6]

On 7 December 1919 the DMP countered with patrols on the city's bridges to check vehicles and ensure that drivers displayed permits; the unions reacted with pickets to ensure that they did not. Not surprisingly, motor vehicles more or less disappeared from the streets, and the *Irish Independent* reported that 'jarveys are having a good time of it.'[7] One reason that the strike was so effective was the small number of vehicles involved: only 109 new vehicles were registered in Dublin in 1919, and there were a further 132 that had changed ownership.[8] Donations for the strikers rolled in from other unions, and the fighting fund stood at £700 by the end of the year. As in the 1918 anti-conscription campaign, many employers took the same stance as their workers. One reason for the employers accepting the drivers' refusal to take out vehicles was the damage being done to them by gunfire, pickets and general mob violence.

In a move to placate the business lobby the British government amended the permit system by excluding all vehicles that weighed more than three tons. But whatever good might have been achieved was largely undone when the Chief Secretary, Ian Macpherson, used the occasion of the announcement to tell the Irish Party MP William Redmond in the House of Commons that the Motor Permit Order 'did not impose any hardship on loyalists,' by which he meant law-abiding citizens; but the distinction was lost on most nationalists.[9]

The dispute was stepped up in the new year. On Sunday 4 January 1920 drivers held a protest march through Dublin. On 16 January, the day after polling in the municipal elections, Macpherson got first-hand experience of the public mood when his own car was attacked on the Cabra Road in Phibsborough. He was rescued only with some difficulty from the mob. Nor was hardship restricted to employers. Having attacked 'the authors and instigators' of the Motor Permit Order for clearing the roads for the 'bad boys' who would break the law regardless, a doctor in the city went on to complain that

> those of us who, from physical or other reason, have to use Fords in our practice, and have disposed of other means of conveyance, have the hardships it entails on the sick poor pushed up to us every hour of the day. Private patients can provide a conveyance as well as a fee. The poor woman in labour, whose agony is prolonged hours and hours, or who is helplessly bleeding to death ... may be merely an academic picture to the protagonists in this fight ... but it seems to me incredible that men born of women can realise the way in which they are crucifying maternity.[10]

The government offered drivers the option of signing an undertaking that they would not knowingly allow their vehicles to be used for unlawful purposes; they would then be safe from prosecution, provided they displayed a permit on their vehicle. However, M. J. O'Connor, secretary of the Irish Automobile Drivers' and Automobile Mechanics' Union, which was leading the dispute, rejected the proposal on the grounds that it effectually left the ability of his members to earn a living in the hands of the police. As a concession, he said drivers would be willing to have a photograph attached to driving licences.[11]

Popular support for the drivers remained strong. While the municipal elections precluded the corporation from debating the issue, the Dublin Board of Guardians, on which several outgoing councillors served, passed a motion demanding the immediate withdrawal of the Motor Permits Order, 'which was entirely opposed to the elementary rights of citizenship and interfered with the livelihood of both motor-owners and motor-drivers.' However, the Dublin Employers' Federation now came out publicly to express 'regret' that some employers continued to pay drivers who refused to apply for a permit.[12]

It fell to the British unions to grasp the nettle. They had reluctantly supported the action by Irish members in what they regarded as a 'political' strike. Those reservations increased in the wake of the attempted assassination of Lord French. In January the Executive Committee of the Amalgamated Society of Engineers, the largest British craft union, withdrew its sanction for the boycott of motor permits, and other unions followed suit.[13] Without their support the smaller Dublin unions could not hold out. What was worse, the British unions went over their heads and negotiated a settlement with the employers and the Chief Commissioner of the DMP, Lieutenant-Colonel Johnstone. The only concession secured was that drivers who had a permit would not have to reapply when changing employment. The Irish strike leaders issued a statement to the newspapers saying that they had no knowledge of the negotiations, 'which have been conducted behind the backs of the Joint [Strike] Committee.'[14]

The motor permits dispute was important not only because it generated support for Sinn Féin in the municipal elections but because it soured relations between British unions and their Irish members. This was especially true of craft workers and would have serious consequences in the coming months.

There was a more satisfactory outcome to another bitter dispute in the city that winter. This was a ten-week strike by barmen and grocery assistants for Sundays off and a pay increase. In a city where pubs were the social fulcrum of working-class communities in which drunkenness and alcoholism were endemic, the dispute was bound to produce some ugly incidents. Both sides adopted a tough stance from the outset. The Licensed Grocers' and Vintners' Association claimed that only twenty-six or twenty-seven houses were willing to settle with the Barmen's and Grocery Assistants' Union, while the latter claimed that half the larger establishments were willing to do so. Whichever figure was the more accurate, the *Irish Independent* observed that 'many houses in which no assistants are employed are enjoying a rich harvest from the closing of close on three-quarters of the larger houses.'[15]

There were several prosecutions in the police courts for intimidation, but few succeeded. An exception involved a mass picket at one of Dún Laoghaire's largest establishments, Thomas Brady's, Upper George's Street. Two strikers were convicted on police evidence and spent fourteen days in Mountjoy. One was Paddy Moran, a 1916 veteran and a captain in the 2nd Battalion of the Dublin Brigade. He became president of the union in September 1920. No doubt his spell in Mountjoy boosted his election prospects, as did his membership of the IRB.[16] Prosecution evidence was usually hard to come by. When four grocers' assistants were charged with being among a group of sixteen men who attacked a strike-breaker called Michael Murray and his boy helper as they delivered porter to Healy's of 39 Parnell Street, Murray refused to identify them in court. The magistrate, Lupton, said he was 'there to protect the public, but if a member of the public was such a coward that he was afraid to have himself protected it was not my business.'

Catherine Clooney of 11 Brabazon Street in the Liberties was made of sterner stuff. She told the court that a grocer's assistant called Duffy stopped her from entering Redmond's public house at 23 Ardee Street and told her it was a 'scab' house before knocking her down with a blow to the chest, after which he ran away. However, she 'got him in Cork Street' and had him charged. She also claimed she had lost a shawl valued at £3 in the commotion. Another picketer, Michael Doran, told the magistrate that Clooney assaulted Duffy, slapping him across the face, and as he thought she was going to strike Duffy again he pushed her away and she fell. A second picketer, Denis Leahy, said she had assaulted him as well, and even the prosecuting sergeant admitted that 'she was excited and might have had drink taken' at the time of the complaint. Nevertheless things looked bad for Duffy until the union's solicitor said his clients 'did not wish any member of the public to suffer through the vindication of their rights. Without admitting the assault, they are willing to buy her a new shawl.' The magistrate, Cooper, made an order for bail on two sureties of £10 and the payment of £3 to Catherine Clooney.[17]

The grocers' and barmen's fortitude was rewarded in March when a settlement was reached through the offices of the Lord Mayor, Laurence O'Neill, in a Sunday conference at the Mansion House—one of many he undertook as chief magistrate of the city. Under its terms the Licensed Grocers' and Vintners' Association agreed to pay an increase of 40 per cent for senior barmen and 33 per cent for junior barmen. Any barman having to move to outdoor accommodation would receive an increase of 30s a week as compensation for the loss of free board and lodging. Each man would also be entitled to an afternoon off a week, something the Drapers' Assistants had secured before the war, and barmen would also be entitled to St Stephen's Day off and every fourth Sunday.[18]

The enforced sobriety of many citizens probably helped cool passions in the municipal elections. When nominations closed there were 61 Sinn Féin candidates, 17 Labour, 12 for the Municipal Reform Association, 2 unionists, 1 socialist, Walter Carpenter, and more than 70 others, 'for the most part supporters of the policy of the old Irish Party.'[19]

It was widely expected that Sinn Féin and the Labour Party would campaign jointly, but Labour entered the contest badly split, with ten 'official' Labour candidates and seven or eight 'unofficial' candidates, who quickly renamed themselves Republican Labour.[20] The immediate cause of the split was the nomination of Tom Lawlor when the Dublin Trades Council election committee met in December 1919 to approve the Labour panel. This was the spark that ignited a division fuelled by years of bitter infighting. Lawlor, a tailor by trade, was a veteran of the 1913 Lockout. He was also a bitter enemy of his fellow-tailor and fellow-veteran William O'Brien. Both men had subsequently joined the ITGWU, of which O'Brien was now general treasurer, which had been riven by internal power struggles. Lawlor was associated with a faction led by P. T. Daly, the head of the union's insurance section for many years; and, like Daly, he had the shadow of financial impropriety hanging over him. A former member of the Supreme Council of the IRB, Daly had used £300 that he collected in America in 1908 to support his family. He was exonerated by an inquiry but O'Brien continued to use the indiscretion against him. Lawlor had indirectly breached a rule of the trades council about accepting 'testimonials' (money payments), which had brought the movement into disrepute and led to allegations of corruption. Lawlor had refused such a testimonial from the Dublin Poor Law Union for his services, in line with the new policy, only to admit that his wife had accepted it 'without his knowledge or consent.' Lawlor's other offence from O'Brien's point of view was that he left the ITGWU to become general secretary of the Municipal Employees' Trade Union, which O'Brien had ambitions of subsuming within his own union.

But the real power struggle was between O'Brien and Daly, whom O'Brien had harried out of his position as secretary of the ITUC&LP and then his job as head of the ITGWU's insurance section. Daly had been accused of misappropriating funds because he sometimes made payments to unemployed members before receiving formal approval.[21] A deficit of £1,400 had been run up, and Daly's accountancy failings had been itemised in detail by Joseph McGrath, Daly's successor. McGrath was a close friend of Michael Collins as well as an ally of O'Brien and the general president of the ITGWU, Tom Foran. Relations between the rival groups had grown poisonous since the Rising. Rumours abounded that Foran had 'forgotten his rifle' in 1916 and gone to the

Fairyhouse races on Easter Monday. The other side went one better and said that Daly had become a British spy. O'Brien publicly denounced Daly as a coward, and Daly, in a reference to O'Brien's club foot, described him as 'a cripple, and he likes to play on his deformity.' The fact that O'Brien was the son of an RIC man was another stick with which he could be beaten.

A split in the union was narrowly averted at a meeting of members in the Mansion House on 22 June 1919, but the row between Daly and O'Brien continued to simmer. A libel action had been begun by Daly against O'Brien over the accusation that he had misappropriated IRB funds and was a spy, and in July both men agreed to refer it to the new courts set up by Dáil Éireann. Some four thousand members of the ITGWU are reputed to have attended the hearing, which took place in the Mansion House. Strenuous efforts were made by the court and by leading figures in the labour and republican movements to resolve the dispute without it going to trial, but both men insisted on their day in court. In one of its earliest and most unusual judgements, the Dáil Éireann National Arbitration Court found that Daly had misappropriated IRB property but in extenuating circumstances, while there was no evidence to sustain the charge of spying.

All the proceedings achieved was to deepen divisions in the Dublin labour movement. When Lawlor was nominated at the Trades Council meeting as a Labour candidate in the Dublin municipal elections, O'Brien, Foran and their supporters walked out and set up a rival Workers' Council to run candidates of their own. The ITGWU's paper *Watchword of Labour* campaigned for them under the slogan 'No twisting, no testimonials, no trickery, and jail before jobs.' It told workers they must choose between two sets of candidates: 'One sails under the disgraced flag of the Dublin Trades Council; the other under the still unsullied banner of the Workers' Republic.' In the event the Workers' Council group of 'unofficial' Labour candidates secured eight seats and the Trades Council's 'official' Labour candidates six.

The majority faction referred to itself briefly as the 'Bolsheviks', until political fashions changed.[22] For all the talk about Bolshevism and a Workers' Republic, the Labour movement had once more, as in 1918, shown that it was not ready to seize power, even at the municipal level.

Meanwhile the main public focus was on Sinn Féin, which began its campaign with a series of meetings and processions on 6 January, the day after nominations closed. The president of the IRB, Seán McGarry, set the tone in the traditional unionist districts of Drumcondra and Glasnevin by promising the electorate that Sinn Féin will use their best efforts to make municipal politics as clean and as straight as they had made national politics. The people who came forward as Independent candidates said politics must be kept out of municipal affairs, but these very people made politics the bedrock of municipal affairs, and now that the parties to which they belonged were dead, they cried: 'Leave out politics altogether.'

McGarry thus made his own lack of political experience a virtue, and of course his 1916 record was cited as a qualification for election. Women were also prominent among Sinn Féin candidates and speakers. Jennie Wyse Power, Hanna Sheehy Skeffington and Constance Markievicz were the best known; Markievicz made a characteristically dramatic arrival by bicycle at her first election rally in Bolton Street. She cycled away equally rapidly, explaining to the crowd that she was 'on the run.' This tactic had the benefit of allowing her to address far more meetings and conduct more business than political propriety—and having to listen to other speakers—would normally allow.

Nor were her precautions unwarranted, as Sinn Féin candidates and election workers were regularly harassed. One of the worst cases involved the City Secretary, Fred Allan, the veteran Fenian who had returned to the politics of his youth. Having agreed to chair the Sinn Féin election committee in South County Dublin he was sentenced to three months' imprisonment in the Police Magistrates Courts for possession of subversive documents after a raid on a Sinn Féin meeting in Kingstown. The items concerned were a local election manifesto and a pamphlet on the party's economic policy.

The Workers' Council faced relatively little harassment; but, not to be outdone by Sinn Féin, or his O'Brienite rivals in the Workers' Council, the flamboyant P. T. Daly began his campaign with a torchlight parade through the North Dock ward. He further boosted his popularity by getting a motion through the last meeting of the outgoing corporation that city employees be given a half day off, with pay, to vote. An attempt by Dr McWalter to have the pay element of the proposal rescinded was comfortably defeated.[23]

The deposed Irish Party MP Alfie Byrne was staging a political comeback after being routed at the general election by Sinn Féin. His hopes were raised by the fact that the Sinn Féin candidate on that occasion, Phil Shanahan, a local publican who had been 'out' in 1916, was not contesting a seat. Byrne ran as an independent nationalist, like many of his former colleagues.

However, twenty-five former members of the corporation did not run for re-election. Besides William Field, among the most prominent absentees from the hustings were another former MP for the city, John Dillon Nugent, national secretary of the Ancient Order of Hibernians, and Sir Joseph Downes, the confectioner, referred to by many Dubliners as 'Lord Barmbrack', who had made a financial killing in his claim for compensation for property destroyed by British artillery in the Easter Rising. The only outgoing nationalist woman candidate, Martha Williams, withdrew her nomination.[24]

But the most striking change in the municipal election scene was the virtual disappearance of unionist candidates. The Unionist Party's ranks in the council chamber had been reduced since 1914 by other councillors blocking the co-option of unionist nominees to replace those who had died in the intervening years. Even some sitting councillors, such as William Coulter, declined to run again, while many activists joined forces with conservative nationalists in the Municipal Reform Association. The exceptions were William McCarthy and William Dinnage, who both ran in Electoral Area 2. Unfortunately there were twenty other candidates fighting for the eight seats. Nor was the unionist vote what it had once been. The departure of Lord Midleton and the other Southern unionist grandees to form the Anti-Partition League in 1919 left the rump of the Irish Unionist Alliance in the city drifting aimlessly in the wake of the Ulster unionists, while traditional supporters looked to the MRA for representation.

Although Dublin and its suburbs were the only region outside Ulster where the Irish Unionist Alliance had a popular electoral base, it chose polling day, 15 January, to debate the proposed new home-rule legislation, the Government of Ireland Bill, rather than to canvass. Predictably, it condemned the bill and called on unionist MPs to vote it down. No Ulster unionist MPs attended the conference, and only one of Dublin's three unionist MPs, J. M. Jellett, member for Dublin University, did so. Despite past promises, the Ulster unionists regarded their Southern cousins as expendable.[25] They suspected that many privately favoured the Anti-Partition League's position of home rule for all Ireland as a lesser evil than partition. There had been the very public falling out on the issue of proportional representation and, while PR had eventually been embraced in theory, the decision to contest only one electoral area in Dublin was an admission of defeat. (See chapter 2 above.)

Law and order had been one of the perennial hobby-horses of unionism in the city, but it was now taken up by the Municipal Reform Association. The situation was not as critical in Dublin as in many parts of the country, but there was a growing perception in the business community that things were deteriorating. On 9 January the chairman of the Visiting Justices Committee for the Dublin Prisons, Sir John Irwin, called for 'citizens to take steps to protect themselves from night marauders' following 'the practical withdrawal of ordinary police patrols and the consequent epidemic of burglaries and robberies in Dublin.' (See chapter 2 above.) Irwin, whose family owned Newbrook paper mill at Rathfarnham, had been a prominent member of the unionist business community but was now running for the MRA. He demonstrated the ambiguity of the association's identity by describing himself variously as a ratepayers' candidate and an independent as well as a member of the MRA.

Inevitably local political issues were overshadowed by national ones, most of which fed into the Sinn Féin agenda, such as a report that the Inspector-General of the RIC, Sir Joseph Byrne, a Catholic, was about to be dismissed. Efforts by Byrne to recruit special constables in rural areas had been as unsuccessful as those of the Chief Commissioner of the DMP in Dublin, but he strenuously resisted pressure from Lord French to recruit ex-servicemen instead. Although a former army officer, Byrne refused to countenance the RIC becoming an adjunct of the military. French regarded Byrne as insubordinate and weak and told Lloyd George he wanted someone 'of less intelligence and more stolidity.' Lloyd George confided to the leader of the Conservative Party, Andrew Bonar Law:

> It may of course very well be that the task in Ireland is a hopeless one and that Byrne has simply the intelligence to recognise [this]. However, until we are through with Home Rule a man of less intelligence and more stolidity would be … more useful.

Byrne certainly had enough intelligence to insist that he be made a permanent civil servant when he left the army to head the RIC. It was not until 1922 that he formally resigned, although he had been sidelined by the military long before then. Rumours that he was being replaced because he was a Catholic were grist to the Sinn Féin mill. His impending departure was compared to the replacement in 1918 of Lieutenant-General Bryan Mahon as General Officer Commanding in Ireland by Sir Frederick Shaw, 'a Protestant of Scotch ancestry.'[26]

The most pressing issue for Dubliners had little to do with politics at all. It was the continuing coal shortage. Despite British production having risen by 10 per cent over the previous year, there was still a fuel famine in the city. The lack of adequate shipping and rolling stock for bringing the product from the mines to the docks was a significant part of the problem. When the British government cut prices by 10s a ton on 12 January 1920 to counter inflation it actually aggravated the shortage, because it disproportionately reduced profit margins in the Dublin market. Irish coal merchants lobbied for the right to charge higher prices so that they could attract suppliers.

However, English and Welsh distributors not only wanted more money but demanded that Irish customers accept consignments containing 25 per cent dross. The result was a price increase of 2s a ton for poorer-quality coal on 13 January, prompting an *Irish Independent* headline: 'Giving Ireland the rubbish'. Storms on the Irish Sea delayed shipments further. Many Dubliners resorted to cutting turf and felling trees, despite the inclement weather.

A serious casualty of the shortage from the point of view of public health was the closure of the public baths in Tara Street, on which large numbers of tenement-dwellers relied for washing clothes as well as maintaining personal hygiene.[27] Distribution of the coal that did arrive was disrupted by the motor permits strike.

Polling day was marked by brilliant sunshine throughout the country, and while there were the usual complaints about personation there were relatively few violent scenes in Dublin, compared with Cork, where ex-servicemen and Sinn Féin supporters clashed. Soldiers were posted at polling stations in the capital. What violence did occur involved the use of motor vehicles to transport voters to the polls, as cars were held up by drivers still out on strike. There was at least one incident in which a car was overturned, but there were no serious injuries. The strikers' action appears to have militated mainly against independents, nationalists, MRA and unionist candidates.

The *Irish Times* conceded that Sinn Féin's electoral machine surpassed those of its rivals, and its election material included 'quite elaborate documents, giving biographical details of the party's candidates—a wise inspiration, seeing that most of the candidates are hitherto virtually unknown to the Dublin public.' Sinn Féin continued to portray itself as a national movement rather than a mere political party. In Rathmines, for instance, where its candidates had formed themselves into the Cuala Group, the *Cuala News* carried the Teutonic-sounding front-page headline 'Ireland over all' and asserted 'our right to speak our minds to our own people in our own country.' It launched a savage attack on Rathmines Urban District as Dublin's 'convalescent home and asylum of Freemasonry and Orangeism.'[28] The group stressed Sinn Féin's commitment to women's rights but failed to mention any other social or economic issues. In this it reflected the composition of the local Sinn Féin coalition, which included figures as diverse as James Dwyer, vice-president of the Family Grocers' and Purveyors' Association, and Thomas O'Connor, accountant and company director, as well as Dr Kathleen Lynn and relatives of 1916 martyrs, such as Áine (Frances) Ceannt and

Joseph MacDonagh. In working-class districts Sinn Féin campaigned strongly on such social issues as housing, better education facilities and greater access to health services, making its programme almost indistinguishable from Labour's.

New women voters in Dublin posed a problem, according to the *Irish Times*. It reported that many inadvertently spoiled their ballots and had to be given new ones. In Electoral Area 4, comprising Inns Quay and Rotunda, 'quite a number of illiterates, mostly women, recorded their votes early ... and put the officials to some little trouble explaining to them how to exercise the franchise.' The method used for people who could not read was that the presiding officer would read out the list of candidates, and the voter would state their preferences. In some instances the voters 'continued to state their preferences ... until they exhausted the entire list.' Some women insisted on their husbands assisting them with the ballot paper.

There was heavy early polling in the South City ward and other areas where business people and clerical workers preponderated. In the townships early voting was certainly the norm. It was slower in working-class areas, such as the North and South Dock wards, where four times as many women as men had voted by 4 p.m. Some employers allowed longer lunch breaks to facilitate voting, but in most cases men had to wait until they clocked out. In Blackrock one perplexed voter entered the town hall and informed the presiding officer that he had a vote in two wards. 'One half of the population tell me I can vote in both wards and the other half say I can't.' The presiding officer replied: 'One half of the population is wrong and the other isn't.'

The city itself was divided into ten electoral areas, which replaced the twenty wards. The counting of votes took two days: the ballot papers for the first five electoral areas were counted on Friday and the rest on Saturday. The police were responsible for the safekeeping of the ballot boxes, and Sinn Féin supporters feared that they would be interfered with. In Howth these concerns were satisfactorily addressed only when the police agreed to leave the boxes in full view through the windows of the counting centre. Sinn Féin supporters maintained an all-night vigil outside. In the event, the contending parties were satisfied that the results accurately reflected the wishes of the electorate. Concern about 'illiterates', the large numbers of new electors and confusion over PR was not entirely misplaced. There were 1,372 spoiled ballots out of 62,503 cast in the city, or 2¼ per cent.

As might be expected, there were striking differences between how the city and the rest of the country voted. Only 63 per cent of the electorate bothered to vote in Dublin, compared with 78 per cent in Connacht and a national average of 72 per cent. Sinn Féin showed itself to be still an overwhelmingly Dublin party, securing 45 per cent of the first-preference votes and 53 per cent of the seats in the capital, compared with only 27 per cent of the votes and 31 per cent of the seats nationally. Ironically, Labour secured only 12 per cent of the votes in Dublin, compared with 18 per cent nationally, yet it won 16 per cent of the seats in Dublin, in large part from strong Sinn Féin transfers.

A more predictable difference in voting patterns emerged in the disparity between the unionist vote in Dublin and elsewhere. In Dublin it secured a mere 1.12 per cent of the vote to win one seat, which corresponded to 1.25 per cent of the eighty corporation seats. Nationally the unionists polled 27 per cent of the vote, within half of 1 per cent of the Sinn Féin tally, but secured only 20 per cent of the seats, because their power base was concentrated in Ulster.

In Dublin the unionists had made a virtue of necessity and concentrated resources in Electoral Area 2. It was quite a come-down from the pre-war years when they made up the second-largest group on Dublin Corporation and had always elected at least two aldermen and two councillors from the wards now constituting Electoral Area 2. (An alderman was the first councillor elected in each ward or electoral area.) The reality was that most unionists in the city were accommodating themselves to the new political realities by defecting to the MRA. A former unsuccessful unionist nominee, J. Hubbard Clark, won the second-highest vote in Electoral Area 2, more than double the combined votes of the two official unionist candidates, by running on the MRA ticket. In number of votes the MRA was now the third-largest political bloc in the city, after Sinn Féin and Labour. It secured 12 per cent of the vote but won only 11 seats, compared with the 14 secured by the warring Labour factions with only 0.1 per cent more first preferences.[29]

Nationalist candidates did surprisingly well in Dublin, as they did throughout the country, considering the rout of the 1918 general election. They won a larger share of the vote than Labour or the plethora of independents who ran in the city. That share was identical to that of their party colleagues nationally: 14½ per cent. But this was not reflected in seats. More than half the 9,132 votes for Irish Party candidates went to two men: the publican and former MP Alfie Byrne, with 3,670 votes, and the tobacconist Lorcan Sherlock, with 1,797. Byrne was already a legendary vote-getter, and many people had been surprised that he lost his parliamentary seat in the Sinn Féin wave of 1918. Sherlock had been a long-serving councillor and a popular former Lord Mayor, nicknamed the 'Lay Pope' because of his constant deference to Archbishop Walsh on spiritual and political issues. The Irish Party ended up with nine seats, or 11¼ per cent.

Independents in Dublin secured 12 per cent of the vote but only four seats, or 5 per cent of the total. Quite a number of independent candidates were former Irish Party councillors, but almost half the independent vote went to the outgoing Lord Mayor, Laurence O'Neill. He had always run as an independent nationalist, free of any taint of association with the Irish Party, and since 1916 as a facilitator of the separatist cause, although not a member of Sinn Féin. Lorcan O'Toole was another popular independent nationalist. Like O'Neill, he had ploughed a lone furrow. The third successful independent was Owen Hynes of the Brick and Stone Layers' Union, who joined the Republican Labour caucus once elected. Although he secured only 450 votes, half the quota, he accumulated enough transfers from eliminated Labour and Sinn Féin candidates to push him over the line. The fourth independent, James Gately, was a former Irish Party candidate.

In the rest of Ireland municipal reformers and champions of the ratepayers tended to be bracketed as independents. The scale of the MRA's success in Dublin sets the capital apart, but it is worth noting that the MRA and independents between them polled 15,165 first preferences, or 24 per cent. If this translated into only 19 per cent of the seats on the corporation it was because political beliefs and allegiances were in flux, and there were no citywide agreements on transfers between candidates outside the Sinn Féin-Labour axis. Nevertheless the strong poll by the MRA showed that there was a large underlying urban middle-class bloc in Dublin that was conservative in outlook, local in political priorities and largely unmoved by the programme of radical nationalism, let alone socialism.

Of course the principal winner in the city was Sinn Féin, with 42 seats out of 80; its effective strength, however, was only 38, because, despite last-minute withdrawals to avert such situations, one Sinn Féin candidate, Kathleen Clarke, was elected in two wards, while two successful candidates were in prison and another, Seán T. Ó Ceallaigh, was in Paris. However, it was expected that the Labour councillors, particularly Republican Labour, would work closely with Sinn Féin and provide a comfortable working majority for implementing a common programme.

In general, the results of the election reflected both the changing fortunes of political parties and the continuing importance of personalities. The Municipal Reform Association, for instance, did well in more prosperous middle-class areas, such as the old unionist heartland of Electoral Area 2 on the north side and Area 3, which included the prosperous Fitzwilliam and Exchange wards, south of the river. Even in those areas its candidates had to settle for second place after Sinn Féin. In Electoral Area 2 it was the surge in Sinn Féin support that put the little-known Seán McGarry, president of the IRB, top of the poll with more than a thousand first-preference votes.

It is hard to know if Dr McWalter's defection from the discredited Irish Party to the MRA helped or hindered him in the struggle for political survival. A former alderman with a socially progressive attitude on many issues as well as a large medical practice, McWalter barely scraped home with the last seat in Electoral Area 8. It seems he lost much of his old nationalist base while failing to attract the admittedly small unionist electorate in a predominantly working-class constituency. By contrast, his former party colleague Sir James Gallagher, the tobacco magnate, romped home as an MRA candidate in predominantly middle-class Electoral Area 3, along with Sir Andrew Beattie, a wealthy former unionist councillor. Yet even in this very comfortable constituency the continuing strength of Sinn Féin, combined with a popular personality, ensured that Alderman Tom Kelly was returned at the top of the poll. His long years of constituency work and chairmanship of the corporation's Housing Committee had made him popular even when Sinn Féin was not. He won 3,438 first-preference votes, the second-highest personal tally in the city. That he was seen as one of Sinn Féin's more respectable candidates no doubt helped with an eminently respectable electorate. His arrest in December 1919 and subsequent detention helped secure the sympathy vote.

Another example of the power of personality was Alfie Byrne. He may have lost his parliamentary seat to Sinn Féin in 1918 but his resolute adherence to clientelism and total dedication to opportunist politics enabled him to top the poll in the overwhelmingly working-class Electoral Area 8, where Dr McWalter had to struggle. Byrne secured 3,180 votes, the third-highest personal vote in Dublin. But the highest vote of all went to the outgoing Lord Mayor and independent nationalist Laurence O'Neill, with 3,672 votes in Electoral Area 4, comprising the relatively comfortable Inns Quay and Rotunda wards.

W. T. Cosgrave, then Minister for Local Government in Dáil Éireann, was the most popular Sinn Féin candidate after Kelly. He secured 2,033 votes. Sinn Féin MPs topped the poll in most electoral areas but with more modest totals: Michael Staines secured 1,675 votes in Electoral Area 1, Seán McGarry secured 1,058 in Area 2 and Joe MacDonagh secured 1,037 votes in Area 5. On the other hand the little-known Joseph McGrath secured only 531 first preferences in New Kilmainham, well behind the poll-topper, Cosgrave, and Peter Doyle, a fitter at the Inchicore railway works who had been an independent member of the corporation before joining Sinn Féin.

The worst-performing Sinn Féin MP was Seán O'Mahony, who secured a mere 136 first preferences in Electoral Area 4, the Lord Mayor's stronghold. He scraped in with another Sinn Féin candidate, Jennie Wyse Power, on the twelfth count. One reason for the low votes of many Sinn Féin candidates was that they were relatively unknown. Their main qualification was participation in the Easter Rising. Another factor was that there were far too many. Seven Sinn Féin candidates ran for nine seats in Area 1; eight pursued eight seats in Area 2; six pursued nine seats in Area 3; and eight pursued ten seats in Area 4. In Area 5 there were six Sinn Féin candidates fighting for seven seats; in Area 6 there were seven candidates for seven seats, while in Area 7 six candidates pursued nine seats. In Area 8 there were eight Sinn Féin candidates for eight seats, and in Area 9 Sinn Féin ran four candidates for six seats. In Area 10 there were six candidates seeking seven seats.

The strength of the Sinn Féin brand ensured that preferences were kept within the party fold. This particularly helped women candidates. Kathleen Clarke topped the poll in Electoral Area 9 with 1,374 votes and came second to Lorcan Sherlock in Area 6 with 937 votes; but other women in Sinn Féin were heavily dependent on transfers. Hanna Sheehy Skeffington, another 1916 widow, secured only 340 first preferences in Area 3 but was elected with 1,551 votes on the second count when most of the other Sinn Féin candidates and independents were eliminated. Jennie Wyse Power, a veteran of the Ladies' Land League as well as of Arthur Griffith's pre-1916 Sinn Féin, started off with 121 first preferences in Area 4 but soaked up transfers from across the political spectrum to be elected on the ninth count. The fact that she was a businesswoman with a respectable Parnellite pedigree no doubt added to her appeal for moderate voters' transfers. The other successful Sinn Féin woman candidate was Mrs Seán McGarry in Area 5. She began with a low first-preference vote, but transfers from eliminated candidates, including Sarah Harrison, put her ahead of two male Sinn Féin candidates to take one of the last seats on the fifteenth count. Finally, Anne Elizabeth Ashton was co-opted to fill the second seat won by Kathleen Clarke.

There were five other Sinn Féin woman candidates who failed to be elected, almost all of them relatives of better-known male activists. The MRA ran two unsuccessful women candidates, and Labour ran no women at all.

In the middle-class townships women candidates were far more successful, securing seats from across the political spectrum. In Rathmines Urban District the unionists retained control in a tightly fought contest. Arguably it was the Irish Party's decision to run a woman that robbed Sinn Féin of victory. Although the nationalists polled only 937 votes, it was enough to put the unionists ahead of Sinn Féin on the first count, by 4,580 votes to the latter's 3,952. Eleven unionists were elected, to nine Sinn Féin and one nationalist. The successful nationalist was Mary Kettle, widow of the former Irish Party MP Tom Kettle. The highest-scoring Sinn Féin candidate was Dr Kathleen Lynn, who came second to the unionist William Carruthers, partner in a prominent firm of solicitors.

The unionists also retained control of Blackrock, where Lady Dockrell headed the poll. In Kingstown the unionists won the largest number of seats, eight, but this was far short of the eleven needed to control the council. Neither the candidate of the local Ratepayers' Association nor the independent, who might have provided them with allies, was elected. Sinn Féin was the next-largest party, with five seats, while Labour and the Irish Party won four each.

Elsewhere the results were equally mixed. Pembroke was the largest of the remaining townships, and the election resulted in deadlock between the unionists, who formerly dominated the council, and Sinn Féin. It was resolved by drawing names out of a hat. A unionist, W. Beckett, won. It was agreed that Nell Humphreys, a sister of the dead 1916 leader Michael O'Rahilly, would be vice-chairman. One unionist was elected in Howth, where Sinn Féin was the dominant party. Labour was the largest party in the other predominantly working-class township, Dalkey. One of the defeated Labour candidates there was the general secretary of the Irish Women Workers' Union, Louie Bennett, a member of a prominent local Church of Ireland business family.

In all, Sinn Féin secured 43 seats in the townships, the unionists 28 (of which 11 were in Rathmines), the Ratepayers' Association 12, nationalists 20 and Labour 17.[30]

Sinn Féin was now in a position to consolidate its grip on municipal power in the capital and to purge the old corporation regime. The council had been fairly inactive in the closing weeks of 1919, and some meetings had struggled to secure a quorum. The last important decision by the old council was the approval of a loan of £160,000 to complete the reservoir at Roundwood, Co. Wicklow. Work had begun in 1908 but wartime shortages of essential materials and inflationary pressures had brought the project to a halt.[31]

When the new council met on Friday 30 January the public gallery was packed, and crowds thronged Cork Hill to witness the arrival of the new members at City Hall, on which a Tricolour was hoisted. Sixteen aldermen were present and fifty-six other councillors. The missing public representatives were imprisoned Sinn Féin members, including Tom Kelly, who was reported to be in very poor health in Wormwood Scrubs Prison in London. There were calls from all parties for his release and talk of electing him Lord Mayor. For the moment, Laurence O'Neill, first elected to the post in 1917, presided. He was a *de facto* ally of Sinn Féin on the corporation but, as an independent nationalist, was acceptable to all sides. Many of the ablest Sinn Féin councillors were also MPs and were heavily committed to the work of Dáil Éireann. All were too busy building the revolutionary counter-state, when not in prison or on the run, to be chief magistrate of the city.

O'Neill's experience came into play at the inaugural meeting when the first of a series of clashes took place between the leader of the Republican Labour group, William O'Brien, and the Town Clerk, Henry Campbell. Campbell was a pillar of the Irish Party establishment. He was sixty-three years old, had been private secretary to Charles Stewart Parnell and had served as a Parnellite MP until he took up the post of Town Clerk in 1893. Always impeccably and even flamboyantly dressed, with a magnificent waxed walrus moustache, he was in form and substance the complete antithesis of the sartorially challenged O'Brien, who was twenty-five years his junior.

The duel began when Campbell formally notified the Lord Mayor that one of the Sinn Féin councillors, Jennie Wyse Power, had 'not subscribed the declaration for Electoral Area Four and therefore a vacancy arose.' In simple terms, she had insisted on signing the form with an Irish version of her name. She told the Lord Mayor that she conducted all her business with this name, and had offered to add her signature in English after receiving a notice of disqualification, only to be told by the Town Clerk that it was too late. He had further warned her not to speak at the meeting, as she could incur a fine of £50, but she said she needed to explain her position to constituents, regardless of the fine, and assure them that she would run again if disqualified.

At this point Alderman William O'Brien rose to propose a motion, seconded by Councillor Lawrence Raul (Sinn Féin): 'That this Corporation is of the opinion that Mrs Wyse Power had been duly and properly elected a Councillor for the Number Four Electoral Area: and, that we hereby direct the Town Clerk to add her name to the List of Members.' It was passed, but Campbell refused to carry out the resolution, 'on the advice given by counsel.' O'Brien, this time seconded by Councillor William Paul (Sinn Féin), proposed the suspension of the Town Clerk. The Lord Mayor ruled the motion out of order.[32] The situation was defused, but the seating of Wyse Power remained unresolved.

O'Brien next proposed that before the council proceeded to its main business members should direct the corporation's officers to remove 'the emblems of feudal authority known as the Sword and Mace, which are only relics of barbarism … originating in the desire of tyrannical monarchs to parade their power before the eyes of a subject people.' O'Neill congratulated O'Brien on getting his motion in so quickly, 'and it was very nicely worded,' but ruled it out of order. O'Brien refused to withdraw it and uproar followed until W. T. Cosgrave rose in support of the Mayor. He told O'Brien that he objected as much as anyone to the presence of those objects but that O'Brien would have to put in a notice of motion like anyone else.

The 'emblems of feudal authority' secured a month's reprieve before being consigned to the muniment room.

It was only now that the corporation reached the first and most important item on the agenda: the election of Lord Mayor. O'Neill made a remarkable speech in defence of the office. He conceded that its 'imperial power' was gone and said that, during his tenure,

> soldiers of the King broke my windows, hammered my hall door with trench tools and clamoured for my blood; my official residence [was] raided by military and police, my family and myself openly insulted at the whim of some under-strapper who pulls the wires in Dublin Castle. [Applause.] But outside of all this the Lord Mayor of Dublin is in an independent position if he maintains it; he signs no pledge, he takes no oath, he owes no allegiance to any power or authority except the people who returned him, and to the members who elected him to the position. Consequently it is a position the most fastidious might occupy without his conscience being annoyed, without his morals being corrupted or his principles being interfered with in any way. Therefore to fill such a position we are called together today, and it is my privilege to propose the name of Alderman Thomas Kelly.

He said he had worked closely with the candidate over the past two years, particularly on the Anti-Conscription Committee, and he had 'never met a man who was so imbued with the spirit of doing what was straight, of doing what was right.'

Cosgrave seconded the motion and called on councillors who might differ in their views from Kelly to put the principle of 'liberty of the subject' first. There was no question of anyone running against the imprisoned Sinn Féin poll-topper, only whether it would be a unanimous decision. O'Brien pledged the support of his 'section of Labour' and added, to laughter, that there were few men who could serve on the corporation for twenty-one years and not be corrupted.

It was when Dr McWalter rose to speak that the resentment of the old guard broke through. He mocked O'Brien as 'the representative in embryo of a workers' republic,' which would 'crumble to pieces' if it ever came to pass. An unidentified member heckled to say that O'Brien 'never had a khaki coat on him.' (Applause.) McWalter replied:

> I had a khaki coat on me, but I am proud of it. [Hisses from the gallery.] Howl away. I had a khaki coat when many members calling themselves republicans were in bed, or under the bed. I except only those who were condemned to death.

He said he would be voting for Alderman Kelly, although

> Sinn Féin is the most infamous tyranny from which Ireland ever suffered. [Laughter.] I am convinced it is worse than Orangeism and Molly Maguireism. Still, if a man be an honest man and a good corporator, I think that the fact that he is a Sinn Féiner should not deprive him of the honour of being Lord Mayor of Dublin.

McWalter's MRA colleague Alderman Sir Andrew Beattie and the sole unionist, William McCarthy, proved more generous in their support for Kelly, and he was elected unanimously after all.

The unanimity proved short-lived, for the old guard were shocked by the next proposal, from Alderman Cosgrave, that the corporation no longer acknowledge the right of the Lord Lieutenant to appoint a High Sheriff. Protests that it was an ancient privilege that, once renounced, might never be restored made no impression on the new councillors. There were 58 votes in favour of Cosgrave's proposal and only 14 against. These fourteen helped define and identify the core opposition grouping to Sinn Féin on the corporation. They were: Councillor William McCarthy (the sole unionist); Aldermen J. Hubbard Clark and Sir Andrew Beattie and Councillors John Russell Stritch, Richard Henry White and Michael James Maxwell-Lemon (all MRA members from a unionist background); James Moran, Michael J. Moran and Dr McWalter (Irish Party defectors to the MRA); John Keogh and Sir James Gallagher (elected on the Irish Party ticket); James Gately (independent nationalist); and William Patrick Delaney and Dr Myles Keogh (former nationalists elected as independents).

They would combine again on the next item on the agenda and the first substantial piece of business for the corporation: the allocation of places on its various committees. A list had already been drawn up by the Town Clerk, Campbell, and it was presented to the aldermen and councillors for acceptance as a *fait accompli*. Dr McWalter, seconded by Alderman Sir Andrew Beattie, called for the list to be accepted *en bloc*, but Aldermen W. T. Cosgrave and Seán McGarry of Sinn Féin insisted on the nominations going before the entire council. They were not going to allow Campbell to rig the committees in favour of the remnants of the old guard. On this occasion 48 votes were cast in support of the Sinn Féin proposal and 20 against. Alfie Byrne tried unsuccessfully to retrieve the situation with a motion to defer a decision until the next meeting, on 2 February.

The increased vote against the axis of Sinn Féin and Republican Labour included some members of the Trades Council wing of Labour. Among these were long-standing opponents of the Irish Party regime, such as Tom Lawlor, John Farren and Daniel Magee. They shared the concern of the MRA and nationalists that they might be excluded from important committees if Campbell's list was not adopted. However, other members of the Trades Council faction, including its leader, P. T. Daly, voted with Sinn Féin and Republican Labour, suggesting that the Dalyites were not as united as the O'Brienites.

The first battleground for seats was the important Housing Committee, over which the absent Tom Kelly had presided since before the 1913 Lockout. It was also by far the largest committee, with two representatives from each electoral area rather than the customary one. In the event the votes reflected significant trade-offs. The solitary unionist, William McCarthy, decided to yield gracefully to Sinn Féin and was rewarded with places on the Electricity Supply and Markets Committees. Ironically, no compromise was possible between the two wings of Labour in Electoral Area 3. The Republican Labour nominee, Joseph Farrell of the Painters' Society, won in a straight contest with John Farren of the Sheet Metal Workers' Society, who had been nominated by the Dalyites and had support from Dr McWalter and his allies. In fact whenever a contest took place for positions on the Housing Committee it was the Sinn Féin and Republican Labour nominees who prevailed over the shifting sands of opposition. Eventually Sinn Féin took nine seats, the Dalyites four and the O'Brienites three, while the MRA and independent nationalists secured two each.

On the crucial Estates and Finance Committee, Sinn Féin took six of the ten seats and Republican Labour took two. There was one MRA member and one independent. By the time the vote was taken on the Electricity Supply Committee, Dr McWalter, the emerging leader of the MRA, decided to bow to the inevitable and withdraw his list in favour of that proposed by the Sinn Féin alderman and MP Joe MacDonagh. This comprised five Sinn Féin members and one each of Republican Labour, nationalists, independent nationalists, MRA and unionists. The message was simple: all parties would receive a share of committee places, but Sinn Féin would rule.

The same formula applied for nominations to public bodies, such as Dublin Port and Docks Board and the voluntary hospitals. P. T. Daly caused a rare upset when he defeated the Sinn Féin absentee Seán T. Ó Ceallaigh for a seat on the board of the Charitable Infirmary (Jervis Street Hospital). Predictably, one committee on which Sinn Féin sought no involvement was the Dublin War Pensions Board. Nevertheless it did object to a former nationalist Lord Mayor, Sir James Gallagher, representing the corporation. The board eventually comprised three Republican Labour councillors, three MRA, two independent nationalists (including the ubiquitous Alfie Byrne), the only unionist on the corporation, William McCarthy, and one Dalyite, John Farren.[33]

Despite the unanimous endorsement of his colleagues, and widespread public outrage over his internment in England, Alderman Kelly was never able to take up the position to which he had been elected. In poor health when arrested, he suffered a complete mental breakdown in prison. He returned to Ireland in April and would not become politically active again for many years.[34] Laurence O'Neill would remain Lord Mayor until Dublin Corporation was dissolved in 1924.

Jennie Wyse Power was able to assume her seat on the corporation at its next meeting on 2 February. The Town Clerk informed members that he now had legal advice that if she was declared duly elected 'the responsibility will attach to the Council and not to me.' There was little comment on Campbell's changed stance, as the proceedings were overshadowed by a wave of arrests in the city the previous night. Three Sinn Féin councillors were among those rounded up, including Joseph McGrath MP. But when William O'Brien put down a fairly routine motion, supported by Sinn Féin, calling on the corporation to publicise the arrests internationally, it was passed only after some bad-tempered exchanges with the MRA, who believed that the best way to stay out of prison was to respect the King's writ.[35]

In the urban districts, which also convened to elect officers on 30 January, Sinn Féin was not able to impose its will so readily. In Pembroke the balance was so tight that a coin was tossed to decide the chairmanship, and luck was with the unionists.

In Rathmines the unionists re-elected Robert Benson as chairman and William Ireland, a former unionist member of Dublin Corporation, as vice-chairman. The Sinn Féin candidates were both defeated, although in the vote for vice-chairman there was only one vote between William Ireland and Áine Ceannt, widow of the executed 1916 leader. The sole Irish Party member of the council, Mary Kettle, abstained on the vote for chairman but voted for Mrs Ceannt as vice-chairman, as did an independent.

In Kingstown the unionists may have come out of the election as the largest party, with eight of the twenty-one seats, but the other parties combined to elect a nationalist councillor, J. M. Devitt, as chairman and a Labour councillor, Edward Kelly, as vice-chairman. There was some consternation when one of the new Sinn Féin councillors, Seán Ó hUadhaigh, a solicitor, addressed the chamber in Irish. He then translated his remarks, saying he sought the co-operation of all members and that they should lose no opportunity to keep before them the aim of ensuring that Ireland remained 'a country self-contained and foreign to every other country, having its own language and traditions.' This led Sir Thomas Robinson, a former unionist parliamentary candidate for South County Dublin, to remark that 'if Mr Ó hUadhaigh continues to address the Council in a language they could not understand I do not see how the co-operation, whether cordial or otherwise, that he has spoken of can be brought about.'

It was a winner-takes-all meeting in Blackrock, where the unionists retained control, while in working-class Dalkey the election of a Labour member as chairman and a Sinn Féin councillor as vice-chairman reflected their relative strengths on the council. In Killiney, A. H. Ormsby-Hamilton, a local businessman who ran as an independent, was elected chairman, and in Bray Joseph Lynch of Sinn Féin comfortably saw off a challenge from the Ratepayers' Association, by nine votes to five.

One other important body held its annual general meeting in Dublin that day: the city's chamber of commerce. It was still dealing with the economic after-effects of the war, including the heavy burden of the excess profits tax and the high cost of freight, which was blamed on continuing military control of the railways and was used as an argument against nationalisation. But local politics intruded as well. There was unanimous concern that the proportional representation introduced for the local elections had been rushed and omitted to provide a 'company' vote for businessmen to reflect the fact that they paid such high commercial rates. The amendment to the Public Health (Medical Treatment of Children) (Ireland) Act making inspections of schoolchildren mandatory was another example of rushed legislation deplored by the chamber, because it failed to take account of the rates burden it would inflict on the business community.

Members also showed unanimity in deploring the state of the country; but when James Brady, a nationalist solicitor, called for the scrapping of the Motor

Permits Order, fissures appeared. While there was general agreement with his call for 'somebody in Government ... who knew something of the trade and commerce of the country' to intervene in the dispute, most members drew the line at his analysis that the order was of 'no earthly use in tracking down criminals.' P. J. Grierson, a major shareholder in the Dublin and South-Eastern Railway who constantly called for tougher penalties on fare-evaders, said he had recently been in Belgium with his wife and had to obtain photographs to travel there. 'I do not see any reason why an Irishman should be ashamed of having his photograph attached to his permit.' (Applause.) Brady rejoined: 'You were a foreigner in Belgium. An Irishman is not a foreigner in his own country.'

Business moved on to the appointment of auditors.[36] Fortunately, the permits dispute would be resolved within a fortnight. (See above, p. 68.)

At the beginning of February the Catholic hierarchy undertook an initiative in Dublin and other cities and towns to confront a more insidious foreign threat than British rule. On 1 February, St Brigid's Day, the city's convents were hosts to 'St Brigid's pledge'. As the most venerated saint in Ireland after St Patrick, it seemed appropriate that her name day should be the occasion for Dublin women and girls to join the newly formed League of St Brigid and sign a pledge designed by the hierarchy to avoid 'all impropriety in the matter of dress and to maintain and hand down the tradition and proverbial purity and modesty of Irish womanhood.' As the Archbishop of Dublin, Dr Walsh, put it,

> the evil to be confronted is a gigantic one, and ... it has gained ground to such an extent that Catholics do not shrink from taking part in the offering of the Holy Sacrament of the Mass and of presenting themselves at the altar rail to receive Holy Communion most unbecomingly dressed, or, rather, one might say undressed.

A few days later, welcoming the response of the city's Catholic womanhood, the archbishop added that if women wished to act 'for the glory of God and honour of Erin' they should wear clothes that were 'distinctly Irish' and 'suitable to the climate, giving a representation of Irish art and Irish modesty.'[37]

February also witnessed a more substantial step forward for women with the establishment of the first General Nursing Council for Ireland. Nowhere had women been more needed during the war than in nursing, but the pay and conditions set by the military authorities were significantly worse than those for unskilled labourers. In contrast, a doctor entering military service received a commission and was paid at least the RAMC rates, and often significantly more, depending on qualifications and experience. Attempts within the nursing profession to set up a register to improve training standards and pay had been disrupted by the war, but the Irish Nurses' Association and Irish Matrons' Association, which tended to share the same leadership, continued to lobby the Lord Lieutenant and the British government on the need for a system of statutory training and registration for nurses.

A relatively high proportion of Irish nurses came from a Protestant middle-class background, which helped account for a strong affinity with the war effort.[38] The Matrons' Association often adopted positions supportive of Britain, as when it endorsed a proposal from Lady Fingall, in her capacity as president of the Conservative and Unionist Women's Franchise Association, to have a woman inspector appointed to monitor 'separation women' and war widows to ensure that they were not cohabiting.[39]

On the other hand, the Matrons' Association had also affiliated to the National Union of Women Workers, the main campaigning body for working women in a wide variety of occupations during the war, and this helped widen its views on women's issues. Nor was it immune to the growing nationalist sentiment in the profession. This fuelled an increasing resentment at the insistence of their British counterparts that Irish nurses should go to London to sit qualifying examinations. It claimed the same professional independence for nurses that the medical profession enjoyed in Ireland and strongly resisted proposals that nurses trained in Voluntary Aid Detachments, who had played a vital role in military hospitals, should be allowed to qualify on the strength of their wartime experience. 'Three years in the wards of a recognised training school or schools is essential to entitle the V.A.D. [member] to the certificate of a trained nurse,' the matrons ruled.

When the war ended, the Matrons' Association secured its objectives with the Nurses Registration (Ireland) Act (1919), which came into effect on 13 February 1920.[40]

If the General Council set up by the Chief Secretary still contained a significant number of male members of the medical profession and the mandatory representative of the Anglo-Irish aristocracy, in this instance the Countess of Kenmare as vice-president, the overwhelming majority were nurses, including representatives of Dublin's leading hospitals.[41]

Chapter 4 ∿

'ON FRIDAY EVENINGS GOD SAVE THE KING WILL *NOT* BE PLAYED'

B y February 1920 it was clear that the DMP no longer controlled the streets, even in the centre of Dublin, although they now patrolled armed. Among the most serious incidents was an explosion at Kevin Street police station on 4 February when a bomb was thrown from neighbouring tenements into the sleeping-quarters. On 13 February a highly organised attempt to steal an arms shipment from a goods train near Newcomen Bridge on the North Strand was frustrated only after a pitched gun battle between the military escort on board and the raiders. All the attackers withdrew in good order with their vehicles.

At 1:45 a.m. on 20 February, two Volunteers, brothers Pat and Gabriel McGrath, were returning home from an unsuccessful attempt to burn down a British army tyre stores on the North Wall. They were challenged by armed DMP constables on Westmorland Street. The policemen opened fire, wounding Pat McGrath and taking him prisoner. Gabriel escaped and, when he ran into another DMP foot patrol on Nassau Street, he too opened fire, killing Constable John Walsh, and wounding his companion, Sergeant Charles Dunleavy. Constable Patrick Dennis, who shot and captured Pat McGrath, was later awarded the King's Police Medal.

Another gun attack took place that night in Marlborough Street, within yards of Sackville Street. In Waterford Street nearby three men with loaded revolvers were arrested by a large police patrol.[1]

At midnight on 23 February 1920 a military curfew was imposed on the city for the first time since 1916. It would last until the Truce in July 1921, occasionally being relaxed but more often extended as the security situation deteriorated. The initial order applied to the Dublin metropolitan area, except for Kingstown. This area extended as far west as Chapelizod, as far north as Glasnevin and as far south as Ballybrack, an area of 36 square miles and 420,000 people. Citizens had to keep off the streets from midnight until 5 a.m. Some twenty military detachments in lorries patrolled the streets each night, equipped with powerful Aldis searchlights. They carried out raids on houses and arrested anyone breaking the curfew and were supplemented by reinforcements as required for additional operations.

These reinforcements soon included British ex-servicemen, brought in as temporary members of the RIC to make up for the increasing number of resignations from the force. Its members would become known from their improvised uniforms as Black and Tans, and in many ways the haphazard mixture of British army and RIC dress epitomised their role over the next eighteen months, for they were neither soldiers nor policemen. Sir Joseph Byrne was sidelined in favour of his more pliant deputy, T. J. Smith, but the real commander of this new paramilitary force was General Hugh Tudor. It was deployed only briefly to reinforce the DMP in the city, and a mere sixteen would serve with the RIC in the county.[2] However, the RIC would soon be augmented by an elite Auxiliary Division, its members classified officially as 'cadets', mainly demobilised junior army officers; and it was this force of 'Auxiliaries', commanded by Brigadier-General Frank Crozier, that became the flamboyantly brutal enforcers of British law and order on Dublin's streets.

Dublin had the distinction of accommodating no fewer than five of the nineteen companies of Auxiliaries in the country, and at no time were there fewer than three in the city. Besides a Depot Company at Beggarsbush Barracks there was one at Portobello Barracks in Rathmines, one in Dublin Castle and another in the London and North-Western Hotel on the North Wall. Many of these cadets had been commissioned from the ranks in the later stages of the Great War, which was a tribute to their combat-worthiness and also helps explain the craving for respect that these 'temporary gentlemen' demanded. In its absence, they would settle for fear.

At first Dubliners were far too concerned about the sheer inconvenience of the curfew to bother too much about its enforcers. The *Irish Times* defended the measure, stating that 'in theory it might be a disagreeable restriction of public liberty, but in practice it affects only a very small minority of the citizens.' It assured readers that anyone engaged in legitimate pursuits after hours would have no difficulty obtaining permits, and pointed out that six policemen had been murdered on the streets of the capital in as many months without anyone being brought to justice. 'A situation in which the police have become hunted instead of the hunters has furnished splendid opportunities for the common law breaker.' Dozens of citizens had been held up by 'highwaymen' and shops and other businesses robbed or burgled.[3] The *Irish Independent* took a different view. It denounced the curfew as one more measure to 'strangle liberty'. It asked: 'How can the friend of a patient at death's door venture out to requisition a doctor, or clergyman?' and called for the resignation of Lord French and the Chief Secretary. 'Without providing either law or order they have thrown the country into a ferment of discontent. Their regime has brought government into contempt.'[4]

The lack of advance notice of the curfew led to thousands of applications from night workers, such as bakers, jarveys and taxi-drivers, who besieged the Permit Office in Ship Street in the hours before it came into force. Permits had been distributed to some employers with large numbers of night workers, such as Guinness's, Jacob's and the newspapers. In other cases permits were issued directly to employees, such as postal workers and the night staff at the telephone exchange. Ironically, the telephone exchange was heavily infiltrated by Michael Collins's intelligence network, including his cousin Nancy O'Brien, who was a secretary in the GPO. Postmen refused to use the permits, because the Dublin Trades Council told members of affiliated unions to boycott the scheme.

Dublin Corporation reacted to the curfew by going into emergency session on Monday 23 February. Alderman W. T. Cosgrave called for 'the necessary steps to be taken to deal with the ... restrictions placed upon the liberties of the citizens ... by the imposition of martial law.' His proposals managed to combine opposition to military rule with significant savings to the corporation's payroll. Under them, employees would be instructed not to apply to the military authorities for permits 'for the discharge of any municipal duties'; all municipal services that might endanger the lives of employees or officials would cease at night, including night watchmen, who were to leave their posts at 11 p.m. and resume at 6 a.m.; all public lamps would be extinguished in time to allow the staff involved to finish work by 11:30 p.m.; and no overtime payment would be made to an employee for work done between midnight and 5 a.m. for which a permit had been obtained.

Any dispute over the implementation of the new measures was to be referred to a joint committee of the Estate and Finance Committees and the relevant corporation committee directly involved.

Councillor Joe MacDonagh, a Sinn Féin MP for the city, said they must make it clear that the 'English military authorities' would be responsible 'for anything that might happen between 11:30 p.m. and 5 or 6 a.m.' in the city. A brother of the executed 1916 leader Thomas MacDonagh, he had resigned from the Customs Service after the Rising to become a tax consultant and insurance broker and to run an advertising agency. MacDonagh would make an important contribution to the work of the corporation and the alternative Dáil Éireann regime in the months ahead. Responding to criticism that switching off the lights would allow the military to do things they would not dare attempt in daylight, MacDonagh said that in his experience 'they had no scruples or shame: if they wanted to shoot people ... they would do it in broad daylight as well as in the dark.' His comments were met with cries of 'Hear, hear' from colleagues.

A series of speeches from MRA members and the sole Unionist, Councillor William McCarthy, questioned the legality of the measures. Councillor Michael Moran (MRA) warned that turning off the lights 'provided a great harvest for the burglars,' while his colleague Dr McWalter said the measure would give the military authorities 'huge delight', as they 'did not care if 300,000 people in Dublin were inconvenienced, burnt or shot if the corporation was foolish enough to do what is proposed.' However, the nationalists backed Sinn Féin, and one of their longest-serving councillors, Coghlan Briscoe, even scoffed that it was a 'very feeble protest', without offering any alternatives. The widow of one victim of martial law in 1916, Councillor Hanna Sheehy Skeffington, told colleagues bluntly that 'martial law is no law.'

Winding up the debate, Cosgrave told the opposition that Sinn Féin now spoke for the majority of Dublin's citizens, and it was saying to the British military authority: 'Clear out, and we will look after burglary and crime, and we will guarantee that this will be the best-governed country in Europe.' He was supported by loud applause. The motion was passed by 37 votes to 11, the opposition coming from the MRA and McCarthy.

The *Irish Times* condemned the proceedings, accusing the new council of being preoccupied with 'schemes to hinder and embarrass the protectors of the law.'[5]

Citizens found the order rigorously enforced from the beginning. Fully armed military pickets were placed at important junctions, including O'Connell Bridge and the other Liffey crossings, from midnight on 23 February. The lights went out, as directed by the corporation, at 11:30 p.m. Most city-centre theatres, cafés, billiard halls, milk bars and pubs closed early, and the O'Mara Operatic Company announced that it would end all performances for the season by

10:30 p.m. However, some dance halls continued opening late, letting patrons decide if they wanted to run the gauntlet of the curfew.

For those dependent on public transport for getting home there was little choice. The time of the last inward train from Bray to Westland Row was brought forward from 10:45 to 10:20 p.m. and the last southbound train from Amiens Street was brought forward from 11:05 p.m. to 10:30. The late trains to the northern townships of Malahide and Howth were discontinued. As the curfew applied only in the city, the GSWR made arrangements with the military that its trains could operate normally from Kingsbridge (Heuston Station), and it was up to passengers disembarking in Dublin to arrange their own permits. Anyone failing to do so could remain at the station until 5 a.m.

However, one group of travellers arriving late at Broadstone station that first night organised themselves into a procession and marched, singing, into the city centre in search of accommodation. They appear to have made the journey safely.

As they did so, the last tram for Kingstown and Dalkey left Nelson's Pillar, shortly after 11 p.m., and the last tram left for Ballsbridge at 11:25. 'At 11.45 p.m. a few jarveys with fares were seen whipping their horses vigorously and driving at full speed across O'Connell Bridge.' Some 'brilliantly lighted motors' also raced through the city centre as slow-moving military vehicles began dropping off men at designated points. After midnight 'there was scarcely an individual to be met in any part of the city.' Nevertheless it was 'standing room only' in military vehicles bringing those violating the curfew to the nearest police station for detention.

In the townships, patrolling was left to members of the DMP, who were out in force, armed and with their identification numbers removed, by order, from their tunics and greatcoats.

There were some unexpected complications arising from the enforcement of the curfew in Dublin port. Thick fog hampered operations on the quays, although the Port and Docks Board had its own power supply for lighting. An even bigger problem than fog was the refusal of dockers to work late if it meant they would be stranded in the port during the curfew. They absolutely refused to berth ships between midnight and 5 a.m., regardless of the tide. As a result the time for turning around vessels frequently doubled. The average delay experienced by colliers rose from 12 hours to 26, exacerbating the coal shortage in the city. The movement of herds for export also required careful timing now that the cattle market could not open until 6 a.m. and animals could enter the city and be driven through the streets to the docks only when the curfew ended.[6]

Frequent arrests continued over the next few days as Dubliners adjusted to the new regime. The most celebrated was that of Rev. T. J. O'Donnell, a former Australian army chaplain. He arrived in the city on 27 February, unaware of the curfew. He asked the magistrate why he had been arrested under the Defence of the Realm Act, which had been passed to prevent people assisting Germany during the war, considering that Germany had surrendered in November 1918.[7] He appears, like many early offenders, to have escaped with a caution. The real penalty for most of those detained was the loss of one or two days' work while waiting for their case to be processed. The greatest danger was being mistaken for someone with a similar name or address who was on the wanted list.

Nevertheless, 'ordinary life and routine went on,' Wilmot Irwin, a young Protestant clerk in the stockbroking firm of Dagg and Dawson, recalled many years later. 'Theatre shows started at absurdly early hours, five thirty or so, and small dances began at much the same hour.' All through the period 'British Tommies off duty still flocked to the first house of the Hippodrome for the British garrison were ever supporters of the variety theatre,' and Irwin believed that the departure of the British army in 1922 was the beginning of the end for Dublin's music-hall culture.

The local vigilance committee, composed mainly of clergymen and members of the city's numerous sodalities, had a very different view. In late 1919 it lodged a complaint with the corporation 'regarding the songs sung by a female performer in a City Theatre.' These were 'of an unsavoury character' and were delivered 'in a voice-tone and inflection, facial expression, gestures etc.' that were 'grossly suggestive all through ... She successfully invests each song with a meaning that cannot be mistaken.' The case was referred to one of the honorary lady inspectors, Mrs E. M. Smith, who reported that she saw nothing objectionable in the performance. However, she did express concern at a Fred Karno review, *Moonstruck*, that was presented at the same theatre some months later.[8]

Films also attracted the attention of the vigilance committee and the corporation censors. Of 164 films examined by censors in the first quarter of 1919, three required excisions before they could be certified for public showing, and two were banned. One film, *When a Woman Sins*, was considered appropriate for screening only after being seen by four censors and referred to Professor William Magennis, lecturer in moral psychology at the National University. He assured the corporation's Sanitation Department that it was appropriate for public viewing. In some cases the films causing concern were early classics, such as D. W. Griffith's *Hearts of the World*, shown at the Gaiety Theatre in August 1918. It was a wartime romance about an American soldier and a French woman that alarmed many respectable Dubliners because of a scene of attempted rape involving a nasty German. It was referred to the Law Agent, Ignatius Rice, but he refused to act, on the grounds that the film had been produced with the support of the British War Office's Department for Propaganda Purposes.[9]

It was not only the increasingly oppressive presence of soldiers and paramilitary Auxiliaries on the streets that alienated the city's conservative citizenry but the image of licentiousness and even lawlessness they increasingly associated with British rule.

Not all Dubliners saw things that way. Wilmot Irwin not only frequented cinemas and theatres but was a regular at dances in the parochial hall near St George's Church in Temple Street. 'Often the gay young things of the period braved ambushes and all sorts of inconveniences to seek forgetfulness … for a couple of short hours, and then scurried off to get home before curfew.' As attacks on British forces intensified, the curfew was brought forward to 10 p.m. and then 9:30. The junction of North Frederick Street and Dorset Street, a stone's throw from the parochial hall, became a regular site for ambushes, and Irwin found himself 'hurrying along Dorset Street at 9.15 p.m. on a perfectly bright evening to get home before the military lorries rumbled out.' Although originally intended as a social function

> for Protestant young people only … during the height of the troubles, Crown forces of any religion were eligible. Very rarely did they come in uniform—it might well have been signing their death warrant—since the parochial hall was situated in a slum area, where the I.R.A. had plenty of supporters, but they came just the same. Often I've watched these members take the revolvers out of their overcoat pockets before they went upstairs to dance. They were not going to be taken unawares. It was somewhat like the conditions of the Old West.

The proceedings always concluded with 'God Save the King'.[10] National anthems were one of a number of useful means by which patrons could identify safe venues for socialising. One 'professor of dancing' who ran classes in Dublin Castle as well as at his own 'academy' would use a discreet code to advertise select subscription dances during the week. On Mondays, evening dress would be worn; on Wednesdays, evening dress was optional; on Fridays, morning dress was worn and, to make sure there would be no misunderstandings, 'God Save the King will NOT be played.'[11]

Besides the music halls and dance halls, the other area where a general truce was honoured was sport, at least where the sport was shared, such as race meetings and soccer matches. Bohemians regularly played fixtures with British army teams, who would be given safe conduct to Dalymount Park when playing away. The compliment was returned when the army teams played at home, with the added courtesy of entertainment for the visitors in the NCOs' mess after the match. On the other hand, GAA matches were subjected to regular harassment.

Friction continued between the old and new regimes in City Hall. Once again the Irish language was a flashpoint between Campbell and the new generation of councillors when the corporation reconvened on 1 March. Having first unanimously condemned the seizure of Alderman Tom Kelly, the duly elected Lord Mayor of Dublin, 'by the English military army of occupation' and the conditions in which he had been held, the councillors moved on to the seemingly innocuous adoption of a report by the Technical Education Committee confirming appointments to the teaching staff for the current year. The Lord Mayor said that the Law Agent had objected to Hanna Sheehy Skeffington being reappointed, as she was now a councillor. She protested that she had been appointed annually for the past five years, and she 'absolutely declined to be bullied into resigning my seat. To resign would be to imply that I was guilty of something corrupt.' Far from feeling bullied, she added that she was 'seriously considering the advisability of putting down a motion to remove the Law Agent, and put him with the Mace and Sword in the muniment room.' (Laughter.)

Even members of the Municipal Reform Association, such as J. Hubbard Clark, Sir Andrew Beattie and Dr McWalter, spoke on her behalf, but the Law Agent was adamant that a member of the corporation could not hold a post financed by the corporation, even though in this instance its contribution was less than a penny in the pound—the rest coming from the Department of Education and a small sum in fees. The councillor had little option but to resign her job or her seat, a difficult decision for a woman of limited means with an orphaned son to raise. She chose to retain her seat.

Resentment was therefore running high with the city's senior officials when the roll call to adopt the report was taken. Things went quietly enough until Councillor William Paul's name was reached, and he replied 'Bíodh.' The Town Clerk refused to record the vote and in this was supported by the MRA. The acting Lord Mayor, Laurence O'Neill, attempted to break the deadlock.

The Lord Mayor—It is up to every Irishman to use the Irish language on every possible occasion, but when they have an ignoramus like myself to deal with I think that a member could answer in Irish and explain in English what he means.

Mr. Paul—I did that already today, but I am out now for principle. There are any amount of influences being brought to bear on me, but I say I would rather see the Council adjourn, and let the Gaelic League and the people of Ireland take up the matter. I am going to see that the principle is asserted, and no consideration can make me withdraw.

Captain Surgeon McWalter—Then let Mr. Paul not speak any more English at Corporation meetings. [Applause.]

The Lord Mayor—This is a matter that has never arisen before in the history of the Corporation, Town Clerk?

The Town Clerk—I think not. My point is that I am bound to keep the records of this Council in the language of the courts—the English language—and a member has answered in a language I do not understand.

Alderman O'Toole—Very well; then send for a member of your staff who does understand Irish.

The Town Clerk—I require no enlightenment from any member of my staff on matters belonging to the Corporation, nor from any member of this Council.

With the meeting on the brink of adjournment, Councillor Paul left his seat, saying, 'I do not like to do it, but I will go outside the barrier.' This allowed the vote to proceed. The report was passed, by 46 votes to 7.[12]

The language war was resumed the next week following a proposal by the Waterworks Committee for a pay increase of £1 for the Chief Turncock. When the proposal was put to a roll-call vote, Councillor Paul answered again in Irish. The Town Clerk said he must have an answer in English, either 'For' or 'Against'. As on the previous occasion, Paul withdrew beyond the barrier that marked off the voting area of the council chamber. Voting continued until it reached John O'Connor, a member of the Republican Labour group, who also answered in Irish. Campbell once more refused to accept the response. O'Connor protested that the Town Clerk had accepted an answer in Irish as to his being present. Campbell replied that when he heard a member's voice it was sufficient proof that he was present, but a division for or against a proposal required a response he could understand.

O'Connor was not amenable to a suggestion from the Lord Mayor that he could answer in English and Irish. After this the meeting quickly fell into chaos and accusations by Sinn Féin and Republican Labour councillors that Campbell was following a Dublin Castle agenda. Campbell protested his impartiality, to little avail. Councillor John Bohan (Republican Labour) even claimed that Alderman William O'Brien had been arrested to ensure he would not be present on this occasion to challenge the Town Clerk. Campbell told the councillors he was not antagonistic to any party in the chamber, and that he had been 'a member of and subscriber to the Gaelic League since it began.'[13]

However, he was now embarked on a collision course with the new council. Even a less conservative official than Campbell would have had difficulty in simultaneously meeting the agenda of the radical new chamber in asserting its independence and that of the Local Government Board, which provided the central funding essential to the municipality.

William O'Brien, leader of the Republican Labour group on the corporation, had indeed been arrested by a raiding party on 2 March in what were now becoming nightly occurrences. The curfew meant the military could move freely through the streets with little likelihood of ambush or interference. However, the raids netted few active Volunteers. O'Brien was not involved in paramilitary activity, but he was transferred next day to Wormwood Scrubs Prison in London, where many activists against whom no specific charges could be laid were detained. Protests by Thomas Johnson on behalf of the ITUC to the Parliamentary Committee of the British TUC and by the British Parliamentary Labour Party had no effect. It was only when O'Brien fell ill during a hunger strike shortly afterwards that he was released. Like his fellow-alderman Tom Kelly, he was forced to convalesce in England and was not allowed to return home until May.[14]

The tempo of war increased noticeably in the spring of 1920. Attacks on police barracks continued in the countryside, as did attacks on individual policemen and patrols. The Government of Ireland Bill was introduced in February, providing the legislative blueprint for partition and the establishment of a unionist home-rule parliament for six Ulster counties. Republicans rejected the measure outright and called on Sinn Féin and nationalist-dominated local authorities in the six affected counties to pledge their allegiance to Dáil Éireann.

If Northern nationalists and republicans were worried about their prospects, they were at least sustained by the continued opposition of Dáil Éireann to partition. But Southern unionists were distraught when the Ulster unionists, led by the Dubliner Edward Carson, accepted the bill. On 8 March 1920 a delegation from the Irish Unionist Alliance met Carson and the Standing

Committee of the Ulster Unionist Council in Belfast to express their concerns; the *Irish Times* reported that a 'frank discussion' took place. That evening Carson spoke at a meeting of Duncairn Women's Unionist Association in his newly adopted Belfast constituency, having abandoned his Dublin University seat in the South. After thanking his hosts for the presentation of a loving-cup and tray of Celtic design, Carson assured them that there was never a time 'when Ulster had better friends, and was better understood in the House of Commons.' He attributed this

> largely to the credit of my Labour colleagues through the city of Belfast. They were able to explain, in an intimate way that I am not competent to do, the real feeling of the Labour element in Belfast, and they are able to bring home ... to those with whom they discuss those affairs in the House of Commons, what the reality of the situation is.

When he came to the plight of Southern unionists, Carson railed against the prospect of handing over 'the lives and properties of those who have been loyal subjects of the Crown to those who have proved themselves the bitter enemies of England and everything that concerns England.' As regards Ulster, however, 'with which, in a sense, I am more immediately concerned,' the only promise he gave was to 'regulate the destinies, the lives and the happiness of our people in future.'[15]

Disappointment was understandably bitterest among unionists in the three Ulster counties of Cavan, Donegal and Monaghan, which were excluded from the new safe haven, and many of them resigned their membership of the Ulster Unionist Council.[16] The response of the *Irish Times* to Carson came in its editorial the next day, which declared that 'for more than thirty years the loyalists of Northern and Southern Ireland have fought a common battle against the enemies of the Union ... Now the link of common interest has been snapped.' The association of interests had been 'so intimate that during the larger part of that time the leader of Unionist Ulster represented Dublin University in Parliament.' Referring to Carson's speech the previous night, it said it 'establishes three things—that Unionist Ulster has resolved to accept the Home Rule [Government of Ireland] Bill, that it has no illusions about the prospects of Southern loyalists under a Sinn Fein Executive and that it recognises its powerlessness to help them.' The paper referred bitterly to sacrifices of recent years, when the devotion to duty of Southern unionists excelled that of any other British community. There was hardly a Southern Unionist household from which a husband or son did not volunteer ... No Southern Unionist made huge fortunes out of the war; many of them it reduced to poverty.

Despite some brave talk of 'the brains and energy of four hundred thousand Southern Unionists' being a powerful force in the fight to save the Union, it had no viable strategy to offer. Nor had its main champions in the House of Commons, Sir Maurice Dockrell and W. M. Jellett.

Dockrell was the more active of the two and had a more direct link with the Dublin loyalist electorate. Although he was a member of the Ulster Unionist group in the House of Commons, much of his time was spent raising issues of common concern to Irish nationalists. For instance, he worked with the only surviving Irish Party MP in the South, William Redmond, to secure extra coal supplies for Ireland. Imports from Britain had continued to fall since the war, as high-quality anthracite from Wales fed international markets and threatened Irish customers and industry alike with a fuel famine. On the day after Carson declared his abandonment of his Southern brethren the British government agreed to ensure an extra 40,000 tons of coal a month for Ireland, after the figures showed a falling off of 16,000 tons since January 1919 and of more than 46,000 tons since January 1918.[17]

Dockrell also worked with Joe Devlin and William Redmond to champion ex-servicemen who found trade unions resisting efforts by employers and the British government to find them jobs. In February 1920 there were still 27,000 able-bodied ex-servicemen unemployed in Ireland, and it was clear from exchanges in the House of Commons that most of the £250,000 spent on providing them with relief work had gone to Belfast and surrounding districts. On 5 March the Board of Works lamely reported in response to parliamentary questions from Dockrell that five recent clerical posts in Dublin had gone to ex-servicemen. By June the number of unemployed ex-servicemen had fallen to 19,127, but this may well have resulted from re-enlistments and emigration rather than successful lobbying by Dockrell and his colleagues. The inadequacy of records makes it impossible to say.[18]

Indeed the strong identification of the unionist MP for Rathmines with the cause of ex-servicemen can have done them few favours with trade unionists in the city, or workers generally, in the battle for scarce jobs. Craft unions were particularly hostile towards ex-servicemen applying for jobs on the strength of qualifications gained during military service: the British army was not a 'recognised house' for serving time as an apprentice. (See also chapter 2 above.)

One way in which many unionists could freely identify with and commemorate the sacrifices of the Great War was in their churches. As early as 1915 figures in military garb began appearing in stained-glass windows representing religious virtues, such as the 'Faithful Warrior' in St Ann's, Dawson Street, designed by Ethel Rhind. By 1920 such representations were increasingly popular, many of them designed by A. E. Child. In that year alone he produced another 'Faithful Warrior', who appeared in the left-hand panel of a triptych at St Philip's in Milltown, and figures representing 'Duty' and 'Sacrifice' at St John's in Clondalkin.[19] Nor were the motifs triumphalist (although the window at Grangegorman is an exception): there was rather an air of resignation and relief that the ordeal of the war was over.

There remained a readiness to assert traditional values and allegiances as well. One such occasion was the opening of the War Memorial Club at 24 Rathmines Road by the Lord Chief Justice, in conjunction with the 1st Dublin Company of the Boys' Brigade and the parish of St Matthias. The unit was thirty years old, and 37 of the 250 former members who joined the colours had died. Thirty parishioners of St Matthias had also died in the war. As Sir Maurice Dockrell said at the inaugural meeting on 25 March 1920, the club would not only be a recreational centre for the 'Old Corps', with a roll of honour on two shields to remind them of past sacrifices, but would provide a 'rallying place' for loyal Dubliners. The building had previously been the Rathmines School, which had educated 2,905 boys, including the current Provost of Trinity College, John Henry Bernard, former Archbishop of Dublin and a unionist of the most determined stamp. More than £1,000 had already been raised for renovating the building.[20]

By contrast, the Old Men's Asylum was £959 7s 6d in debt. This somewhat less prestigious Protestant institution was over a hundred years old and, like many such bodies, faced relentlessly mounting costs for basic provisions and fuel. An added problem was the government's withdrawal of the old-age pension from inmates, which may have saved the exchequer money but made it impossible for the institution to admit new applicants. All hopes turned on the ability of Sir Maurice Dockrell to persuade the government to relent. Meanwhile an appeal went out to 'the Protestant merchants of the city, and to the wider circle of the charitable Protestant public to assist them in wiping out this very serious debt.'[21]

Protestant charities continued to colonise other activities, inevitably leading them to assume a political hue. The Royal Dublin Fusiliers Prisoner of War Committee flourished long after the memorable welcome-home dinner at the Mansion House on the same day that the first Dáil Éireann assembled in

January 1919. Lady Arnott, now a dame of the British Empire, presided, and by early 1920 it had provided assistance to 251 of the 291 men on its books. Its door at 28 South Frederick Street remained open to supplicants.[22]

Inevitably, Southern unionists blamed the weakness of the government in tackling subversion for their woes. And yet on the very day that Carson cut the umbilical cord with the South at Duncairn Women's Unionist Association a special inquiry was beginning under a retired resident magistrate, Alan Bell, into the funds of Dáil Éireann and the infant Republic. Bell was believed to have had a hand in another blow against the enemy when, on 19 March, the Lord Mayor of Cork and Irish Volunteers commander in the city, Tomás Mac Curtáin, was shot dead in his home. The killing was widely attributed to the RIC. A week later, in a further escalation of the war, the first Black and Tans were deployed on the streets of Dublin to assist the RIC and DMP in maintaining law and order. Five days after that the IRA, as the Volunteers were now popularly known, issued a general order proclaiming all RIC members 'spies and traitors,' and it warned recruits that they joined the force 'at their peril.'[23]

Bell posed a different and ultimately more serious threat than the Black and Tans. A former RIC district inspector and resident magistrate, he had acquired great experience in combating subversion from as far back as the land wars of the 1880s. He was brought out of retirement in 1919 to join a select committee advising Lord French on how to take the war to the enemy. Bell also reported to Sir Basil Thomson, head of the Special Branch in London. Assassinating the assassins was one of the measures discussed by the committee, and its deliberations may well have played a part in Tomás Mac Curtáin's death. But Bell's main objective was finding and seizing enemy funds, especially the money raised from the public and from the Irish diaspora, not to mention foreign sympathisers, through the Dáil loan. More than a million dollars had been raised by the Friends of Irish Freedom in America during 1919. Bell was probably unaware that it had been made clear to the Dáil by hard-boiled Irish-American politicians that this money would be spent promoting the cause of Irish freedom in America, not in Ireland. With some reluctance, $10,000 was eventually sent to help the Irish to free themselves at home. Meanwhile Sinn Féin lent the Dáil £1,300 to cover the cost of its launch at the Mansion House in January 1919, and a few wealthy sympathisers, including members of Michael O'Rahilly's family, also lent substantial sums. But this was a small fraction of what was required to build a civil administration and fight a war.

There had been hopes that the Republic might be able to appropriate the £250,000 left over in various funds from the anti-conscription campaign of

1918, but most of the trustees on local committees were clergymen, and the Catholic hierarchy made a pre-emptive strike. Sinn Féin secured a mere £17,000. Attempts to divert taxes from the British exchequer were more successful in encouraging Irish citizens to stop paying tax to the old enemy rather than in persuading them to hand over hard-earned cash to the new Republic. The launch of republican bonds was therefore a financial necessity if the new state was to function; and, unlike taxation, it gave the prospect, however distant, of the investment one day yielding a return. The Minister for Finance, Michael Collins, undertook the task with the same gusto he applied to the murder campaign against the police. A newsreel was made by the Irish Film Company, at a cost of £600, showing patriotic citizens buying bonds from the minister, with the widows of 1916 martyrs featuring prominently among them. The Catholic Archbishop of Dublin, Dr Walsh, gave 100 guineas (£105) and wrote to Cardinal William Henry O'Connell, Archbishop of Boston, asking him to spread the word to the Irish in America.[24]

IRA units made sure that cinemas in Dublin and throughout the country showed the fund-raising films. On a more prosaic level, Collins told Sinn Féin cumainn and IRA units to 'get the painting squads who did such service in the general election at work.' A ferocious propaganda war broke out, with the police desperately trying to pull down posters, block out painted slogans and seize promotional literature as quickly as they appeared. The minister advertised in the provincial and separatist press, but the *Cork Examiner* was the only daily to defy the censor and publish the prospectus. It was banned for three days as a result. Up to forty-two publications suffered temporary or permanent closure for publishing the Dáil Éireann prospectus, according to Sylvain Briollay, a French journalist in Ireland.

A target of £250,000 was set when the campaign began in September 1919, and £19,160 was raised by the end of October. Collins set 17 July 1920 as the closing date for the purchase of bonds. By then 150,000 people throughout Ireland had contributed £371,849 and a further £78,000 had been raised in straightforward donations to the cause. Another £750,000 had been raised in America and almost £12,000 in Britain and France, and even a gold reserve was accumulated and secreted around Dublin by the master builder Batt O'Connor. This totalled more than £25,000 by the time of the Truce in 1921.

A large factor in the success of the loan was the fact that the country's farmers were convinced it was not alone patriotic to buy bonds but a sound investment. The average amount raised from each constituency was £3,629, but none of the eleven constituencies in Dublin city and county came near this figure. The relatively low total from Dublin reflected the poverty of many supporters of the Republic in the capital, as well as the hostility of unionists, who made up almost a fifth of the population. The massive military and police presence was a further hindrance. Funds were forwarded to nominees of Collins, often IRA officers and Sinn Féin councillors, such as Jim Lawless in East Wall. The work of the collectors was both difficult and dangerous. Raids on Sinn Féin premises and suspected business fronts, such as the New Ireland Assurance Society, were frequent.[25]

The counter-attack by Dublin Castle culminated in raids on a thousand premises in January 1920, resulting in eighty-six arrests, including six members of the Dáil and several members of local authorities. In March £11,116 in cash was seized from the Sinn Féin Bank and another £7,204 in deposits. Most ominously, senior officials in all the banks received summonses to attend Bell's inquiry, which opened on 8 March. They were told to bring records of all deposits with them. The *Freeman's Journal* and its sister-publication, the *Evening Telegraph*, castigated the government and Bell for conducting a 'Star Chamber'. The *Freeman* called on those summoned to stand firm and not compromise the 'privacy and confidence which are essential to the proper relations between banker and clients.' But, as proceedings were held *in camera*, with no-one present except Bell and an official shorthand-writer, there was no way of knowing for certain if the bankers were standing firm.

Collins could not afford to take the chance. The *Freeman's Journal* was good enough to publish a photograph of Bell as a somewhat younger man, and Collins managed to obtain a more recent picture from Michael Knightly, a 1916 veteran now working as a journalist with the *Irish Independent*. This enabled members of the Squad to track their prey from Dublin Castle to his home at 93 Belgrave Square, Monkstown. Aware of the potential threat, the DMP posted a guard on Bell's house. He was escorted to his tram each morning and was met by another police escort when he alighted in Grafton Street for his walk to his office in Dublin Castle, or to the hearings he was conducting at the Bridewell. Incredibly, he had no police protection on the tram.

It was an indication of how seriously Collins took the threat that the most experienced and senior members of the Squad were assigned the task of Bell's elimination. Firstly, though, they had to dispose of a new British spy in the city. Fergus Bryan Molloy, a soldier in the Service Corps, had managed to meet Collins on the promise of being able to supply weapons to the IRA. Unfortunately for Molloy, Collins had added a new source to his intelligence network: Lily Mernin, a member of the Women's Army Auxiliary Corps who, like Ned Broy in the DMP, had the lowly but vital task of typing intelligence reports, in her case for the intelligence section of the Dublin Garrison District

Adjutant's office. She was able to identify Molloy as an *agent provocateur*, and he was shot dead in Wicklow Street on 24 March. On 26 March it was Bell's turn.

The plan was simplicity itself. Two members of the Squad, Paddy Daly and Tom Keogh, waited discreetly with their bicycles near Bell's home in Belgrave Square to make sure he caught his regular 9:30 tram from Dalkey into the city centre. They then followed on their bicycles—with some difficulty, as the tram travelled at speed. As it approached the junction at Aylesbury Road they were able to signal to Mick McDonnell, Liam Tobin, Vinnie Byrne, Jim Slattery and Joe Dolan, waiting at the stop, that Bell was on board. The five men boarded the vehicle. Byrne and Slattery went upstairs to make sure there would be no interference from that quarter while the rest positioned themselves around their target. McDonnell sat in the seat behind Bell, who was reading a newspaper, tapped him on the shoulder and asked, 'Are you Mr Bell?' On Bell assuring him that he was, the group stopped the tram and bundled him towards the exit. Eye-witnesses on the tram said Bell looked 'aghast' but was 'unable to do or say anything. He looked in blank astonishment at his assailants.' One of the latter said, 'Come on, Mr Bell, your time has come,' but he failed to move, and after a second prompting of 'Ah, come on,' he was dragged off the vehicle. Passengers and passers-by heard at least three shots as he fell near the railings of the RDS grounds at the corner of Merrion Road and Simmonscourt Road. The body was taken to the City of Dublin Hospital in Baggot Street. He had bullet wounds to the wrist and groin, but it was a bullet behind the ear that killed him. The dead man had a revolver in his pocket.

Although it had done most to identify Bell in the public mind as a threat to both Dáil Éireann and the Irish banking industry, the *Freeman's Journal* published the briefest account of his killing. In its editorial next day it hypocritically commented that 'it behoves all who have influence with the people, and especially with our young men, to counsel restraint.' It placed the primary blame for the situation on Lord French and his coterie, who 'have made up their minds that the short cut to peace is through an exploded insurrection.' Predictably, the *Irish Times* raged against 'Another Shocking Crime in Dublin', but the *Irish Independent*'s headline was a matter-of-fact 'Mr. A. Bell, R.M., Shot Dead in Dublin,' with a heading promising readers a 'Thrilling Story of Tragedy'. In fact the *Times* gave its readers a much more comprehensive account of events, but the *Irish Independent*'s editorial, like that of the *Freeman*, showed that Catholic middle-class opinion was without any sympathy for the powers that be. It emphasised the other violent deaths throughout the country over the previous week, especially that of the Lord Mayor of Cork, Tomás Mac Curtáin.

Such things did not happen in countries 'where the people are responsible for the management of their own affairs.' The 'Irish Executive and the British Cabinet who have subjected the nation to "an iron rule of oppression as cruel and unjust as it is ill-advised and out of date" must bear full responsibility for the consequences.'

Unfettered by the sensitivities of its rival, the *Independent* sent a reporter to interview the widow at Monkstown, but she was too distressed to comment and was being comforted by the wife of Sir John Taylor, the Under-Secretary for Ireland, and one of Bell's colleagues on the select committee advising Lord French on how to implement the 'iron rule of oppression.' In general, the country's largest-selling newspaper was more in sympathy with the nascent Republic than with Dublin Castle, even when the Republic's agents resorted to serious acts of violence.[26]

A colleague of Bell's, John Gray, a resident magistrate in Belfast, fulminated next day that 'the men on the tramcar must either have been cowards or sympathisers with the criminals.'[27] The situation certainly contrasted with that when Fergus Molloy had been killed two days earlier in Wicklow Street. A domestic servant, Annie Hughes, had tried to get between the injured man and his killers, and some passers-by in Grafton Street gave chase to members of the Squad. Unused to such a reaction, they concluded subsequently that people might have thought they were undercover government agents after all the publicity attracted by the death of Tomás Mac Curtáin.

Ironically, some of the passive passengers on the Dalkey tram were colleagues of Bell, as the police discovered when they began interviewing them. One was a Mr Terney Jr, who worked in the Chancery Office at the Four Courts; another was F. W. Francis, a civil servant in the Accountant-General's Office at the Four Courts. Francis lived in Dalkey and regularly saw Bell catch the inbound tram. Both were upstairs on the tram that morning. Terney refused to give a statement and, when pressed, referred them to Francis. Francis told them he went up to the top deck of the tram to have a smoke. He told the DMP he was

> smoking a cigarette and reading a newspaper. At Sandymount Avenue I heard a shot. I was very upset, as I am not strong since my only son was killed in the late war. I looked down on the road and saw a man lying dead. I know nothing further.

He declined to sign even this innocuous statement. He also failed to mention that two members of the Squad, Vinnie Byrne and Jim Slattery, went upstairs to cover the passengers and ensure that no-one interfered, possibly because he knew he would then be asked to identify them. The DMP investigating detectives were convinced that the men had seen more, and they felt strongly enough to send a memo to the Chief Secretary's Office with transcripts of the interviews with the two men.

> The attached statements show what little help poor Mr. Bell received from parties whose position … would lead one to expect something more. It shows how little assistance they intend giving (even confidentially) in the interests of society to track down these desperate assassins.

Field-Marshal French was exercised enough to consult the Lord Chancellor on the 'very extraordinary' behaviour of these men, which he believed was 'incompatible with their continued employment as public officials.' The Lord Chancellor, however, the former unionist MP Sir James Campbell, refused to interfere. As he saw it, the men were on the top deck of the tram and did not witness the shooting. If he discussed it with them it could be interpreted as

> putting official pressure on them to supply information with the knowledge that each had distinctly stated he had no information to give. If I took such action they would, I am certain, bring the matter before the Whalley [sic] Council of the Four Courts staff, which has recently been constituted with the result of raising a public agitation in which my action would, unfortunately be misrepresented.

In a DMP memo the Chief Commissioner, Lieutenant-Colonel Johnstone, reported that Bell had been offered police protection, 'two good constables' between his home in Monkstown and Dublin Castle, as well as on his forays around the city. He had refused the offer, on the grounds that the escort would only attract attention. He also declined the offer of motor transport, on the grounds that the number of the vehicle would become known. He would only allow the police guard outside his house and a phone call to be made to notify the DMP when he left, so that an escort could meet him at the stop beside the Thomas Cook office in College Green.[28] It appeared that the Lord Chancellor, along with Messrs Terney and Francis, had a better grasp of the new realities than either the Field-Marshal or Alan Bell.

Bell's investigation ended abruptly with his death. The failure of the government's policy of repression was starkly illustrated by the fact that fifty houses had been raided and forty arrests made in the city only hours before he was shot. The houses raided included the homes of some leading military activists, such as Richard Mulcahy, Chief of Staff of the IRA, Frank Henderson, who had taken over the 2nd Battalion after Dick McKee became commander of the Dublin Brigade, and Liam Tobin, one of Bell's assassins. Naturally, none of them was at home. Other raids seemed provocatively futile, such as the arrest of two Sinn Féin MPs. One was the Dublin publican Phil Shanahan; the other was Laurence Ginnell, who represented Westmeath. Ginnell was arrested at the home of Dr Kathleen Lynn, where he was recuperating from a bout of ill-health brought on by imprisonment the previous autumn. Lynn expressed grave concern at the consequences for Ginnell, a 66-year-old veteran of the home-rule movement and land war, if he had to endure another term of imprisonment.

There was also a comical aspect to the raids. Large numbers of young men waiting on the North Wall for passage to America were arrested, on the grounds that they might be fugitive IRA men fleeing undetected crimes. At Liam Tobin's house in Munster Street, Phibsborough, a brother was dragged away as a result of mistaken identity, the second time this had happened. A similar incident almost occurred at the Henderson household in Fairview until a DMP constable, who knew the wanted man, persuaded the army officer in charge of the raid to release the prisoner. The family, however, were complimentary about the conduct of the military during their search. This contrasted with a letter Henderson had written to the former General Officer Commanding in Ireland, Lieutenant-General Shaw, complaining of a similar raid the previous year and the attitude of the soldiers to his parents. It seems to have had the desired effect, and on this occasion Henderson's family were treated politely and everything carefully put back where it was found.

Dublin was 'in the grip of a murder association,' Mr Justice Moore had told the grand jury when it assembled in February 1920. It was a common perception among an embattled establishment. In her memoir published anonymously in 1921, Caroline Woodcock, an army officer's wife, wrote miserably of her sense of isolation as she sat in a car at a military road block waiting to be waved through.

> It was a strange scene, and an unpleasant one. Crowds of scowling, sullen looking men and women, and just a handful of very youthful soldiers and one lorry ... I felt distinctly anxious. There was always a chance of a shot in the back from the crowd too. Doubtless, a good many of them carried revolvers.[29]

In reality, very few Volunteers had weapons of any sort. The organisation never recovered from the massive loss of weapons in the 1916 Rising, and this was particularly true in cities and large towns, including Dublin. The ability of the IRA to conjure up this sense of omniscient power was one of its most important achievements in the War of Independence; but it took its toll on the mental health of the city's inhabitants.

The very lack of resources forced many leading figures in the Dáil government and the IRA to follow the example of Michael Collins and hide in plain sight. Bicycles and trams were the main forms of transport. Máire Comerford, a member of Cumann na mBan whose work for the White Cross would allow her to travel extensively on behalf of the Republican government and the IRA,[30] could tell by the bicycles parked outside a venue who she would find inside. So could many members of the DMP. On one occasion Éamon de Valera was stopped for not having a light on his bicycle and told by a sympathetic constable that it was too dangerous for him to be out after dark. Nor did someone need to be part of the inner circle to spot key figures in the rebel government. The French journalist Sylvain Briollay wrote that 'it was a very common thing to recognise an Irish "Minister" in a cheerfully juvenile figure which flits past on a muddy bicycle, in a faded waterproof and a little cleft hat dripping under the pelting rain.'[31] This was quite apart from the promotional film for the Dáil loan that featured the Minister for Finance, Michael Collins, in the leading role.

Bicycles, being ubiquitous, were a relatively safe way to travel, although they could be hazardous, as Richard Mulcahy discovered. On one occasion his wheel caught in a tram track, the bicycle fork broke, and he was thrown off. Passers-by picked him up and one pointed out his dentures, which had landed a few yards away. Afterwards he returned to the safe house he had just left to recover some essential documents. He had to escape over the rooftops when a raiding party arrived. The officer in charge, realising they had uncovered an important rebel refuge, ordered an NCO to fetch assistance from Portobello Barracks. The NCO jumped on Mulcahy's bicycle but travelled only a short distance before it collapsed. He was knocked unconscious by the fall, and the reinforcements never arrived.[32]

Over the night of 3/4 April 1920 the Irish Volunteers celebrated the fourth anniversary of the 1916 Rising by burning down some 150 small RIC barracks and police posts, most of them abandoned for some time as indefensible. Seventeen income tax offices were also destroyed, along with all the files within. While there was little scope for incendiarism against abandoned police posts in Dublin, seven tax offices in the city were destroyed. Most were in commercial premises, but two were in private residences, where the documents were burnt in fireplaces.[33] Charlie Dalton's group was tasked with burning the office opposite the Abbey Theatre. The raiders had to wait for the theatre to open and absorb the queue of theatre-goers before they could break in without attracting attention.

> We soon located the office we wanted and proceeded to set the papers on fire. But the progress of the fire was so slow ... Jimmy Conroy went round to a nearby shop and bought a bottle of paraffin oil. After that we had no difficulty and the office was well on fire before we left.

Dalton was keen to get the blaze well under way, as the office was near the Central Fire Station in Tara Street. This was little consolation to Conroy, who found he had to walk home after spending his tram fare on the kerosene. The *Irish Times* rightly saw the night of destruction as 'enormously injurious' to British authority. The rebels had 'forced the Executive ... to surrender the law-abiding inhabitants to the de facto supremacy of revolution,' which represented 'startling progress for the Republican Party's guerrilla campaign during the last three months.' The paper denounced the burning of the tax offices as 'a new and clever act of war' that further undermined the state and drew attention to the lack of a similar drive and initiative by the forces of law and order.[34]

The same forces faced another challenge the next day, 5 April, when more than sixty men who were known or suspected Irish Volunteer officers in Mountjoy Prison began a hunger strike to achieve their release or be given the status of prisoners of war. The demand could be traced back to the death of the 1916 leader Thomas Ashe during a hunger strike in the same prison in 1917. It was the largest scale on which this form of struggle had ever been attempted. At the time no-one knew how long a hunger-striker could hold out, or what the physical and psychological effects on participants would be. Ashe had died as a result of forcible feeding, so his example provided no yardstick. His death had turned him into a secular saint for the republican movement, and thousands of Dubliners, particularly women, had gathered outside the prison each day to show their solidarity with the men and to recite what must have seemed to the young British soldiers on duty endless decades of the Rosary.

The situation soon resembled a siege. The barbed-wire entanglements and tanks deployed in support of the helmeted Tommies with fixed bayonets guarding the approaches to Mountjoy provided Sinn Féin propagandists with an opportunity they used to the full.

On Monday 12 April a general strike began in Dublin in support of the hunger-strikers. It quickly spread throughout the country, apart from the north-east. By the following day most of Ireland had come to a standstill, apart from a very limited railway service on the Great Northern line. Railway services elsewhere had stopped, postal deliveries ceased, and in Dublin the labour exchange in Lord Edward Street closed when mass pickets arrived at 1 p.m. on 13 April, forcing the staff to leave. 'All through the day the churches of Dublin were crowded and many trade union sections marched to the churches en masse to pray for the prisoners,' the *Irish Independent* reported. When the Drapers' Assistants' Association heard that some shops in Grafton Street had remained open, a large flying picket was organised, only to find that the reports were false. However, a number of smaller shops in Parnell Street did open, only to be forced to close again by the angry public reaction.

By Wednesday even the civilian clerks in the Army Pay Office came out rather than face the pickets. All sailings from Dublin had stopped, including live cattle exports, and such essential items as bread and milk were only available directly from the suppliers, or from vans and shops for an agreed period in the afternoons. Fishing-boats caught up in the dispute were forced to sell their catches for very little on the North Wall.[35]

On the same day the army estimated that the crowds outside Mountjoy had swollen to twenty thousand. Regular contact between the outside world and the prison enclave, which included the warders' homes and the DMP police station, was now possible only by telephone. The subsequent report in the army's *Dublin District Historical Record* spoke of the

> futility of committing troops to hold back such a crowd … Rapidly constructed obstacles were soon trodden down by the leading ranks … being pressed from behind; even tanks were no obstacle. The troops thus found themselves in the unenviable position of either being overwhelmed or having to open fire on a somewhat passive, but advancing crowd of men and women.

Tribute was paid to the 'intrepid work' of the Royal Air Force in flying just above the eaves of the houses, despite 50 m.p.h. winds, to help drive back the protesters. 'This clearly demonstrated that aeroplanes could be used for clearing streets by dropping warning notices and, if necessary, using Lewis gunfire,' the report added ominously.[36]

Meanwhile large demonstrations of Irish Volunteers in military formation took place in streets leading to the prison, while thousands of striking railway workers marched in procession through the city centre to be addressed by the general secretary of the National Union of Railwaymen, J. H. Thomas MP, outside union offices in Middle Abbey Street. Thomas, who had earned the opprobrium of the left for his support of the British war effort, could nevertheless tell his Irish members that 'they had given the greatest demonstration of manhood and true comradeship that it was possible to give.' He skilfully dodged the question of why the prisoners were in Mountjoy by pointing out that there was 'no justification for condemning people without a trial. The men who were at this moment suffering and risking all were doing so because they were guided by their conscience.' But he urged members to continue their protest 'in a dignified and manly way' and not provide any excuse for the authorities to move against them.

The authorities offered to transfer prisoners to Wormwood Scrubs in London with political status, and then offered to grant them political status in Mountjoy. But the leader of the hunger-strikers, Peadar Clancy, Dick McKee's second in command of the Dublin Brigade, rejected the offer outright. 'I know the risk I'm taking,' he told the other hunger-strike leaders, 'but there are men here who must get out before they are recognised.' He conceded that 'the Castle isn't done by a long chalk, but they're done for the moment. The general strike has them beat.'[37] Unlike the Castle, he was thinking several moves ahead.

The new General Officer Commanding in Ireland, Sir Nevil Macready, arrived to take up his duties in the middle of this maelstrom. He had been chosen not so much for his distinguished war record as for his experience of policing, including his success in handling a post-war mutiny in the London Metropolitan Police. He was seen as the ideal candidate for managing a situation where the British government was seeking to camouflage a policy of increased state repression by handing the worst aspects of the job over to the new paramilitary Auxiliaries and Black and Tans. He would subsequently blame the Assistant Under-Secretary, Sir John Taylor, for much of the mess he found, and he discovered a badly needed if distasteful temporary ally in the Lord Mayor, Laurence O'Neill, who had been calling on the authorities to release the men.

O'Neill was now summoned by Field-Marshal French to the Viceregal Lodge. The Lord Mayor was in Mountjoy visiting prisoners at the time, and speculation grew among the crowd as he left the prison at 1:30 p.m. to meet French and Macready. The latter would later write in dismissive tones about his first encounter with O'Neill, but his observations said more about his own prejudices and preconceptions where Ireland was concerned than they did about the Lord Mayor. At the interview Macready found that O'Neill was full of protestations that peace would result from the liberation of the hunger strikers, painting their condition with that colour that only a master of Irish blarney can achieve, accompanied by the trickle of an occasional tear down his cheeks.

According to Macready, O'Neill promised to obtain the prisoners' parole to be of good behaviour if released. 'Several telephonic conversations took place with Downing Street, but there was not much help from that quarter,' Macready wrote, 'the decision being left to the Lord Lieutenant.'

O'Neill returned to Mountjoy at 3 p.m. with the parole proposal, only to be told by Clancy that they were remaining adamant that every prisoner must be released. To sign a parole form would be to concede the principle that the armed struggle was a criminal conspiracy rather than a legitimate war for independence. Despite Macready's dismissive account, O'Neill, who certainly had the traditional quota of sentimentality expected of Dublin's Lord Mayors, may well have been going through the motions of exhausting the negotiating options. He certainly had no illusions about what the British thought of him. Indeed the only senior British official with whom the Lord Mayor and his staff struck up a strong rapport was Sir James McMahon, Under-Secretary for Ireland, and his private secretary, Walter Doolin.

At this point O'Neill proposed that the authorities accept a verbal pledge. Macready, who was convinced that the authorities in London would release all the prisoners anyway if one of them died, felt there was little option but to accept, subject to the proviso that it would apply only to men being held under the Defence of the Realm Act and not those serving time for specific offences. The situation soon turned to farce when a phone call was received from the prison at 6 p.m. to say that the first prisoner released, Patrick Sheils from Derry, had been serving a prison sentence.

French and Macready effectually capitulated by delegating the decision about who should be released to the doctors charged with examining the hunger-strikers. All sixty-six hunger-strikers were released that evening and the rest of the prisoners the next day. One of the former, Frank Gallagher, who worked on Dáil Éireann's *Irish Bulletin* and could therefore be considered one of the revolution's elite, recalled the crowds coming in through the gates to 'the very steps of the gaol itself,' and then

> loving hands came up to receive me and there is a memory of Anna Fitzsimons smoothing for my head a very white pillow; of Frank Kelly, who had helped to bring Dev out of Lincoln [Prison], sitting beside the driver of

the taxi; and of my brother Dick, in his full clericals at my side, and a sense of fantasy over it all.

Morale in the enemy camp hit rock-bottom. The *Irish Times* contrasted the absolute refusal to concede the prisoners' demands by the leader of the Conservative Party, Andrew Bonar Law, in the House of Commons twenty-four hours earlier with the mass release of prisoners on Wednesday. 'It will be claimed as a great triumph by Sinn Fein and the Irish Labour Party.' The paper predicted it would weaken the resolve of the British government on both sides of the Irish Sea. It certainly convinced Macready that the Chief Secretary, Macpherson, who had played no meaningful role in the proceedings, would have to go. The official military history of the Dublin garrison concurred: it recorded the hunger strike as an important psychological victory for the enemy that resulted in the 'Military and Police Secret Services personnel' being 'virtually driven off the streets,' as many of the released prisoners could 'identify our agents.' The IRA's 'morale and truculence began to increase accordingly.'[38]

That assessment was confirmed by a sinister coda to the strike. On the day the hunger-strikers were released, Henry Kells, an ambitious DMP constable operating as a 'buckshee detective' in the hope of promotion, was shot dead by Paddy Daly, on the specific orders of Michael Collins. He was hit three times, and although the attack happened at 9:45 a.m. at the busy junction of Camden Street and Pleasants Street, there were no witnesses. A few days earlier Kells, also on this occasion wearing plain clothes, had visited Mountjoy to identify prisoners suspected of criminal offences. Peadar Clancy recognised him and called out his name from across the prison yard. Kells, a married man with no children, had twenty-two years' service in the DMP.[39]

Six days later Detective-Constable Laurence Dalton, a recent recruit to G Division, aged twenty-six, was shot dead on his way to the Broadstone terminus of the Midland and Great Western Railway to watch for suspected rebels travelling on the trains. He was the chief prosecution witness in a case to be brought against J. J. Walsh, a 1916 veteran and Sinn Féin MP for Cork. He had arrested Walsh in a raid shortly before and refused to withdraw his statement against him.[40]

Chapter 5 ∼

'NOT THE EMPIRE BUT THE IRISH REPUBLIC'

On 3 May 1920, Dublin Corporation declared its allegiance to Dáil Éireann. The declaration may well have been prompted by Kevin O'Higgins, W. T. Cosgrave's very able deputy in the Republic's Department of Local Government.

In June, local elections were due throughout Ireland, and O'Higgins planned to request newly elected councils to declare their allegiance to the Dáil. A Dublin declaration would provide a boost for such an initiative. The motion to recognise the Dáil came from a relatively junior Sinn Féin councillor, Michael Dowling, who represented the Inns Quay and Rotunda wards. It was seconded by another junior member, Thomas Cassidy, representing South Dock. Many senior Sinn Féin members of the corporation were either in prison or on the run. Cosgrave, the Dáil's Minister for Local Government, was one of those regularly arrested. He had been released on parole in April because of ill-health and on condition that he refrain from political activity.[1]

The absence of so many councillors seriously disrupted the corporation's work. Cosgrave was chairman of the powerful Estates and Finance Committee, which determined budgetary matters. In March, Laurence O'Neill, once more formally installed as Lord Mayor because of Tom Kelly's continuing ill-health, wrote to Lloyd George complaining of the increasing difficulty in conducting business because so many councillors had been arrested. He received short shrift. Lloyd George replied: 'Ireland today is menaced by a formidable organisation which seeks to promote its ends by terrorising public officials and the Irish people.' The authorities certainly do not wish to arrest the guiltless. On the other hand their first and imperative duty is to leave no stone unturned to enable them to lay their hands on those who are terrorising society, and they may at times have no option ... but to dislocate in some degree the normal life of the community.

The only sop Lloyd George offered was to 'make as easy as possible the task of those who are endeavouring to carry on the administration of the country on reasonable lines.'[2] Dowling's resolution confirmed Lloyd George's worst suspicions. It declared:

> That this Council of the elected representatives of the City of Dublin hereby acknowledges the authority of Dáil Éireann as the duly elected Government of the Irish people, and undertakes to give effect to all decrees duly promulgated by the said Dáil Éireann so far as same affects the Council.

Predictably, the leader of the Municipal Reform Association, Dr McWalter, objected, on the grounds that the proposed change of allegiance was illegal. He warned Sinn Féin councillors that he would not allow his office as High Sheriff to be used to distrain (i.e. seize) the goods of ratepayers who refused to contribute to the city's upkeep.[3]

The risk that some ratepayers might boycott the corporation was a serious if indeterminate one. Already the city's largest property-owner, His Majesty's Government, was refusing to pay rates. There was also a strong possibility that the Local Government Board would cease subsidising the rebel municipality. Its subvention accounted for a fifth of all funds. On the other hand, Dublin Corporation might not see this money anyway, because in October 1919 legislation had been introduced making Irish local authorities liable for all malicious damage claims in their jurisdiction. It came into force in 1920, and the Local Government Board was empowered to pay successful claimants from central exchequer subventions. The Dáil had already instructed local authorities not to increase rates to meet such claims, and most, including Dublin, followed its advice. A contest of wills was under way between rival regimes. Individual councils and councillors had to decide to which they owed allegiance.

O'Neill readily admitted to McWalter that the Law Agent had advised him that Dowling's motion was out of order, and ordinarily he would not have allowed it.

> But as the country quite recently elected as its representatives to Parliament—I am not going to say what parliament—the vast majority of

the Sinn Féin party, and as the citizens of Dublin more recently still have elected to represent them in the Corporation a majority of the Sinn Féin party in the city, the position I take up is that the city and the country must be prepared to put up with the actions of their representatives, and consequently I am not going to rule the motion out of order.

Dowling made no attempt to answer McWalter's objections when he proposed his motion, and Thomas Cassidy said he was seconding it

as one who answered the call of an Irish Republic in 1916, and who recognises that the people of Ireland had pledged themselves to Government of the Dáil in 1918, and that the people of Dublin, at a later date, sent forward as their representatives to this council a Republican majority. It is up to us to say that we took every opportunity of forwarding their views and showing that we kept our pledges of 1916 and later years, and that we reaffirm them at the meeting today.

McWalter pointed out that £1.1 million in city rates could be at stake. He, for one, would make no attempt to collect them 'if such rates are to be collected with the authority of the Dáil Éireann.' Another MRA member, John Russell Stritch, said that any councillor who was a justice of the peace, like himself, had an obligation to uphold the law. But looking around the chamber he could not refrain from commenting that 'whenever anything of a disloyal nature came on' his fellow-justices 'were not to be seen—generally they did a bunk.' (Laughter.) At the vote there were thirty-five councillors in favour of the declaration of allegiance to Dáil Éireann, including all Sinn Féin members present and those from both wings of the Labour group. Only the five MRA councillors present voted against. Nationalist and independent members abstained.

The corporation was soon brought down to earth by the arrival of a deputation representing a broad alliance of groups calling for the establishment of a municipal coal store to help tenement families. They included the Society of St Vincent de Paul, the Ladies' Association of Charity, the Indigent Room Keepers' Society, the Infant Aid Society and the Irish Transport and General Workers' Union. It was led by the former Parnellite MP William Field, who said that a coal famine was upon them and 'even ... the new poor could not get coal.' Frank Sweeney of the Society of St Vincent de Paul said the society had always been able to care for children but, owing to high prices, the springs of charity are frozen up and one of the most appalling things we have to meet is the growing number of ill-clad and bootless children who are sitting before empty grates or fanning the embers of a sod of turf.

Séamus Hughes of the ITGWU said there was no shortage of coal in England but that it was being diverted 'for statesmanlike reasons to other places,' where it commanded a better price.

It is for the municipality to put up the demand from the people of Dublin that they should get a fair share of the means of livelihood. On behalf of the self-reliant poor represented by the Transport Workers' Union I endorse the demand for a municipal coal depot.

In a written submission, the Women's Civic Union drew attention to the particular problems of tenement-dwellers, who, even when they could afford coal, had nowhere to store it. In Britain the Coal Controller facilitated schemes by local authorities for helping poor families. There need be no extra cost to the ratepayer if coal merchants agreed to hold stocks on behalf of the corporation and absorbed the expense of storage within their profit margins.

The Lord Mayor latched on to Hughes's interpretation of the situation and likewise attacked the British coal industry and Dublin Castle for the shortages. So long as it suited both to 'keep the camp fires ... burning' in France, Italy and even Germany, 'the poor of Dublin would suffer and the babes would die.' While he was all in favour of setting aside the law when he could, the city lacked the resources to establish a coal depot. Instead they should set up a public fund, and he would personally contribute the first £100. Unfortunately there was no statutory basis on which the corporation could establish a municipal coal yard, as the Law Agent, Ignatius Rice, confirmed subsequently.[4]

Another pressing problem was the demand by unions representing all corporation employees for a pay increase of 10s a week, with provision for an extra 3s if an anticipated pay rise for building workers was conceded on 1 May— as indeed it was. This provoked a letter from the absent Alderman Cosgrave (which technically put him in breach of the terms of his parole), who warned that the pay increases could not be conceded without violating a commitment he had given to two directors of the Bank of Ireland, the Deputy Governor, H. S. Guinness, and Andrew Jameson, both staunch unionists, that the corporation would live within its budget for the year. They had advanced credit after Cosgrave had been rebuffed by the Munster and Leinster Bank, 'which was regarded as the most National of all these [financial] institutions.'⁵ Cosgrave told his colleagues they must either rescind the pay increase or appoint someone else to represent them in negotiations with the Bank of Ireland.

The corporation did neither. The Lord Mayor, seconded by Sir Andrew Beattie of the MRA, proposed that the matter be put to a committee of the whole house. Alderman Tom Lawlor, whose nomination as a candidate in the local elections had sparked the split in the Labour group, demanded to know when the workers would be paid; they had been waiting since July 1919 for the increase. 'Are you going to compel us to take such action as will compel you to pay?' he asked. O'Neill said that manual workers had been paid the increase from the previous week and promised that arrears due to them would be paid within three weeks. A combination of Sinn Féin and MRA councillors ensured that a final decision on the pay rise was deferred. All fifteen Labour councillors present opposed the delay. It was the first division on class lines.

There was consensus, on the other hand, over a resolution proposed by Councillor Michael Staines MP (Sinn Féin), 'hailing with joy the approaching canonisation of Joan of Arc, who was burnt to death for the crime of endeavouring to free her country.' The members called for Sunday 16 May, the day of her canonisation, to be declared a national holiday in memory of her fight against English tyranny. The Catholic Archbishop of Dublin, Dr Walsh, was urged to contact the Cardinal Archbishop of Paris to convey their good wishes to their French co-religionists, while George Gavan Duffy, Ireland's representative in France, was asked to give their felicitations to Rouen, where Joan was burnt, to Rheims, where she witnessed the coronation of Charles VII, and to Orléans, which she had saved from the English. Not to be outdone, Councillor Thomas Loughlin, also of Sinn Féin, proposed that a deputation travel to Rome to attend the celebrations on 23 May for the beatification of an Irish victim of English tyranny, Oliver Plunkett. It was agreed that the Lord Mayor, Alderman Cosgrave, Councillors John Forrestal and Mrs McGarry should attend. All except for the Lord Mayor were members of Sinn Féin.⁶

The following month the corporation would condemn the New York courts for their persecution of one of Dublin's living secular saints, Jim Larkin. He had been found guilty of advocating criminal anarchy and was given an indeterminate sentence of five to ten years' imprisonment. It was his old disciple P. T. Daly who moved the motion, which was passed by 28 votes to 11, with the MRA and remnants of the old Irish Party establishment voting against it and probably only sorry that Larkin had always been let off more lightly by the Irish courts.[7] The corporation asked Éamon de Valera to use his good offices in the United States to lobby for Larkin's release. However, it would be 1923 before he was released and returned to a very different Dublin.

The wage claims by corporation employees were part of a wider movement within the city that recorded a number of successes on the industrial front. During the same week that the 10s claim went in to City Hall the Dublin United Tramways Company increased wages for adult male workers by 8s a week and for boys by 4s a week. It was agreed to pay a Sunday premium as well. This brought the weekly pay of drivers to £3 18s 5d and of conductors to £3 16s 11d. Another major employer in the city, the Alliance and Dublin Consumers' Gas Company, would shortly concede pay increases of 15s a week to shift workers, 10s 8d to tradesmen and 10s to general labourers.[8] As we have seen, building workers had already secured substantial increases, so that a builder's labourer was now receiving £3 4s 7½d a week, compared with £2 13s for a corporation labourer, rising to £2 18s after ten years' service.[9] What was unusual about the gas workers' claim was that for the first time it was made on behalf of all the unions representing manual workers as well as the recently formed Irish Clerical Workers' Union, which represented junior white-collar employees. Despite Cosgrave's protestations, the corporation agreed to an arbitration process that resulted in increases of up to 13s a week for adult male workers and a reduction in the working week from 47 to 44 hours. Boys under eighteen and women were paid an extra 7s 6d a week.[10] As the arbitration process was under the auspices of Dáil Éireann, Cosgrave could hardly object.

The success of the ITGWU, the Irish Municipal Employees' Trade Union, the Building Labourers' Union and the Irish Clerical Workers' Union prompted the Municipal Officers (Ireland) Trade Union, representing middle-ranking white-collar staff, to renew its claim on behalf of members. This too had gone to arbitration and had hung fire since the previous November. Alderman Joe MacDonagh MP (Sinn Féin), recently released from prison, successfully proposed the suspension of standing orders to hear a deputation from the union, led by its general secretary, Éamonn Price. A comment by Price that the union had treated the corporation 'with kid gloves' did not go down well. When the delegation withdrew, MRA members were quick to question the element of the arbitrator's award that sought to link municipal officials' pay with that of the civil service. Dr McWalter objected 'to the attitude of some of the delegation from our employees who waited on us this morning … I should not have to put up with insolence in my public capacity which I have not to put up with in my personal affairs.' While the award was accepted by the councillors, the MRA won the argument on refusing to pay the element linking municipal employees' rates with civil servants' rates. This would have meant conceding the civil service 'war bonus,' and allowing it to be consolidated into basic pay.

The city's officials now decided it was time to demonstrate more of the 'insolence' that McWalter found so objectionable by demanding the war bonus, which, the MOITU pointed out, had been provided for in the city estimates for manual workers. Strike notice was served, and action by the 450 members involved began on 22 June. Apart from the Town Clerk, the new Chief Medical Officer, Dr Russell, and the three senior officers of the fire service, who were excused to provide emergency cover, the strike was remarkably comprehensive. It incurred the wrath of Alderman William O'Brien, recently released from prison, as well as the MRA. O'Brien saw the members of the MOITU as well-heeled middle-class bureaucrats, many of whom had actively worked to break the ITGWU in the 1913 Lockout. Nevertheless, his attitude jarred with some trade unionists, and William Richardson, a Labour renegade from the lockout days, asked if the officials were 'to be victimised because they refuse to recognise the OBU ['one big union'—the ITGWU] as the ultimate goal, and that only under "permit" from … Liberty Hall are we to be permitted to draw our breath?'

The dispute certainly demonstrated that to be effective a dispute did not need the imprimatur of Liberty Hall. By the end of the month the corporation had been forced to reach a settlement. Nor did all the officials fit O'Brien's categorisation. One of the leading negotiators was Harry Nicholls, who had supported the strikers in 1913 and participated as a Volunteer in the Howth and Rathcoole gun-running operations. In 1916 he had fought alongside the Irish Citizen Army contingent in St Stephen's Green after failing to reach his Volunteer unit in time. He was, in short, the epitome of a rebel.

The fact remains that the salaries of officials were comparatively high, and so were the increases they secured. For those on less than £100 a year the increase was 130 per cent. All other officials would also receive 130 per cent on their first £100, followed by a sliding scale of between 50 and 25 per cent on existing salaries up to £700 a year. Salaries for higher-paid officials were to be the subject of further negotiation.

What this meant in practice was that a municipal official who had been earning £100 a year in 1914 and who had received an interim pay rise of £92 a year in July 1919 would now be earning £232 a year. Corresponding increases would be as follows:[11]

Pay in 1914	Pay in 1920
£150	£305
£200	£380
£250	£455
£300	£520
£400	£650
£450	£715
£500	£780
£550	£847 10s
£600	£905
£650	£967 10s
£700	£995

Senior officials earning more than £700 a year in 1914 had to make do with the interim award of July 1919 and whatever increases they had received individually during the war years. This left them with salaries ranging from £1,035 to £1,360, and the possibility of further increases. As it stood, the offer to the corporation's white-collar staff would add another £38,888 to the wages bill of a city in which the commercial rate (business property tax) was 21s in the pound, up from 18s in the pound in 1919, itself a record.

Councillors of all political complexions fumed at news of the award. The Sinn Féin businesswoman Jennie Wyse Power asked the Lord Mayor how long it would be before the corporation knew if the MOITU would accept the proposals. Councillor John Russell Stritch (MRA) wondered what the five high-earning officials who had still to be dealt with were receiving, at which Alderman William O'Brien snarled, 'They are starving on a thousand pounds a year.' (Laughter.) Sir Andrew Beattie (MRA) said, 'If these men do not like to do their work on their present salary, let the corporation give them to understand that it could get other Irishmen in Dublin to take their places.' (Loud applause, and cries of 'Sack the lot!') The Town Clerk, Sir Henry Campbell, protested that his staff could be relied upon 'to run the British Empire,' to which a member shouted back, 'Not the Empire but the Irish Republic.' Councillor George Lyons (Sinn Féin) described the MOITU as a 'bogus' union, 'an unholy alliance of Freemasonry and Hibernianism, which has disgraced and ruined the city.'

W. T. Cosgrave, who was once more attending corporation meetings, despite his parole, reminded councillors that the corporation had to pay £25,000 to bond-holders by 1 July, that it owed a further £37,000 to the Dublin Union, £10,000 to the Richmond Asylum, and a week's wages to all employees.

Meanwhile the bank overdraft was 'practically exhausted.' Nevertheless he felt they should accept the proposal, and offer the senior officials on more than £1,000 a year £25 a year each. His proposal was seconded by Councillor Coghlan Briscoe, a remnant of the Irish Party regime, but was defeated, by 8 votes to 40. The majority comprised the rump of the Irish Party, some members of the Dalyite faction of Labour, including Daly himself, and a couple of Sinn Féin members. Even those voting for Cosgrave's motion made no attempt to defend the tactics of the officials, which were designed to cause the maximum disruption and loss to lower-paid employees and the public alike.

Concluding the debate, the Lord Mayor said he was

> sorry for some of the lower officials, but there are certain higher officials of the Corporation whom I will see are dealt with as they deserve in the future. The meanness of some of the latter, and the tactics they employed during the week, rendered them unworthy of recognition by any union.

An *Irish Times* editorial predicted that 'this straw may break the ratepayers' back altogether.'

By August, despite Cosgrave's assurances to the directors of the Bank of Ireland, the corporation's overdraft had reached £100,000, and it would need another £160,000 to reach the end of the year. It was Harry Nicholls who helped negotiate a settlement, allowing the corporation to withhold a quarter of all wages and salaries from September 1920 until the beginning of the next financial year in April 1921, together with cuts in services. Nicholls managed to push a resolution through the Dublin Branch of the MOITU that the union, 'recognising the national importance of the fight in which the Corporation is engaged, undertake to help the Corporation in every way in its power.' But the clinching argument was simply that there was no money to meet the pay bill.[12]

The dispute with the municipal officers' union undoubtedly damaged relations between councillors and senior officials, including the Town Clerk, Henry Campbell, and his assistant, John J. Flood, although neither man was directly involved in the industrial action.

The short shrift given to a claim by nurses in the city's hospitals for an eight-hour day makes an interesting contrast with the treatment of the municipality's senior officials. It came up at the same meeting of the corporation on 7 June at which the 'insolence' of Éamonn Price and his municipal officers' union so shocked Dr McWalter. Although the nurses' claim came with an endorsement from the corporation's Public Health Committee that was as strong as that from the Estates and Finance Committee for the municipal officials, no deputation of nurses was invited to explain their case. Dr McWalter had recovered sufficiently from his encounter with the MOITU to protest that conceding an eight-hour day to nurses would result in the city's hospitals, and even the Hospice for the Dying, having to turn patients away. The chairman of the Public Health Committee, P. T. Daly, responded by pointing out that it was not so long ago that 'it was held to be inconceivable for a tradesman to work less than fifty-eight hours a week.'

But the project was sunk once William O'Brien said, 'We all know the Dublin hospitals are bankrupt, and it's ridiculous for a man to come here and ask an eight-hours day for nurses when he knows it is impossible.' O'Brien's intervention was as much concerned with settling scores with Daly as with the justice of the nurses' claim. All the latter could hope for was a review when the city's finances improved.

In fact all the city's hospitals faced a financial crisis, not just those supported by the corporation. Faced with the need for severe cut-backs, the government refused 'even a penny' extra to the House of Industry hospitals, which it effectually owned, let alone Dublin's voluntary institutions. All were caught in the dilemma of frozen public finances while the average cost of a bed had risen from £75 a year to £120. As we have seen, the three House of Industry hospitals now charged for their services, although, as the *Irish Independent* commented, 'to compel the patients to pay for their treatment would be to inflict a grievous hardship upon those for whom the hospitals were primarily intended—the poor of the city.'

The voluntary hospitals had a larger and more prosperous pool of paying customers, together with the resources of the religious orders that ran them, but they still faced rapidly increasing deficits. On 31 May there was a meeting in the RDS Theatre at which Viscount Powerscourt proposed a fund-raising drive to clear the £100,000 debt that now afflicted eleven hospitals in the city, both publicly and privately owned. He told the audience that it was 'the biggest thing of its kind ever attempted in Dublin.' To achieve their objective would require 'all classes of people ... to put in its quota of subscriptions.'

The speakers and the public sponsors of the meeting were overwhelmingly unionist in affiliation. Of the more than forty prominent people listed in the *Irish Times* as attending, only Dr Richard Hayes MP, Sinn Féin's joint Director of Public Health, Dr McWalter and Rev. Thomas A. Finlay SJ came from outside the city's unionist community. The hospitals on the list—the Adelaide, Dr Steevens', the Meath, Mercer's, the Royal City of Dublin (Baggot Street),

Sir Patrick Dun's, the Coombe, the Rotunda, Cork Street Fever Hospital and the Eye and Ear, as well as the House of Industry institutions—came from the same tradition. None of the Catholic voluntary hospitals appear to have been involved, or to have suffered from such a severe financial crisis.

The initiators of the fund-raising campaign did not allow their politics to inhibit their criticism of the government for not stepping into the breach. However, Viscount Powerscourt acknowledged that if the government did give more money to the Dublin hospitals it would have to give money to hospitals everywhere, and 'the result would be that taxation would go up by leaps and bounds.' At the same time he was 'entirely opposed to the idea of compelling all patients to pay for their treatment, because I think there is a great deal of poverty in this city.' Private philanthropy was the only alternative.

Sir Henry McLaughlin and the Lord Chancellor, Sir James Campbell, who were the moving spirits behind the project, had more ambitious plans in mind than a mere fund-raising campaign. McLaughlin, whose building empire extended to Belfast and Britain, called for the development of occupational health insurance schemes. 'Labour in Ireland does its share, and a bigger share than most people realise,' he said. A higher proportion of hospital funding came from trade unions than anywhere else in the United Kingdom, but most of the money was generated and spent in Belfast. He did not see why the Belfast scheme should not apply in Dublin, with each working man contributing 1d a week to a Hospital Fund. He advocated a greater rationalisation of services and specialities between the Dublin hospitals, and urged the committee to seek funding throughout Ireland, as the hospitals were involved in relieving 'suffering humanity not only in the City of Dublin but throughout many of the counties as well.' Financing hospitals by charity fund-raisers was not sustainable. 'I do not believe that a complete solution will ever be arrived at unless the institutions are developed on better lines and that contributions are paid by the patients themselves.' (Applause.)

Father Finlay's approach diverged significantly from McLaughlin's. He accepted that 'the well-paid working classes' could make a large contribution to financing voluntary hospitals.

But below that class there is a very large residuum which has no resources out of which to contribute and which, when sickness or disablement come, are plunged into utter and absolute destitution. From that class we can hardly expect any serious contribution towards the upkeep of the hospitals, and it is for that class especially that the hospitals were set up.

Like Viscount Powerscourt, he saw little merit in greater government involvement. 'The relief of the poor comes best not from official sources but directly from the heart of the benevolent.' Similar sentiments were expressed from the floor, and Dr McWalter stressed the primary role of the new committee as a fund-raising body. For, he warned, if hospital finances were not restored, patients would have to be admitted to the workhouse wards of the Dublin Union, at the expense of the ratepayer.

Given the limited role it had set itself, the Dublin Associated Hospitals Fund performed admirably well. Sir Henry McLaughlin took over the practical management of the campaign, and his firm's offices in Dartmouth Road, Rathmines, became the hub of operations. A great fete at the RDS grounds in October was the main fund-raising event, but musical societies, football clubs and swimming clubs also contributed. By the end of the year £35,000 had been raised, more than £15,000 from the fete itself. This was well below the target of £100,000, but McLaughlin accepted that the latter figure was unachievable, and there was general agreement that more could have been raised but for the effects of the curfew in the city.

One small advance in public-health finances was the belated acceptance by local authorities outside Dublin of the need to make contributions towards the treatment of patients referred by them to the city's hospitals.[13] The IRA had already introduced a similar measure for its members in June 1920. In one of its periodic drives to promote greater efficiency and reduce costs, GHQ had issued a directive informing brigades of the procedures to be followed if they were sending wounded Volunteers to Dublin for treatment. The men were required to have a satisfactory false identity and a referral from their GP. Full particulars of the injury and the treatment required were to be sent before their arrival, as well as dates on which the patient could travel. Units were advised to allow one or two nights for accommodation in Dublin before the Volunteer was admitted to hospital. Most importantly, brigades were informed that they 'must arrange to bear the expenses of any such case.' The Dublin battalions also had to meet their own medical expenses.[14]

Among the 'well-paid working classes' to which Father Finlay looked so confidently for contributions to the Associated Hospital Fund were the city's craft workers. But their attention was concentrated elsewhere. On Sunday 9 May 1920 a public meeting was held in the Abbey Theatre for fitters, turners, boilermakers, electricians, moulders and kindred trades interested in forming a new Irish union. The meeting was packed, and no doubt one topic of conversation was the shooting of Detective-Sergeant Richard Revelle in

Phibsborough earlier that morning on his way to work in College Green.[15] Revelle would have been well known to many of the union activists in the Abbey. He had been a note-taker at trade union rallies and Sinn Féin meetings since the Dublin Lockout of 1913, and he had been the main prosecution witness against Jim Larkin when the latter was sentenced to seven months' imprisonment for making seditious speeches.

Revelle was shot four times that morning. When the ambulance arrived he insisted on being taken to the Adelaide Hospital in Peter Street, on the other side of the city, rather than the Mater, run by the Sisters of Mercy, which was less than two hundred yards away. As a member of G Division he may have known of the Mater's links with the IRA and have feared another attempt on his life. In the event, he survived, but his note-taking days were over. On his discharge from the Adelaide he retreated into the safety of Dublin Castle until the Truce. The unionist stockbroker's clerk Wilmot Irwin, who lived locally, thought he might be able to identify one of the men who shot Revelle, but his brother advised him to 'forget all about what you saw.'[16]

Policemen and loyalists were not the only people having difficulty adjusting to the changes in the city. Many of its craft workers were in British unions that had little sympathy for or understanding of the problems facing Irish members. The British unions had reluctantly supported what they regarded as the 'political' strike over motor permits and withdrew at the first opportunity. There was also resentment among Irish craft workers at the ease with which union cards were being issued in England. In large part this was because of a 'dilution' of the crafts between 1914 and 1918, when women, semi-skilled and even unskilled workers were employed in engineering to meet the demands of a war economy.[17] It was allowed at the time on the grounds that the arrangement would be temporary, but it proved impossible to turn the clock back when the war ended. Now there were complaints that temporary men, including ex-soldiers, were arriving in Ireland with union cards to take jobs. Mutual incomprehension and very different political and economic conditions fuelled the growing breach between British craft unions and their Irish members.[18]

The idea of an independent Irish craft union for the engineering and technical trades had first been mooted in 1917 by Constance Markievicz, inspired by what Larkin had achieved for general workers through the founding of the ITGWU in 1909. But the initiative came from within the ranks of the craft workers themselves. The committee that organised the meeting at the Abbey Theatre covered most of the engineering trades. John (Jack) Redmond, a fitter living in Lord Edward Street, appears to have been the prime mover. He was born in Dublin but served his time with Camel-Laird in Liverpool. He was subsequently employed in a workshop of the Dublin United Tramways Company. He developed a critical attitude towards his own union, the Amalgamated Society of Engineers, even before the Great War imposed strains on cross-channel solidarity. As district secretary he publicly criticised the ASE's lack of support for the 1913 Lockout at the following annual conference of the Irish Trades Union Congress and told delegates that Irish engineers, such as himself, were representing the ASE at their own expense.[19]

Other pioneers included Joseph Toomey, a fitter, and Michael Slator, a brass-moulder, who both lived in Ballybough Road, Patrick McIntyre, an iron-moulder from Arbour Hill, Thomas Leahy, a boilermaker, and Thomas Maguire of the Stationary Engine Drivers' Society. All had strong links with the independence movement: McIntyre had been elected a councillor for Sinn Féin in the January municipal election, while Toomey and Slator had stood unsuccessfully for the party. Toomey, Slator and Leahy had been out in 1916. Leahy, who had learnt his trade, like Redmond, in England, came home to avoid conscription and worked in the Dublin Dockyard. Although he was a member of the Irish Citizen Army he canvassed for Phil Shanahan of Sinn Féin in East Wall during the 1918 general election and for James Lawless, another successful Sinn Féin candidate in the same area, during the 1920 municipal elections, rather than for Labour. Leahy recalled later that the aim was 'to make a start to break this connection with the British trade unions and to devote our future to that work, as it is considered most important to the industrial side of the march of independence.'[20]

Maguire was a long-standing member of the Irish Republican Brotherhood, and Toomey was almost certainly in the IRB as well. Both men were part of an IRA group that used their specialist skills to manufacture hand grenades and ammunition.[21] The Minister for Labour, Constance Markievicz, encouraged the men and collaborated in what became the most important initiative undertaken by the government of the Irish Republic in the industrial relations arena and would have lasting consequences for craft unionism in the country.[22] The political climate was certainly favourable. Dáil Éireann was receptive to any initiatives that strengthened its ties with the labour movement and that did not unduly alarm business or church leaders. Not only Markievicz but many leading figures in the Dáil government subscribed to a vision of Ireland as a co-operative commonwealth, spurning the worst excesses of both capitalism and class warfare. National unity was the priority in the struggle for independence. But efforts to 'discourage the exploitation of Irish Industries by Foreign Capitalists by every means in their power' were to be welcomed, as the Minister for Industry, Ernest Blythe, told the Dáil, and displacing foreign unions with native ones was a natural extension of this policy.[23]

The task of liaison with the dissident craft workers fell to Joe MacDonagh, who had already met representatives of the organising committee in early 1920. They put their views in writing in a letter dated 9 March 1920, asking him to bring their concerns

> before An Dáil at the earliest opportunity. For some years it has been the opinion of a great number of members belonging to Amalgamated Societies, particularly in the Engineering Trades that it was advisable to have one large Irish Union for these trades. There have been great difficulties in the way of forming such a Union, financially and otherwise, and we believe that this is a favourable opportunity for starting such a project. This is due to the fact that for some time past the attitude of the English Executives has been one in keeping with the attitude of the English Government towards this country.

Among the grounds cited for complaint was the refusal of the ASE to issue strike pay during the 1918 general strike against conscription and the motor permits dispute.

> This continued policy has created in the minds of a great number of our members [the idea] that the time had arrived when we should have a Union of our own, governed and controlled in Ireland by Irishmen ... The same dissatisfaction exists among the Iron Founders. It is the opinion of this Committee that the only binding link at the present time between Ireland and England is that of the Amalgamated Unions, whose executives, some of us believe, are in league with the British Government. There are ten sectional unions in the Engineering Industry in Ireland, who are all Amalgamated Societies, and our proposal is to bring about a fusion of members of those ten different trades into one big Irish Engineering Union.

The letter then raised the thorny issue of funding. It pointed out that

> as members grow older in these Amalgamated Societies so their benefits become greater, and unless we are prepared to offer some of these men immediate benefit in the new Union ... we would not be able to break up the influence of the English Societies in this country.[24]

A loan of £2,000 was proposed with which to create a reserve fund 'so as to point out ... that we are able to offer immediate and equal benefits.'[25] The organising committee believed the majority of engineering craft workers would join the new union, 'not only in Dublin, but throughout the whole of Ireland, with the exception of Belfast.' Admitting that breakaway unions had a poor record in the past, the committee said it believed the present conflict had transformed the situation and that the new organisation 'will spell the death knell for English Unions in this country.'[26]

Two thousand pounds was an enormous sum for the Ministry of Labour—more than twice its own running costs in 1920. However, the new union may have been pushing at a half-open door, because of the involvement of the IRB in the engineering trades. Diarmaid Ó hÉigeartaigh, secretary of the Department of Labour, was an IRB member, as was the Minister for Finance, Michael Collins. Ironically, one of the few people involved who was not in the Brotherhood was Markievicz, as it did not admit women.

In any event, further information was required by Collins, and Markievicz met the organising committee on 5 May 1920, along with Seán Etchingham and Art O'Connor, who had collaborated with her in establishing the Republic's rudimentary mediation and arbitration structures.[27] The craft workers' group wanted the Dáil to advance £100 to finance an inaugural meeting in the Abbey Theatre as well as to guarantee the loan of £2,000.[28] Members spoke with some authority. Besides Redmond's position as district secretary of the ASE, Toomey was a district delegate of the union. McIntyre was secretary of the Southern District of the Ironmoulders, 'from Dundalk to Cork,' and Slator was president of the Dublin Branch of the Founders and Brass Finishers. They were able to provide a detailed assessment of the southern branches of the craft unions, identifying potential opponents as well as supporters. Although they accepted that most of the 22,000 ASE members in the North would remain loyal to the British connection, they were confident that at least 1,000 of the 8,000 in the South would join the new union immediately and that the rest would follow.

A major reason was dissatisfaction over delays in the payment of unemployment and sickness benefits to Irish members from London.[29] Besides Dublin, they predicted mass defections in Cork, Passage West, Queenstown (Cóbh), Waterford, Wexford and Dundalk. The committee had the support of Irish unions, including the ITGWU. Not only was the latter the largest union in the country, and itself a breakaway from the (British) National Union of Dock Labourers a decade earlier, but it enjoyed strong links with Dáil Éireann and cabinet members through William O'Brien.[30] Another leading ITGWU member, P. T. Daly, had supported the engineers during the motor permits dispute and now used his position as an alderman on Dublin Corporation to advocate the need for an Irish craft union. Another important contact was Thomas Foran, general president of the ITGWU, who would become president of the Irish Trades Union Congress in 1921.[31] The organising committee stressed to Markievicz its commitment to Dáil Éireann's industrial relations structures. Members would use 'every means in their power to induce their members and employers to accept ... arbitration.' Their only reservations were about lodging funds with an Irish bank.[32]

On a more positive note, the organising committee told Markievicz that if a thousand men defected from the ASE the estimated income would be £3,900 a year, compared with running costs of only £500. The request for the loan of £2,000 was based not alone on the need to reassure older members who might be afraid of losing benefits if they switched unions but to guard against the possibility of recognition disputes if British unions decided to black the new organisation and received support from employers.[33] On 7 May the Ministry of Labour approved the £100 loan for the public meeting.

The work of the dissidents did not go unnoticed in Britain, and when more than seven hundred men gathered on 9 May 1920 in the Abbey Theatre, officials attended from the parent British organisations to warn members against joining a 'political' trade union. They received the backing of the unionist press in the North. The *Northern Whig*'s denunciation of the new initiative as a Sinn Féin plot was more accurate than it may have realised, but it also underlined the fact that separatism and sectarianism were becoming indivisible in a trade union movement that offered no political challenge to Ulster unionism or Sinn Féin. However, there was support from several left-wing trade union leaders in Britain, including Willie Gallacher. He was one of the best-known members of the Clydeside shop stewards' movement during the Great War and travelled to Dublin to speak in favour of the new union.[34] But its main advocate was Joseph Toomey, who said that the interests of Irish workers clashed increasingly with those 'across the channel'. The Irish and English were

> two separate and distinct peoples and could not always view matters from the same standpoint. Some people might say that the interests of all workers were common. That might be so, but workers in different countries often saw things in a different light. They were progressing in the labour movement in Ireland far quicker than the men in England were, and the question was whether they were going to be held back by the people in England because the latter were not progressive enough.

Patrick McIntyre said they were not out for trouble but warned British unions to recognise them or 'start fighting them here on Irish soil.' The meeting agreed that the organisers should continue as a provisional committee, to draw up rules and to recruit members. The name Irish Engineering, Shipbuilding and Foundry Trades Union was adopted. It was to be 'an exclusively Irish trades union' and would include 'fitters, turners, pattern-makers, boilermakers, blacksmiths, brass finishers, iron and brass moulders, electricians and machinists.'[35]

At its inaugural meeting next day the provisional committee distributed a thousand contribution cards, and the following Saturday it held a 'financial meeting' in the National Foresters' Hall at 41 Parnell Square, a popular meeting-place for advanced nationalists of all hues, where it began signing up members.[36] In the meantime meetings were organised in the provinces, and the new union put the English craft unions on notice of its intention to seek recognition in work-places where they were recognised.[37] The weekly subscription was set at 1s 6d, and it was agreed to admit semi-skilled members of British engineering unions. McIntyre was appointed full-time general secretary, with a salary of £6 a week, and a 'vacant' list was opened for unemployed members. The Colmcille Hall in Blackhall Street provided a temporary office. Other tenants included the 1st Battalion of the Dublin Brigade of the IRA and a local unit of Cumann na mBan.[38] The £2,000 loan guarantee from Dáil Éireann proved more difficult to obtain than the £100 for the Abbey Theatre meeting. The Ministry of Labour wanted more information on the financial viability of the new union. Markievicz undertook to obtain the information,[39] met Redmond shortly afterwards,[40] and satisfied herself that 'the men are sincere republicans and capable of the work that they are undertaking.' In return the committee decided, despite earlier reservations, to put its funds into the Irish National Land Bank rather than any British financial institution. Toomey and Leahy were appointed trustees.[41]

Leahy later wrote of the 'bitter opposition' from the British unions but added that Sinn Féin cumainn and IRA units assisted in securing acceptance of the new union by employers. Although the spectre of a strike over recognition did not materialise, there were isolated cases of members losing their jobs. In one instance a man was sacked from Gallagher's tobacco factory in Dublin after pressure from a British union. He was found a position in the Dublin Corporation workshops; when the corporation's blacksmiths were instructed by their British union not to associate with him, they joined the new union. Attempts to block the union at the Inchicore works of the Dublin United Tramways Company were faced down when the union threatened to pull out members at the Ringsend and Ballsbridge depots of the company.[42]

The ASE attempted a fight back. It organised a meeting in Dublin on 6 June 1920, at which the legendary general secretary Tom Mann told members: 'Men should be prepared to forget the county or country in which they were born and look to the international question of organised labour.' But it was the wrong message for the times in Ireland, and the contributions from other British ASE leaders denouncing nationalism and reminding their audience that the bulk of the members were in Belfast and were remaining loyal were counter-productive.[43] The ASE replaced Toomey as district delegate with James Freeland. Freeland predicted in the Irish section of the 1920 annual report: 'The proposed Irish Engineering and Foundry Trades Union is foredoomed to failure.' However, the report itself showed there were no ASE members left in Arklow, and there were incomplete returns for Dublin, where the state of the union was classified as 'bad'. The situation elsewhere in the South was largely categorised as 'poor' or 'bad'; Drogheda was the only centre outside Ulster with a 'good' accreditation. At the end of the year the ASE could claim only 1,762 paid-up members left in the South.[44]

Freeland's prediction proved wrong, in large part because the IESFTU appears to have been particularly successful in recruiting younger craft workers and apprentices, who were attuned to the political radicalism sweeping the country. Some of them were active in the IRA. The one sector where the new union met strong resistance was the ship repair yards of Dublin, Cork and Passage West, where many men were originally from Belfast and the Clyde. But the public tide was running against these isolated groups. Terence MacSwiney, who had succeeded Tomás Mac Curtáin as local IRA commander and Lord Mayor of Cork, encapsulated the mood when he presided at the organising meeting of the IESFTU in the city. He said it was 'the duty of all Irish trade union men to be able to manage their own affairs and way of life; by joining and strengthening the union they were also helping on the work of Irish independence.'

By 1921 the IESFTU had 4,500 members in Dublin, Cork, Dundalk, Drogheda, Cóbh, Passage West, Limerick, Wicklow, Galway, Sligo and Wexford.[45] It also became the main union representing electricians after a mass meeting of the Electrical Trades Union in Dublin on 20 June decided to join the IESFTU in a body. Overnight the IESFTU became the main electricians' union in the South, with 99 per cent of electricians in the Dublin Corporation power station at Ringsend signing up. The union also agreed to accept members of other crafts. The plumbers and brass-finishers came over in a body in June, the Vehicle Builders' Union did so in August and the Irish Stationary Engine Drivers' Society in November.[46] The union recruited among a wide range of engineering employments and secured a number of pay increases, some through Dáil Éireann's industrial relations machinery and some by direct negotiation. It frequently liaised with the ITGWU on recruitment and industrial relations strategy and with left-wing union leaders on Clydeside, where headline rates for shipbuilding were struck that applied in Ireland as well as Britain.[47]

A breakthrough was the first working rule agreement with the Dublin Building Trade Employers' Association.[48] This became the predecessor of the National Joint Industrial Council for the Electrical Contracting Industry, which negotiated minimum rates for the industry for the rest of the century. The first rate, negotiated on 31 March 1922, was 1s 10d an hour for a basic 44-hour week.[49] Meanwhile, on 24 July 1920, the union held a rules conference in the council chamber at City Hall, by courtesy of the Lord Mayor. Allowing the union to use the chamber was an important acknowledgement of its legitimacy by the new Republican regime in the city.[50]

While the engineers were the most dramatic manifestation of the new sense of confidence and national self-awareness among organised workers, it was by no means the only one. These new organisations reflected the rapidly growing strength of workers in the labour market. As we have seen, white-collar groups such as the Irish Bank Officials' Association, which had been formed on 17 March 1918 at a meeting in the Mansion House, had won recognition and improvements in conditions by merely threatening a strike.[51] The Dublin Municipal Officers' Association was already well on its way towards forming a national public-service white-collar union.

But trade union militancy did not necessarily translate into political radicalism. The IBOA had a staid, lower-middle-class membership. Its first secretary was C. H. Denroche, a solicitor who had been part of Captain John Bowen-Colthurst's defence team when he was tried for the murder of Francis Sheehy Skeffington in 1916.[52]

Meanwhile the most significant of all labour disputes during the War of Independence had begun in Dublin. In a way it originated in England, where William O'Brien had been studying the labour situation while convalescing after his hunger strike. At the beginning of May the new General Officer Commanding in Ireland, Sir Nevil Macready, decided to allow O'Brien to return home. (See chapter 4 above.) Before his departure he was interviewed by a journalist at the London office of the *Freeman's Journal* about the political situation, and he referred approvingly to the London dockers who were refusing to load a ship, the *Jolly George*, with arms for Poland to be used in the war against the new Soviet government in Russia. Shortly afterwards a Citizen Army veteran of 1916 and member of the dockers' section of the Number 1 Branch of the ITGWU, who had read the article, called to Liberty Hall and told O'Brien that two shipments for the British army had arrived in Dublin port. He wanted to know if the union would back the men if they refused to work the ship. O'Brien contacted the general president of the ITGWU, Tom Foran, and they agreed that the ship would be blacked. The second vessel was diverted to Kingstown, where soldiers unloaded the cargo, but on its arrival at Westland Row station the porters refused to touch it. All four hundred workers at the station came out on strike.

As O'Brien recalled in his memoirs, the action of his own members did not pose a problem, as they were all casual workers who could be reallocated to work other vessels, but the railwaymen were permanent employees, who would be looking for strike pay from the National Union of Railwaymen if they were laid off, and their own union was unlikely to support yet another 'political' strike.

O'Brien made an unsuccessful attempt to raid the remnants of the anti-conscription fund for strike pay. Control rested jointly with Arthur Griffith, Acting President of the Irish Republic in de Valera's absence, and John Dillon, the last leader of the Irish Party. According to O'Brien, Dillon blocked the payment. Faced with the prospect of the strikers being forced back to work, O'Brien persuaded the NEC of the ITUC&LP to raise a special strike levy from members that would guarantee every docker or railwayman sacked or suspended from work £3 a week in strike pay. This was as good as a full week's wages for some men, although higher-paid workers, such as train drivers, would suffer considerable loss during the dispute. Altogether £120,000 was subscribed to the fund by the end of the year.[53]

There was significant support for the munitions strike in Britain, where unions already had their embargo in force on military supplies to Poland. The 50,000-strong South Wales Branch of the National Union of Ex-Servicemen called for the withdrawal of troops from Ireland and advised reservists to refuse mobilisation papers if called on to serve in Ireland or in the Russo-Polish war. Despite the unexpectedness of the 'political' strike in Dublin, the Executive Committee of the NUR supported its members, at least to the extent of calling on its allies in the Triple Alliance of railwaymen's, dockers' and miners' unions to consider sympathetic action. The Alliance in turn referred the dispute to the Parliamentary Committee of the TUC 'so that the attitude of British Labour towards the production and handling of munitions of war for Ireland and Poland may be determined.' There it died a bureaucratic death.

Meanwhile pickets spread in Dublin. The premises of the London and North-Western Railway at the North Wall, where most munitions entered the country, were among the first targets. The pickets were so effective that the strike committee had to issue permits for the release of perishable goods, such as eggs, tea, confectionery and medical supplies, to local traders and provincial firms. Other items, such as agricultural implements, remained strike-bound. Military guards were posted on the LNWR power house, but the dynamo was idle because the maintenance craft workers came out in sympathy with the dockers. Passengers were allowed to board ships and trains in the capital but they had to carry their own luggage.

Inevitably, the strikers sometimes adopted inconsistent positions on the transport of goods. For instance, a consignment of rifles for the RIC in Wexford was blacked on 31 May by porters at Harcourt Street station, but they agreed to carry quantities of gelignite and a consignment of sporting cartridges for a merchant in the town. The same train took wagons laden with sugar, cocoa, jam and other foodstuffs *en route* from Kingstown pier to the Curragh, including provisions for the garrison.[54]

As the *Irish Times* pointed out, the transport workers were challenging 'the fundamental security of the state and the fundamental rights of employers.' Railway workers would come under extreme pressure to carry munitions and soldiers. Not only were they sacked or suspended from duty but those still at work were assaulted, subjected to mock executions or, in some instances, shot.[55]

Incidents such as the attack on the British military post at King's Inns the day after the munitions strike began further infuriated the authorities. Slack discipline, with soldiers entertaining girl-friends at the post on fine summer days, gave Dublin Volunteers their opportunity. The guard of thirteen soldiers was held at gunpoint while twenty-five rifles, two Lewis machine guns and five hundred rounds of ammunition were removed. Among the raiding party was a young medical student, Kevin Barry, who was later to be involved in a similar raid a few hundred yards away, with tragic results.

The military authorities in Dublin decided to reduce the number of public buildings that had a small military guard to avoid a repetition of the raid. One of the posts from which they were withdrawn was the Custom House; that decision too would have unfortunate consequences.

After the King's Inns raid the *Irish Times* fulminated at 'the railwaymen [who] refuse to handle munitions for the troops [while] the flying columns of the Republic continue to handle them with despatch and dexterity.' The *Times* reported ruefully that the weapons at King's Inns were taken away in two motor cars, while 'the raiders, who were undisguised, departed calmly through a cheering crowd.'[56]

At the end of the week Sinn Féin swept the board in the elections for Poor Law guardians, winning nineteen of the twenty-two seats. Labour won two seats, and one independent was elected. The unionists did not contest the election, and the only MRA candidate was unsuccessful.[57]

A deputation from the Labour Party was sent the following weekend to Britain to secure sympathetic action in support of the munitions strike. Unfortunately, claims that a strike was necessary 'to combat Prussianism' failed to convince the TUC. It probably did not help that the signatories of the ITUC&LP manifesto included Jack Redmond, president of the breakaway engineering union. For the TUC to support its Irish counterpart would have been a declaration of war in a cause that did not directly affect it. Lloyd George made it clear to the British unions that capitulating on the munitions strike was not an option for the government.[58] Even without the support of the TUC the strike was extremely effective, forcing British army transport onto a treacherous road network unsuitable for heavy motor traffic but ideal for ambushes. A large proportion of the occupation forces had to be employed in keeping supply routes to local garrisons open; this in turn prevented a serious counter-offensive against IRA flying columns until 1921.[59] Without the leading role taken in the munitions dispute by Dublin workers, the guerrilla war in the provinces would have been conducted under much less favourable circumstances in 1920.

Of course not all Irish trade unionists agreed with the munitions strike. On 12 June carpenters and joiners at the Workman Clark shipyard in Belfast strongly dissociated themselves from a vote by the union's NEC in Manchester supporting 'the aspirations of Sinn Féin' and the 'boycott in the manufacture and transport of munitions.' Carson may have secured partition for the six north-east counties of Ulster, now being redesignated Northern Ireland, but many unionists in the new statelet felt deeply insecure. More than thirty years of relative communal calm in Belfast was about to give way to unprecedented sectarian violence.

An aggravating factor was the increasing competition in the labour market. By the middle of 1920 the postwar recession had begun to bite. During the war significant numbers of Catholics had moved into the engineering and shipbuilding industries to replace men serving in the British army. They were still there when the cut-backs in spending on armaments began. Some Catholics were also involved in the revitalised labour movement, which was perceived as a threat to unionist hegemony in the city. Nationalist publications provided plenty of ammunition for convincing the doubters. As Old Ireland put it in the aftermath of the 1919 engineering strike, 'the best service both in the interests of Sinn Féin and the people would be to tackle the enemy with the labour weapon.' An Ulster Protestant, W. Forbes Patterson, who had served in the Canadian army in the Great War and become convinced of the justice of the Sinn Féin case for independence, suggested that the best way to undermine unionism was to establish a newspaper advocating the Democratic Programme of Dáil Éireann. The Sinn Féin leadership gave the idea a cold shoulder, although it had commissioned Patterson's report. As Arthur Mitchell put it, only one member of the Sinn Féin leadership, Constance Markievicz, had even a fleeting acquaintance with unions, and promoting the Democratic Programme would leave them open to the charge

> that they were crypto-Bolsheviks … How would the grocer, the priest and the farmer react to such a programme? Flaming nationalism had got them this far, and flaming nationalism would see them the rest of the way.

Flaming unionists certainly bought in to the argument of fighting fire with fire. In 1920 the Belfast Protestant Alliance began to mobilise workers in the city on sectarian grounds. The spark was provided inadvertently by the Divisional Commissioner of the RIC in Munster, Lieutenant-Colonel Gerald Smyth. He provoked a highly publicised mutiny of RIC constables in Listowel, Co. Kerry, by telling them that the more rebels they shot the better he would like it. The leader of the mutiny, Constable Jeremiah Mee, had to flee to Dublin. Smyth's inflammatory activities were cut short when he was shot by the IRA in the Cork Country Club.

For many Ulster unionists, primed by months of reports about attacks on their Southern brethren, Smyth's death not alone confirmed their worst fears but demanded a response. When the news was received, Catholic homes were attacked by loyalist mobs in Smyth's home town of Banbridge, Co. Down. The rioting soon spread to Belfast. One of the survivors reported:

> Men armed with sledge hammers and other weapons swooped down on Catholic workers in the shipyards and didn't even give them a chance of their lives. The vests and shirts of those at work were torn open to see if the men were wearing any Catholic emblem, and then woe betide the man who was. One man … had to swim the Musgrave Channel … pelted with rivets … to emerge in streams of blood and rush to the police office in a nude state.

Attacks on Catholics in engineering firms such as Mackie's Foundry and in the textile mills followed. When unions sought to restore evicted Catholic workers to their jobs the workers were often required to sign a loyalty oath. This left many in an impossible situation: if they refused they would be locked out; if they signed it would quickly be known in the Catholic ghettoes and they would face ostracism in their own communities, which were mobilising against the pogrom.

The question of the loyalty oath aroused as much anger in Dublin as the actual pogrom and the 'industrial evictions'. For organised workers and their unions the oath carried echoes of the declaration demanded from workers by employers in the 1913 Lockout to renounce membership of the ITGWU.

At first the police and military acted firmly to disperse loyalist mobs, but the latter had the endorsement of Carson and the Ulster Unionist leadership, and government forces quickly slid into 'indecision and vacillation'.[60] As Arthur Mitchell says, the decision by the British government to abandon Belfast Catholics to the tender mercies of loyalist militias was even more irresponsible than the decision to introduce the Black and Tans to the South as a means of bolstering the RIC. More than eight thousand workers were driven out of the shipyards and engineering plants for being either Catholics or socialists, or both; a quarter of those expelled were Protestants. However, the critical weight of organisations involved in providing relief, such as the Catholic Protection Agency established by the Catholic Bishop of Down and Connor, Joseph MacRory, and the Ancient Order of Hibernians inevitably gave a confessional overtone to the effort. Even trade union funds were often subsumed in bodies such as the Irish White Cross, set up at de Valera's instigation as an alternative to the Red Cross. Although strenuous efforts were made to include figures from outside Sinn Féin and Labour ranks, these were very few, and the president of the White Cross was Cardinal Logue.

By October 1920 the Expelled Workers Register was assisting 8,400 workers, of whom 4,000 were heads of families. Union structures proved a broken reed. After the Amalgamated Society of Carpenters and Joiners served strike notice on employers who refused to reinstate sacked workers, 3,000 out of its 4,000 members in the city passed union pickets.[61]

A boycott in response to the prospect of partition had already begun in parts of the west of Ireland, with some shops no longer stocking Northern products. Indeed some loyalists cited this boycott as one of the reasons for the pogroms against 'disloyal' elements in Belfast. Once the pogroms began, the Dáil cabinet found itself in a dilemma. It could not ignore the calls for reprisals in the South to curb the Orange mobs, but as the one Northerner in the cabinet, Ernest Blythe, pointed out, a commercial blockade of Belfast 'would destroy for ever the possibility of any union.'[62] Constance Markievicz and Desmond Fitzgerald also felt that a general boycott would be a vote for partition. A further problem was the impossibility of distinguishing between Belfast firms that had expelled Catholic workers and those that had not. The latter would eventually be harder hit by the boycott, as they tended to be in industries that catered for the domestic market, such as brewing, whereas engineering and shipbuilding firms, which were the main offenders, relied on export markets.[63]

Eventually it was decided to confine the boycott to banks and insurance companies with head offices in Belfast. In practice this proved impossible, and the boycott soon extended to other businesses and to farming. The Dublin MP Michael Staines, who was still active as Quartermaster-General of the Volunteers as well as a member of Dublin Corporation, was given the job of directing the national boycott. It was good news for Southern banks. Staines found himself frequently asked to arrange for the transfer of Northern accounts to the Munster and Leinster bank. The Bank of Ireland was able to expand its services significantly in Ulster and especially the border counties as unionist businesses switched accounts.[64]

Dublin Corporation discussed the pogrom on 9 August. P. T. Daly proposed that 'an agitation ... be initiated ... to prevent the commodities and products of Belfast from being bought until such time as the embargo upon the workers of Belfast is withdrawn.' He moved that 'an All-Ireland Conference be called for the purpose of taking joint action to protect the interests of the Roman Catholic, Nationalist and Socialist workers in the City.' It was seconded by councillor Peter Doyle (Sinn Féin) and might have sailed through except for an amendment from another Sinn Féin councillor, Andrew Lyons, asking that steps be taken to provide housing for refugees from the North. The Lord Mayor was quick to point out the futility of making such offers in a city with seven thousand families on the housing list and thousands more living in conditions unfit for human habitation. In fact the number of refugees coming to Dublin at this time appears to have been relatively small. It was rather the prospect of a mass exodus that alarmed city councillors, many of whom shared the Lord Mayor's hope that 'the people in Belfast were prepared to stand their ground and face their Gethsemane.'

Dr McWalter went even further and suggested that 'the question of exclusion of any trade unionists from work in Belfast is best left ... to the good sense of the trade union bodies of Belfast.' Daly told the doctor he might feel differently if he had been 'held before a furnace,' as happened to expelled shipyard workers, but he accepted a relatively mild compromise proposal from the Lord Mayor, 'that in the opinion of the Council a religious or political test should not be made a condition of industrial employment.' This was passed unanimously.

On a less contentious note it was agreed to rename Great Brunswick Street after its most famous native, Patrick Pearse. Not content with this, the Sinn Féin majority went on to propose that the adjoining Queen's Terrace and Queen's Square be renamed Pearse Terrace and Pearse Square, respectively. Disharmony arose only when Councillor George Lyons (Sinn Féin) proposed that Townsend Street be renamed James Connolly Street. This was too much for Councillor Michael Bohan (Labour), who said that if they wanted to name a street after Connolly it should be Dame Street. He found an unlikely ally in Dr McWalter, who said there 'was no honour conferred on James Connolly to associate his name with such a filthy, loathsome, dirty den' as Townsend Street.[65]

One issue on which there was unanimity was the success of the RDS Horse Show in August. In 1920 there was a record number of entries for the jumping competitions. The department stores in the city did extremely well out of the event, and a Motor Show was organised by the Dublin Motor Company in Kildare Street. Models on display included the Dodge Brothers' Landaulette, Limousine and Roadster. The *Irish Times* believed that the Horse Show,

> with its good fellowship, grace and charm, its harmonious prosperity, is not alas the whole of Ireland. Nevertheless it is what the whole of Ireland might be, if the faith, courage and Catholic patriotism that created the Show could be applied by all Irishmen to all the problems of Irish Life.

One Catholic Irishman who would not be attending the Horse Show or any other event in Ireland was Dr Daniel Mannix, Archbishop of Melbourne and former president of St Patrick's College, Maynooth. He had led the anti-conscription campaign in Australia during the Great War and met de Valera in America before proceeding on his trip to Ireland to receive the honorary freedom of the city of Dublin, among other honours. He was not allowed to keep his appointment. The transatlantic liner *Baltic* was intercepted by the Royal Navy as it entered the western approaches. Mannix was arrested and deposited in Penzance. Inevitably his captors were dubbed the 'pirates of Penzance' in the nationalist press. The archbishop was forbidden entry to Ireland and prohibited from addressing meetings in any part of England that had a large Irish immigrant population.

Crowds defied the curfew and lit bonfires in protest at news of the archbishop's arrest. In one confrontation with soldiers at Mary's Lane 23-year-old Thomas Farrell of Church Street was shot dead and 19-year-old Thomas

Clarke of Green Street was seriously wounded in the knee.[66] Despite these shootings, on 9 August the military considered the curfew a success. It had 'a pacifying effect ... Even when sniping occurred it was only spasmodic and very ineffective.'

The curfew was shortened during the summer months, operating only from midnight to 3 a.m., to ameliorate the effects on the civilian population and the strain on soldiers charged with enforcing it. Nevertheless increased hostility towards off-duty soldiers led to the army issuing them with automatic pistols for personal protection.[67]

The Belfast boycott had a generally unsettling effect on Dublin, especially the business community. In mid-September the chairman of the Markets Committee, Councillor William Paul (Sinn Féin), banned the use of cheques drawn on Belfast banks and banknotes issued by them. As the munitions strike was now causing serious disruption to imports from Britain, and Northern suppliers had been making up much of the shortfall, the extension of the boycott severely affected business in both cities. The loss to Dublin's corporation markets alone was estimated at £3,000 a week. In response to critics such as Dr McWalter, Paul said the sanctions were no more severe than the 2½ per cent commission that English banks were charging customers for changing Belfast notes.[68] Nevertheless, sanctions in the city never reached the proportions seen in some areas, where Volunteers banned Northern participants from fairs and markets as well as Northern commercial travellers and their goods from shops.

The boycott surfaced at Rathmines Urban District Council in October when Sinn Féin members proposed its introduction 'until the imposition of political and religious tests as a condition of employment was removed' in Belfast. It had been a testy enough meeting already, with the unionist majority opting to keep street lights on during the curfew and appointing a Protestant as a temporary engineer without a public competition. The unionist chairman, Robert Benson, ruled the boycott motion out of order, and W. W. Carruthers declared that such a resolution would never be tolerated in Rathmines.

When Alderman Joe MacDonagh[69] moved the suspension of standing orders, Benson ruled this motion also out of order and left the chamber, along with unionist colleagues. The clerk then declared the business of the meeting over, but Sinn Féin members elected one of their own, William Sears, to the chair.[70] The clerk protested at the proceedings and collected up his papers, only to have MacDonagh insist that he leave the minutes book. Among those who remained was the sole nationalist councillor, Mary Kettle. She said she was in thorough agreement with the proposers of the resolution that political or religious tests for public-sector employment should be banned but pointed out that the Dublin Technical Education Committee had imposed an oath of allegiance to the Republic as a condition on teachers. Previously the oath had been to the King. MacDonagh told her the taking of an oath of allegiance to the King was not a political matter but 'a matter of treachery.'

Not all teachers agreed, and neither did the Department of Education, which meant that technical schools failed to open for the autumn term. But all politics are local, and it was clear that the real target of Sinn Féin's anger was not so much the Belfast pogroms as perceived religious discrimination in Rathmines, where Councillor Sears claimed that Catholics obtained fewer than 5 per cent of council jobs although they made up half the population. Mrs Kettle voted with Sinn Féin, and the new acting Chairman recorded in the sequestered minutes book that the decision to implement the Belfast boycott was unanimous.[71]

The pogrom affected all sorts of organisations. The new engineering union, the IESFTU, was a case in point. By September the question of acquiring premises had become urgent, and the delay was affecting plans to organise up to five branches in Dublin.[72] When the President, Jack Redmond, and Vice-President, Joe Toomey, proposed that the union acquire the Plaza Hotel at 6 Gardiner Row, a mass meeting of Dublin members agreed to a levy to meet the costs. By October the Executive Committee had secured a loan of £2,500 from the National Land Bank to close the sale. Part of the cost of the Plaza Hotel was met by transferring the deeds of 10 Upper Abbey Street to the union's solicitor, James O'Connor.[73]

The Abbey Street premises were leased, but not owned, by the Stationary Engine Drivers' Society, whose members were in the process of joining the IESFTU *en masse*. As we have seen, this was also the building where the Squad was based, operating under the cover of 'George Moreland, cabinet-maker'. Members of the Squad appear to have continued using the premises after the deeds were transferred. The fact that Collins was Minister for Finance as well as founder and controller of the Squad suggests that funds for acquiring the Plaza Hotel, or at least for providing security for the purchase, may have come from him. Details of the transaction are not recorded in the minutes of the Executive Committee of the IESFTU; nor do they mention that among new tenants at 6 Gardiner Row was the Dublin Brigade, which transferred there from the Dublin Typographical Society premises after the death of Dick McKee in late 1920. The new tenant was officially registered as Number 1 Branch of the Clerical Workers' Union.[74]

Whatever secret arrangements may have surrounded the acquisition of the Plaza Hotel, renamed the Irish Engineering Hall, it put severe pressure on the union's finances. On the same day that the deal was closed a mass meeting of IESFTU members passed a motion 'that in view of the amount of levies being paid by our members at present we find it would hardly be wise for E.C. [Executive Committee] to decide on any amount to be paid to Belfast Victimised Fund, but we strongly recommend all members to subscribe to same.' The following night the EC decided to continue paying the levies nevertheless, at least in respect of craft workers driven out of their jobs in the Belfast shipyards and of transport workers victimised for refusing to carry munitions or troops. Within a week it also reinstated the Belfast victims levy. However, an attempt to increase the levy from 6d to 1s was narrowly defeated.[75]

This suggests that the leadership of the IESFTU was more committed to supporting the Belfast pogrom victims and following the policy of Dáil Éireann than was the general membership. Of course the Executive Committee would have been mindful that if Collins was subsidising the hall, or even acting as guarantor, it was important not to alienate him or his colleagues. The real story of how the hall was financed remains a mystery. As with so many secrets of the Irish revolution, especially financial ones, the full details of these transactions were probably known fully only to Collins and died with him at Bealnablagh less than two years later. It is no wonder that the military authorities in Dublin were finding it 'difficult to differentiate between a labour and Sinn Féin meeting' in late 1920.

Meanwhile in September 1920 the Dáil took another major step in consolidating trade union support by establishing a Labour Arbitration Tribunal.[76] The tribunal operated in situations where both sides agreed to be bound by the outcome. The extent of the collapse of British civil administration by 1920 was such that it made the arbitration system quite appealing to employers as well as trade unionists, providing rudimentary state machinery for resolving disputes in an otherwise chaotic world.[77] One of the first people appointed to the arbitration panel was an IRB member, Thomas Maguire of the IESFTU.

Chapter 6 ~

'WE CANNOT HAVE A ONE SIDED WAR'

'The alternative government of Dáil Éireann blossomed in the summer of 1920; its growth was rapid and the season short.' This is how Arthur Mitchell describes the civil administration of the Republic. It received a boost with the local elections in June, when Sinn Féin won control of 29 out of 33 county councils and 172 out of 206 rural district councils.[1] The Dáil cabinet now had the opportunity to establish a dual-power structure and to apply some of the lessons learnt in cities and towns, such as Dublin, that had fallen to Sinn Féin in January.

The central question was finance. Quite apart from the internal opposition of senior full-time officials, such as the Town Clerk of Dublin, Henry Campbell, his deputy, John Flood, and office-holders nominated by Dublin Castle, such as the High Sheriff, Dr McWalter, the corporation encountered serious problems in obtaining access to British government funds. A conference organised by W. T. Cosgrave's deputy, Kevin O'Higgins, before the June elections had recommended that any local authority with a Sinn Féin majority should declare for the Republic. However, O'Higgins soon realised that this could lead to financial disaster.

Many councils, including Dublin Corporation, tried to have it both ways, giving their political allegiance to Dáil Éireann but continuing to draw on Crown funds. Cosgrave, mindful of the financial hazards, wrote in his capacity as chairman of Dublin Corporation's Estates and Finance Committee to the Republic's Minister for Finance, Michael Collins, requesting that trustees be appointed, with authority to use Dáil Éireann funds to buy bonds under the

Dublin Corporation Loans Act (1889). These funds could then be used by the municipality to finance capital projects. The main project Cosgrave had in mind was slum clearance. The cost would be £200,000 a year 'at the outside'. The contradiction involved in citing British legislation as a financial vehicle for the scheme does not appear to have struck Cosgrave. He even assured Collins that 'Corporation stock is a perfectly legal security and one easily disposed of if the necessity arose.' Collins disagreed, and the proposal was 'negatived' at a session of the Dáil on 29 June.

Cosgrave continued to press for funds. On 28 July he warned Collins that the corporation was facing bankruptcy and that the situation was now so serious that 'the only solution would be for me to retire altogether from public life as it would not be in the interests of the Republic that such a failure in the Corporation could continue to function as head of local government.' Collins called Cosgrave's bluff and replied on 29 July that there was no question of the Dáil Éireann loan trustees investing in corporation stock. The only sop was that housing investment might fall under the Dáil's remit at some future date.

On the same day the secretary of the Local Government Board, A. R. Barlas, issued a circular notifying all local authorities that further grants would be conditional on the submission of accounts for audit in conformity with LGB rules. On 4 August the British administration went even further. The Under-Secretary for Ireland, Sir James McMahon, wrote to Dublin Corporation informing members that the Lord Lieutenant, Field-Marshal Sir John French, would 'withhold any further payments from the Local Taxation (Ireland) Account ... until a definite assurance [of loyalty] was received.' Similar letters were sent to every county, borough, urban district and rural district council in the country as well as boards of Poor Law guardians.

Two days later the Deputy City Treasurer, John Murphy, sent a confidential memo to Cosgrave telling him that the current account was now £100,000 overdrawn, 'entirely due to the Government policy recently adopted of withholding all grants, even those ... due in respect of services already rendered; as well as the non payment of rates on [British government] property in the city.' On the capital side he said the Electricity Supply Committee had to spend £81,000 on 'absolutely necessary' new equipment for the Pigeon House power station and warned that contractors at Roundwood reservoir would not continue unless they were assured that the loan of £150,000 required for completing the project was sanctioned. On the housing front, contractors were threatening to stop work on 202 houses in the former McCaffrey estate at Mount Brown and sixty houses at St James's Walk unless their accounts were paid.

Murphy pointed out that the new equipment for the Pigeon House had been sanctioned by the 'old Council', and that it would be disastrous for the city if the waterworks were not upgraded. If the contractors pulled out of the housing projects the half-completed houses would be useless by the time winter came. He could not resist pointing out that no difficulty would have arisen 'but for the Dáil Éireann resolution' passed the previous May. The only way to make good the deficit was 'by strict economy' on current expenditure and by refusing to undertake new capital projects. Like Cosgrave, he put forward a schedule for issuing corporation stock to raise £500,000 but, unlike Cosgrave, he put his trust in the banks rather than Dáil Éireann.

In the meantime the financial crisis was not an opportunity that Sinn Féin's opponents in the council could ignore. On 9 August Dr McWalter proposed 'that the necessary assurances be given to the Local Government Board' for securing funds. But Cosgrave, who had recovered his nerve, was now pursuing the bank loan option and put forward an amendment that the correspondence be simply marked 'read'. This was passed, by 17 votes to 4, with only McWalter's MRA colleagues supporting him.

The next day, 10 August, Cosgrave made a virtue of necessity by calling, in his capacity as Minister for Local Government, on all local authorities to affirm their allegiance to the Republic. A Dáil decree followed on 17 September and a declaration from Cosgrave accompanied it, telling local authorities that 'the stoppage of grants in aid of local taxation by the enemy government is a last despairing attempt to bribe the people of Ireland back into slavery.'[2]

Beneath the rhetoric, the basic facts had not changed. While the Bank of Ireland was still providing overdraft facilities, there was no change of heart by the other banks, and no desire to buy corporation stock by anyone. On the positive side, unionist ratepayers in Dublin, both residential and commercial, do not appear to have taken advantage of the position adopted by McWalter as High Sheriff, that he would not sanction the seizure of property in lieu of payments. As with so many changes being wrought in society, they accepted the new regime for fear of something worse, and paid up.

Nevertheless the withholding of LGB funds was imposing severe strains on the city's finances. Even with the pay freeze agreed with the staff until 1 July 1921, the current deficit now stood at £200,000, and drastic budgetary surgery was required. Among the cuts proposed were:

Paving:	£20,000
Lighting:	£15,000
Improvements and services:	£4,820

Construction of a ladies' lavatory:	£5,000
Housing:	£3,000
Markets:	£1,490
New TB clinics:	£10,000
Waterworks:	£10,600

Besides these cuts, school meals for between seven and ten thousand children were to be discontinued when funds were exhausted, as were subsidies to the Dublin Union, the Richmond Asylum and the technical schools. The school meals scheme and Richmond Asylum were heavily dependent on corporation funds but the Technical Schools were largely financed by the LGB. As we have seen, teachers in technical schools—significant numbers of whom were Protestants—inadvertently came to the assistance of the corporation by going on strike over the introduction of a new oath of allegiance to the Dáil, replacing that to the Crown.[3]

The motion to implement the cuts was proposed by the Lord Mayor and seconded by Cosgrave. Even then James Gately, one of the longest-serving of the old-school nationalists, now an independent, proposed an amendment that councillors 'place the present intolerable financial position before the representatives of the British Treasury.' The amendment was defeated, 30 votes to 22. Those reluctant to cut the umbilical cord with the LGB coffers included not only the MRA and independent nationalists such as Gately but even some Labour councillors, from both factions, who put the protection of jobs and services before the Republic.[4]

The stalemate with the LGB continued, but in September there was good news for the corporation on the financial front. Once again the Bank of Ireland came to the rescue. Despite, or perhaps because of, the assassination of one of the directors of its Dublin board by the IRA in July (see below), and threats of sanctions from the corporation if it breached the Belfast boycott, its secretary, Thomas Lanphier, had been in correspondence with the City Treasurer, Edmund Eyre, about the purchase of stock on the very same terms that Dáil Éireann and Collins had 'negatived'. The offer was timely, for by September the corporation was owed £70,000 in unpaid rates by the Crown and its overdraft had grown to £220,000, although publicly it was admitting only to £200,000. Not alone did the Bank of Ireland agree to continue covering the overdraft given to Cosgrave earlier in the year (see chapter 5 above) but it offered to advance £200,000, the equivalent of the LGB grant, in return for corporation stock carrying a dividend of 3¼ per cent.

The Bank of Ireland had already facilitated the establishment of the National Land Bank, and Sinn Féin leaders were learning that 'the Bank's Anglicanism was never of the bitter, partisan, exclusive kind.' Whether it was through Cosgrave or separately, Collins appears to have struck up a good working relationship with one of the directors, Andrew Jameson. In many ways they were kindred spirits. Jameson was a Scot by birth and a Cambridge rugby blue who had gone big-game hunting with Theodore Roosevelt as a young man and plunged into the African bush in search of a brother lost on one of H. M. Stanley's expeditions. A member of a Scottish distilling dynasty, he had looked after the family's Irish business interests since 1887. He was open to new ideas and largely untainted by the traditional prejudices of his class, incurring the wrath of many unionists for his conciliatory approach to nationalists in the abortive Irish Convention of 1917–18.

Moreover, the Bank of Ireland was a lot better off than its 'nationalist' rivals and in fact had money to invest. Having adopted a more cautious investment and loan policy during the post-war boom, now turning rapidly into a slump, it could afford to hedge its bets by taking a gamble on the corporation, as it did on several smaller local authorities. In the event, the other banks now offered the corporation loans on the same terms, and the risk was eventually spread between them.[5] For the Bank of Ireland it was relatively small change; it bought almost £900,000 in British Treasury bonds during the same period. What was important was that both the Bank of Ireland and the Munster and Leinster Bank now believed in the long-term solvency of the corporation. Their investment decision was a serious setback for the strategy being pursued by Dublin Castle, just as it was a victory for Sinn Féin.

Dublin Castle appears to have been unaware of the nature of the financial transactions taking place under its nose. On 26 October 1920 the Auxiliaries raided the branch offices of the Munster and Leinster Bank in Palace Street in search of documents relating to corporation finances. They came away empty-handed. No such raid was made on the Bank of Ireland around the corner. This operation was deeply resented by the business community, not only for the disruption it caused but for the humiliation inflicted on customers, including the Chief Justice, Sir James Campbell, who were briefly exposed to the tender mercies of the new Auxiliary police.[6]

The restored creditworthiness of the corporation was no doubt due in part to the budgetary cuts agreed by councillors and the pay freeze accepted by the staff. But Bank of Ireland directors seem to have been sufficiently impressed by the calibre of the Dáil and corporation representatives to feel that it made more sense to subsidise a rebel administration than see the capital descend into chaos.

At the same time the inability of Dáil Éireann to give meaningful financial support to the city exposed the fragility of the dual-power strategy and added to personal tensions.

At the height of the crisis Cosgrave chided Collins for failing to attend a meeting with corporation councillors and officials. 'There was a suspicion that we were not getting any assistance from An Dáil,' he wrote. Collins replied tartly:

I should have thought my absence from an interview at the gate of Dublin Castle would not need very much explaining, and if the Members of the Committee think they are not getting any assistance from the Dáil, I am sorry for people who have such minds as to make a view point like this possible.

Access to banking finance allowed the corporation to contemplate a start on slum clearance. During the war a handful of small developments had been completed, mainly in the south inner city, with the assistance of the former Chief Secretary, Henry Duke, who was appalled at conditions in the tenements. However, the new scheme would be mired in controversy when it emerged that the largest site bought by the corporation had been owned by Alderman Patrick Corrigan, one of the biggest slum landlords in the city. It paid £10,000 for his twenty-two acres at Fairbrother's Fields, just south of the Dublin Union, which already had open space available for housing. The generosity of the old home-rule corporation to one of its own was revealed in 1920 when the Housing Committee considered acquiring a 39-acre site at Killester owned by the Lord of Howth. It was valued at £3,500, much less than Corrigan received, even before allowing for wartime inflation.

In 1915 Corrigan had been able to hide his identity as the beneficial owner behind the ground landlord, the Earl of Meath.[7] As a result of the revelation the new corporation passed a motion requiring members to declare an interest in any property that was insanitary or 'being considered for acquisition' in future. While the initiative for this was taken by P. T. Daly, leader of the Trades Council Labour group, J. Hubbard Clark of the Municipal Reform Association proposed an amendment that broadened and strengthened the motion. When it came to municipal reform, champions of the business and unionist interests in the city were as zealous as any Labour or Sinn Féin representative. Unfortunately the report was not published until 1923, when it was revealed that the Lord Mayor, Laurence O'Neill, another independent nationalist, Alderman William O'Connor, and Councillor James Moran (MRA) also owned

slum tenements. But the biggest surprise was Alderman Thomas Patrick
O'Reilly of the Republican Labour group, who not only owned more tenements
than anyone else but had been served with notice to carry out extensive repairs
to roofs, floors and windows 'and provide adequate sanitary accommodation.'
Daly was probably well aware of the connection at the time and no doubt hoped
to embarrass William O'Brien by his motion.[8]

Because of lack of funds, Fairbrother's Fields had been handed over to the
Dublin Vacant Lot Cultivation Society during the war for growing vegetables.
In 1920 the new corporation managed to secure an extension of the deadline
by which work must begin to be eligible for LGB funds. Further progress was
stymied because funds for building the houses also had to come through the
LGB, until the prospect of bank loans opened up.

Yet new delays arose immediately over naming the streets. Now that Great
Brunswick Street was to be renamed Pearse Street, language enthusiasts in Sinn
Féin proposed that streets in the new housing developments should carry the
names of national martyrs as well. There was a precedent in housing
developments for which the LGB had already sanctioned funds at St James's Walk
and in the McCaffrey estate beside the Dublin Union, which bore the names of
Irish Volunteers who died in 1916. A further refinement of the process was that
each of the new streets should bear the Irish version of the names selected.[9]

Inevitably some councillors wished to declare their approval for this motion
in Irish, and equally inevitably the Town Clerk, Henry Campbell, refused to
accept their votes as valid. Nor, he informed councillors, would contributions
to the debate in Irish be recorded. Previous confrontations between Campbell
and Irish-speakers still rankled. Councillor John Forrestal (Sinn Féin) moved
a series of motions in English to force the Town Clerk's hand. These included
proposals that, in future, correspondence received by the corporation in Irish
would be replied to in Irish, that the corporation chequebook be replaced with
a new one in Irish, with appropriate typefaces and designs, and finally that the
roll-call for councillors attending meetings or voting at meetings be recorded
in Irish as well as English, with 'Bíodh' for 'Aye' and 'Ná bíodh' for 'Nay'. As the
motions were with reference to future business rather than that immediately
in hand, they constituted a declaration of war rather than the outbreak of
hostilities.

Other, more practical measures taken at the meeting to implement Sinn Féin
policy included endorsement of the Belfast boycott, adoption of the new Dáil
Éireann Ministry of Labour system of Conciliation and Arbitration Boards for
resolving industrial and trade disputes, and adoption of a Dáil Éireann decree
on new rent schedules for corporation tenants.

It was agreed that the cost of running the new Ministry of Labour bodies would be borne by the ratepayers, most of whom were businessmen and employers. In a very public acceptance of the new order, the sole surviving unionist councillor, William McCarthy, proposed that the conciliation and arbitration system set up by Dáil Éireann's Ministry of Labour be used for dealing with proposed fare increases by the Dublin United Tramways Company, a proposal that received enthusiastic cross-party support. Nor was there disagreement with a proposal from P. T. Daly early in 1921 that the corporation examine the possibility of the 'municipalisation' of the DUTC. There was an option in the legislation for a corporation takeover, but it was discovered that this could not be exercised until 1948.

On the other hand, the setting of rents for local authority tenants resulted in members being divided along party lines. There was a consensus that rents must rise to take account of inflation and ease the burden on the rates during the current financial crisis; however, opinions diverged on how much of that burden the tenants could bear. Without increases, the ratepayers would have to provide a subsidy of £56,000, equivalent to a quarter of the shortfall in the LGB subsidy. The increases sanctioned were relatively modest. For instance, in the case of the largest development, Corporation Buildings in Foley Street, which had 376 dwellings and where rents in 1914 were between 1s and 1s 6d a week, the increases were to 1s 3d and 1s 10d, respectively. Altogether, the rent increases agreed for corporation tenants would save 1s 2d in the pound for the ratepayer.

Because of the financial crisis, further cuts had to be agreed to those sanctioned in July. These still only achieved a reduction of £175,524 in expenditure. In some areas, such as the treatment of TB, the budget was cut by 40 per cent and in housing by over 80 per cent. A series of measures was agreed, ranging from the imaginative to the radical and the desperate. It was agreed, for instance, to sell more than £25,000 in railway investment stock, including £15,800 in GSWR shares. Dr McWalter and his MRA colleagues protested, not unreasonably, that it was bad timing to sell railway stock in the middle of a munitions strike and the end of the post-war boom. P. T. Daly proposed that the corporation sell its 'pictures and other paraphernalia of, or from, British Kings and their representatives' at public auction, but this proved impossible, as most were held in trust. Another radical measure, which was agreed, involved diverting £5,000 voted for beginning work on the Marine Promenade at Clontarf 'to the use of the Housing committee for the purpose of building houses for the working classes.' This was moved by Councillor Michael Dowling (Sinn Féin), who had proposed that the corporation recognise Dáil Éireann. Being specific to one electoral area, it produced some interesting cross-party voting and was passed by only 21 votes to 18. Seventeen Sinn Féin representatives voted for it, along with three Labour (Trades Council) councillors and one independent. The only councillor representing a Clontarf ward who voted for the proposal was John Farren (Trades Council Labour), who lived at Blackhall Place in the north inner city; every other member representing Clontarf, including the three Sinn Féin councillors, voted against.[10] The MRA and Republican Labour were the only groups to vote *en bloc* against diverting the funds. So, surprisingly, did Hanna Sheehy Skeffington, who represented South City ward.

There were also increases in charges for services, such as fees on beds for the treatment of infectious diseases at Cork Street Fever Hospital. The rate rose from 4s a day to 5s. Budgets were reduced for other services, such as the treatment of sexually transmitted disease. Both cuts were advocated by Jennie Wyse Power and Anne Elizabeth Ashton, Sinn Féin councillors. On the other hand, another Sinn Féin councillor, Hanna Sheehy Skeffington, who had put the construction of the Clontarf promenade before 'housing for the working classes,' managed to persuade colleagues not to close three public libraries—although corporation scholarships for academically bright working-class children were halved. Strong opposition to library closures was voiced by the newly founded James Connolly Labour College, which provided adult education for trade unionists. Its submission had the backing of the Labour councillors, who stressed the importance of the library service for self-improvement.[11]

In some respects these debates represented the normalisation of local politics and an implicit acceptance of the new order by unionists in the city and by traditional home-rulers through their joint surrogate, the MRA. By the same token, in seeking to balance the interests of ratepayers and tenants, and to reconcile the conflicting interests of different constituencies, Sinn Féin was reinforcing its claim to political legitimacy.

A couple of weeks later the new regime received a tribute from an unexpected quarter when Sir Andrew Beattie, addressing the Dublin Rotary Club on 'Civic Finance', admitted that

> the present Corporation is a better Corporation than the old one. The present body is an honest, straightforward one, trying to do its best … I admire the work of the present Sinn Féin party … there is no jobbery and I venture to say that if they could keep their finances going for some time to come, the rates of the city would soon become quite normal.[12]

Not that the struggle for independence was being neglected. In the same communication that asked the corporation to use the new Dáil Éireann arbitration machinery the Minister for Labour, Constance Markievicz, appealed for assistance in finding positions for members of the RIC who had resigned rather than implement the new repressive policies. This was circulated to all the relevant corporation committees, but there is no evidence that action was taken. There were few enough jobs for Dubliners, and these were the subject of intense lobbying.[13]

Meanwhile the war of wills between the Sinn Féin and Republican Labour majority on the corporation and the Town Clerk, Henry Campbell, continued. It completely dominated the quarterly meeting on 4 October, despite far graver problems, such as the threatened closure of the TB sanatoriums, which, as Alderman Tom Lawlor pointed out, would result in the spread of the disease 'among the citizens of Dublin, especially the poorer classes.'

The renewed clash arose out of a vote on pay increases for staff in the Electricity Supply Department. The motion was defeated by 21 votes to 11. Councillor Forrestal, the Sinn Féin member who in September had pushed through the motions on the greater use of Irish, said that, as there were far more members present than votes recorded, he wanted to know how many had voted in Irish. Campbell replied that he and his officials were governed by the standing orders and statutes, which required that votes be taken in English, to which Forrestal's response was that the corporation 'had declared their allegiance to Dáil Éireann, and if there was anything against that in standing orders the standing orders must go overboard.' Alderman Cosgrave said that Irish 'was not going to be proscribed in Dublin,' while an old adversary of Campbell's, Jennie Wyse Power, pointed out that votes had been recorded in Irish during his absence. Dr McWalter and Sir Andrew Beattie of the MRA strongly supported the Town Clerk's right to abide by standing orders, as did P. T. Daly, leader of the Trades Council faction of Labour.

When the dominant Sinn Féin-Republican Labour group insisted on another vote, Campbell recorded it as far as the first declaration in Irish, by Alderman Michael Staines. He then retired, and his assistant, John Flood, was ordered to take the vote, only to retire as well. The Law Agent, Ignatius Rice, refused to carry out the duty, as it was not in his remit, and no official in the Town Clerk's department could be found to deputise for Campbell. Councillor Forrestal was then deputed to record the vote.

The Lord Mayor, Laurence O'Neill, said he wanted to

protest in the strongest possible manner against the position in which the Council has today been placed by the officials of the Corporation. By a unanimous voice of the Council, a resolution was passed at the last meeting that the votes of the representatives of the people here should be recorded in Irish. We now find that the language of our country is to be trampled upon by our officials, and it is up to us to see that, if every official of the Corporation leaves us, we are then going to discharge our own business. [Applause.]

The situation continued to deteriorate over the following weeks when Campbell and Flood sought to avoid the consequences of the corporation's resolutions to boycott the LGB. On 2 November, when the LGB auditor, Cyril Browne, arrived at the City Treasurer's offices to collect the accounts he was told that Edmund Eyre was 'indisposed' and given a letter signed by a junior official, 'by direction of the Right Hon. the Lord Mayor.' It stated that the matter was due for consideration by a committee of the whole house. Campbell had refused to write the letter and told Browne that the Lord Mayor and Corporation were acting illegally. In doing so he handed the LGB man all the evidence needed to seek a writ of *mandamus* (compelling officials to perform their duties correctly) from the courts.[14]

At the monthly meeting of the corporation two days later, 4 November, Alderman William O'Brien (Republican Labour) proposed that Campbell and Flood be suspended for co-operating with 'the English Local Government Board' auditor in his efforts to examine the corporation's financial records. Predictably, both officials refused to record the votes cast in Irish for suspending them, but the motion was passed anyway, by 26 votes to 12. The MRA councillors voted against the suspensions; so did Daly and the Trades Council Labour councillors.

The vote of the MRA members is easily understood. As McWalter pointed out, the issues involved thousands of pounds, and the financial health of the corporation was in jeopardy. Significantly, neither McWalter nor Beattie made a direct attack on the use of Irish. As a former member of the IRB and Sinn Féin, Daly could hardly do so either; but personal friendship, or at least mutual respect built over a long number of years working with Campbell, probably influenced him, as well as natural antipathy towards anything William O'Brien was proposing. And, like the MRA councillors, Daly and his Trades Council colleagues would have been more anxious to maintain services for the city than to fight over the Irish language.[15]

One of Daly's major initiatives, the establishment of a new treatment centre to combat the epidemic of sexually transmitted disease, was among the projects at serious risk from budget cuts. It relied for three-quarters of its funding on the LGB, and expenditure in the year ending 31 March 1921 was expected to reach £5,000 rather than the £3,000 budgeted for. The number of patients, particularly women, showed that these diseases were now a serious health threat to the city, but the service had fallen foul of the battle of conflicting allegiances.

Cases of STD treated at Dr Steevens' Hospital, 1919–20

	31 March 1919		31 March 1920	
	Men	Women	Men	Women
Attendance at out-patient clinics	452	59	2,298	529
Aggregate in-patient treatments	231	143	1,296	292

Source: Dublin Corporation, Report No. 152, vol. 2, 1920.

Relations between the Town Clerk, his assistant and the councillors continued to deteriorate rapidly. By 15 November the naturally cautious W. T. Cosgrave felt he had no option but to propose that the corporation 'dispense with the services' of the Town Clerk and Assistant Town Clerk. One of the officials in their office, Michael J. Walsh, who had signed the letter to the LGB auditor on behalf of the Lord Mayor, was directed to act *pro tem* until new appointments could be made. O'Neill had long since lost patience with Campbell and Flood, but he told councillors he had been advised by the Law Agent that the proceedings were illegal. To further confuse matters, both Campbell and Flood had sent in letters of resignation the previous day, only to withdraw them.

The actions of the Town Clerk and his deputy are understandable in the light of the confrontation with the LGB. The legal millstones were grinding inexorably closer to City Hall. Neither could serve two masters. For Campbell, a man of considerable private means but with a substantial pension at risk, the personal stakes were high. His attitude towards Irish is less easy to understand, as was his tendency to lock horns with such members as William O'Brien, Hanna Sheehy Skeffington and Jennie Wyse Power. Subsequent events suggest that Campbell had already decided that his interests and loyalties lay elsewhere. However, when he wrote his letter of resignation he discovered that he was already the subject of a High Court writ of conditional *mandamus* directing him to produce the corporation's documents. In fact he was the only individual named in the writ. Therefore he had to withdraw the resignation, and he declared he would fight any dismissal in the courts, by which of course he meant the British courts.

The IRA, however, came to everybody's rescue. When the case came before the Lord Chief Justice, Sir James Campbell, in December he was told of an unexpected development. In a sworn affidavit the chief bookkeeper of the Estates and Finance Section of the City Accountant's office, Matthew H. de Courcy, said that shortly before 1 p.m. on Saturday 20 November, as the staff prepared to leave, a group of armed men entered the office, menaced them with revolvers, and took away all the accounts. (See chapter 8 below.) De Courcy 'had never seen any of them before or since. They had no authority from the Corporation or the City Accountant to remove the books and vouchers.' This had happened just before the conditional order of *mandamus* had been served. An affidavit by the City Accountant, Henry Mangan, stated that he did not think it possible to carry out an audit until the accounts had been recovered, while the auditor, Cyril Browne, said he was not aware of any decision by the corporation not to make the records available as required by the order. The question of another writ of *mandamus* was put back for judgement.[16]

It says something for the urgency of the crisis facing the corporation that the raid took place on the eve of Bloody Sunday, when suspected British intelligence agents would be shot at different locations around the city by the IRA in a carefully planned coup. As Henry Campbell had repeatedly warned the corporation that he would not defy the courts if they granted a writ of *mandamus* for the accounts, the obvious solution was for the IRA to seize them on behalf of the rival jurisdiction in a city where power was now contested on the streets rather than in the courts.

If IRA attacks in Dublin were on a smaller scale than in rural areas, they made up for it in frequency and in ferocity. Volunteers used crowds as camouflage to get close to enemy targets. A good example was on 29 July 1920, when three military police patrols converged on College Green before returning to Ship Street Barracks. Volunteers managed to approach one patrol of three soldiers outside Trinity College and another group of three soldiers at the corner of Westmorland Street, without being spotted, and disarmed both groups. The third patrol, however, consisting of five soldiers outside the Bank of Ireland, saw the Volunteers approach and, taking cover behind the pillars of the bank, opened fire. The Volunteers replied, and civilians scattered in all directions as the brief gunfight left three soldiers wounded. The IRA Volunteers made off with six captured revolvers.

Similar tactics were used to close with motorised patrols. Cages for Crossley tenders were introduced to prevent hand grenades being lobbed into them. Surprisingly, the IRA never tried to petrol-bomb these vehicles. Armour plating was fixed to the sides of the tenders to guard against gunfire and grenade shrapnel. Body armour was issued to drivers. The extra weight of the tenders was not the problem on Dublin's roads that it proved on country roads. Tanks were also used from time to time, especially in support of foot patrols and security cordons, but their movement was hampered by narrow laneways and the city's bridges, many of which could not take their weight. Relatively few armoured cars were used in Dublin, but the arrival of five new Peerless vehicles in December 1920 to supplement ageing Rolls-Royce models 'were invaluable' for giving protection to convoys and raiding parties. The military found the vehicles 'practically unstoppable'. Their only disadvantage was a noisy engine, which gave the enemy early warning of their arrival.

Unlike the countryside, there were relatively few attempts to dig up roads or damage bridges, an activity that played a major role in hobbling military operations in rural Ireland. Among the few exceptions were the Dublin Mountains and parts of south Co. Dublin, such as Foxrock and Dundrum. Communities could find themselves isolated for days until repairs were carried out. However, local Volunteers were sometimes accommodating, as when they agreed to move a trench they were digging in 1920 outside Sir Horace Plunkett's house at Foxrock to facilitate his daily drive into the Co-Operative Society offices in the city.[17]

Worse still were raids for arms, which were a constant hazard. On 9 September 1920 forty houses in Kingstown, Killiney, Glenageary, Glasthule, Blackrock, Dalkey, Sandycove, Monkstown and Bray belonging to members of the gentry and police and army officers, retired and still active, were raided. They included the residence of Sir Horace Plunkett's land steward.[18] The British military authorities were well aware of the problem, and efforts were made from time to time to encourage the owners of legally held weapons to surrender them.

More importantly, the British command structures for Dublin had been upgraded since the beginning of the year, from brigade to divisional status. The 24th Brigade was made responsible for the city and county north of the Liffey along with Co. Meath, and the 25th Brigade was responsible for the city south of the Liffey, south Co. Dublin and parts of Co. Wicklow. While this meant more troops on the ground, many of them were raw recruits; some had not even undergone a musketry course.[19]

Incredibly, Dublin Castle had closed the military intelligence office, run by Temporary Major Ivon Price, when the war ended and he returned to his duties as an RIC inspector. Thereafter the British army relied on the DMP for intelligence. By February 1920 the Dublin command had realised that G Division was a broken reed, and it set up its own organisation.[20] It had a breakthrough in the same month when the headquarters of the IRA Chief of Staff, Richard Mulcahy, was discovered at Cullenswood House in Ranelagh, where Pearse's school, St Enda's, had moved after the Rising. Mulcahy escaped, but not his files, which included the names and addresses of thousands of Volunteers throughout the country.[21] This valuable if somewhat unwieldy data was supplemented by information received from army raiding parties. The Cullenswood haul enabled the military to undertake widespread raids in the city during the following couple of months, although relatively few senior IRA activists were lifted, as they rarely slept at home.

Considerable military resources in the city were absorbed by crowd control in April during the mass protests in support of the Mountjoy hunger-strikers. In May the munitions strike put another disproportionate burden on the Dublin garrison. Soldiers were required to unload and guard military supplies to meet not just their own needs but those of other Crown forces in Ireland. They even had to provide escorts for military units from other districts passing through the capital. While the logic behind providing protection for battalion-sized combat units is not explained in the British army's own historical record of the campaign, it may have been to avoid over-reaction by these units to any IRA attacks or to public demonstrations of hostility. Incidents similar to that at Bachelor's Walk in 1914, when dozens of civilians were killed or injured, were to be studiously avoided.

Static guard duty on important buildings was another drain on mobile reserves. It was estimated by the Dublin command that four hundred men were tied up each day on such duties, quite apart from guards on the main barracks and the escorts required to accompany the few trains carrying military supplies to other parts of the country.

Inevitably, the Dublin garrison served as part of a general reserve, and troops could even be redeployed to Britain. The 2nd Battalion of the Duke of Wellington's Regiment was despatched to Belfast to help deal with disturbances in April and sent to England in May in relation to the coalminers' strike. Overall responsibility for maintaining communications in Ireland was another duty that devolved on the Dublin garrison. Besides telephone, telegraph and wireless services it looked after carrier pigeons. These were housed in a loft at Dublin Castle. Railwaymen did not object to transporting the birds and, much to the surprise of the military, no pigeons were shot or poisoned by the IRA.[22]

The Restoration of Order (Ireland) Act, introduced on 13 August 1920, gave the military extensive new powers. It underpinned the primacy of the army for all practical purposes. The collection of information on the IRA now rested firmly with the army rather than the DMP. A plain-clothes Dublin District unit of the Special Branch was established under Lieutenant-Colonel Walter Wilson, a former English rugby international who made up in drive what he lacked in expertise. The increasing passivity of DMP members on military patrols to maintain the fiction that the troops were acting in aid of the civil power made army officers complain at having to carry 'passengers'.

In October 1920 members of the DMP approached Collins for protection from retaliation for participating in these raids. Collins sent Jeremiah Mee, the former RIC constable who led the Listowel mutiny, to meet them. They asked Mee for assurances that, if they stopped carrying arms, participating in military raids and identifying Volunteers for the military, they would no longer be targets. Collins provided the assurances sought, and attacks on the uniformed branch of the DMP ceased.[23] So did their value to the British forces.

If the DMP was a spent force, the army certainly felt it benefited from the arrival of F Company of the Auxiliaries in May. Although administratively part of the RIC, this unit was placed under the operational control of the General Officer Commanding Dublin District, Major-General Gerald Boyd, and was quartered in Dublin Castle. In November two extra companies, I and J, arrived and were allocated to the 24th and 25th Brigades, respectively. These were subsequently rotated with N, C and R Companies. Whatever Dubliners or the British liberal press thought of them, the Dublin District military command concluded that 'the work of the Auxiliaries in Dublin was excellent, and the happiest relations existed between them and the troops.'[24]

The commander of the Auxiliaries, Brigadier-General Frank Crozier, was less generous in his assessment and would ultimately resign in protest when the government refused to support his efforts to impose discipline. However, he attributed some of their problems not just to a lack of adequate command structures and poor discipline but to the failure of the authorities to provide elementary services, such as canteens. His superior and paramilitary supremo, General Hugh Tudor, had no qualms about the men under his command; nor had the man appointed Deputy Chief of Police and Director of Intelligence, Colonel Ormonde de l'Epée Winter.

Winter's arrival marked the re-entry of Dublin Castle to the intelligence war. Like Tudor and Crozier, he was part of a new team introduced by Greenwood and his Under-Secretary, Sir John Anderson, to make Ireland 'hellish' for rebels. Winter was almost a caricature of a spy. He cultivated an air of mystery, liked to be known as O, wore a monocle rather than glasses, was captivated by the cloak-and-dagger tricks of the trade, enjoyed the good life and made up for his lack of a moral compass by dividing the world into enemies and friends—some of the enemies inevitably on his own side. One of the latter appears to have been the head of Dublin military intelligence, Walter Wilson, who eventually resigned rather than continue working under Winter. His successor enjoyed equally bad relations with him.[25]

A much-decorated officer, Winter, like many war heroes, had a penchant for violence. He had been acquitted as a young man of the manslaughter of a boy who had thrown stones at his boat, and this seems to have rubbed off on subordinates, who were mainly former army officers or young serving officers on secondment or liaising between their own units and Winter's operatives. Such activities inevitably attracted a disreputable tail of touts, including unemployed Irish emigrants in Britain attracted home by easy money.

Meanwhile G Division of the DMP was moved to Dublin Castle, where one of Collins's spies, David Neligan, said it seemed that 'the British flooded the place with secret service men.' He was not mistaken: Winter later recounted employing almost a hundred agents in the office of the Dublin Military District alone. While a significant number appear to have been from a loyalist background, unionists and respectable citizens generally steered well clear of Winter's menagerie, a task made easier by the latter's tendency to patronise select cafés and bars in the city, where, inevitably, some of those they encountered were IRA intelligence officers anxious to get a look at their new enemy.[26]

The IRA's intelligence operations in the city had already been transformed by Michael Collins and were managed without the internecine warfare that affected their British counterpart. An intelligence office was set up above J. F. Fowler's printing works at 3 Crow Street in the heart of the city's commercial district, half way between the Bank of Ireland and Dublin Castle. Collins tended to avoid calling there, relying on one of his closest assistants, Joe O'Reilly, to liaise with Tobin's team. As intelligence operations increased, a second office was opened at 5 Mespil Road, another impeccably respectable venue, which Collins favoured. Although he frequently initiated and undertook projects, Collins's activities augmented rather than superseded those of Tobin as Deputy Director of Intelligence. Tobin had a clearly defined chain of command, with brigade intelligence officers reporting to him and his subordinates. Much of the work was routine and systematic, allowing the IRA to build a picture of the enemy that was more comprehensive than that constructed by the British of the IRA. One advantage the IRA enjoyed was that so much of the enemy's activities, including the appointment of officers and officials, addresses and transfers of units, were in the public domain. This was supplemented by information from members and sympathisers in the postal and telegraph services. By contrast, British military intelligence and Winter had great difficulty putting names and faces on the enemy's order of battle.

What the British had, on the other hand, was overwhelming superiority in conventional military force. The application of rigorous and continuous raiding was the most effective way of simultaneously harrying and collecting information on the enemy. In August 1920 a Raid Bureau was set up to co-ordinate this important activity, and Winter claimed that between then and the Truce, in July 1921, 6,311 raids were carried out in the Dublin district, an average of nearly nineteen a day.[27] Unfortunately it was also an important contributory factor in further alienating the civilian population.

Like its intelligence system, the IRA's battalion structure in the city remained relatively unchanged during the War of Independence. The army had been reorganised after the Rising. The process began under Richard Mulcahy and was continued by Dick McKee, who took over the Dublin Brigade on Mulcahy's election as Chief of Staff. Mulcahy always gave priority to Dublin, as it was 'by far the most important Military Area in Ireland.' He believed that 'the grip of our forces in Dublin must be maintained and strengthened at all costs.' Lacking the opportunities to disrupt communications or to carry out large-scale operations that existed in rural areas, the Dublin Brigade believed that the best way of inhibiting British army movements in the city was constant small-scale actions and the threat of attack. By May 1920 most of the city centre, the inner-city tenement areas and even such suburbs as Fairview, Inchicore and Glasnevin had been classified as dangerous by the British and were entered only in force. Without such constraints, many activities of Dáil Éireann and the operation of its alternative state structures would not have been possible. There was the bonus that attacks on British forces in the capital registered more forcefully with British public opinion and the international press. The curfew, the constant presence of troops on the streets and fortified public buildings presented a constant image of a government under siege.

The good working relations between McKee, Mulcahy and Collins played a crucial role in ensuring that additions to organisational structures, such as the creation of the Squad and active service units, were implemented relatively smoothly. It also facilitated the easing out of 1916 veterans who had scruples about employing the mafia-style killings that replaced the more conventional tactics of the Rising. Frank Henderson, who took over the 2nd Battalion from McKee, referred to 'some sincere men who refused to take part in street ambushes. They had to retire.'[28] These included quite a number of older Volunteers, who had to make serious choices about whether to put the movement or increasing family commitments first. Many a husband who went off with a few sandwiches for a route march on Easter Monday 1916 and did not return for six months now found himself under house arrest outside working hours.

By the summer of 1920 the emphasis of the Squad's activities had switched from G Division of the DMP, whose members were now largely quiescent, if not active agents of the IRA, to military intelligence, to Winter's agents and even to political opponents of the regime. Nevertheless, the attack on the Right Honourable Francis H. Brooke, a director of the Dublin Board of the Bank of Ireland and chairman of the Dublin and South-Eastern Railway Company, on Friday 30 July surprised as much as it shocked the business community.

The previous day Dublin Chamber of Commerce had passed what for it was a revolutionary resolution, calling on the government 'to give a pledge in Parliament to concede a measure of complete self-government for Ireland, subject only to the restrictions ... that Ireland should remain within the Empire and that Ulster should not be coerced.' There was implicit criticism of British government policy as well as that of the new Republic when it condemned 'the crimes and reprisals which are rapidly making life intolerable in Ireland.' The conflict 'gravely imperils all industrial and commercial interests. It is obvious that peace and contentment can only be secured by a change in the form of government.' It pointedly rejected the latest Government of Ireland Bill, which had tinkered with the 1914 settlement and 'does not meet with the approval of any section' of the community.[29]

The chamber's position was strongly endorsed by the *Irish Times*, which contrasted renewed assurances from the Prime Minister that law and order would be restored with the disarming of military police patrols by the IRA a few yards from its own offices. 'The truth is that, apart from a political settlement, law can be restored only by military operations on a big scale.' The paper recognised that 'the Government's hands are tied by the sentiment of the English people—especially of English Labour'—and that 'the Government must consider its military resources in relation to the disturbed conditions of Europe as a whole.' But when the government spoke of law and order

loyal Irishmen find exasperation rather than comfort in the words.

These circumstances explain the resolution of the Council of the Dublin Chamber. It is a startling resolution: two years ago—one year ago— it would have been impossible ... The Legislative Union, which these men championed so sturdily in the past has been killed by the secession of North East Ulster.

The Victory Parade on 1 August 1919 was the last great demonstration of imperial power, but thousands of Irish ex-servicemen refused to participate, and only one member of Dublin Corporation, Surgeon-Captain James McWalter, accepted an invitation to attend. That evening serious rioting occurred in which two policemen and several members of the British armed forces were seriously injured. In one incident Sinn Féin supporters were led by Australian soldiers awaiting repatriation and demobilisation. (© *RTE Stills Library*)

A rare Irish cartoon in praise of British rule. Here the *Sunday Independent* welcomes the intervention of the Board of Trade to prevent profiteering by Dublin coal merchants. (*Courtesy of the National Library of Ireland*)

Mountjoy Ward Municipal Election
15th JANUARY, 1920.

STRIKE A BLOW FOR

IRISH INDEPENDENCE

BY SUPPORTING THE FOLLOWING

SINN FEIN AND LABOUR CANDIDATES

BYRNE, JOHN, Electrician, 582 North Circular Road.

CLARKE, KATHLEEN, Richmond Ave., Fairview (Widow of late Tom Clarke, who was executed Easter, 1916).

O'SHEA-LEAMY, LILLIE, Shopkeeper, 78a Summerhill.

MAHON, PATRICK, Printer, 71 Summerhill (Chairman City of Dublin Technical Education Committee).

O'MAOILFHINN, JAMES, Provision Merchant, 107 Summerhill.

SLATER, MICHAEL, Brass Finisher, 41 Summerhill Parade (President Brassfounders' Society).

TOOMEY, JOSEPH, Engineer, 31 Clonliffe Avenue (Member Amalgamated Society of Engineers).

THE ABOVE CANDIDATES ARE PLEDGED TO CARRY OUT THE SINN FEIN MUNICIPAL PROGRAMME:—

(1) TO SECURE THE EXPENDITURE INSIDE IRELAND OF THE RATES RAISED IN IRELAND.

(2) TO SECURE EFFICIENCY AND PURITY OF ADMINISTRATION.

(3) TO ESTABLISH THE PRINCIPLE OF FREE AND OPEN COMPETITION FOR PUBLIC APPOINTMENTS.

(4) TO CARRY INTO EFFECT THE DEMOCRATIC PROGRAMME APPROVED BY THE ELECTED REPRESENTATIVES OF IRELAND.

Vote Early and Solid for this Republican Ticket.

DIA SAOIR ÉIRE.

[IRISH PAPER.]   [TRADE UNION LABOUR.

'Strike a Blow for Irish Independence by supporting Sinn Fein and Labour candidates,' proclaims this poster for the municipal elections in January 1920. It even states that it was printed by 'Trade Union Labour,' but all the candidates listed are Sinn Féin members. Four are indeed trade unionists and at least two of these, Michael Slater and Joseph Toomey, are IRB members. The Labour Party was widely regarded by craft workers as representing general labourers and the low-paid. (*Courtesy of the National Library of Ireland*)

City Hall with the Tricolour flying over it was a symbol of defiance on Dublin Castle's doorstep. (© *Bettmann/Corbis*)

From big-game hunting in Africa to banking in Dublin, Andrew Jameson brought determination and a willingness to take risks. He advanced loans to Dublin Corporation during the War of Independence when 'nationalist' banks shied away and was heavily involved in opening peace negotiations between Éamon de Valera and David Lloyd George. However, he naïvely believed that the 'Welsh Wizard' would protect Southern unionist interests in the Treaty negotiations. (*Courtesy of the Bank of Ireland*)

Crowds trampled down barbed-wire barricades outside Mountjoy Prison during the 1920 hunger strike. At one stage RAF planes flew at rooftop level to drive back the crowds, but British Government resolve collapsed when faced with the prospect of prisoners dying. (© *Bettmann/Corbis*)

British troops regularly occupied rooftops when large military contingents passed through Dublin in order to reduce the risk of sniping or ambushes. (© *Bettmann/Corbis*)

Mobile checkpoints were one of the most effective means of disrupting IRA activities, but they could be dangerous places for civilians. It was at a checkpoint near this one that the accidental discharge of a rifle dropped by a British soldier led to two civilians being killed and seven wounded in January 1920, when soldiers thought they had come under attack from gunmen in the crowd. (© *Bettmann/Corbis*)

The American Relief Commission see the results of the Auxiliaries' activities in Balbriggan after the fatal shooting of Head Constable Peter Burke. (*Courtesy of the National Library of Ireland*)

Middle-class schoolboys
collect money for
Republican prisoners, an
eminently respectable
activity in 1920 Dublin.
(© *Bettmann/Corbis*)

Coming just a week after the death of Terence MacSwiney in Brixton Prison, the execution of Kevin Barry on 1 November 1920 in Mountjoy was another political debacle. Young, brave and handsome, the new martyr appealed on many levels to the nationalist populace, especially women. Here crowds recite the Rosary, inadvertently demonstrating the growing Catholic ethos attached to the independence struggle. (© *Bettmann/Corbis*)

The coffins of British officers killed on Bloody Sunday being loaded on the destroyer *Sea Wolf* in November 1920. (© *Getty Images*)

Members of the Dublin Brigade at the funerals of Dick McKee and Peadar Clancy, a demonstration of strength made possible because thousands of British soldiers were attending the funeral of British officers and RIC members killed on Bloody Sunday. (© Underwood & Underwood/Corbis)

After Bloody Sunday the Auxiliaries systematically wrecked Liberty Hall, rendering it unusable by the Irish Transport and General Workers' Union or its Republican allies. They took anything of value, including the band's instruments. (© RTE *Stills Library*)

The sudden arrival of Crown forces could ignite panic, as evidenced by this raid in Abbey Street in January 1921. Nervous soldiers frequently ignored standing orders that restricted the circumstances in which they could open fire on civilians, while the Auxiliaries were a law unto themselves. (© *Getty Images*)

Auxiliaries in
buoyant mood
after the failure
of one of several
attacks on their
base at the LNWR
Hotel on the
North Wall.
(*Courtesy of the
National Library
of Ireland*)

Belfast refugees elicited sympathy at first, but proposals to rehouse them in Dublin were quickly rejected in a city that could not provide decent accommodation for its own citizens. They were advised instead to 'stand their ground' at home. (© *Bettmann/Corbis*)

The mother of Thomas Whelan being comforted by Maud Gonne outside Mountjoy Prison after she had seen her son for the last time. She said of his demeanour: 'You would imagine he was going to see a football match.' Note her traditional clothes, which underlined the large cultural gap between the capital and the impoverished West, which many advanced nationalists idealised. (© *Getty Images*)

Despite failing health, the Catholic Archbishop of Dublin, Dr William Walsh (centre), continued to exercise a powerful influence on his clergy, his flock and a new generation of Irish politicians. He was arguably the ablest Irish political strategist of his era. His secretary, Michael Curran (*left*), had to resign after refusing to condemn IRA tactics in a press interview. Walsh secured him the post of vice-rector of the Irish College in Rome. (*Courtesy of the National Library of Ireland*)

A phalanx of priests leads the funeral procession of Archbishop William Walsh. His funeral, which he probably planned himself, was a massive demonstration of clerical power. No representatives of the British government were allowed to attend, and Irish Volunteers provided the stewards needed to manage the estimated crowd of 200,000 mourners. (*Courtesy of the National Library of Ireland*)

'The stupidest thing the Sinn Fein ever did' was the verdict of Sir Henry Robinson, vice-president of the Local Government Board on the Custom House attack. He led a charmed life, leaving the building to award trophies at the LGB golf tournament at Dollymount five minutes before the IRA arrived. The prisoners contained many members of the Active Service Unit and Volunteers from the 2nd Battalion of the Dublin Brigade. (*Courtesy of the National Library of Ireland*)

Auxiliaries collecting weapons at the Custom House after their battle with the IRA. A DMP sergeant assists while firefighters look on. Several members of the Dublin Fire Brigade were Volunteers, and relations with the British forces were always strained. (*Courtesy of the National Library of Ireland*)

'He hath delivered my soul in peace from the battle that was against me.' The sacrifices of the Dublin unionist community in the First World War were commemorated in several freshly commissioned stained-glass windows for the city's churches. Few possess the pathos of this panel by Ethel Rhind in the nave of St Ann's, Dawson Street. (*Courtesy of St Ann's Select Vestry*)

The crowds outside the Mansion House during the Truce talks in July 1921 gave a warm welcome to the leader of the Southern unionist representatives, Lord Midleton, and his colleagues. (© *Bettmann/Corbis*)

Lawrence O'Neill, Lord Mayor of Dublin (centre), was the only member of the first Irish peace delegation to London who was not a member of Sinn Féin. This was a very public tribute to the role of the city and its chief magistrate in the War of Independence. The other figures in the photograph (from left to right) are Arthur Griffith, Robert Barton, Count Plunkett and Éamon de Valera. (*Courtesy of the National Library of Ireland*)

If the present Home Rule Bill becomes law, it will doom three-fourths of Ireland to Crown Colony government, enforced by a permanent Army of Occupation—in other words to a permanent state of guerrilla warfare.

Referring to the Council of the Chamber of Commerce, the *Times* supposed 'that the majority of them are still Unionists,' but they had been forced to recognise 'that the issue is no longer between Union and Home Rule, but between any tolerable form of government and no government at all.'

The shooting of Brooke was appallingly timed, in the light of the Chamber of Commerce's revised view of the political situation; that it was the first overtly political assassination of a member of the unionist community in Dublin made it all the worse. He had been relaxing in his office at Westland Row station with a fellow-director, Arthur Cotton, after a board meeting when Paddy Daly entered with three other members of the Squad shortly before midday. Cotton dived under the table while Brooke, who was sitting by the fire, tried to escape. He was hit by a volley of shots. One of the Squad, Jim Slattery, later recalled that as they were

going down the stairs again Daly said to me, 'Are you sure we got him?' I said I was not sure, and Daly said, 'What about going back and making sure?' [Tom] Keogh and myself went back.

They fired a warning shot at Cotton, who had emerged from under the table, and then Slattery 'fired a couple of shots at Brooke' to satisfy himself that he was dead.

Although I did not wound the other man who was in the room, I was informed afterwards that it would have been a good job if he had been shot, as he too was making a nuisance [of himself].

The noise of the trains below drowned the sound of the gunfire.

While Cotton undoubtedly shared Brooke's hostility towards the independence movement, he was not actively involved in its suppression, as Brooke was through his membership of the advisory committee on security set up by Lord French. Brooke was also a member of the Irish Privy Council, which had banned Sinn Féin, the Irish Volunteers, Cumann na mBan and the Gaelic League (by mistake for the Gaelic Athletic Association) in November 1919. He was under no illusions about the risks he was taking or which side he was on. A loaded revolver was found in his coat pocket after his death.[30]

Brooke's widow would subsequently be awarded £9,500 in compensation under the malicious damages legislation: in other words, the ratepayers of Dublin Corporation, Dublin County Council and Pembroke Urban District Council footed the bill. The evidence in the case gives an interesting insight into the various sources of income open to a senior member of the Dublin business community. Brooke was sixty-eight at the time of his death and left a widow, a son, who was serving as a colonel in South Africa, and a daughter, whose husband succeeded to some of the dead man's business interests. Brooke lived in Shillelagh, Co. Wicklow, where he received a salary of £900 a year as agent of the Fitzwilliam estate. He received another £500 as agent of the Fitzwilliam estate in Dublin and had 'the use of a very beautiful house, all repairs and upkeep being done by the estate, while he had free fuel and free lighting, as well as some grazing land.' These benefits were estimated as worth another £292 a year. As chairman of the Dublin and South-Eastern Railway he received a salary of £900 a year. He received fees as a director of the Norwich Union Life Insurance Society, which in 1919 amounted to £87 4s. He was also an agent of the company, and his commission averaged £439 a year. He received a further salary of £19 19s a year in connection with the Railway Clearing House.

This provided a gross income of £2,748 17s 8d, or £2,248 17s 8d net after a notional £500 was deducted for personal expenditure. The award of £9,500 went in its entirety to Brooke's widow.[31] He does not appear to have received any income from his directorship of the Bank of Ireland's Dublin Board, which sent his family a letter of condolence.[32]

The lack of public outrage at Brooke's death suggests that, much like the indifference to the wave of attacks on G Division detectives in 1919 and the enthusiastic popular response to the IRA raid on the King's Inns garrison in June, there was far greater tolerance for republican violence in the city than for that of the Crown forces. The presence on the streets of the flamboyantly belligerent Auxiliaries was especially resented by Dubliners.

During August, events in Cork overshadowed those in Dublin or Belfast. On 12 August the Lord Mayor and local commandant of the IRA Terence MacSwiney, was arrested by a British raiding party. The next day the Restoration of Order Act came into force. MacSwiney was quickly convicted by a British military court of being in possession of various incriminating documents, including an RIC cipher. Other republican prisoners in Cork had just begun a hunger strike to secure political status, and MacSwiney began refusing food from the time of his arrest. Unlike other republican prisoners, however, his protest was to secure his unconditional release. It was done without consultation with or sanction by IRA headquarters,[33] an individual act of war that could result only in his death or the collapse of British authority. Eventually it helped achieve both.

The British government's handling of the dispute was disastrous from the outset. The conviction was legally unsound, and the decision to transfer MacSwiney to Brixton Prison in London on 18 August, two days after the trial, far from isolating him helped attract international attention. British black propaganda suggesting that the hunger strike was a charade and that the prisoner was hoping desperately for a royal pardon further enraged public opinion at home and abroad. While the focus of events was inevitably in London and Cork, Dubliners were moved as much as anyone by his ordeal. Masses and protests took place throughout the city. One of the largest protests was by four thousand Guinness workers, who held a special Mass on 9 September. On 6 September Dublin Corporation adjourned for a week in protest at 'the slow murder of the Lord Mayor of Cork ... in Brixton' and sent 'the heartfelt sympathy of the citizens of Dublin ... to the Lady Mayoress and the MacSwiney family.' It was proposed by Alderman Joseph MacDonagh (Sinn Féin), brother of the 1916 martyr Thomas MacDonagh. Before adjourning, however, the corporation was mindful to pass a vote of sympathy for Councillor Sir Andrew Beattie (MRA) and his family on the death of his father, Lieutenant-Colonel Beattie MC.[34]

Another event on the same day as the Guinness workers' special Mass, and even more remarkable in its way, was a meeting of the magistrates of Dublin city and county in the Gresham Hotel. This unanimously passed a motion

> requesting the immediate release of the Lord Mayor of Cork and [we] earnestly pray that the Government may be granted wisdom to avert the widening of the breach between the two countries which the death of the Lord Mayor would undoubtedly cause.

Only fifty of the five hundred magistrates and justices of the peace attended, but another twenty-five sent their apologies, with most pledging their support for the motion. Although the meeting had been called solely to discuss this motion, it quickly developed into a debate on the state of the country. It was generally agreed that there had been a 'complete collapse of the Petty Sessions Courts.' Another motion was put:

> That we, the magistrates of the City and County of Dublin, convey to the Government our firm conviction that the continuance of martial law and military rule in this country will lead to absolute ruin and disaster. That the

attempt to rule against the will of the people has destroyed all respect for and confidence in the operation of the Petty Court Sessions. That until the restoration of Constitutional Law and a national settlement of Ireland's rights which will fully satisfy the Irish people is enacted; law or government in this country will remain inoperative and the holding of Petty Sessions a farce.

Both motions were passed and forwarded to the Prime Minister, the Chief Secretary for Ireland and the Home Secretary. Those present passed a further motion proposed by the former Home Rule stalwart P. J. Kettle resigning their commissions 'as against the present misgovernment of the country.' Only one magistrate voted against.[35]

The heavy military concentration in the capital made IRA operations difficult and well nigh impossible after dark, when the curfew removed the cover of crowds in camouflaging attacks. The first major operation after the King's Inns raid was the ambushing of a bread detail in Church Street on 20 September 1920.

As Kevin Barry's nephew and biographer Dónal O'Connor recounts, it all began with a business transaction between a member of the Lancashire Fusiliers offering to sell a couple of rifles and two Volunteers interested in buying them. The Volunteers were waiting to meet a go-between in North Brunswick Street when a military work party pulled up outside Monk's bakery at 79–80 Old Church Street to collect a daily bread ration. It was a detachment of the Duke of Wellington's Regiment, which had come from their base at Collinstown aerodrome. The Volunteers, John Joe Carroll and James Douglas, noticed the sloppy procedures as the two NCOs disappeared inside, leaving the rest of the escort to their own devices. The Volunteers continued watching the routine for the next three days, noting the position of the telephone in the bakery office and the best escape routes.

A total of twenty-four men were assigned to the ambush—a large group. They were so confident of success that one of Collins's intelligence contacts in the *Irish Independent*, Michael Knightly, was given a tip-off that it was about to take place.[36] One of the raiders was an eighteen-year-year old medical student, Kevin Barry, who had travelled back to Dublin from the family farm in Co. Carlow to repeat an examination at University College. The exam was at 2 p.m., but Barry reckoned he could make the raid at 11 a.m. with plenty of time to spare. He had participated previously in the King's Inns raid a few hundred yards away. Like some of his colleagues, he went to Mass beforehand, and he arrived at the assembly point a little late.

That morning the lorry was also late, and members of the ambush party had difficulty remaining inconspicuous as they waited at various places along the street. Some bought newspapers to read or to more easily conceal their weapons. Barry had been issued with a .38 Mauser pistol. When the ration detail arrived there was only one NCO in it. He climbed down from the driver's cab, lowered the tailgate and walked into the bakery. Two unarmed bandsmen on fatigue duty jumped down from the rear of the lorry and followed him. There were five armed privates left sitting in the rear of the lorry, together with the driver from the Royal Army Service Corps with another soldier in the cab. They too were armed.

Things immediately began to go wrong. When the IRA officer in charge, Seán O'Neill, ordered the soldiers to drop their arms, one soldier opened fire. A general firefight followed, during which Barry's pistol jammed. He ducked beside the lorry to clear it. With the Lancashire Fusiliers based in the old North Dublin Union a couple of streets away, all hope of capturing weapons had to be abandoned, and the attackers fled—all except Barry, who now hid under the lorry. A widow who owned a small coal and vegetable shop on the corner of Church Street, Catherine Garrett, spotted him and shouted, 'There's a man under the lorry.' It was more probably a warning not to run him over, or to see if he was hurt, than a deliberate attempt to identify him to the military; but Mrs Garrett would be known for the few years she had left as the woman who spotted Kevin Barry.[37]

While three members of the ambush party suffered minor wounds, three of the soldiers had been fatally wounded. They were aged twenty, nineteen and fifteen.[38] It was the first time a Volunteer had been captured red-handed at the scene of an ambush. When he received the telephoned report of the incident the British army commander, Sir Nevil Macready, scribbled on the margin, 'Colonel Toppin. Try for murder.'[39] Toppin was the Assistant Adjutant-General of the Dublin District, responsible for courts-martial.

At the time Barry's arrest was overshadowed by other events. Terence MacSwiney was entering the final stages of his 73-day ordeal in Brixton Prison, which had the nation transfixed. Even in Dublin, Barry's arrest attracted less attention than other happenings that day. A few hours after the bakery raid two sergeants in Portobello Barracks were killed by a third sergeant in what appeared to have been a lovers' quarrel over a woman.

Later still it emerged that a nineteen-year-old member of the Volunteers, Seán Doyle, had been shot dead in the Dublin Mountains on the previous Sunday in an ambush by a mixed party of plain-clothes soldiers and

Auxiliaries. Forty men had been arrested at the ambush site. The undercover military-cum-paramilitary unit claimed it had been returning fire when Doyle was killed. However, no weapons or ammunition were recovered at the scene. The dead youth was a son of Councillor Peter Seán Doyle of Sinn Féin, the man who a fortnight before had proposed at a corporation meeting that new roads in the city be named after dead Volunteers.[40] It is not clear whether the men arrested were on their way to a training camp or simply on a Sunday excursion. Despite the best efforts of the British military authorities to delay and then subvert the coroner's court, the jury at the inquest found that Doyle had died as a result of shock and haemorrhage 'following a gun shot fired by the Crown forces.' His funeral on Thursday 23 September was made a demonstration of solidarity by the local community as well as the IRA. Six Sinn Féin MPs attended, including Michael Staines and W. T. Cosgrave, the Lord Mayor and many councillors. Large contingents of Volunteers, Cumann na mBan and Fianna Éireann were followed by more from the ITGWU, employees of Inchicore railway works, where Councillor Doyle was a fitter, and Dublin Corporation's workshop in Stanley Street, where his son had been an apprentice. Local shops and businesses in Inchicore and Kilmainham closed, and so did businesses in Lucan, where the dead youth was buried.[41] A claim in some newspapers that the officer in charge of the undercover group had been admonished by the General Officer Commanding Dublin District, Major-General Boyd, was denied by the Dublin Castle Press Bureau. It appears that it was an operation initiated by Brigadier-General Crozier, commander of the Auxiliaries, who claimed in his memoirs to have received Boyd's congratulations on the outcome.[42]

Worse was to come. At 3 a.m. on Thursday a group of soldiers entered the Exchange Hotel in Parliament Street and asked to book a room. When the night porter told them all the rooms were occupied they held him at gunpoint and examined the register. Having identified the guest they were looking for, John A. Lynch, they went to his room and shot him. Afterwards they said they had returned his fire when he resisted arrest. However, there was no evidence that he was armed, nor was there any warrant in existence for his arrest. Lynch was a member of Limerick County Council and had served as local Sinn Féin director of elections. He was also a justice of the Republican Court and collector for the Dáil Éireann loan. He was in Dublin to deliver loan funds.

The leader of the raiding party was believed to be Captain Geoffrey Baggallay. One of his companions, Lieutenant Henry Angliss, thought they had killed the commandant of the 2nd Cork Brigade, Liam Lynch. On this occasion the army succeeded in preventing another embarrassing inquest in the city, but

Collins's moles in the DMP soon made him aware of the identity of this new British 'murder gang'.[43]

But the most shocking event of the week was the 'Sack of Balbriggan'. This occurred on Monday night and Tuesday morning, 19 and 20 September 1920. It followed a gunfight on Monday evening when Head Constable Peter Burke, his brother Michael, who was an RIC sergeant, and some companions from the newly formed Auxiliary Division arrived in Mary Smith's pub in Balbriggan and were refused service. The local RIC could not persuade Burke's group to leave, and local Volunteers acting as Republican Police were summoned. In the fight that followed, Burke was shot dead in the doorway of the pub and his brother seriously wounded. Their companions fled in their waiting taxi to Gormanston, where Black and Tans and Auxiliaries were undergoing training.

Soon afterwards a large police detachment arrived to exact vengeance. They ran berserk through Balbriggan, defying efforts by the local RIC to restrain them.[44] They killed a local barber, James Lawless, and a dairy proprietor, Joseph Gibbon. Both men were Volunteers. They beat up other civilians and proceeded to burn more than thirty houses, most of them small cottages. Four licensed grocery premises were burnt down, including one owned by a Sinn Féin town commissioner, John Derham, but not apparently the one where Head Constable Burke was refused a drink. The hosiery factory of Deedes, Templar and Company, the largest employer in the town, was destroyed.

In all, £200,000 worth of damage was done, four hundred people were thrown out of work and many families were rendered homeless.[45] The incident was a disaster for the authorities, not least because Balbriggan was near enough to Dublin for newspapers to despatch photographers, and because a Canadian tourist staying with relatives could corroborate the testimony of local people. Not surprisingly, the authorities used the Restoration of Order Act to ban a coroner's inquest. There was an internal inquiry into the incident, but the Chief Secretary for Ireland, Sir Hamar Greenwood, refused to publish the findings. He subsequently told the House of Commons: 'I have yet to find one authenticated case of a member of the Auxiliary Division being accused of anything but the highest conduct.'[46] In response the editorial of the *Irish Independent* declared:

> The circumstances under which two civilians were killed—not shot but butchered ... were singularly horrifying and brutal. For weeks past other towns and districts have been subjected to terrorism of an equally ferocious character ... Are the armed forces of the Government to be given immunity to play the role of terrorists, to kill Irishmen and burn their property as they

please? A Bill was enacted recently for the 'Restoration of Order.' Considering what has occurred since it was passed it ought to be described as a Bill 'for the creation of disorder and anarchy and the abolition of law.'

Certainly police disorder continued to be the order of the day in north Co. Dublin. Before Christmas the Auxiliaries were prime suspects in other serious incidents, including the murder of a boy, John Sherlock, thought to be carrying messages for the rebels, and a quarry labourer, Thomas Hand, secretary of the local branch of the ITGWU, who had also served on Sinn Féin arbitration boards and was active in the Gaelic League. The tempo of IRA attacks also increased in north Co. Dublin in a spiral of mutual retaliation.[47]

In spite of Balbriggan and the new 'murder gang' tactics of British officers and their Auxiliary allies in the city, a remarkable initiative was launched that week in Dublin. Even as news of Balbriggan was breaking, a meeting was launched in the Mansion House by the Lord Mayor to help victims of the Belfast pogrom. It received cross-community support. Besides Laurence O'Neill, who chaired the meeting, the main speakers were Dr McWalter, Charles Eason, Joe MacDonagh MP (Sinn Féin) and the Earl of Fingall. McWalter said he was proud to have served with men from the Ulster Division in the last war and he had never thought to see the day when fellow ex-servicemen would be driven out of their homes, or thousands of young girls thrown out of work. The only way to help victims of the pogrom was to

> create such a feeling in the country as would make it imperative on employers to take back those people, with the assurance of safety in the future ... I think that the meeting is prepared also to testify that there is no idea of reprisals in Dublin. [Hear, hear.] I think that the meeting is prepared ... to assure everyone that a Unionist in Dublin is as safe as the best Nationalist.

As one of Dublin's leading Protestant employers, Charles Eason felt that Dublin's citizens

> should all condemn unreservedly the throwing out of employment [of workers] on account of their religious beliefs. I do not think that employers have a right to put a question of that kind to their staffs. I have for many years employed persons of all creeds, and they work together with the utmost friendliness, faithfulness, honour and integrity. I feel that it is only

right that the Protestants of Dublin should join in support of those families who are in distress.

What was happening in Belfast was not only mistaken 'but entirely out of harmony with the Christian religion, which they all profess.' He cautioned against the equally unchristian, if understandable, impulse to retaliate.

Sinn Féin's boycott of Belfast goods was already a reality in Dublin, and its director, Joe MacDonagh, made no apologies for it. It was up to nationalists and Catholics to show they would no longer suffer in silence.

> If the country were rid of the enemy tomorrow, I am perfectly certain there would be no question of bigotry or intolerance. I do not believe any Irishman is intolerant. This intolerance is dinned into their ears from the other side. I blame Sir Edward Carson less for this intolerance than I blame Lloyd George and Bonar Law. It is a deliberate attempt ... to split the Irish nation at a time when Ireland is more united than ever it was before.

It was a classic statement of the Sinn Féin position. 'The Irish people have ... decided that so long as ... intolerance and bigotry should exist in Belfast the rest of Ireland is not going to have anything to do with Belfast.' At the same time MacDonagh was anxious to assure his audience that there was no danger of Sinn Féin engaging in reprisals. 'A unionist and a Protestant is as secure in the south and west of Ireland as he would be in Sandy Row, Belfast. [Hear, hear.]'

The Earl of Fingall abhorred 'bigotry of any description, whether political or religious.' He would not touch upon the political issues alluded to but endorsed the Lord Mayor's call 'as a matter of humanity.' There was agreement among speakers from the floor, ranging from trade unionists to businessmen, that the British government was at fault for not ensuring that those expelled from their jobs were able to return. 'Is there any Government in this country?' the Right Honourable Thomas Lough asked rhetorically. A voice answered 'No.'

But tension did arise when it came to appointing a committee to administer the Lord Mayor's fund. Charles Eason, on being nominated, said he could not agree with MacDonagh 'that the crimes are all on one side,' and he disagreed with the boycott. Nevertheless he agreed to serve. A call was made from the body of the hall for the first meeting of the committee to be in City Hall, Belfast. But Councillor William Paul of Sinn Féin said, 'If we send this group of decent, tolerant Protestants to preach toleration in Belfast there would be a rush for their scalps.' Instead the boycott 'must be carried out ... close and stringently.'

Citing his experience as chairman of the corporation's Markets Committee (see chapter 5), Paul said that sending money to pogrom victims alone would not make Belfast 'fall into line.'

Ever the peace-maker, O'Neill reiterated that the meeting was solely to organise funds for pogrom victims, 'no matter to what religion they belong,' and it was not in its remit 'to interfere in any way whatsoever to boycott this body or that body.' The committee eventually consisted of the Lord Mayor (Laurence O'Neill), the High Sheriff (Dr McWalter), Michael Staines MP, Sir Thomas Myles, John Farren, Sir Horace Plunkett, Charles Eason, Blacker Douglas, Sir Nugent Everard and Edward Lee. It was neatly balanced, with Staines, O'Neill, McWalter and Myles representing various nationalist strands, Farren representing Labour and the balance composed of three liberal unionists, a Northern unionist (Blacker Douglas) and a military man (Sir Nugent Everard, Honorary Colonel of the Prince of Wales's Leinster Regiment).

The voice of Southern unionism, the *Irish Times*, welcomed the formation of a fund and the ability of the meeting to overcome political differences for a common humanitarian goal. It asked:

> Can we not make the fund a peace offering—a proposal of amnesty—from South to North? ... Murder must cease; reprisals, from whatever quarter and in whatever province, must cease ... Our earnest hope is that the fund which was opened yesterday will achieve simultaneously the re-employment of all banished workers and the removal of the Southern boycott of Belfast.

But not everyone proved so ecumenical. When Dublin County Council met to consider helping the inhabitants of Balbriggan, Lady Dockrell questioned the need. The Chairman, Friel, asked in amazement, 'Do you deny the town was sacked?'

'I don't know,' Lady Dockrell replied. 'I have no evidence. There are plenty of people committing murder on both sides; but I will admit nothing until I have absolute proof.'[48]

And yet the creation of the Mansion House fund for the relief of distress in the North was a minor political miracle: it was reassurance to Dublin unionists that the primary Sinn Féin response in the city would be a boycott rather than reprisals.

It also helped pave the way in the following month for the establishment of the Irish White Cross. This was the brainchild of Éamon de Valera, who saw the creation of a body along the lines of the Red Cross Society for relieving suffering in Ireland as a means of simultaneously obtaining funds from American sympathisers and uniting leading figures from the nationalist and unionist communities in a large-scale good-works project. As we have seen (chapter 5 above), the organisation's Executive Committee was heavily loaded with leading figures from Sinn Féin. These included Arthur Griffith, Michael Collins and W. T. Cosgrave. On the General Council there was a sizeable Labour contingent, including the party's secretary, Thomas Johnson, some token nationalists, such as Mary Kettle, and a sprinkling of liberal unionists, such as Sir Horace Plunkett.

The White Cross proved a tremendous financial success and helped relieve distress in the most disturbed parts of the west, south-west and Belfast. Dublin received only £53,906 from the personal relief fund, compared with £362,356 for Belfast and £548,862 for Cork. Two of the main beneficiaries in Dublin were Temple Street Children's Hospital and St Ultan's Hospital for Mothers and Infants, which received £1,000.

Despite all the military activity in Dublin it remained a relatively civilised place, unlike Belfast, which was cursed by large-scale sectarian violence, or large areas of Connacht and Munster, where Crown forces and Volunteers alike became a law unto themselves.

Anyone who thought that the military and their paramilitary allies might not have approval for their activities from the highest authorities was soon disabused. Not only the Chief Secretary, Sir Hamar Greenwood, but the Prime Minister, David Lloyd George, robustly defended the police and army. In a speech at Caernarvon Town Hall in his own constituency on 9 October the Prime Minister said:

> Policemen and soldiers do not go burning houses and shooting men down wantonly without provocation ... If it is war it is war on both sides; we cannot have a one sided war ... In war men wear a uniform, but in Ireland a harmless-looking citizen might pass a policeman in the street, and there is nothing to indicate that he has murderous weapons or to arouse suspicion. When he has passed the policeman he will pull out a revolver and shoot him in the back. Scores of policemen have been killed in this way. This is not war, but murder. If it is war, give the soldier and the policeman a fair chance, and they will give a fair account of themselves.

He warned the enemy that the government would 'restore order ... by methods however stern.'[49]

Dublin was the only city in which such attacks on soldiers were frequent. As the attacks on the King's Inns garrison in June and the military police patrols in College Green in July had shown, the aim was to disarm the enemy rather than kill him. Dáil Éireann's *Irish Bulletin* responded vigorously along these lines in its critique of Lloyd George's speech, pointing out that between January 1919 and the Prime Minister's speech the IRA had taken 441 soldiers and policemen prisoner and had released all of them either unharmed or after providing first aid to those wounded. By contrast, prisoners of the army or paramilitary police were often ill-treated or even killed. The *Bulletin* claimed that, besides forty-one IRA members killed by the Crown forces, there had been seventy-eight civilian fatalities.[50]

The two sides would continue to trade statistics and insults until the Truce. The impossibility of each accepting the legitimacy of its opponents' tactics would become the twentieth-century norm in conflicts between aspiring nation-states and empires in residence.

The tempo of raids increased as winter closed in; the longer nights and curfew extensions allowed mobile military patrols to dominate the streets. Active Volunteers lay low and stayed as much as possible in safe houses. Charlie Dalton, who worked full-time for IRA intelligence, managed to find a safe billet through a sympathetic relieving officer, who let Dalton and his comrades use empty rooms over a health dispensary. 'There was no furniture at the dispensary beyond two double beds and a few chairs,' Dalton recalled. Food consisted of 'anything easy to cook.' In north Co. Dublin, safe houses were supplemented by dug-outs, and many Volunteers paid a high price for periods spent in these cold, wet conditions through ill-health and premature death in later years.[51]

Meanwhile the Crown forces blundered into situations that further alienated the local population. A raid on St Andrew's Catholic Club at 114 Pearse Street was typical. It began shortly after ten o'clock on Saturday 25 September. The *Irish Independent* reported:

The raiders, who were accompanied to the street by a large force of military, with an armoured car, shouted 'Hands Up!' The caretaker's wife, standing at the top of the stairs leading to the basement, and seeing one man with a revolver in each hand approach, became so terrified that she fell down the stairs, injuring her back. She has been confined to bed since.

Entering the card room they held up eight men playing cards and placed them against the wall with their hands over their heads. In the billiard room players and onlookers were similarly treated. The floor was torn up and the ground underneath searched; the billiard table cloth and cushions were ripped and left useless, while other furniture was smashed. A photograph of Mr. De Valera was torn from the wall and burned, as were pictures of The O'Rahilly [Michael O'Rahilly] and Con Colbert in the uniform of Irish Volunteers. Strangely enough, pictures of Padraic Pearse, Thomas Clarke and the others executed after the Rising were left untouched, possibly because the subjects were not in uniform. A portrait of the Irish Volunteers of 1782 was gashed. In another room a piano was left a wreck.

The raiders were looking for Alderman Charlie Murphy, who was also a Volunteer officer, but they had to make do with his brother, Tom. They removed the club's safe, having failed to open it, and also thirty thousand Christmas Goose Club tickets. Meanwhile soldiers outside held up vehicles and searched passing civilians. 'A revolving searchlight from a motor lorry played on the crowd.' When the search party eventually left, at about 11:15 p.m., there were shouts of 'Balbriggan' from local onlookers nonchalantly defying the curfew order.[52]

Whether the Goose Club ever regained possession of its tickets, or the club its safe, is not clear, but one major cause of resentment of raiding parties was the cavalier way in which soldiers and police took anything that caught their fancy. Leon Ó Broin's home was raided in late December 1920. The seasonal goose had just been delivered and was being readied for the oven when the raiders arrived. Failing to find anything more incriminating, the raiders seized it 'together with the other comestibles my mother had laid in for the Christmas.'[53]

Of course things looked different from the other side. Caroline Woodcock, wife of a serving British officer, described how her husband and his colleagues would dress

in filthy old clothes and rubber soled shoes, especially kept for what was frequently very dirty work … If the house was moderately clean this work was bearable, though unpleasant.

There is another side to this picture, and some descriptions given to me by officers, to whose unhappy lot had fallen the searching of some filthy tenement houses in which Dublin slums abound, made me quite ill. A dozen people in a room, and five or six to a bed was quite usual; imagine searching such a bed and pulling the mattress to pieces. One officer told me that he had found four human beings, two ducks and a lamb in one bed, not to speak of hundreds of smaller and unmentionable animals. A few days in hospital subsequent to a raid such as this, to get rid of a complaint common among the great unwashed, were often necessary.

She also complained of the indignity of men returning from a raid being searched because of complaints of stolen or damaged property. She implicitly acknowledged that the army operated to a higher standard than its paramilitary allies.

> The occupants of the house ... were generally terribly frightened, but when they realised the raiders were soldiers, and not the much feared Auxiliaries, they became calmer.

The daylight raids were on a much larger scale. Soldiers

> picqueted [picketed, i.e. patrolled] every corner, a house to house search was made and usually numerous arrests effected. Throughout tanks waddled slowly up and down the street ... During these raids, ever the most awe-inspiring sight for me was the car loads of Auxiliaries: eight or ten splendid looking men in a Crossley tender, armed to the teeth ... I know little of what the Auxiliaries have done or left undone but I do know that they have put the fear of God into the Irish rebels. When criticising them, it should never be forgotten that these men are the survivors of the glorious company of those who fought and died for England.[54]

As the wife of a British officer serving in Ireland, Woodcock brought a different viewpoint to the impact of the War of Independence on civilians caught in the crossfire and, for understandable reasons, one that lacked any sympathy for Irish women. In her book *Renegades*, Ann Matthews has raised the question of the 'war on women'. She makes a cogent argument that combatants on both sides not alone physically abused women but sexually ill-treated and even raped them. Reports by visiting delegations from the American Committee for Relief in Ireland and the British Labour Party allude to such incidents, but the social shame attached to rape meant that very few complaints were lodged. The evidence Matthews has assembled suggests that many of the most serious incidents happened in rural areas and villages rather than Dublin; but in Dublin too the advent of curfew made women fearful to leave home after dark, or even made them feel unsafe within their homes. The veteran Dublin suffragist Margaret Connery reported to the Irish White Cross:

> Women and children were in a constant state of depression and nervous breakdown, and in the case of expectant mothers, it produces very grave results for the mothers and children ... Women know that it is during curfew

hours attempts of a sexual character have been made, it is difficult to appreciate the effects which this continued strain is producing upon the health of women.

Women were also subjected to humiliating rituals by combatants on both sides, such as having their head shaved for fraternising with the enemy. Again this seems to have been more prevalent outside the capital, although Matthews mentions a couple of incidents in Ranelagh and East Wall that appear to have been the work of IRA and Cumann na mBan members.

The British government was particularly sensitive to allegations of rape, the 'most serious charge that can be laid at the door of any white man,' as Sir Hamar Greenwood told the House of Commons in February 1921. The equal reticence of Sinn Féin propagandists to use anything more than innuendo in most instances allowed the issue to be quietly shrouded in forgetfulness after the independence struggle.[55] Only one formal complaint of rape was made, and that was by the wife of a Protestant farmer in Co. Tipperary against IRA members during the Truce. Three Volunteers were subsequently found guilty of what had been a very brutal gang rape, but as the punishments meted out to the culprits consisted of a £3 fine in one case, being bound over to keep the peace in another and a caution in the third, it hardly encouraged other victims to come forward.[56]

In the meantime there could be no meeting of minds in the situation that had developed by late 1920. If Lloyd George fumed at the way soldiers and policemen were shot in the back and used it to justify reprisals, Republican propagandists contrasted the indiscipline and licentiousness of British forces with the humane way the IRA treated military and police taken prisoner. Neither side would accept the legitimacy of the other's cause, and neither side was desperate enough, yet, to reach an accommodation. Things would have to get worse before they got better.

On 12 October 1920 a military intelligence party raiding a house in Drumcondra got more than it bargained for. This was Fernside, the modest two-storey residence of Professor John Carolan, who lectured at St Patrick's College nearby. Earlier that day two of the most wanted IRA men, the Tipperary Volunteers Seán Treacy and Dan Breen, bumped into a Cumann na mBan member, Kay Fleming, in a cinema near Nelson's Pillar. As always, both men were living largely on their wits and the generosity of friends such as the Flemings. She invited them back to her parents' grocery shop in Drumcondra for a meal. The Flemings were a well-known Republican family and were regularly raided, so it was decided afterwards to send the men the short distance up the road to Professor Carolan, a sympathiser. There is strong circumstantial evidence that they were followed there by an ex-soldier, Robert Pike, who lived nearby and was on Colonel Winter's payroll.[57] But Fernside had previously been the residence of Richard Mulcahy, and this may have been a factor in its being singled out that night, as some of the raiding party thought he still lived there.

Shortly after 1 a.m. soldiers surrounded the house and demanded access, smashing the glass panelling in the front door before Carolan could open it. The raiders ran upstairs, to be met by a hail of gunfire. The two officers leading the charge were killed and a corporal just behind seriously wounded. Breen had run onto the landing and engaged the military party at point-blank range. Some of the soldiers covering the rear rushed to the front of the house to assist the main party. Treacy, realising their mistake, called Breen back into the room and told him to jump through the window into the garden while he provided covering fire. Breen, bleeding profusely from bullet wounds, suffered further injuries as he crashed through the roof of the conservatory below. Treacy followed amid further exchanges of fire and stumbled over the bodies of two badly wounded soldiers in the back garden as he fled. He assumed in the darkness that Breen was dead, as Breen did Treacy.

Treacy, who had not had time to put on his shoes, headed barefoot away from the city streets and curfew patrols towards a safe house in Finglas. Breen managed to cross the Tolka River, despite his injuries, aiming for the only house he could see that had a lighted window. It turned out to be the home of a retired policeman and confirmed unionist. He threatened to call the military, but his wife said, 'If you do I'll report you to Michael Collins.' Instead they called a neighbour, Nurse Long, who staunched Breen's wounds and then called to the Flemings, only to find the military there. She managed to let the family know where Breen was without arousing the suspicions of the raiders. The latter were probably too shaken by the disastrous end to the raid for the significance of her arrival to register.

Kay Fleming and her sister Dot were treated to a rare view of the war from the other side when the officer questioning them broke down and said, 'We have lost five of our best men in the fight at "Fernside", including Major Smyth, my best friend.'[58] Kay Fleming later recalled that the officer 'rambled on, telling and retelling the story and asking odd questions, now and then, but not with any great malice.'

Professor Carolan was less fortunate: he had been shot dead before the raiders left. In what was now becoming a habit, his death was explained by saying he was caught in crossfire. Unfortunately for the raiding party, Carolan lingered long enough to give a statement that he had been made face the wall and then shot in the back of the neck. His wife and children were not harmed in the affray. Many years later one of the surviving intelligence officers who took part in the raid, Captain Robert Jeune, described it as 'a most unfortunate accident': the professor was 'shot by mistake while being questioned.'[59]

The other fatalities that night were Major George Osbert Smyth and Captain Alfred White. Smyth was a brother of the former RIC Divisional Commander for Munster, Lieutenant-Colonel Gerald Smyth, who had been shot in Cork some months earlier after making the notorious speech that caused mass resignations from the RIC in Listowel. Both men were members of a well-known unionist family in Banbridge, and Gerald Smyth's death had sparked the rioting in the town that subsequently spread to Belfast. The Cork shooting had been widely but mistakenly attributed to Dan Breen, and Major Smyth successfully sought leave from regimental duties in Egypt to serve with Winter's intelligence network and track down the man he thought had killed his brother.[60]

His colleague Captain White had also recently returned from Egypt. Taken in conjunction with a tendency by some British undercover operatives to frequent the Cairo Café in Grafton Street, it inevitably gave rise to stories that a special group of secret agents had been brought over from Egypt to hunt Michael Collins, giving birth to the myth of the Cairo Gang. While it was a handy nickname that helped IRA intelligence target a group of agents for liquidation, most members of the 'Cairo Gang' had prosaic English addresses, and some were home-grown Dubliners.

Breen was subsequently smuggled into the Mater Hospital for treatment, where Collins's foresight in establishing a private health insurance scheme for Volunteers was proving its worth by keeping them off the official books. Breen was treated in the private nursing home attached to the main hospital. Although soldiers raided the hospital, as they did others in the city, they did not search the nursing home. Breen's amazing luck continued to cause discomfort to the enemy. Shortly afterwards an engineering officer of the 5th Battalion, Matt Furlong from Dunboyne, was brought to the Mater badly injured during trials on a trench mortar. When he died, two Co. Tipperary RIC men were sent to Dublin to see if the dead man was Breen. One of them, Detective-Sergeant Comerford, took one look at the body and said immediately that it wasn't Breen: 'I'd know his ugly mug anywhere.'

Unfortunately for Comerford and his companion, their escort in Dublin was David Neligan, one of Collins's agents in the DMP. Comerford was shot dead the next day by the Squad on the quays while his companion managed to flee.[61]

Treacy, who had survived relatively unscathed from Fernside, was less fortunate. He was due to return to Co. Tipperary to marry a local woman, May Quigley, on 25 October, her birthday. But he was reluctant to leave Dublin while Breen was in danger. Besides, McKee wanted him to attend a meeting with senior officers of the Dublin Brigade to discuss future operations, and Treacy, ever the dutiful soldier, agreed. The meeting was at Peadar Clancy's shop, the Republican Outfitters in Talbot Street. It was a suicidal venue, regularly raided and kept under surveillance. Clancy was McKee's deputy and was well known to the enemy. On the previous day soldiers had carried out intensive searches of nearby tenements and Miss Hughes's Hotel around the corner in Lower Gardiner Street. They were looking for the Dublin Brigade headquarters but missed the real site in the offices of the Dublin Typographical Society. McKee was a member of the union, and this served as headquarters of the Dublin Brigade until his death in November 1920. Liberty Hall in Beresford Place nearby was also used for meetings. Once again the fact that these were union offices in constant use facilitated the IRA strategy of hiding in plain sight.

For the moment, British forces were still groping their way through the urban labyrinth, and the Dublin Brigade was relying increasingly on luck as much as native cunning and greater familiarity with their combat environment to keep one step ahead.

Apart from the badly wounded Breen and the men guarding him at the Mater Nursing Home, luck was not with the IRA that day. An attempt to rob a British army payroll at the Munster and Leinster Bank in Phibsborough in the early afternoon ended when a Volunteer was fatally wounded by machine-gun fire from an armoured car, whose crew then proceeded to spray the street with bullets, shooting out most of the windows in the bank and narrowly missing passing civilians. This was followed by angry exchanges minutes later between ambulance men from Dublin Fire Brigade and soldiers when the latter refused to allow the dying man medical attention.

McKee had been considering an attack on the funeral procession for the two British officers killed at 'Fernside' that day. It was rumoured that the Chief Secretary, Sir Hamar Greenwood, and Sir Hugh Tudor would attend. But both refused to oblige.[62]

Treacy had barely arrived at the shop, shortly after 4 p.m., when an armoured car and two lorries turned into Talbot Street from the Sackville Street end. The lorries were filled with soldiers, accompanied by military intelligence officers and some Auxiliaries in plain clothes. McKee told everyone to make a run for it. All succeeded except Treacy, who grabbed a bicycle at the kerb that was too big for him. As he stumbled, a British intelligence operative who had been keeping Clancy's shop under surveillance all afternoon, Colour-Sergeant Francis Christian, grabbed him. As the pair grappled, two more intelligence officers ran to Christian's aid. Treacy managed to draw his gun and shoot Christian and another of his attackers, Lieutenant Price, before the soldiers and armoured car opened fire on the mêlée, firing indiscriminately, just as the armoured car crew in Phibsborough had done shortly beforehand.

Among the fatalities were a fifteen-year-old messenger boy, Patrick Carroll, and 57-year-old Joseph Corringham, who ran a tobacconist's shop in Gardiner Street. Price and another intelligence operative were killed, along with Treacy. Christian survived, although badly wounded. Seán Brunswick, a young Volunteer who had passed the afternoon liaising between McKee and the men guarding Breen at the Mater, arrived in Talbot Street just in time to see the shambles unfold. On this occasion the ambulance men were not prevented from going to the aid of the wounded, and Brunswick, posing as a medical student, searched Treacy's pockets and removed all documents while assisting with the wounded.

Treacy's determination not to be taken prisoner was unusual among Volunteers, some of whom seemed to regard a gun as a fashion accessory, to be deposited with a female companion or even a casual passer-by when caught in a dragnet operation. But one of Treacy's formative experiences had been the Mountjoy hunger strike of 1917, in which Thomas Ashe had died. After their release a group of hunger-strikers visited Ashe's grave and swore that if arrested again they would go on hunger strike; Treacy simply vowed he would never be taken alive.

As a result of Brunswick's endeavours it took a while for the British to confirm the identity of the dead rebel. When it was known, there was considerable interest, with Colonel Winter being among those who went to view the body. Nora O'Keeffe, a cousin of Treacy's, was called to identify the man whose single-minded determination had precipitated the War of Independence. She found him laid out neatly on clean sheets in King George V Hospital at Arbour Hill, his fatal head wound carefully plugged. A soldier on guard duty told her they had done all they could. He gave her a ring Treacy had been wearing and a lock of hair. The body of William O'Connor, the Volunteer killed in the raid on the Munster and Leinster Bank in Phibsborough, was laid out with equal ceremony in the same room.[63]

Chapter 7 ∿

'THAT NIGHT I SHOULD HAVE UNDERSTOOD, AND FORGIVEN, ANY ACT OF REPRISAL BY OUR MEN'

The tactic of taking the fight to the enemy created a new reign of terror for Dubliners, who found they were no safer in their homes than on the streets. It was increasingly unclear who was killing whom, or why. Only when it emerged that the victim had connections with either the British state or the Republican movement was it possible to make an informed guess.

One of the shootings that caused most outrage was that of Peter O'Carroll at 1:50 a.m. on Saturday 12 October. O'Carroll was a 56-year-old invalid, confined to his home in Manor Street. Armed men forced their way in and questioned him on the whereabouts of his two Volunteer sons. When he refused to tell them he was shot with a pistol with a silencer attached and his body dumped, with a note claiming he was an informer. His wife, Annie, was invited to attend a military inquiry under the Restoration of Order Act. Instead she went to the local alderman, Michael Staines, for O'Carroll was an old Fenian. Dublin Corporation condemned his death and demanded a coroner's inquest, to no avail. Annie O'Carroll had no doubt that her husband 'was murdered by members of the Army of Occupation. Not content with this, they placed a label on his body which maligned the living and defamed the dead.'

Proposing the vote of sympathy, Staines said, 'An Englishman's home is his castle, but an Irishman's home is either his fort or his death bed.' In an uncharacteristically muted response, Dr McWalter suggested that there should be a proper inquest into 'every death of a citizen ... in the streets of Dublin.' Not even the Municipal Reform Association was prepared to defend such excesses by Crown forces.

Dubliners became increasingly fearful of the dangers that even casual proximity to the military could bring. When a youth 'got the wind up' in Charlemont Street at the sight of a motorised patrol approaching on Saturday 13 November, his fear quickly infected the crowd. The officer in charge of the patrol, suspecting that the fleeing civilians were Volunteers, ordered his men to open fire. Two girls playing nearby were hit: six-year-old Teresa Kavanagh was wounded in the arm and eight-year-old Annie O'Neill in the chest. The soldiers raced to the Meath Hospital with the eight-year-old but she died on the way. A DMP inspector was sent to the girl's home with a military order prohibiting any flags, 'marching or procession,' even by children, at the funeral. Her mother, whose husband had died of TB shortly before, said the family had no political affiliations. The policeman's response was to tell her, 'In that case it will not be necessary to bring force to see that the order is enforced.'[1]

Meanwhile there was a very public judicial execution in Mountjoy Prison, that of Kevin Barry. It followed the death of the hunger-striker Terence MacSwiney, Lord Mayor of Cork, a week earlier in Brixton Prison, London. Two other IRA prisoners had already died on hunger strike in Cork. The protest would be called off after MacSwiney's death, but his ordeal had captured the world's attention. Sinn Féin and the Irish Volunteers carried out a similar campaign in support of Barry. In large measure the circumstances of his arrest and the deaths of three young soldiers were successfully glossed over. On Dick McKee's instructions, Barry gave a statement of his rough handling in custody and interrogation, which was then portrayed as torture. It was certainly brutal, although nowhere near as bad as the treatment inflicted on some Volunteers taken prisoner. It still managed to shock British public opinion.

Young, handsome and undoubtedly brave, Barry cut a far more sympathetic figure than the elder statesmen making the case for his execution. It also brought home the republican message that the IRA was waging a war in which it adhered to the rules more closely than its opponents did.[2] The scenes outside Mountjoy Prison resembled those during the April hunger strike, but the atmosphere was, if anything, even more emotional. A large party of Cumann na mBan members, many of whom would have known Barry, assembled in Dorset Street as the hour of execution approached at 8 a.m. They marched up the North Circular Road to the prison and joined the early-morning crowd, some of whom still hoped for a last-minute reprieve. Several women began to recite the Rosary aloud and it was taken up by the whole gathering, with men in the crowd taking off their caps and uttering the responses. Any hope of a reprieve ended when the prison bell began to toll.

Immediately there was a movement in the crowd. Everyone—men and women, youths and girls—knelt down upon the muddy roadway, and the chorus of prayers became louder and more fervent. Many of the women were in tears, and even men displayed signs of emotion. While the prison bell was tolling the crowd remained on their knees.

When the first priest who had attended the prisoner emerged he was immediately surrounded for news. The crowds did not disperse until the official notice of execution had been posted on the prison gate. The *Irish Independent* reported:

> He was steadfast and unflinching to the end, walking to the scaffold without a tremor in voice or body.
>
> It is recorded that when being pinioned and blindfolded he objected to both processes, saying that as a soldier he was not afraid to die. The chaplains pay the highest tributes to the manner in which he met his death, his piety and bravery being unsurpassable.

Even Dr McWalter lent a hand with the demonisation of the enemy. He issued a statement saying that he had no official notice to attend Mountjoy Prison that morning as High Sheriff, and in the circumstances it would appear 'very doubtful if the execution proceedings were at all legal.'[3]

Events such as the deaths of MacSwiney and Barry played a major role in the propaganda campaign at home and abroad, but they had less effect on the progress of the war and on people's daily lives than the munitions strike, which was now entering its sixth month. Ireland was heavily dependent on the railways. Thanks to the excellent tram network, many Dubliners were less affected than people in rural areas. But there were fewer than 250 registered motor vehicles in the city in 1920, so that those living in the suburbs beyond the tramways' reach were thrown back on traditional horse-drawn transport.[4]

The military had their own vehicles, but the poor state of the roads, made worse by trenching and the demolition of bridges by the IRA, severely restricted movement. This was one of the main reasons why pressure was applied remorselessly on the railwaymen. As the British army commander in Ireland, Sir Nevil Macready, conceded, their refusal to carry troops or equipment had prevented large-scale winter counter-offensives against the IRA. On occasion the army had to use the navy to transport men and supplies to garrisons in the south and west. At first the railwaymen enjoyed the support of the National Union of Railwaymen in Britain, which had sanctioned the blacking of military supplies to Poland in the fight against the Bolsheviks. But there was a big difference between industrial action opposing military adventures abroad and taking it in opposition to a war at home. As Sir Hamar Greenwood put it in November, 'no Government can allow railways subsidised out of the pockets of the taxpayers to refuse to carry police and soldiers.' The Irish railways had been under direct military control since 1916, and if the strikers refused to carry troops, police or munitions, Greenwood warned, the government would use the Restoration of Order Act to exclude such items as the Royal Mail and old-age pensions. It might even close down the system completely.

Food committees were set up in all the cities and principal towns, including Dublin, to deal with the anticipated shortages that would ensue. The Dublin committee was established by the corporation and included members of every political group. It co-opted the Chief of Staff of the IRA, Richard Mulcahy, the commandant of the Dublin Brigade, Dick McKee, and the Secretary of the Irish Labour Party and Trades Union Congress, Thomas Johnson. John J. Devine of the corporation's Electricity Supply Department was appointed Secretary.

McKee appears to have taken charge of the deliberations, and one of the committee's first decisions was to compile a census of citizens to establish the essential needs of the city. However, the military seized the questionnaire forms before they could be distributed. The committee also made efforts to establish alternative routes for the supply of food to the city by motor lorries, canals and ships. A figure of £5 10s a day was struck with Dublin hauliers for collecting essential goods, but the motor permit regulations would confine them to a twenty-mile radius of the city. The canal system could deliver significant quantities of milk and eggs but was not geared to the delivery of meat and other food items. The corporation's steam vessel *Shamrock*, normally used for dumping raw sewage in Dublin Bay, was to be pressed into service, and plans were made to hire tramp steamers, but this would mean reliance on imports from Britain rather than on native produce. Nobody was under the illusion that normal life could continue without the railways.

Not surprisingly, on 15 November the corporation joined the growing chorus in trade union as well as business and British government circles for the strike to be called off. A special all-Ireland trade union congress was held in the Mansion House the very next day to discuss the crisis. By then the mass dismissals and suspensions of workers meant that railway services had finally begun to break down. On the day of the conference at least fifteen trains failed to run on the Great Southern and Western Railway, while the Midland and

Great Western Railway had put all staff on notice the previous day. If the railways closed, not alone would Dublin lose access to traditional sources of food but the provinces would lose access to vital imports as winter drew near.

Handsome tributes were paid to the railwaymen at the trade union conference. Thomas Farren, chairman of the NEC of the ILP&TUC, said that

> the railwaymen of Ireland should be proud of the part they played during this dispute. It is a common practice for the military ... to get up upon the footplate of an engine and say to a driver, "You have got to drive this train," in many cases with revolvers presented at their temples. They still asserted their manhood.

But there were warnings too. Thomas Johnson told delegates frankly that if the railway strike continued 'it would mean throwing back the social life of Ireland ... perhaps for a hundred years.' Communities would have to become self-supporting, and 'a complete change to the social outlook' would be required 'while the struggle lasted.' The conference pledged continuing support to the railway workers but also mandated the National Executive Committee to take the necessary measures to protect workers' wider interests.

Exactly one month later, on 14 December, the NEC advised railway workers 'to offer to carry everything that the British Military Authorities are willing to risk on the trains.'[5] The biggest, most protracted and most effective campaign of passive resistance to British rule was over; but in the meantime there had been a renewed surge of violence in Dublin and the provinces.

More ink has been spilt over Bloody Sunday than on any other event in the War of Independence, except possibly the Kilmichael ambush, which took place a week later. Retrospectively, both events were seen as part of a resurgence by the IRA, which had been wilting under combined military and Auxiliary pressure. In a triumphalist speech at the Mansion House in London on 9 November, Lloyd George declared that the government had 'murder by the throat.' On the same occasion the Secretary of State for the Colonies, Winston Churchill, included the Auxiliary Division in his response to the toast for the armed forces.[6]

On the very next night, 10 November, a raid on the home of Professor Michael Hayes at Longwood Avenue, off the South Circular Road, netted another cache of documents belonging to Richard Mulcahy, Chief of Staff of the IRA. Mulcahy narrowly escaped capture by climbing through a skylight. It was on this occasion that he had his bicycle accident and almost lost his dentures.[7] While only a relatively small number of names and addresses were obtained, proposals to carry out reprisals in England for the destruction of Irish property by Crown forces were discovered. These included plans to blow up Liverpool docks, one of the largest dock complexes in the world at that time. Arson attacks by IRA units in Britain had already begun, and the docks were promptly put under military protection.[8]

At the time the events of 21 November in Dublin had a more immediate impact than those on a remote country road in west Cork on 28 November. Bloody Sunday involved the deaths of twelve British officers, two members of the Auxiliary Division of the RIC and ten civilians. Well over sixty other people, most of them civilians, suffered serious injuries in the capital that day, and four died subsequently. The fact that all the assassinations were planned to take place on a Sunday morning at 9 a.m., when most of the targets could reasonably be expected to be at home, added to the general revulsion against the shootings. Yet Collins had at first wanted to kill far more suspected intelligence officers. The number of potential targets was drastically reduced because of a convergence of moral and logistical factors.

The moral-cum-political aspect came into play because an operation on this scale could not be sanctioned in the usual informal way that served for individual executions delegated to the Squad. A joint conference of senior cabinet and GHQ personnel was convened at which the Minister for Defence, Cathal Brugha, insisted that many names on the list be deleted because of insufficient evidence. On two occasions Brugha himself planned to assassinate the British Cabinet, but, like his colleagues, he was constantly torn between the need to use sufficient force to make the enemy sue for peace and the need to avoid undermining the legitimacy of the cause by resorting to methods that forfeited popular support.

Many ordinary Volunteers shared Brugha's ethical concerns, and their attitude had to be taken into account, because an operation on the scale of Bloody Sunday could not be carried out by members of the Squad and other active-service Volunteers alone. When the purpose of the mobilisation on Bloody Sunday was explained, some Volunteers were reluctant to participate. Even some senior officers, such as Simon Donnelly, deputy commandant of the 4th Battalion, within whose area many of the targets lived, expressed doubts to McKee. McKee told him to 'do your best. If we don't get them, they will get us.'

One member of the 4th Battalion was nineteen-year-old Christopher 'Todd' Andrews, who believed that 'the prospect of killing a man in cold blood was alien to our ideas of how war should be conducted.' He admitted also to being apprehensive because of the dangers involved. 'We were already being affected

psychologically by the terror of the Tans.' The execution of Kevin Barry three
weeks earlier for his part in the Church Street raid meant that Volunteers such
as Andrews knew they might be hanged for murder if taken prisoner. Most
Volunteers who did participate in Bloody Sunday went to confession
beforehand, to be 'in a state of grace' should they die.

Andrews was doubly fortunate in that he honoured his commitment to go
on a raid but his quarries, Lieutenant William Noble and Captain William King,
were out. Ironically, both men were hunting IRA suspects when Andrews arrived
with his fellow-assassins at 7 Ranelagh Road, the lodging-house where they
lived. The raiders raced through the house looking for their quarry. Andrews
found himself in a room

> empty except for a half-naked woman who sat up in bed looking terror
> stricken … I was very excited but, even so, I felt a sense of shame and
> embarrassment … I was glad to get out quickly and moved to the next room
> where there was a man shaving. He was literally petrified with fear. His safety
> razor froze in mid-air. Thinking he was Noble, I was going to pull the trigger
> of my .45 when Coughlan [Andrews's company commander] shouted, 'He's
> all right.' He was a lodger in the house and was apparently one of our
> intelligence sources.

The Squad members present were less conscientious. Cheated of their prey, they
ransacked the house looking for files. Apparently Noble and King were not as
careless as some of their colleagues and had no papers on the premises. Squad
members behaved 'like Black and Tans,' tearing furniture apart and, whether
deliberately or not, setting fire to a room with children in it. In fact one member
of the Squad, Joe Dolan, infuriated at King's escape, used the missing man's
sword scabbard to beat his unfortunate lover. 'Coughlan was furious at their
conduct,' Andrews wrote, and local Volunteers found themselves forming a
bucket chain to douse the fire with water from a tap in the basement. On his
way home Andrews wondered

> whether I was glad or sorry that Noble had not been at home. I would
> certainly have felt no remorse at having shot him but I found it hard to get
> the memory of the terrified woman and indeed, the equally terrified lodger
> from my mind.[9]

Andrews and Coughlan were unaware that the missing men were among the
most feared enemies of the Squad and that their absence was a serious setback.

King was doubly lucky, because he had scooped Dick McKee and Peadar Clancy in a raid a few hours earlier on the other side of the city. McKee's prediction to Simon Donnelly was about to come true, for himself at least.

The first inkling that one officer's wife had that it was not going to be a normal Sunday morning came when she looked out her third-floor rear bedroom window in another large lodging-house, 28 Upper Pembroke Street, and saw a man climbing over the garden wall. Caroline Woodcock could hear church bells ringing in the distance. 'My husband had hurried over his dressing, as he was to take a Church Parade at the Commander-in-Chief's,' she wrote. At first she thought the man 'had come to see one of the maids. But directly I saw him take a revolver out of his pocket my fears were aroused, and I rushed to the door, and shouted to my husband.'

But he had gone down to breakfast and it was already too late. Some twenty-two Volunteers had been mobilised for the operation, as there were several officers staying at the house. Their job was inadvertently made easier by the porter, who opened the front door at 9 a.m. to shake out the mats. By the time Caroline Woodcock rushed to the landing

the hall was full of armed men, dressed in overcoats ... and wearing cloth caps and felt hats. My husband was ordered to put his hands up and to give his name. He did so, and added, 'There are women in the house.' The murderers answered, 'We know it.' At that moment the door behind my husband opened, and he, fearing that one of the officers he had hoped to warn was coming out of his room, shouted, 'Look out, Montgomery.' As he spoke they fired and shot my husband through the shoulder, and he fell at the foot of the stairs. He scrambled up, but he was shot again through the back. Getting up again, he half walked and half crawled upstairs.

The man her husband had tried to warn, Lieutenant-Colonel Hugh Montgomery, was shot twice. He collapsed at his wife's feet and a bullet grazed her knee. Charlie Dalton, who was primarily an intelligence operative rather than a gunman, ran upstairs, where he saw more officers shot.

Shaking, I said to the Officer of my party: 'Wait for me. I have to search for papers.'
    'Wait be damned! Get out of here as quickly as you can.'
    I was only too glad to take his advice ... In the hall three or four men were lined up against the wall, some of our officers facing them. Knowing

their fate I felt great pity for them. It was plain they knew it too. As I crossed the threshold the volley was fired.

Recalling events from the other side, Caroline Woodcock wrote:

> Never to my dying day shall I forget the scene in the hall and on the stairs, where four officers had been shot ... There were great splashes of blood on the walls, floor, and stairs, bits of plaster were lying about, and on the walls were the marks of innumerable bullets.
>
> Fortunately, the murderers had been so panic-stricken themselves and their hands so shaky that their firing had been wild in the extreme.

Although her husband had been hit four times, he survived, as did Captain Brian Keenlyside, his adjutant. Both men were regular army officers, but the two officers killed in the upstairs shootings that shook Dalton, Lieutenants Leonard Price and Charles 'Chummy' Dowling, were intelligence men. Unlike Woodcock and Keenlyside, they were armed but never had a chance to use their weapons.[10]

Captain William Newberry's pregnant wife was less fortunate than Caroline Woodcock. Two members of the Squad burst into the couple's flat at 92 Lower Baggot Street and shot him, still in his pyjamas, as he tried to escape through the window. They then questioned him as he lay dying about where he kept his papers.

Luck on this occasion was with Captain Jeune, the man who had bungled the raid at Drumcondra a month earlier. He had rooms in the same house as the Woodcocks but received last-minute information on Saturday night that ammunition was stored in the railway works at Inchicore. After hours of fruitless searching, his Saturday night ruined, he decided to grab a few hours' sleep in a railway carriage. When he returned to Upper Pembroke Street he saw

> the body of my friend Chummy Dowling, a grand ex-guardee, wounded three times in the war, lying full length on the floor. As he was to have relieved me he was in uniform and had been shot through the heart, probably by a small Sinn Feiner because there was a bullet hole in one corner of the ceiling.[11]

Captain Baggallay, who had lost a leg in the Great War, was another fatality. He was shot in his bed, just as his own alleged victim, Councillor John Lynch, had been shot in bed at the Exchange Hotel by mistake for Liam Lynch on 22 September. One of the young Volunteers who took part in this attack was the future Taoiseach Seán Lemass.

The worst encounter of the morning was at Lower Mount Street, where members of the Squad sought out two other officers involved in the shooting of Lynch. They were now operating under cover. One was Lieutenant Henry Angliss, who was going by the name of McMahon and posing as the landlord. The raiders succeeded in killing Angliss, but the screams of other residents and the shots attracted the attention of a passing lorryload of Auxiliaries. In the gunfight that followed, two Auxiliaries were killed and one Volunteer, Frank Teeling, was wounded and captured. One of his captors had a gun pointed at his head and was giving him to the count of ten to name his accomplices when the commander of the Auxiliaries, Brigadier-General Crozier, arrived on the scene. He told his men he had no objections to Teeling being executed, but it would have to be after a court-martial. The evidence against Teeling was even more overwhelming than that against Kevin Barry, and the verdict was not in doubt.

The easiest executions were those of two officers in the Gresham Hotel, where the gunmen forced the hall porter to point out their rooms. They were led by Captain Paddy Moran, a 1916 veteran and recently elected president of the barmen's union.[12] He was the only part-time Volunteer officer to lead one of the successful execution squads that morning. At another hotel, the Eastwood in Leeson Street, the job had been left to the 4th Battalion. The officer in charge took the word of the manager that their target was not at home and left.

Altogether twelve British army officers and two Auxiliaries had been killed, while one IRA Volunteer had been wounded and taken prisoner. The death count would have been much higher if all the targets had been at home and if all the IRA units had pressed home their attacks. How many of the officers were actually engaged in intelligence operations has been contested ever since. However, volume 2 of the British army's own *History of the Rebellion in Ireland*, covering intelligence operations, states:

The murders of November 21st, 1920, temporarily paralysed the Army Special Branch. Several of its most efficient officers were murdered and the majority of the others resident in the city were brought into the Castle and Central Hotel for safety. This centralisation in the most inconvenient places possible greatly decreased the opportunities for obtaining information and for re-establishing anything in the nature of a secret service.[13]

After the encounter at Lower Mount Street, Crozier rushed to Dublin Castle with the news.

> Never shall I forget the scene in the mess when I walked in and announced the three murders. I was in uniform … The superior intelligence crowd at breakfast, mostly 'hoy hoy lah-di-dahs' were in mufti … They were generally afraid to wear uniform for fear of being 'spotted.' I had just finished my story, during which the eggs became cold and the mouths opened wider and wider when the telephone rang. 'What!' I heard as the speaker paled ashy white, 'in Leeson Street? … Yes … yes … Hold on. About fifty officers are shot,' he said as he turned round, staggering as he clutched the table, 'in all parts of the city—Collins has done in most of the secret service people.'[14]

An emergency meeting of senior military officers and civil servants was convened, at which it was decided to seal all roads and stop trains for twenty-four hours. The mail boat was to be searched before being allowed to sail for Holyhead, all British officers living out were to be brought into Dublin Castle or moved to hotels that would be commandeered in the city centre. There was to be a round-up of as many IRA 'Extremists'

> (i.e. known Gunmen, not officers) as possible, irrespective of actual charges against them for any specific 'tryable' act, to go into detention camp already arranged at Ballykinler near Newcastle.

The curfew in Dublin was increased to extend from 10 p.m. to 5 a.m. instead of midnight to 5 a.m. Dublin Corporation was singled out for particular attention as a stronghold of the enemy. City Hall and adjoining offices at Cork Hill and in Castle Street were to be commandeered. One of those attending the meeting, Mark Sturgis, a senior British civil servant seconded to Dublin Castle as part of the revamp under Sir Hamar Greenwood, relished the prospect of seizing City Hall. He commented in his diary: 'I have long coveted it—we want room for a garrison and it's too near the Castle to be in enemy hands.'[15]

The other concern of senior officials in the Castle was to make sure there were no reprisals, such as had happened in Balbriggan and other towns after members of the Crown forces had been killed. The fact that it was a Sunday was a considerable advantage in this regard.

Unfortunately, by a cruel coincidence a friendly challenge match had been arranged for the afternoon in Croke Park between the Tipperary and Dublin football teams. It had been organised as a testimonial for a GAA steward, a member of the 2nd Battalion, who had been seriously injured refereeing a match.

Because of increasing unrest, fixtures had become intermittent and attendances at Croke Park poor. In early November matches had been suspended as a mark of respect following the deaths of Terence MacSwiney and Kevin Barry. The GAA organisers were actually advised by the IRA to call off the match but decided to go ahead, on the grounds that a last-minute cancellation would confirm British suspicions that the organisation was a front for the IRA. It was a no-win situation, because the British now concluded that the match was contrived to allow IRA gunmen from Co. Tipperary to enter the city undetected to carry out the shootings. In fact there were two Volunteers on the Tipperary team, both of whom received some inkling in a bar on Saturday night that a 'big job' was to be pulled off next morning.

That Sunday afternoon there was a larger turn-out for the match than usual, which was surprising, given that trains into Dublin had been cancelled by 11 a.m. and motor vehicles were ordered off the roads from midday.

As with the morning's shootings, most of the events of the afternoon are contested. The mixed convoy of soldiers and Auxiliaries arrived in anything from ten to seventeen lorries, accompanied by two armoured cars. One group approached the grounds from the north-east, down Clonliffe Road and Fitzroy Avenue, while the other group arrived from the direction of the North Circular Road. Both groups deployed at about 3:30 p.m., shortly after the match had begun. The convoy coming from the North Circular Road stopped at the bridge over the Royal Canal. As members of the Auxiliary Division jumped down from the lorries a group of men standing outside, described in the British accounts as 'pickets', ran through the turnstiles into the grounds. According to Auxiliary witnesses at the subsequent military inquiry, held *in camera*, some of these 'pickets' opened fire as they fled, and fire was returned. To add to the confusion, some Auxiliaries were in plain clothes. One of these, who vaulted over the closed turnstiles in pursuit of the fleeing men, told the inquiry that he opened fire only after being fired upon from within the grounds.

Harry Colley, who would become Adjutant of the Dublin Brigade in the reshuffle following Dick McKee's imminent death, described the period before the shooting differently. He said a warning had been received from a DMP sergeant 'who, while not in any way in sympathy with us, had been so horrified when he discovered what was about to happen' that he 'thought it his duty to get word to us to see if the calamity could be avoided.'

As it happened, the 2nd Battalion normally provided stewards at Croke Park, but they had been stood down because of the operation planned for the morning. Colley, along with two other senior IRA officers living locally, Seán Russell and Tom Kilcoyne, went to the match and warned the organisers to call it off. However, the GAA officials were reluctant to do so, as they were afraid the crowd would want a refund and if they were to give the real reason for its cancellation there might be panic. According to Colley, they did agree to close the turnstiles, but a breakdown in communication meant that this did not happen before the military and Auxiliaries arrived. Meanwhile Colley went to his mother's house in Clonliffe Avenue nearby for his Sunday dinner. He had just begun eating when the firing began.

Inside the grounds the crowd had been distracted from the match by a military aircraft that circled the pitch twice at low altitude. This caused no alarm, as it was now a common enough occurrence at large public events in the city; nor did the firing of a Very pistol by the pilot cause concern. Only later would this come to be regarded as the signal for an attack. Almost immediately afterwards sustained gunfire broke out from the Jones's Road entrance. Panic erupted. Michael Hogan, one of the two Volunteers on the Tipperary team, was killed as he tried to crawl with other players across the open ground. Another player, Tommy Ryan, who was with Hogan when he died, managed to climb a paling and find refuge in a house in Clonliffe Road adjoining the pitch. He was taken prisoner when the house was surrounded. His shorts and shirt each had a Tricolour sewn into them; these were torn off and he was made to walk naked back to Croke Park, where the rest of the team were detained. Meanwhile hundreds of civilians had 'swept like an avalanche onto the pitch.' Many prayed aloud as they ran. Some, like Ryan, climbed over the paling and tried to hide in adjoining houses, only to be rounded up and brought back. Others tried to escape through the turnstiles closest to Clonliffe Avenue, to be confronted by soldiers with fixed bayonets. Some received bayonet wounds as they were forced back into the grounds. The *Irish Independent* reported:

> Everyone was subjected to a minute search, being first ordered to put their hands up. Most of the men bore marks of the terrible experience. Some were bleeding profusely from the face and hands, others were hatless, while more had their clothes torn and [were] blood spattered ... When any motion took place in the crowd a volley of shots was fired over their heads.

Ten people were killed immediately and fourteen died in total, mirroring the British fatalities earlier in the day. Apart from Hogan, one other Volunteer was killed: Joseph Traynor of F Company, 4th Battalion. Another sixty-four people were injured seriously enough to require treatment in hospital. Among the wounded were Tom Keogh, who had led the attack on McMahon's house in Lower Mount Street that morning and then returned across the city on the Liffey ferry to attend the match. He received a flesh wound in the arm. Other spectators were not so fortunate: some were trampled in the rush to escape once the firing began. The figures could have been worse, but some of the GAA officials redeemed themselves by managing to restore calm, telling the crowd that the military were firing blanks and to lie down. In fact the military and Auxiliaries fired 278 live rounds, including 50 machine-gun rounds.

The number of casualties would have been much higher if dozens of spectators, mainly local people, had not escaped down the railway line beside the Royal Canal. The badly wounded Joseph Traynor was carried along the track to 5 Sackville Gardens. An ambulance was called, but the Auxiliaries, now aware of the new escape route, sealed it off and refused to allow the ambulance through. Traynor sank into a coma and subsequently died in Jervis Street Hospital. Meanwhile the householder, Christopher Ring, another Volunteer, was made to stand in the middle of the street by the Auxiliaries and sing 'God Save the King'.[16]

The youngest victims were ten-year-old Jerome O'Leary from Blessington Street and fourteen-year-old John Scott, who lived almost opposite Croke Park in Fitzroy Avenue. The latter appears to have been fatally injured in the confrontation with soldiers at the lower exit from the grounds nearest his home. A man who obviously did not realise the boy lived nearby carried him to the home of a Mrs Coleman in James's Avenue, some distance away, where he was placed on a table. Dr Monahan, the Mater house surgeon, told the inquest:

> Mrs Coleman and her two girls knelt down by his side and said prayers, and the little boy made responses. All the time the rattle of shots was heard outside and they were unable to get out for a drink of water for the dying child. He was suffering greatly and moaning a lot and died three quarters of an hour later.

Only one woman was killed, 26-year-old Jane Boyle, who lived in Lennox Street on the south side of the city and had been due to marry the following Wednesday; she was shot in the back and trampled in the stampede.

Croke Park presented an eerie sight that evening, strewn with

overcoats, umbrellas, walking sticks, hats, caps, ladies' jewellery etc., as well as about 200 bicycles. Evidently getting news of this a mob swept down on the park and rushed the gates. The few officials could do nothing to prevent the wholesale looting that followed. Women, girls and young men carried away handfuls of coats.

Predictably, the Castle bulletin next day claimed that gunmen had travelled to Dublin to carry out assassinations under cover of the match, and that '30 revolvers were collected on the field, besides the few captured on spectators.' However, no-one was charged with possession of a firearm, although a number of guns were put on display for the press. According to two DMP members present, there was no gunfire from the crowd and the Auxiliaries ceased firing only after being ordered to do so by an army officer.

The death toll for Bloody Sunday was not yet over. At 11:45 p.m. an eighty-year-old man, William Barnett, was shot through the heart in Mountjoy Square, not far from Croke Park, while walking from his home on the North Circular Road to his business premises in Summer Hill. No-one claimed responsibility for this shooting, and it had no obvious motive.

But the killings connected with Bloody Sunday were not at an end. On its eve, the commandant of the Dublin Brigade, Dick McKee, and his deputy, Peadar Clancy, had been lifted in the city centre and taken to Dublin Castle by a raiding party led by Captain William King and his constant companion, Captain Jocelyn Hardy. King was intelligence officer for K Company of the Auxiliaries, and Hardy was an Irish officer who had served with the Connaught Rangers. The two men were among the most efficient and most ruthless British intelligence operatives in the city. McKee and Clancy managed to burn documents they had brought from the meeting held a few hours earlier to complete details for the Bloody Sunday operations even as the door of their safe house in Gloucester Street was being broken down. Clancy was well known by sight to the British, because he had led the Mountjoy hunger strike earlier in the year. They were at first unsure of McKee's identity.

When the two men arrived at the Castle they found other Volunteers arrested earlier in the night, including some who had been detailed to take part in the assassinations. There was also a young man, Conor Clune, head clerk of Raheen Rural Industries in Co. Clare, who had been lifted in Vaughan's Hotel. He had come to Dublin on business and was not a member of the IRA. He had gone to Vaughan's for a drink and attracted attention by his belligerent attitude towards the raiding party, declaring that he was as willing as any man to 'die for Ireland.' Unfortunately for him, Captain Hardy decided to look at the hotel register and found that Clune was not listed. He then searched him, declaring, 'This bloody fellow hasn't even got a toothbrush with him,' before adding him to the bag for the night.

Over the next few hours McKee and Clancy were interrogated and tortured by King and Hardy, but they did not betray the operations planned for a few hours' time, nor did any other Volunteers in custody. The latter included Ben Doyle, a Volunteer officer who had been arrested at work in his insurance office on Saturday morning. Doyle said:

> From noon to night that Sunday the scene in that Dublin Castle guard room is beyond description.
>
> The stark mad Auxiliaries lost all traits of being human. Suffering from the effects of the blow that had been struck ... combined with the fact that they were drinking whiskey or gin, they simply could do nothing except shoot, shoot, shoot and drink more whiskey and gin. There was nobody in control but somehow they were making plans for the coming tragedy. Apparently they could not execute up to twenty prisoners out of hand so they were setting the stage for something 'explainable.'

Doyle took his mind off what he thought was his own inevitable end by reciting mentally Pearse's last poem, 'The Mother'.

At about 5:30 p.m., after the shootings at Croke Park, most of the prisoners were sent to Beggarsbush Barracks. One Volunteer, Patrick Young, could not find his cap. Witnessing his dilemma, McKee 'took off his hat and gave it to me, saying "I don't think I will want this any more".'

Next morning at eleven o'clock McKee, Clancy and Clune allegedly tried to fight their way out of the guardroom at Dublin Castle and were killed. Captain King gave evidence corroborating the account given by the Auxiliaries on duty at the time that they killed the men in self-defence. Clune's death was particularly embarrassing: not alone was he innocent of any rebel activity but he was a nephew of the Catholic Archbishop of Perth, Australia, Dr Patrick Clune, who was involved in discreet peace initiatives by the British government.

The official statement issued from Dublin Castle after the Bloody Sunday attacks on army officers said the men were 'connected with the administration of military justice, or as court martial officers concerned in preparing cases for trial.' It went on to give accounts of the shootings, including such details as the death of Captain Newberry in front of his wife. It was less forthcoming on the events at Croke Park, insisting that soldiers and Auxiliaries were returning fire from the crowd.

Unfortunately for the Castle, another death came to light that weekend that could not be explained away, that of Father Michael Griffin, a curate in Galway who had been abducted from his home on Sunday 14 November. His body was found the following Saturday night in a bog at Cloch Scoilte, four miles away. He had been shot through the head. Like a number of local curates, Griffin had become an advocate of Sinn Féin policies. Lieutenant-Colonel Evelyn Lindsay Young, like Jocelyn Hardy an Irish-born officer with the Connaught Rangers, said many years later that the identity of the killers was common knowledge in military circles. Griffin was shot because he had identified to the IRA a well-known loyalist as an informer. The internal military inquiry into Griffin's death failed to identify those responsible.[17]

Unusually, the Republican propaganda machine failed to respond effectively to its Dublin Castle rival on Bloody Sunday. For one thing, Sinn Féin publicists had not been briefed in advance, for obvious reasons. For another, the results had been too disappointing to boast about. Quite a few important targets had slipped the net, either through luck or through the incompetence of those sent to kill them.

How many of the officers killed were intelligence agents has been contested ever since. The figure may have been less than half, as Jane Leonard suggests in a detailed examination into their backgrounds. Collins himself publicly accepted that one man shot at the Gresham Hotel, Captain Patrick McCormack of the Veterinary Corps, was probably not a spy. McCormack's misfortune was his involvement with the Gezira Sporting Club and Alexandria Turf Club in Egypt, a possible case of guilt by association with the so-called Cairo Gang. With peculiar symmetry, his death, like that of Conor Clune, was particularly embarrassing, as he belonged to a prominent Catholic family. He was a nephew of the late Bishop of Galway, Dr Francis McCormack, and a cousin of Michael Davitt, founder of the Land League.

On the other hand, Collins had numerous sources for cross-checking information, including Lily Mernin, a typist for the British Military Intelligence office. (See chapter 4.) She was conscientiously typing detailed notes on military intelligence operations with equal efficiency for both sides. Rather than risk making extra carbon copies in the office, she would go to an empty house in Clonliffe Avenue after work and repeat the exercise there. Her reports would then be left on the typewriter for collection. She was further protected by her *nom de guerre*, 'Little Gent', which in correspondence was shortened to 'Lt G', further obscuring her identity should incriminating documents be captured.[18]

On the other side of the balance sheet, the IRA had lost Dick McKee and Peadar Clancy. Collins was devastated at McKee's loss, and his replacement, Oscar Traynor, was widely regarded as no match for his predecessor. Although he undertook frequent organisational initiatives, with varying degrees of success, Traynor lacked McKee's political standing and his ability to inspire a fierce loyalty among Volunteers. If McKee had a weakness it was for taking on too many tasks: at the time of his death he was Director of Training and editor of the IRA's newspaper *An tÓglach* as well as commandant of the Dublin Brigade. Had McKee survived the War of Independence, the role of the Dublin Brigade in the Truce and in the Civil War would have been far more significant, whichever side he would have taken on the Treaty. Like Collins, he combined ruthlessness with charm, and adherence to the Fenian tradition with pragmatism. According to Harry Colley, who took the anti-Treaty side, McKee told him that a republic was unattainable, but that was all the more reason for an effective military campaign to drive the hardest political bargain possible.[19]

If McKee's death demoralised many of his comrades, fear of retribution cowed most Dubliners. Even after the Croke Park blood-letting people were far from sure that the vengeance of the Auxiliaries was sated. As Caroline Woodcock made her way in an armoured lorry to visit her wounded husband in hospital on Sunday evening she recalled:

> Never, if I live to be a hundred, shall I forget the Dublin streets that night. They were crowded, though one would have thought only fools would have been out at such a time.
>
> There was firing everywhere, and occasionally the crash of a bomb. We dashed along at a terrific pace. The driver was longing to run over some one. The men were longing to shoot. They were mad with passion. One motor car did not stop when challenged, and they fired at once. Fortunately they missed it. It was an RIC car, going from one hotel to another, collecting luggage belonging to the survivors of the morning's massacre, who had already been moved into the Castle and other safe places.

On the return journey, as the lorry roared past,

> people fell on their knees on the pavements. I could feel no pity for them. I hated them. I know nothing about reprisals ... but I do know that night I should have understood, and forgiven, any act of reprisal by our men.[20]

Revulsion and incomprehension at the attacks on army officers spread far beyond the British establishment and unionist community: it deeply affected many nationalists. Despite almost two years of political violence in which the only rules of engagement were that there were no rules, shooting men in their beds in front of their wives on a Sunday morning was still considered beyond the pale.

Even families of Volunteers felt revulsion at these activities. Pat McRae was a driver for the Squad. He explained his early departure on Bloody Sunday by telling his wife he was going on a fishing trip. Later, while trying to catch up on sleep on a couch after a late breakfast, she

> came into the room crying with a 'Stop Press' in her hand.
>
> I woke up and asked her what was the matter. Before speaking she handed me the 'Stop Press' and wanted to know was this the fishing expedition I had been on … I said: 'Yes, and don't you see we had a good catch' … She then said: 'I don't care what you think about it, I think it is murder.'

McRae insisted she was talking nonsense and added, 'I'd feel like going to the altar after that job.' But that night he found himself sleeping in St Anne's demesne, Raheny, and did not return home for a week.[21]

It had certainly been the most lethal day of the War of Independence, with thirty-five people killed in a little over twenty-four hours in Dublin and more than sixty seriously wounded, not to mention the discovery of Father Griffin's body in Co. Galway and five fatal shootings elsewhere.

Like most of the British press, the *Irish Times* accepted the Dublin Castle version of events at face value.

> Yesterday was Dublin's most dreadful day since Easter Week of 1916. Fourteen persons were done to death, of whom twelve were servants of the Crown … Some of them were torn from their beds and murdered in the presence of their wives.

It fully accepted the Castle's version of what happened at Croke Park and swallowed the story that the shootings were aimed at officers engaged solely in the administration of justice, through the courts-martial system. Although it condemned the 'mysterious murder of the Reverend Michael Griffin, in County Galway,' for being 'as foul a deed as any that was done yesterday in Dublin,' the emphasis was overwhelmingly on the capital, which 'has reached the nadir of moral and political degradation.'[22]

By contrast, the *Freeman's Journal* emphasised the happenings in Croke Park and compared them to the massacre at Amritsar in 1919, where British soldiers killed 379 people and wounded more than 1,100 others during the suppression of a proscribed protest by Indian nationalists. With unconscious irony regarding the disparity in casualties, the *Freeman* pointed out that, unlike the Indians, the people in Croke Park had done nothing illegal. There were 'no proclamations, no warnings, no legalities defied.' The Auxiliaries had gone there in search of trouble and found it. 'The slaughter was a classic sample of a Government reprisal—the innocent were shot down in a blind vengeance.' It offered an olive branch of sorts: with reference to Dáil Éireann's objective of an independent republic the *Freeman* counselled that 'people do not expect miracles—they would expect peace with honour, peace with full freedom in those affairs that are their aim.'[23]

The other main nationalist paper, the *Irish Independent*, dwelt on the death of Father Griffin, which it described as the 'most appalling' event to come to light that weekend.

> There have been several instances lately of Catholic clergymen being threatened and insulted, but that one should be done to death and buried by stealth is an occurrence without parallel in the history of Ireland for at least 120 years.[24]

Another near-fatal casualty was the GAA. Very few major fixtures would be played in Croke Park before the Truce in July 1921. The takings from the Bloody Sunday game were seized by Auxiliaries, according to one of the collectors, although it is impossible to say where they ended up in the murderous chaos of the day. What is certain is that by the end of 1920 the GAA faced bankruptcy. It was bailed out by the Dáil Éireann cabinet, which agreed to pay off debts of £1,700 and advanced the association a loan of £6,000, at 5 per cent interest.[25]

The following Thursday saw a massive demonstration of military power in honour of eight of the officers shot on Bloody Sunday, along with the two Auxiliaries killed that day. Ten gun carriages bore the bodies, while three police tenders carried the remains of three Black and Tans shot in Cos. Cork and Clare during the previous week. All thirteen bodies were being returned to England for burial. The funeral procession began at 10:30 a.m. from King George V Hospital, where double ranks of soldiers lined Infirmary Road, along with detachments from the Royal Air Force, DMP, RIC, regular army and RIC Auxiliary Division. The advance party was formed by representatives from the regiments of the dead officers, as was the firing party. A single artillery round marked the opening of the obsequies, followed by Chopin's Funeral March and the Dead March from Handel's *Saul*. After a series of hymns the military bands changed to a quick march as the coffins, draped with Union Jacks, proceeded down the quays to the North Wall, where the destroyer *Sea Wolf* waited to receive the remains.

A thousand men from the 24th and 25th Brigades of the Dublin garrison followed the funeral cortege. Behind them came cavalry units, more detachments of the DMP, RIC and Auxiliaries and a rearguard of soldiers with an armoured car. It was meant to overawe the citizenry, and it did. Union Jacks flew at half mast in the city centre. The *Daily Telegraph* correspondent reported: 'As a token of respect and fitting reverence to men whom all regard as martyrs to the sacred principle of duty every business house within the city closed its doors … between 10 a.m. and 1 p.m.' The few businesses that 'thought to offer insult to the dead were brought to reason if not to a mood of reverence' by visits from the Auxiliary Police.

While there was a general 'attitude of reverence' among spectators, the Auxiliaries ordered any man in the crowd wearing a cap or hat to remove it, or removed it themselves and threw it in the Liffey, so that the river carried a flotilla of confiscated headgear on the tide. At the Four Courts the Lord Chancellor, the Master of the Rolls and the Lord Chief Justice waited to pay their respects. Parties of infantry, Auxiliaries and DMP were posted at all the bridges, and tram services north of the river were suspended. The Under-Secretary for Ireland, Sir John Anderson, and Assistant Under-Secretary, Andy Cope, paid their respects as the procession reached O'Connell Bridge. There was also a large contingent of clergy from all the Protestant denominations in the City, many of them former army chaplains; but the Catholic archbishop, Dr Walsh, was not represented, nor was the Lord Mayor. The public were not allowed near the destroyer on the North Wall, but selected journalists were invited to witness the bodies being brought aboard and the playing of the Last Post.

Meanwhile the funeral Masses of twelve of the civilians killed at Croke Park took place quietly at various churches around the city. They included those of 26-year-old Jane Boyle, fourteen-year-old John Scott and ten-year-old Jerome O'Leary. The military banned any displays at the funerals or any processions to Glasnevin or Mount Jerome cemeteries. However, there were large crowds at Thurles and Clonmel to greet the Tipperary Gaels on their 'marvellous escape' from Croke Park, bringing the remains of their dead team-mates with them.[26]

Two other men were buried that day: the former commandant of the Dublin Brigade, Dick McKee, and his deputy, Peadar Clancy. Despite the risks, Michael Collins insisted on attending the Requiem Mass and giving a brief funeral oration. Ironically, the huge concentration of British forces at the removal of the dead officers not alone facilitated Collins's homage to his dead comrades but allowed hundreds of Volunteers from the Dublin Brigade to march in formation behind the coffins to Glasnevin. When a photograph of Collins carrying one of the coffins appeared in the *Evening Herald* that afternoon Volunteers raided its offices, smashed the offending block and in a citywide trawl of newsagents managed to scoop up thousands of copies of the paper. Miraculously, the British failed to obtain a single copy of the most up-to-date photograph of Ireland's most wanted rebel.[27]

After Bloody Sunday, British intelligence operations in Dublin were brought largely under the control of Colonel Winter, whose rule was much resented and judgement mistrusted by the military. Most of his new operatives were based in Dublin Castle and its environs. Never again would the IRA be presented with easy targets. One result of the reorganisation was that Lily Mernin found little current intelligence material coming across her desk. However, she got to know many of the new arrivals and identified them to senior IRA intelligence personnel.

Her first rendezvous was with Collins's Deputy Director of Intelligence, Liam Tobin, at a rugby match in Lansdowne Road; but most of her work was with Frank Saurin. A dandy, always immaculately turned out and sometimes scandalising colleagues by wearing lavender gloves, Saurin was bespoke for the job. He had already made hotels, restaurants, sports meetings 'and such places' his special field. He would accompany Lily Mernin on window-shopping expeditions and meals in fashionable watering-holes around Grafton Street and Dame Street, such as the Wicklow, Shelbourne, Fuller's, Moira and Central Hotels. The Central was one of a number of smaller hotels taken over by the military to accommodate officers who had been living in private quarters before Bloody Sunday. The bar at Jammet's restaurant in Nassau Street was a particular haunt of off-duty Auxiliaries. The strong attachment of British spies and paramilitaries to what the best hotels, restaurants and cafés Dublin had to offer left them exposed, but mounting attacks was risky and there were few successes. The Auxiliary garrison in the Castle also organised in-house smoking concerts and whist drives, at which Mernin volunteered her services. She brought along Sally McAsey, Saurin's girl-friend and future wife, to help out.[28]

A crackdown on Sinn Féin and its allies began in the week after Bloody Sunday. On Wednesday 24 November, the day before the great funeral march through the city, the Auxiliaries raided Liberty Hall, head office of the ITGWU, and arrested every man found on the premises, including the union's General

Treasurer, Alderman William O'Brien, its General President, Tom Foran, and the Secretary of the Labour Party and Irish Trades Union Congress, Thomas Johnson. All were subsequently released, but during a five-hour search from roof to basement the Auxiliaries meticulously smashed furniture, equipment and fittings, rendering the hall uninhabitable. A revolver, bombs, ammunition and a rifle rest were found behind a fireplace, although the search parties missed bomb-making material. The Auxiliaries carried union publications, flags and banners into Beresford Place and used them for a bonfire. Altogether £5,000 worth of damage was done, and the union had to move its offices to Parnell Square. While partially renovated as a branch office, Liberty Hall would not resume its role as head office of the union until it was rebuilt in 1965.[29]

Two days after Liberty Hall was sacked, Arthur Griffith was arrested in a raid on St Lawrence Road, Clontarf, much to the chagrin of Sir John Anderson and the British political establishment, who saw Griffith as a moderating influence within the Republican leadership. His place as Acting President of the Irish Republic was taken by Michael Collins for the rest of de Valera's sojourn in the United States.

One decision taken at the emergency meeting in Dublin Castle on Bloody Sunday that would have an impact in the months ahead was to expedite the building of internment camps at Ballykinler, Co. Down, and Collinstown and Baldonnel, Co. Dublin. In the absence of more sophisticated methods, the IRA would be ground down by the indiscriminate use of coercion. By the first week in December regular consignments of internees were being despatched from the North Wall by destroyer to Belfast, *en route* for Ballykinler. The first contingent was put on board the *Sea Wolf*, which had taken the coffins of the officers killed on Bloody Sunday to Holyhead. Each night approximately a hundred men were transported by lorry with an armoured car escort to the North Wall during curfew, to minimise the risk of protests or rescue attempts. Nothing was allowed to interfere with the schedule. Even gales of up to 70 miles per hour did not delay the sailing of the destroyer *Valorous* later in the week. The *Belfast Telegraph* reported with some relish that the prisoners 'must have suffered tortures from sea sickness.'[30]

Reliance on internment is understandable, given the inadequacies of the legal process, even one that rested on the Restoration of Order Act. This is illustrated by the experience of Caroline Woodcock, whose husband had survived the attack in Upper Pembroke Street. 'GHQ suddenly got agitated about me … Apparently they wanted me later as a witness, so I became … quite precious.' After a fortnight in England she was asked to return as a witness for the prosecution in a field court-martial of those charged with the murder of

Lieutenant-Colonel Montgomery. She insisted that she would do so only if she was allowed to stay with friends in Dublin Castle or the Royal Hospital at Kilmainham, rather than the hotel on offer. There was no response to her request; instead she heard on the grapevine that the accused man had been released and then rearrested and charged again, which was 'rather hard on the prisoner and hard on me.'

On the second occasion she was offered accommodation at the Chief Secretary's Lodge in the Phoenix Park, and she returned with her husband on a night crossing, only to be left waiting at Dún Laoghaire pier for over an hour. When an apologetic escort arrived and told them they would be accommodated in a well-guarded hotel on the quays, she rejected it as 'a pot house—twenty sentries on the roof of that morally deficient establishment would not make it any cleaner.' Her persistence prevailed, and the Woodcocks were accommodated after all at the Lodge. However, it proved to be only a preliminary hearing for summary evidence. There followed a tour of the prisons to undertake identity parades. Most of the prisoners, whom she observed through a felt-covered window with a slit, 'seemed absolutely terror stricken.' She was outraged that the suspects were allowed to smoke. At the same time she was struck by the stance adopted by some men.

> One in particular had a wonderful face. He looked straight at the hut and at the same time through it and beyond it. He stood with his head up without a trace of fear. ... Whatever he had done he was not ashamed of it. But then, alas! No Sinn Feiner is ashamed of murder.

She was unable to identify any of the gunmen who had shot her husband or his colleagues. The only person she could identify clearly was James Greene, the porter in Pembroke Street who had inadvertently opened the door on Bloody Sunday. He had no connection with Sinn Féin or the IRA, but she was convinced he had colluded with the gunmen, and he was lucky to get away with ten years' imprisonment.[31]

Meanwhile the net was closing on the more sedentary target that was City Hall. Any doubts about the corporation's allegiance were removed by the Lord Mayor's riposte to the extended curfew hours. He announced that, despite its parlous finances, the City would switch on public lighting throughout the night to give added protection for citizens. No longer would they grope down streets trying to dodge the searchlights of the military patrols. O'Neill's uncharacteristic silence on Bloody Sunday's events was due to his attendance at a special Mass in Finglas that day, where a very frail Archbishop Walsh laid the foundation stone of a new parish church. O'Neill paid generous tribute to the long-serving prelate for his efforts to save the life of 'a noble boy', Kevin Barry. Unaware of events unfolding in the city, he had thanked the archbishop for his work for peace, which had 'prevented the streets of Dublin from being deluged with blood.'[32]

At 3 p.m. on Monday 6 December 1920 a joint military-Auxiliary raid took place on the monthly corporation meeting in City Hall. Shortly beforehand all approaches to the building and Cork Hill were sealed off. Councillors were unaware of events taking place outside, and there was quite a large attendance, as one of the items on the agenda was a motion tabled by Dr McWalter and Sir Andrew Beattie of the MRA calling for a truce. Several leading Sinn Féin members, such as Michael Staines, Quartermaster-General of the IRA and organiser of the Belfast boycott, were there to ensure the defeat of what he regarded as a motion that was little better than an abject act of surrender.[33]

However, the first item on the councillors' agenda was the exact status of the Town Clerk, Henry Campbell, and his assistant, John Flood, who had both resigned temporarily in November. They left the chamber while the debate on their status took place, and two Sinn Féin Councillors, Michael Dowling and John Forrestal, were deputised to take the minutes in their absence. The leader of the Trades Council Labour group, P. T. Daly, was in the act of enquiring about the exact status of the officials when Captain William King and another intelligence officer entered the chamber by the same door that Campbell and Flood had used to leave. King was accompanied by an escort of heavily armed Auxiliaries.[34] His activities, including the torture of prisoners, were not yet public knowledge but would have been known to some councillors. By using the same door as Campbell and Flood the raiding party immediately controlled the members' reserved area.

The Lord Mayor summoned the Law Agent, Ignatius Rice, to act as a witness to events. Meanwhile these uninvited guests spread out to cover the exits from the public and press galleries. Campbell and Flood now returned and resumed their customary seats. When King demanded the roll-book, Campbell handed it to him. Looking down the list, King asked, 'Is Alderman Staines here?' There was no response, and another officer, probably Captain Jocelyn Hardy,[35] who worked assiduously with King in the interrogation of prisoners, said, 'Surely there is somebody here who can identify the members?' After a pause he turned to King and said, 'We shall probably have to take the whole lot.'

King then produced photographs of Staines and went up with the other officer to arrest the Alderman where he was sitting. They took several Sinn Féin members into custody and aggressively questioned other councillors, including Dr McWalter, Sir Andrew Beattie and J. Hubbard Clark, much to the amusement of the crowd in the public gallery.

P. T. Daly suggested that the corporation resume its discussion of the minutes and the Town Clerk's employment status. 'There is a more important point,' O'Neill replied, indicating the Auxiliaries and military around them.

A visibly angry Jennie Wyse Power, the Sinn Féin councillor whom Campbell had tried to bar from the first meeting of the year because she had signed the election declaration form in Irish, remarked: 'I see the Town Clerk and his friends are here.' Campbell jumped to his feet and shouted:

> How dare you, Mrs Wyse Power, use that expression, 'that the Town Clerk and his friends are here'! What have I to do with the military gentlemen here? How dare you!

'How dare you speak to me like that!' she retorted, and other members rallied to her support. As the Lord Mayor tried to restore order, Daly proposed an adjournment, as it was impossible to conduct business. But Sir Andrew Beattie demanded that the MRA's truce motion be debated. He may have hoped it would be passed in the presence of King and his men. Daly said he wanted it perfectly understood that he wished to debate the motion too but not in the present circumstances, and it was clear that the majority of remaining members agreed.

Dr McWalter then made the serious tactical blunder of asking for a roll-call vote of members who wanted to debate the motion. 'Is he out to spot the people?' Wyse Power asked. 'No, no,' McWalter assured her. 'I will take the sense of the meeting.'

The Lord Mayor then brought the proceedings to a close; but any illusions O'Neill and his colleagues had that they would be allowed to leave were rudely shattered. King added Daly and the seconder of the adjournment motion, Tom Lawlor, to his haul. Meanwhile a trawl of the building yielded several new suspects, including a young Seán Lemass.[36] King was obviously acting on good intelligence, and Staines was a particularly valuable catch, as he was known to be an important associate of Collins.

As soon as King left, O'Neill, mindful of the officer's reputation, telegraphed Lloyd George, informing him that he would be held personally responsible for the safety of the arrested men. Shortly afterwards an army detachment arrived at Dublin Castle to take the prisoners into military custody. According to Staines, King was 'very upset' at not being able to interrogate his prisoners in depth. He insisted on questioning Staines before he was taken away, but with so many witnesses present he could not indulge his penchant for torture. Asked where he had slept the previous night, Staines replied, 'A haystack.' In fact he had spent the night in St Ita's Mental Hospital in Portrane, where he was chairman of the board, but he did not want to invite King's retribution on the institution.

By the time the corporation reconvened on Tuesday 14 December 1920 Staines was safely behind bars for the duration of the War of Independence, along with his fellow-councillors Joseph Clarke, James Lawlor, Michael Lynch and James Brennan, all of whom had been identified by King as IRA officers.[37] Campbell and Flood had resubmitted their resignations, and another official, Michael J. Walsh, had been allocated to carry out the secretarial duties of the meeting until a new Town Clerk could be appointed.

While Flood restricted himself in his new letter of resignation to a brief if pointed reference to those councillors, 'a majority', whose activities prevented him from discharging his duties 'according to the law', Campbell had written a tirade. The Lord Mayor read it out.

> The illegalities, irregularities, and indecencies perpetrated or attempted to be perpetrated by the Councillors in reference to my position as Town Clerk, and the duties and obligations connected therewith have forced me to the conclusion that I shall best serve the citizens of Dublin and my own honour and dignity by severing my connection with the Municipal Council.
>
> I have always performed my duties in accordance with the Law, the Statutes, and the Standing Orders, under which alone the Municipal Council and its officers can act, as such: for this reason the Council has decided to make my position as Town Clerk an impossible one.

By now few councillors were in a mood to humour Campbell. Alderman William O'Brien (Labour) and Councillor John Forrestal (Sinn Féin) questioned how the Town Clerk could be allowed to resign after refusing to carry out the corporation's instructions and failing to provide essential cover until replacements could be found. O'Brien proposed that Campbell and Flood be dismissed.[38]

Their dismissals took place at a meeting of the whole house on 10 January. The proposer was O'Brien's arch-rival, P. T. Daly. Dr McWalter and Sir Andrew Beattie, on behalf of the MRA, resisted the decision, mustering only seven votes in favour of a motion that the former Town Clerk and his assistant be asked to 'reconsider' their resignations. By then other events had confirmed most councillors in their suspicions of the treachery of Campbell and Flood.

On 20 December 1920 a special meeting of the corporation had been convened by the Lord Mayor because of a threat by the military authorities to requisition City Hall and other corporation offices under the Defence of the Realm Act. The notice had been issued on 7 December, the day after Captain King's raid.

In the meantime a writ of peremptory *mandamus* had been served on the corporation, requiring it to present all the books, accounts and documents that remained in its possession to the Local Government Board for audit. Aldermen William O'Brien and Thomas O'Reilly (both Republican Labour) proposed that the Lord Mayor take no further action over the writ—effactually boycotting the LGB and the courts. McWalter and Beattie then proposed an amendment that the order be complied with. The resulting vote was surprisingly close, with the amendment defeated by 14 to 11. Three members of the Trades Council faction of Labour, John Farren, Tom Lawlor and John Lawlor, voted with the MRA, as did Michael Brohoon of O'Brien's Republican Labour faction. On the final motion there was a more comfortable majority of 16 to 10,[39] but both votes showed how tight the Sinn Féin-Republican Labour working majority on the corporation had become from the attrition of repression.

The threat posed by the military takeover was too imminent to ignore. Barbed-wire barriers had already been erected in Lord Edward Street and Castle Street. The army plan for requisitioning the corporation complex included the City Treasurer's department, the Rates Office, Public Health Office, City Accountant's Office and corporation telephone exchange, as well as City Hall. Besides the inconvenience of such a move it posed serious administrative problems, because the city's funds, some £1¾ million, passed through these offices, including £50,000 a week in cash. The strong room that housed the cash and important documents was on the premises as well.

An initial request for vacant possession from Captain Herbert Quare on behalf of Dublin Military District was followed by a more peremptory demand from the commanding officer, Major-General Boyd. Dr McWalter, seconded by his MRA colleague Richard Henry White, proposed compliance with the order but added a proviso that the military authorities allow the corporation access to the strong room and lower portions of the buildings. Alderman Kathleen Clarke put forward an amendment that the corporation not act on the military order. This was carried by 18 votes to 7. On this occasion the MRA minority was joined only by the solitary unionist councillor, William McCarthy, in offering to co-operate with the army.

The army had at first demanded occupation of the buildings from 13 December, but the Lord Mayor played for time, citing the need to consult fellow-councillors and senior officials. It was now so close to Christmas that he clearly hoped nothing would happen before the new year, and to be on the safe side it was decided to close City Hall for the holiday from Friday 24 December to Tuesday 28 December.

However, Major-General Boyd had other ideas. At 7:30 a.m. on Wednesday 22 December the army posted sentries on the corporation's premises and forbade entry to anyone except Henry Campbell and a handful of officials nominated by him, including John Flood, to take charge of corporation records. The military also removed the Tricolour from the flagstaff, where it had flown since Sinn Féin obtained a majority on the council in February. The caretaker, Mr Powell, and his family, the only residents, were given until 6 p.m. to leave. On arrival, Campbell announced that he would be performing the statutory duties from which he had resigned twice in as many months.

Large numbers of soldiers spent the day unloading barbed wire and sandbags to convert the municipal offices into an extension of the defences around Dublin Castle. As usual, crowds of curious citizens gathered to watch. Later in the day the Estates and Finance Committee announced the transfer of administrative offices to other sites in the city. The caretaker and his family were accommodated in Tara Street fire station, and O'Neill made the Oak Room in the Mansion House the new venue for corporation meetings.

In a reversal of roles, the military now refused to release any records from the seized premises to the corporation. The Estates and Finance Committee expressed concern that 'all their efforts to carry on the civic administration would be futile unless the officials were to have the use of the books and documents in their various offices,' and they applied to 'the Competent Military Authority' for their release. The committee, which was chaired by Alderman Beattie, reserved its strongest comments for Henry Campbell.

> The most extraordinary part of the whole proceeding was the fact that they [the military authorities] allowed the Town Clerk and his staff to remain in their offices, and when all the other officials presented themselves this morning they were refused, not only admission to their offices, but were not allowed to procure the morning correspondence.

Despite his public statements to the contrary, it soon emerged that Campbell was acting for the Local Government Board, his new paymasters. All sympathy for him evaporated. Even members of the MRA would only argue the merits of accepting his resignation versus dismissal, on the grounds that the corporation should do nothing precipitate that might secure him extra pension entitlements or expose the ratepayer to punitive damages in the courts.

On 15 February the Deputy City Treasurer, John J. Murphy, would replace Campbell as Town Clerk. After protracted legal proceedings the old Parnellite MP, who had served as Town Clerk for twenty-seven years, secured a full pension in November 1921. The back money awarded, £1,152 18s, was only £3 less than the annual fees the corporation paid to the Royal College of Surgeons for its services in treating the epidemic of sexually transmitted disease in the city. Campbell's final vindication came with a knighthood in the same year for his services to the Crown. As far as the dapper, moustachioed Town Clerk is remembered at all by Dubliners it is for a passing reference in James Joyce's *Ulysses*, no doubt repayment for the help he gave the author's father during the latter's time as a corporation rate-collector.[40] Dublin had lost one of its most colourful characters.

Chapter 8 ∿

'THE BLACK AND TAN GUARDS ARE DECENT TO US, AND WE THOUGHT WE MIGHT AS WELL ORDER IN A DRINK FOR THEM'

Despite the British army making clear its intention of taking over City Hall, its actions seem to have taken Dáil Éireann by surprise. On the very day of the occupation the Dáil's Department of Local Government issued guidelines to all public bodies advising them to approach their banks and seek an extension of normal overdraft facilities to bridge the shortfall in funding from the Local Government Board, worth on average 20 per cent of budgets.

The circular advised public representatives to find up to twenty individuals willing to pledge £50 each as collateral security against these overdrafts. Such a proposal was totally inadequate to meet Dublin's needs, and the discrepancy was inadvertently emphasised at a meeting of the Dublin Board of Guardians on the same day over funding for the Richmond Asylum. The annual budget had soared from £30,000 to £200,000 since 1914. Despite this, the dominant Sinn Féin-Republican Labour group on the corporation had rejected all attempts by the Municipal Reform Association, the Trades Council Labour group and some nationalists to seek a larger subvention from the LGB.

Now the chairman of the board, Alderman Thomas O'Reilly (Republican Labour), tried to reassure colleagues that banks would provide credit on the strength of the Dáil guidelines, although Councillor James Gately (independent nationalist) continued to question the wisdom of Sinn Féin policy. If the Board of Guardians took what is due to them from the Local Government Board they would not want any bank to make them any concession so far as an overdraft is concerned. The Richmond Asylum had agreed to submit their books ... and they had received the necessary sum of money to carry on—£33,000.

Failure to do so would cause the loss of up to 160 jobs.[1] Gately's stance raised the spectre of other public bodies in the city defecting to the LGB and recognising British rule in order to remain solvent.

In fact the officials in the Richmond Asylum had pre-empted Sinn Féin. They managed to sell the pass without losing their jobs in the process, unlike Henry Campbell or John Flood. Their situation epitomised the dilemma every local official faced. The Richmond Asylum was run in conjunction with its sister institution, St Ita's in Portrane, with patients split equally between them. When the Joint Committee of the Richmond Lunatic Asylum met on 16 December 1920 members were presented with a letter signed by the Resident Medical Superintendent, Dr Donelan, the Accountant, Mr Doyle, and the Chief Clerk, Mr Murphy, stating that, after being advised that the decision of the board to boycott the LGB was not legally binding, they had submitted the accounts for audit, in the interests of the patients.

Dr Donelan told the board that in an effort to economise he identified 32 patients out of 3,252 who, 'though not actually cured, with safety might be removed and left in the care of friends.' However, only the friends of five patients had taken on this onerous duty of care. Dr Donelan said he dreaded the thought 'that unfortunate patients would be left without a dinner, tea or fire.' Councillors 'could not ... carry on "high-falutin" language and indulge in heroics at the expense of the most unfortunate people' in the community.

Doyle, the accountant, assured the board 'that there is no intention on the part of officials to override its functions.' The LGB had already approved the accounts for the year ending 31 March 1920. Grants of £40,000 were involved and, crucially, Doyle reminded them that the Finance Subcommittee had approved their action. 'Bearing in mind only the welfare of the patients, and that if anything terrible happened as a result of the withholding of the necessary money a large part of the blame would be put on the officials,' Doyle concluded that there was no option.

The Chief Clerk, Murphy, made the same defence. 'Officials cannot absolve themselves of the responsibility of doing certain things, because their duties are laid down by law, and according to statutory rules.'

There was little that board members could do retrospectively except vent their anger. Councillor Jennie Wyse Power (Sinn Féin) said it was the first time in the history of the joint board that its senior officials had gone behind the backs of board members and assumed the right to reverse a decision. Not only were the officials guilty of withholding information but 'a grievous wrong was done to their absent colleague Alderman Staines,' who had chaired the St Ita's board. The action of the officials was equally embarrassing to Michael Dowling, the councillor who had proposed that Dublin Corporation pledge its allegiance to Dáil Éireann and now presided over the joint board.

Sinn Féin councillors were equally angry with their colleagues on the Finance Subcommittee of the asylum, which had condoned the officials' action. The subcommittee included the MRA councillors Michael Maxwell Lemon and Bernard Shields, as well as P. T. Daly of Trades Council Labour. In an effort to be placatory, the Lord Mayor, Laurence O'Neill, who was also a member of the board, said he felt that the officials and the subcommittee were 'between the devil and the deep sea.' Sinn Féin councillors pressed for a vote of sanction on the officials and the Finance Subcommittee, but the Lord Mayor's proposal to simply note what happened was passed, barely, by 13 votes to 12.[2]

Although most local public bodies in Dublin and elsewhere adhered to the Dáil's boycott of the LGB, the Richmond Asylum and St Ita's were not alone in breaking it. It was one thing to vote for Sinn Féin, or even actively assist the IRA; it was another to allow institutions to close, jobs to be lost and the infrastructure of society to collapse for want of funds.

Whatever Sinn Féin members of Dublin Corporation thought of the actions of the Board of Guardians, it soon had to grasp the same nettle in relation to the city's technical schools. Only £4,200 of the budget of £52,200 came from the rates; the rest was from the LGB. On 3 January 1921 P. T. Daly, leader of the Trades Council group, proposed that the Technical Schools Committee be allowed to submit its books to the board to obtain the £48,000 needed to keep the schools open. The proposal was defeated, by 19 votes to 14, but on this occasion not only did the MRA vote with Daly's group but so did all the independent nationalists present and one Sinn Féin councillor, Lawrence Raul.

At a meeting two weeks later the Lord Mayor renewed the proposal. There were angry exchanges between members of the dominant Sinn Féin-Republican Labour group, perhaps sensing that they would lose the vote, and the rival MRA and Trades Council opposition. But the sharpest clash was between the rival Labour leaders, William O'Brien and P. T. Daly. The latter said he could not see any 'high political principles' involved in allowing the committee to keep the schools open. O'Brien retorted: 'We are not all renegades.' In a pointed reference to O'Brien's late father, a head constable in the RIC, Daly said:

I don't mind what peelers' sons say. If the Technical Schools are closed down it will mean that the workers' children are to be deprived of a necessary adjunct to their education, and the responsibility will fall on the right shoulders.

The motion allowing the Technical Schools Committee to submit its records for audit was passed on this occasion by 13 votes to 10. No Sinn Féin councillor voted for the proposal, but several absented themselves from the meeting. As with the railway strike, the limits of resistance to British rule were being defined by what civilians could endure, not by what militant republicans demanded.

A pragmatic approach also prevailed when it came to unemployment. While Dáil Éireann was keen to set up an alternative to the British labour exchange system, even its staunchest ally in the trade union movement, William O'Brien, said it was impractical to ask workers to risk forgoing the benefits they could obtain from the British social insurance scheme simply to make a gesture, especially if they were unemployed. When Sinn Féin councillors proposed setting up a committee 'to investigate the problem of unemployment in the city and to bring forward such recommendations as they think necessary,' Daly was quick to propose an amendment that part of its remit would be 'negotiating Ireland's share of the amount earmarked for the relief of the unemployed in Great Britain.' This was too explicit an acknowledgement of the British link for Sinn Féin to stomach, but its councillors did agree that the committee could 'take such steps as they deem desirable to secure funds for the unemployed.'

It was also agreed to establish a Labour Bureau, where men who had worked casually for the corporation over the previous two years might register. However, the list was limited to six hundred. In a concession to the Minister for Labour, Constance Markievicz, it was agreed that members of the RIC resigning for political reasons could be added to the bureau's waiting list. There is no evidence that any benefited from the decision. Regardless of political persuasion, there was little prospect of councillors passing over constituents in favour of RIC men from Listowel, or anywhere else. Throughout the revolution, patronage and concern for the ratepayer's pocket continued to provide the main basis for consensus in the council chamber.

Of course there could never be consensus between the MRA and the dominant coalition of Sinn Féin and Republican Labour on the big question of allegiance to Dáil Éireann or the Crown. But this too played itself out in the mundane conflict over finances rather than support for, or opposition to, the 'war'. The killing of 'peelers' and soldiers grabbed headlines but did not intrude on the corporation agenda, except when votes of sympathy or condemnation were being passed. Policies that jeopardised jobs, children's education or benefits for the unemployed were another matter. As a municipality struggling to survive in the political front line, Dublin Corporation was discovering the limits of civil resistance. In the process, members were learning that it was sometimes easier to die for the Republic than to live according to its writ.[3]

The same meeting at which the corporation allowed the Technical Schools Committee to submit its books to the LGB witnessed a significant change of heart by Republican Labour and Sinn Féin councillors towards Dublin's ex-servicemen. Like technical school pupils and their parents, ex-servicemen had been caught in the crossfire between the corporation and the LGB. The corporation had been refusing for almost a year to allow the transfer of 39 acres at Killester to the LGB for the building of 160 houses, at a cost of £176,000, for ex-servicemen in the city, although it had the support of Dáil Éireann's Minister for Local Government, Alderman W. T. Cosgrave. The scheme was part of Lloyd George's wartime promise to create a land fit for heroes. The situation was further complicated by the fact that the land was the subject of a dispute involving the corporation, the ground landlord, Gaisford St Lawrence, Lord of Howth, and the long-term lessee, Sir Henry McLaughlin, one of Ireland's leading builders and developers. Both men, particularly McLaughlin (see chapter 5 above), were prominent in unionist circles, but there is little doubt that many councillors opposed the scheme because it involved ex-servicemen receiving what they regarded as preferential treatment in a city full of slums.

After the corporation finally rejected the proposal in January 1921 and decided to dispose of the lands, the Irish Federation of Discharged and Demobilised Sailors and Soldiers requested that the councillors receive a deputation so that they could put their case. The exchanges that took place when they were given a hearing were illuminating. Mr Walker of the Dublin Branch of the federation said it had 5,200 members, many of them living in the city's slums,

> and the attitude of the Corporation up to the present is that they should continue to remain in that state ... If the Corporation persist in their refusal to grant facilities to the Local Government Board ... I wish to ask what steps the Corporation propose to take to give us an alternative.
>
> In regard to the political conditions of the country, the attitude of the ex-servicemen is one of neutrality, and we feel it is not just or right that the Corporation should victimise us.

His colleague, Mr Hounan, said:

> Ex-servicemen are Irishmen first and citizens of Dublin next, and they all
> love Ireland as much as the members of the Corporation themselves. All we
> ask is that the Corporation give all facilities to the Local Government Board
> and not turn down a grant of £176,000.

Support from MRA members, such as Dr McWalter, himself a Great War veteran,
was to be expected, but when confronted with the reality as opposed to a
preconceived view of ex-servicemen the attitude of Sinn Féin councillors
softened appreciably. Margaret McGarry said she was

> pleased to see the two members of the deputation coming here as Irishmen
> and not as English soldiers. On that consideration the matter has now a
> different meaning. [Hear, hear.] I do not call Ulstermen Irishmen.

Mr Hounan, interposing, said that as he belonged to Ulster he considered
himself as good an Irishman as any of those who spoke in the council chamber.
(Applause.) Councillor McGarry said that might be, but it was Sir Henry
McLaughlin she took exception to.

As was so often the case, O'Neill smoothed over difficulties, observing that
it was not corporation policy 'to prevent anyone from building houses ... At
the earliest possible moment I will call a special meeting of the corporation.'

At that meeting, convened the next week, the decision to refuse permission
for the development was rescinded.[4] By 1924 Killester would be Dublin's first
modern working-class suburb, with 465 houses in a landscaped estate providing
an oasis of stability in the aftermath of revolution and civil war, by courtesy of
the British War Office.

The dilemma posed by housing for ex-servicemen underlined the inadequacy
of resources for tackling slum clearance on a serious scale. In contrast to the
War Office, Dublin Corporation built no houses between 1918 and 1921 and
managed to build only 162 between then and 1925, the year after the Killester
development was completed. By the end of 1920 the corporation barely had
enough funds to meet day-to-day bills. Dáil Éireann had established a fund of
£100,000 from its own resources to help meet the deficits of local authorities,
but this was nothing like enough to meet the £220,000 shortfall of Dublin
Corporation, let alone all the other rebel authorities; hence its suggestion that
local authorities ask wealthy individuals to underwrite their debts.

In theory there was more than $5 million in the United States, raised from Michael Collins's Dáil loan. Although the surprisingly large amount of $1.4 million had been spent financing the Republic's activities in America, including President de Valera's tour, that still left $3.7 million. Because of logistical problems, not the least of which was the need to keep the money out of the hands of the British authorities, only $300,000 (£75,000) made it to Ireland. Renewed efforts to raise money by diverting British tax receipts and by levying direct taxes in Ireland were as disappointing as previous ones, and by the summer of 1921 the Republic would be broke.

Dublin Corporation was not afraid to think big. One of the first acts of the Housing Committee was to appoint a special subcommittee consisting of Laurence O'Neill (Lord Mayor), Alderman Joe MacDonagh TD (Sinn Féin), William O'Brien (leader of the Republican Labour group and General Treasurer of the ITGWU) and J. Hubbard Clark (company director and member of the MRA) to consider 'ways and means for raising money for housing purposes.' Alderman W. T. Cosgrave was asked 'to give his assistance in the matter' as Dáil Éireann Minister for Local Government.

The first thing the group did was approach the head of the Guinness dynasty, Lord Iveagh. The Guinness family had been the foremost providers of social housing for the working class in the city before the Great War, but Iveagh replied that, regrettably, 'it was out of the question ... to accede to the proposal that I should advance money to the Corporation for building.' It was one thing to provide houses for philanthropic purposes and quite another to support a rebel regime, even indirectly. In some ways what was more significant than the refusal by Lord Iveagh was the fact that another Southern unionist, J. Hubbard Clark, would actively canvass the scheme on behalf of the corporation. The fundamental difference between the two men, of course, was that, unlike Clark and his MRA colleagues, Lord Iveagh did not have to live in the city.

Undeterred, the group then asked the City Treasurer, Edmund W. Eyre, to make a new approach to the banks for a loan of up to £1 million for slum clearance, against a security of bearer bonds at 6 per cent interest. Despite his experience from the previous year, Eyre appears once more to have made his first approach to the 'nationalist' banks, with the usual response. He then stated that only £68,603 was needed immediately to complete the first phase of 134 houses at Fairbrother's Fields, and this could be met out of the Improvement Rate. The Hibernian Bank expressed a willingness to make funds available for this limited objective. It was 'pressed ... pretty hard' by Eyre, but it eventually declined, because the National Bank and the Munster and Leinster Bank refused to commit themselves.

The risk was minimal. Even though the LGB had withdrawn the facility for future capital funding it had not withdrawn loan approval for housing schemes sanctioned when the old corporation was in office. The board was even prepared to provide a subsidy of £1 7s 6d for every £1 the corporation collected in rent on new housing developments. It agreed to relax the building by-laws and offer subsidies of £230 for a three-room house, £240 for a four-room house and £260 for a five-room house. This was significantly higher than the subsidy for similar schemes in Britain.

The continued willingness of the LGB to assist a local authority that refused to recognise its authority was due to a combination of concern at the enormous health threat the slums posed and a conviction dating from the official inquiries into the Lockout and Easter Rising that bad housing was a major factor in Dublin's civil unrest. As General Sir John Maxwell put it in 1916, 'as long as the labour questions, the incidence of wages, the housing of the poor, remain as they are, rioting and disorder can be expected on the least provocation'; and the town planner Patrick Geddes believed the expenditure of £100,000 on housing before 1914 would have removed any thought of rebellion. Of course Dublin Corporation placed on British misrule the responsibility not alone for Dublin's appalling housing but for every other social problem in the city as well—and it could point out that during the Great War almost all slum clearance funds went to British cities.

The Bank of Ireland came to the rescue once more. (See chapter 6 above.) It advanced £70,000 for capital expenditure, of which £30,000 was earmarked for housing and the rest could be drawn down as required. This cleared the way for work to begin on the Fairbrother's Fields scheme and the completion of the McCaffrey estate, begun during the war. Again the financial wing of Southern unionism was showing more faith in the Sinn Féin project than its nationalist counterparts, reflecting the Midletonian view that some form of dominion rule was inevitable. It also made sound financial sense. Local authorities did not have to pay interest on overdrafts from the banks, as these were normally regarded as deferred payments from the LGB. The times were not, of course, normal, and the alternative of driving Dublin Corporation into insolvency and the city into chaos remained the stark choice on offer from the previous autumn. Besides, a dividend of 6 per cent was not to be sneezed at when British Treasury securities were yielding between 4 and 5 per cent.

Unfortunately the stalemate between the corporation and the LGB was not free of cost for the city or, more particularly, the ratepayers. Continuing inflation saw the cost of building a typical three-bedroom house at Fairbrother's Fields increase by more than half between August 1918, when the first tenders were received by the old Home Rule corporation, and February 1920, when the 'nationalist' banks refused credit, or from £439 to £659. As we have seen, the extra costs could be partly offset by rent increases, which had the bonus of ensuring a higher top-up from the LGB's scheme for matching funding.[5]

Unfortunately, by now the housing programme was beset by another problem, a bricklayers' strike, which lasted from the beginning of October 1920 until 13 June 1921 and brought virtually all building work in the city to a standstill. The bricklayers were seeking 2s 6½d per hour, but the employers offered only 2s 2d. Most of the strikers availed of a shortage of bricklayers in Britain to work there during the dispute, but this option was not open to thousands of other workers laid off as a result of the nine-month battle. Eventually the end of the post-war British building boom saw the return of the bricklayers, who accepted an offer of 2s 3d per hour, which by 1 January 1922 was reduced to the 2s 2d figure.[6] The narrow militancy of the bricklayers had secured them a temporary increase of 1d per hour, at considerable expense to thousands of other workers, not to mention keeping the city's modest slum clearance programme on hold. Likewise, employers made meagre savings on their wages bill but lost out on potential building contracts.

Another hidden cost, not alone to the housing programme but to most corporation activity, was the disruption caused by the arrest and internment of city councillors and employees. In April 1920, for instance, five members of the Housing Committee were in Crown custody. Employees were regularly arrested, at home or at work. Normally the corporation paid them for their time in custody, following the precedent introduced for employees who joined the British army in 1914 or were arrested after the 1916 Rising. The practice became so frequent that at a corporation meeting on 17 January 1921 Councillor Lawrence Raul (Sinn Féin) proposed that the corporation direct 'the payment of their full remuneration to all permanent and quasi-permanent employees of the Council who have been or may be arrested, detained, or otherwise precluded from attending to the duties of their positions as a result of existing military operations.' It was passed by 15 votes to 3, but the three dogged MRA defenders of the ratepayer pointed out that a quorum was not present. Raul waived his automatic right to have the motion put again at a subsequent meeting. Presumably colleagues dissuaded him, fearing that the cost would become crippling as the numbers interned grew by hundreds every month.[7]

However, this did not debar individual employees from applying for assistance. The first successful applicant after the vote was Noel Lemass, an apprentice fitter in the corporation's Stanley Street workshops, released following a year in Mountjoy Prison for Volunteer activities.

As in so many mundane areas of corporation activity, the work of the Housing Committee could prove a unifying factor. J. Hubbard Clark, one of the three MRA representatives to vote against paying employees in military custody, was proving a very effective Chairman during Tom Kelly's enforced absence through ill-health. When he submitted the first phase of the Fairbrother's Fields scheme for implementation he endorsed a suggestion from W. T. Cosgrave 'that the Dublin Building operatives should be asked to undertake in competition with a contractor the building of a certain limited number of houses,' using the trades guild scheme operating in Britain, which 'it is claimed ... can build better, cheaper and quicker than Master Builders [employers].' Clark's MRA colleague John Russell Stritch even seconded a motion from P. T. Daly to allow the Stanley Street workshops to tender for the work, although they were bedevilled with management problems and were not cost-effective.[8]

It was also proposed that the Dublin Building Trades Guild, which was still in the process of being established, be allowed to quote for a contract to build ten of the four-bedroom houses and provide foundations for fifteen others. This work was costed on the Glasgow model, which used time and materials plus 5 per cent. If the cost exceeded estimates, the corporation would pay for the excess, while the guild would receive half of any savings on the contract. The corporation would pay for insurance against accidents or fires on site. The successful guild quote came in at £1,200, or 10 per cent, below that from the corporation workshops.

Unfortunately, budgetary constraints and the continuing bricklayers' strike meant that the Fairbrother's Fields development had to be put on hold again.[9] The only significant housing initiatives in the city, besides the War Office project for ex-servicemen in Killester, were those by public utility societies. The first of these was launched by Rev. David Hall, Church of Ireland canon in East Wall. He raised £1,000 to launch St Barnabas' Public Utility Society in one of the poorest Anglican parishes in the country, as one of his flock, Seán O'Casey, testified so vividly in his autobiography. The first scheme, of ten houses, was launched in June 1921 and completed by December. It cost £10,700, significantly below prices quoted for yet uncompleted corporation houses—although the real difference was much less, as the sites were fully serviced by the local authority. Canon Hall pioneered other publicity utility schemes in the city, winning the soubriquet of the 'Housing Parson'. East Wall provided not only a financial and engineering template for other schemes but an exercise in local democracy as well, with tenant-dominated management committees and an ecumenical approach to housing that provided homes to families of all denominations.[10]

It was a tribute to the belief that many citizens, most of them Protestants, still had in the city that Canon Hall could raise the initial funding of £1,000 required for his social housing project from a public appeal. Dublin Corporation had no such recourse. Towards the end of 1920 the LGB brought rate-collectors into the firing line by instructing them not to hand over sums collected to unauthorised bodies or persons, which included local authorities that had given their allegiance to Dáil Éireann. Cosgrave's understudy, Kevin O'Higgins, riposted with an equally severe warning.

> Officials are reminded that their pensions are paid from the rates, not by the English Government, and no pension from public money can be granted to any official who is dismissed for endeavouring to thwart the will of the people of Ireland.[11]

Nevertheless many Dublin councillors expressed fears for the safety of funds in the hands of rate-collectors. Once more the Republican Police came to the rescue.

The Dublin Brigade had informally begun seconding Volunteers for police duties since mid-1919 as DMP members increasingly restricted themselves to maintaining a semblance of law and order in the city centre. When the Chief of Staff of the IRA, Richard Mulcahy, instructed brigades to establish Republican Police units in May 1920 it merely formalised the situation in large areas of Dublin. Not alone Irish Volunteers but members of the Citizen Amy, such as Larry McLoughlin, had been policing their localities for months. McLoughlin was a big, gruff docker, a veteran of the 1913 Lockout and the 1916 Rising whose beat included the docks, the North Wall and the neighbouring community of East Wall. He was also a shop steward for the ITGWU. The arrangement suited the port companies, because men like McLoughlin kept the perennial problem of pilfering under control while at the same time the new dispensation allowed them to smuggle arms and personnel through the port unhindered.

Life became more difficult from April 1921 when Q Company of the Auxiliaries was based in the London and North-Western Hotel on the North Wall to counter IRA activities, but it hindered operations rather than halting them. McLoughlin's arms-importing activities sometimes took him as far as Co. Kerry to ensure the safe delivery of weapons. His Republican Police unit also had the somewhat unusual remit of organising armed robberies. The proceeds from the robbery of banks and post offices were taken to Joe McGrath, Finance Officer of the ITGWU, in Liberty Hall, where he acted as a bagman for the Minister for Finance, Michael Collins.

The overall commander of the Republican Police in Dublin was Peter Ennis, whose brother Tom was a member of the Squad. Ennis reported to the Department of Home Affairs, overseen by Austin Stack. Stack had been a solicitor's clerk in Tralee, and a crucial responsibility of the Republican Police was protecting the Sinn Féin courts. They also executed court writs. It was much harder to run courts in Dublin than in the provinces, and the risk of apprehension was high. Nevertheless there was one based in the Billiard Room of the Mansion House, run by the journalist P. J. Little, who had been the only unsuccessful Sinn Féin candidate in Dublin in 1918.[12] The Lord Mayor sometimes escorted members of the court and important witnesses through the military cordons that enmeshed the building under the pretext that they were visiting him.

Other duties of the Republican Police were enforcing the licensing laws, carrying out raids for stolen goods and enforcing the Belfast boycott. Perishable goods seized from Belfast firms were usually distributed in poor areas, either directly or through the agency of religious communities. Some of the latter reciprocated by providing shelter and food for Volunteers on the run. In this way the Republican administration negotiated a tightrope, balancing the need to make Ireland ungovernable by the British with the need to reassure important interest groups, such as the business community and the Catholic Church, that the war was not descending into social chaos.[13]

Nowhere was the balancing act more difficult than in the area of public finances. By early January 1921 several rate-collectors had succumbed to pressure from the LGB and resigned their position with Dublin Corporation. On 5 January members of the Republican Police made synchronised visits to their homes at 8:30 a.m. and persuaded them to sign cheques making over all rates money in their possession to the corporation. The cheques were then taken to the appropriate banks and cashed while the collectors remained at home and completed their records before handing them over to their uninvited guests. Some £11,000 was collected from eight different premises in this way. One of the collectors whose records and funds were sequestered, William Duffy of Broome Bridge, Cabra, said that the armed contingent that called to his house consisted of 'very courteous and well-behaved young men, and during their stay they partook of tea, which they insisted on paying for.' Another collector, Charles

Sutton in Kiltiernan, Co. Dublin, was impressed by his visitors' knowledge of the system. They accurately computed the amount he was holding for Dublin County Council but took nothing from the funds he held for Killiney Urban District Council, which still recognised the authority of the LGB.[14]

New collectors were elected by the corporation in March to replace the defectors. Near the top of the list was Harry Colley, a 1916 veteran who was now Adjutant of the Dublin Brigade. But, like the seizure of the corporation's accounts in November, these measures bought time rather than resolved the underlying problem of how long a rebel local authority could function at the very heart of the British administration in Ireland.

Inevitably this finely judged campaign to defy the Empire produced anomalous and sometimes ludicrous situations, such as the incident in which the Auxiliaries found seven men 'in suspicious circumstances' at 100 Seville Place. Four turned out to be Republican Police and the other three claimed to be prisoners detained for trying to emigrate. All seven were charged with possession of a revolver and ammunition found on the premises. A sceptical court-martial sentenced them to prison terms of between three and five years each. The campaign to stop men of military age leaving the Republic was a significant drain on the resources of the Republican Police in Dublin without producing any obvious political dividend. Not surprisingly, it was unpopular with Volunteers tasked with the job.[15]

More importantly, a situation now existed in which it was often impossible to know which side the various armed groups roaming the streets were on. When William Kennedy, a clerk in the military stores at Islandbridge Barracks, was shot during a performance of the pantomime *The House That Jack Built* at the Empire Theatre no-one went to his aid; instead there was 'a stampede of people from the theatre.'[16] Kennedy survived, one of his ribs deflecting the bullet intended for his heart. William Doran, the gregarious head porter at the Wicklow Hotel, was less fortunate: a fortnight after Kennedy he was shot by the Squad as a suspected informer. When his wife contacted Michael Collins, believing her husband had been shot by British agents, he had not got the heart to tell her who the real culprits were and authorised financial help for her family.[17]

In some instances it was not difficult to discern ordinary criminals, such as the men who held up the staff and customers at the Dublin Savings Bank in Lower Abbey Street on a Saturday evening in November 1920 and took £790. The fact that it was a mutual bank with a mainly working-class and trade union clientele, and that customers were forced to hand over the money in their pockets, showed that it was not the IRA. On the other hand the military precision with which the same gang was suspected of carrying out other robberies with apparent impunity fuelled rumours that those concerned were off-duty Auxiliaries. The gang was still robbing banks almost up to the Truce in July 1921.[18] Nor were fears of such skulduggery unfounded. The *Irish Bulletin*, published weekly by Dáil Éireann, reported cases in which members of the Auxiliaries and Black and Tans were prosecuted for robbery and other crimes. Eventually the commander of the Auxiliary Division, Brigadier-General Crozier, resigned when he discovered that twenty-one 'cadets' he had dismissed for looting and for attacks on civilians in Trim, Co. Meath, had been reinstated by the British government after the men threatened to reveal worse scandals.

A handful of Auxiliaries were tried and convicted of offences, some of them veterans broken (sometimes literally) by their experience of war in Europe. One such was Ewan Cameron Bruce, a former major in the Tank Corps who robbed £60 from a dairy in Kells at gunpoint. His war record was put forward in mitigation at the field court-martial in Dublin. His defence counsel said Major Bruce had won the Military Cross and the Distinguished Service Order with two bars in 1917, had been mentioned three times in despatches, was wounded five times, was gassed and had lost an arm at the front. He had received decorations also from the Japanese and Russian imperial governments for his services but had nothing to show for his endeavours after he was invalided out in 1919 except his decorations. In many ways the Auxiliaries were his natural home; the only wonder is that he was accepted for 'police' work with only one arm.

Simultaneously, back in Dublin a group of five armed men claiming to be Republican Police searching for hidden weapons robbed the Maypole Dairy in Dorset Street and the Colonial Stores in South Great George's Street, stealing a total of £116. The leader of the gang was a publican called John Carroll; the other members were among his regular customers and drinking companions. He told the field court-martial:

> I am in very bad straits. My business is gone to the dogs on account of the name of the place, the Republican Bar, which had been raided and often smashed up. I wanted money. I planned the two raids ... selecting these firms because they were English, as a return for the damage done to my business by the English authorities.[19]

Banks were badly affected by the breakdown in law and order. The Bank of Ireland's Pembroke Branch lost £2,789 on 16 November 1920 and another £1,286 on 7 February 1921, while smaller amounts were taken from other branches by armed gangs. The National Bank lost £8,000 in the first half of 1921, including more than £3,000 from its branch in Lower Camden Street on 9 May 1921. The situation was so serious that in late 1920 the Bank of Ireland considered closing all sub-offices in the Dublin district. However, it seems to have failed to persuade competitors to do likewise and opted instead to seek police protection 'on Market and Fair Days' as well as installing bars on windows and other precautions. These proved inadequate deterrents. Staff members, on the other hand, did occasionally frustrate the robbers. During the second Pembroke raid they managed to apprehend one of the raiders, although the rest of the gang escaped with the proceeds. During the Camden Street raid a teller, A. P. Swaine, showed quite exceptional courage, grappling with one of the robbers, Terence Byrne. The field court-martial that subsequently tried Byrne was told that another robber

> called out "Shoot that man." The cashier was shot in the temple, and lost his grip of Byrne, who stood over him for a moment or two and then left. The cashier jumped up and followed the men out … He pursued them into Pleasants Street, Synge Street and Grantham Street. At the corner of Grantham Street, Byrne turned and shot at the cashier, but unsuccessfully.

Swaine continued to chase the robbers into Heytesbury Street and Harrington Street, where they hijacked a butcher's van, and Swaine gave chase after he 'persuaded a boy to give him a bicycle.' He followed the robbers until they abandoned the van. He recovered £997 from the vehicle, together with a bag of silver they threw into a garden during his pursuit. Nevertheless they succeeded in holding on to £2,336 14s 6d. Swaine subsequently received a letter of commendation and a reward of £250 from the bank, and had his medical bills paid. Three men were convicted on the evidence of Swaine and other members of the bank's staff. Byrne was released in January 1922 as part of the Treaty settlement, suggesting that it had been an IRA operation.[20]

Some robberies were unequivocally the work of the IRA, such as the raid on the military mail at Ballsbridge Post Office on 14 December by the 3rd Battalion. After four Auxiliaries arrived in a car to collect it they came under attack from men armed with rifles and grenades. The Auxiliaries beat a hasty retreat inside the post office, and the attackers made off in the car with the mail. Besides the intrinsic attraction of military mail, the other indicator that this was an IRA operation was the large number of raiders involved, some of whom were deputed to hold back the public and stop a passing tram so that passengers would not be caught in the crossfire. These measures proved necessary, because during the attack a grenade bounced off the Auxiliaries' car, exploding on the pavement.[21] It was the first attack on an Auxiliary patrol in Dublin, and its success was a significant boost to Volunteer morale.

The IRA campaign in Dublin received a further boost with the creation of the Active Service Unit. Its formation had been delayed by the death of Dick McKee but it was finally established in December 1920, with each battalion contributing fourteen men, two of them officers. Like the Squad, members were paid £4 10s a week, more or less the going rate for a craftsman in the city. The first OC was Paddy Flanagan of the 3rd Battalion, and the Adjutant was Seán Gibbons of the 4th Battalion. Meanwhile the new Dublin OC, Oscar Traynor, was being initiated into the high command, attending his first meeting of the Army Council at the Cúig Cúigí branch of the Gaelic League in Ely Place. The Minister for Defence, Cathal Brugha, presided. Although the council appointed Traynor, at his own request brigade officers were given the opportunity to confirm his appointment by a ballot. Besides establishing the ASU, Traynor changed most of the battalion commanders and moved the brigade headquarters from Dick McKee's old base at the Dublin Typographical Society offices, 35 Lower Gardiner Street, to the IESFTU offices at 6 Gardiner Row. The move was arranged by Mick Slator, a 1916 veteran who had been an unsuccessful candidate for Sinn Féin in the municipal elections and was a founder-member of the IESFTU. The tenancy was held in the name of Number 1 Branch of the Irish Clerical Workers' Union, one of whose officials was a Volunteer.

The close relationship between the Dublin Brigade and the craft unions was further proof of the continuing legacy of the Fenian tradition in the city and underlined the fact that the IRA leadership consisted primarily of the upwardly mobile members of the skilled working class, white-collar workers and lower professions among whom the IRB was based.

With the creation of the ASU the tempo of attacks in the new year increased. The first operation, on Wednesday 12 January, was typical of the form that combat now assumed in the city. The target was an Auxiliary patrol driving along Bachelor's Walk at about 4:30 p.m. Shots were fired and grenades thrown at the lorry before the ASU escaped through Scannell's auction hall, where the proprietor, James Scannell, had to suspend proceedings while the Volunteers pushed their way through the largely female attendance. The Auxiliaries returned fire in the general direction of the shops along Bachelor's Walk. One bullet crashed through Scannell's shop front, causing several members of the crowd to scream; other rounds hit the interiors of Walsh and Sons, cabinetmakers, and the O'Brien Brothers' pub, where the clientele were in a more soporific mood. There were no civilian casualties.

Bystanders were less fortunate the following day when Crown forces set up a checkpoint outside the Ballast Office at the corner of Westmorland Street and Aston Quay at 4:30 p.m. to examine motor permits. Despite the danger, crowds of curious Dubliners gathered, as usual, to watch proceedings. As the soldiers were about to leave with a confiscated motorbike and side car in tow, firing broke out. When it was over, 22-year-old Martha Nowlan, head bookkeeper at Mitchell's Restaurant in Grafton Street, was dead, and so was sixteen-year-old James Brennan of Mary Street. Seven other people, five men and two women, had suffered gunshot wounds. It was thought that the accidental discharge of a rifle dropped by a soldier from a lorry sparked a burst of gunfire by his comrades, who thought they were under attack.[22]

Of course the IRA also had bad days. When a detachment of the ASU launched an ambush on a contingent of Auxiliaries on the Drumcondra Road just above the bridge over the Tolka at 11 a.m. on 21 January 1921 one Volunteer was killed and five taken prisoner. The dead man, Michael Magee, and two of those taken prisoner, Patrick Doyle and Bernard Ryan, had been involved in IRA operations ever since the arms raid on Collinstown aerodrome in March 1919, the first major operation by the Dublin Brigade after 1916. (See chapter 1 above.)

The commander of the unit, Lieutenant Frank Flood, was also its youngest and least experienced member. His handling of the operation subsequently came in for strong criticism. He had been instructed to ambush a patrol at Binns Bridge further south but had to call it off after two Volunteers fired prematurely at a vehicle carrying Auxiliaries. Instead of dispersing, the group redeployed at Drumcondra Bridge, leaving them open to a counter-attack by Auxiliaries.

Flood came from a prominent republican family that owned a shop in Summer Hill. He was a scholarship engineering student at the National University, where he had known Kevin Barry. Like Barry, he now faced the hangman's noose, as did his three companions. Patrick Doyle was the oldest member of the group, at twenty-nine. He was just married at the time of the Collinstown raid and now had a young daughter, while his wife, Kathleen, was expecting another child at the time of the ambush. Bernard Ryan was a twenty-year-old apprentice tailor and the sole support of his mother and sister. The other man taken prisoner was Thomas Bryan, a 22-year-old electrician who had married a month before the ambush.

This setback did not stop ambushes in the city, but more of them took place in the evenings to take advantage of the dark. A week later nine soldiers were wounded in an attack on the Terenure Road at 7 p.m.[23] The basic technique was to fire a volley or two at close range from cover, throw grenades, and then retreat before the enemy could respond or before reinforcements could arrive.

Following another ambush at 7:50 p.m. on 7 February 1921 at the corner of Lennox Street and South Richmond Street in which a boy was injured in the crossfire, the General Officer Commanding Dublin District, Major-General Boyd, brought forward the beginning of the curfew from 10 p.m. to 8. The effect on Dublin life was drastic; even the *Irish Times*, which normally supported the authorities, was appalled.

> The existing order has throttled social life and has done much harm to trade. The dismal hour ... falls on the city like an extinguisher on a candle and the last trams are crowded with people in flight as it were from an infected area.

While the leader-writer admitted that something had to be done to counter the evening attacks, he warned that the extension of the curfew

> would be a staggering blow for Dublin. It would mean a sore loss for trade, with resultant unemployment ... the disappearance of the tramway services and local train services after half-past seven o'clock. It would cripple the hotels and restaurants, and would put the theatres wholly, and the picture houses partly, out of action. In a word, it would abolish most of the surviving amenities which make life just tolerable for the citizens of Dublin.

Dubliners did not even have to be shot to fall victims of the curfew. Its most distinguished victim was Dr McWalter, High Sheriff of Dublin and leader of the Municipal Reform Association on the corporation. On Friday 4 February he attended a private meeting with MRA colleagues and supporters in Merrion Square to discuss the political situation. When he left the meeting his host, Dr Ashe, described him as 'the picture of health'. But it was after 9 p.m., and the last trams had left the city centre. McWalter managed to beat the curfew but arrived at his home on the North Circular Road in a state of exhaustion. He collapsed shortly afterwards. A local priest and a medical colleague, Dr Cook, braved the military patrols to attend him before he died.

McWalter was one of the last survivors of the old Home Rule establishment in the city. A man of many parts, he was a doctor, a barrister and an engineer. He had been a founder-member of the Catholic Association, which had propelled him into politics. He had served as a member of the Senate of the Royal University, a member of the Royal Irish Academy and a Governor of

Apothecaries' Hall. But his life revolved around the corporation and his north inner-city dispensary, where he had treated many of those injured on Bloody Sunday in 1913 at the start of the great Lockout. Incensed at police brutality, he had called for the immediate withdrawal of the DMP and RIC from the city, had generally supported initiatives to relieve distress and mediated in industrial disputes. He had also championed the Hugh Lane gallery proposal.

It was his wholehearted endorsement of Redmond's pro-war stance in 1914 that changed McWalter's political trajectory. In 1915 he took a commission as a lieutenant in the Royal Army Medical Corps. He served mainly in Iraq and Palestine, witnessing the capture of Jerusalem in 1918. He took great pride in his military service and often on formal occasions insisted on being addressed as Surgeon-Captain McWalter. On his return to civilian life he was one of the prime movers in establishing the Municipal Reform Association, along with such former unionists as J. Hubbard Clark and Sir Andrew Beattie.[24] His impetuous temperament caused him to clash with Sinn Féin members of the corporation more frequently than his MRA colleagues from a unionist background. However, he retained a good working relationship with P. T. Daly and the Trades Council wing of the Labour Party from the days of the Lockout and remained progressive on social issues—provided they did not impose what he felt was an undue burden on the ratepayer. The two groups formed the *de facto* opposition to the Sinn Féin-Republican Labour majority on the corporation.

McWalter had been made High Sheriff by Lord French in recognition of past services, although, in spite of threats to do so, he does not seem to have used his powers to obstruct the work of the corporation. On his death Alderman J. Hubbard Clark replaced him, but by then the MRA was more or less reconciled to working with their rebel colleagues on most issues, and the new High Sheriff adopted a more conciliatory stance to the ruling factions.

The corporation adjourned its meeting on 7 February as a mark of respect for Surgeon-Captain McWalter, who was buried the same day. It was to be the first in a series of adjournments that followed the execution by firing squad of six IRA prisoners in Cork Prison on 28 February, the shooting of George Clancy, Mayor of Limerick, on 7 March and the execution of six more IRA prisoners in Mountjoy Prison on 14 March. Four of the latter were the Volunteers captured in the Drumcondra ambush in January; the others—Thomas Whelan and Patrick Moran—were convicted of murdering Captain Geoffrey Baggallay and Lieutenant Peter Ames, respectively, on Bloody Sunday.

Unlike other Volunteers executed in Mountjoy, Whelan and Moran were not native Dubliners. Thomas Whelan was from Clifden, Co. Galway. He worked at the Broadstone railway works and had five witnesses to place him two miles from the scene of the Baggallay shooting at the time. One was his landlady, who saw him leave the house for Mass that morning at 8:55 a.m., while the other four confirmed that he attended Mass at Ringsend shortly afterwards. He was convicted on the evidence of an officer who stayed in the same house as Baggallay and had been spared by the gunmen because he was not on their list. Whelan, a deeply religious man who sang at early morning Mass on the day of his execution, readily admitted he was a Volunteer but insisted on his innocence to the end.

Moran, a native of Crossna, Co. Roscommon, had no less than seventeen witnesses to establish his movements on the morning of Bloody Sunday, several of them barmen and grocers' assistants, like himself, and members of the Irish National Union of Vintners', Grocers' and Allied Trades' Assistants, of which he had recently been elected President. Most of the witnesses testified that he presided at a union meeting on the morning of Bloody Sunday. He was so confident of acquittal that he gave up his place in a successful escape attempt the night before his trial to another prisoner, Frank Teeling, who had been captured red-handed on Bloody Sunday.

Teeling's escape may in fact have sealed Moran's fate. General Macready was furious that no-one had yet been found guilty of the Bloody Sunday shootings, and the case against Teeling had been a cast-iron one. Moran's trial took place in City Hall, where the council chamber had been given over to the field court-martial. The case against Moran was based on the shaky eye-witness evidence of Major Frank Hallowell Carew and two privates, all of whom claimed they saw Moran in Mount Street on Bloody Sunday. A picture of him in Volunteer uniform holding a revolver found at his lodgings cannot have helped the defence.[25] In fact it was impossible for Moran to have shot Lieutenant Ames, because at the time he was supposed to have done so he was involved in the assassinations of Captain Patrick McCormack and Leonard Wilde in the Gresham Hotel, on the other side of the city. From there it was only a few minutes' walk to the Banba Hall, where he presided at the union meeting.

As many as forty thousand people gathered outside Mountjoy Prison on 14 March, the day of the executions, and tens of thousands more attended Masses in the city and in the coastal townships as far south as Bray, where there was a Requiem Mass at the Church of the Holy Redeemer preceded by a march by railwaymen down the Main Street. The crowds outside the prison were even bigger than those at Kevin Barry's execution. The Labour Party and the two rival trades councils in the city called a half-day strike in protest at the hangings.

No trams, trains or ferries ran. Shops and public houses closed as a mark of respect for Moran, as president of the barmen's and shop assistants' union.

People began to gather outside the prison even before the curfew was raised at 5 a.m. The *Irish Independent* reported:

> The stars were still shining. The air was chill—a slight snowfall had covered the ground between 3 and 4 a.m.—the darkness being relieved only by the electric lamps …
>
> One felt an eerie and depressed feeling approaching the gloomy prison portals. Then, at that early hour a vast, silent mass of humanity was moving towards Mountjoy Jail. Many were young boys and girls, a great number early workers, who, but for the impending sacrifices would have been going to their workshops, but, above all were the working women, especially those who came from their humble homes to pray for the happy repose of the six whom the gallows awaited.

Inside the prison a grim but moving ritual was followed. The prison chaplain, Canon Waters, accompanied by two other priests, Father McMahon and Dr Dargan, gave spiritual consolation to the men. The first pair to be executed, Patrick Moran and Thomas Whelan, were brought to Mass at five o'clock. They both served at the altar, and Whelan sang. An Auxiliary co-religionist, Lester Collins, who had guarded them, knelt beside the two men at the altar rail to receive communion. The *Irish Independent*—which appears to have been given most of the details by Canon Waters—reported:

> Following the Mass, Ellis, the executioner, and an assistant approached to make the usual preparations before the prisoners would be led to execution.
>
> Both men bade good bye to the Chaplains and others in the cell, including Auxiliary Police and warders and finally bade farewell to one another.
>
> Then began the procession to the execution chamber, which was situated only a short distance away. Both men walked firmly and fearlessly to the scaffold, where final words of comfort and consolation were uttered by the attendant chaplains.
>
> The executioner completed his arrangements, the heads of the doomed men were covered, and promptly at 6 o'clock, just as the new dawn was breaking, the bolt was drawn.

At 6:15 a.m. Father McMahon celebrated Mass for Patrick Doyle and Bernard Ryan before they followed Whelan and Moran to the execution chamber. Flood and Bryan had slept so soundly that they had to be wakened at 7:20 a.m. This still left time for Dr Dargan to celebrate Mass before they were executed at 8 a.m.

'The manner in which the condemned men went to their deaths made an extraordinary impression on those present,' Canon Waters told the press. Mixing his metaphors, he added that 'they seemed as children receiving their first communion ... walking to the scaffold like lions.'

There seems no doubt that the men underwent a deep religious experience similar to that of the Easter Week leaders and others condemned to death in 1916, such as Thomas Ashe. The latter had expressed regret that his death sentence had been commuted, because he had never felt himself to be better prepared spiritually for his fate. The fact that these deaths occurred in Passion Week would have contributed to the men's elevated state of spiritual awareness and acceptance of their fate.

Moran was understandably outraged on discovering he was to be executed despite the lack of evidence against him, but Whelan said: 'Never mind, Paddy. Tomorrow you will be accustomed to it, and by Sunday you will not wish for a reprieve.' Father McMahon said that these words proved true, and both men went to their deaths freely forgiving those who condemned them.

Even young Frank Flood's only regret, expressed in a letter to his brother Seán, was 'to have done so little for Ireland, but this thought is outweighed by the thought of how much we can do in heaven for Ireland in the great fight.'

Having no dependants, Flood, Whelan and Moran could at least concentrate on reconciling themselves to their fate. Bernard Ryan, on the other hand, was the sole support of his mother and invalid sister, while Doyle and Bryan were married. The fact that family members had very restricted access to the condemned men, while priests and nuns were regular visitors, no doubt reinforced the religious mood. None of the men smoked or drank as they awaited execution. When a member of the Sisters of Charity entered Frank Flood's cell and saw two empty porter bottles, he told them, 'You know our friends can bring us in anything we ask for. The Black and Tan guards are decent to us, and we thought we might as well order in a drink for them.'

Members of the order also visited Patrick Doyle and Bernard Ryan.

We found both men sitting before a cheery fire; they were resigned, but sad. Doyle spoke of his dear wife and twin babies and his darling little girl aged three-and-a-half. He said: 'You would love her, Sister. She has lovely golden hair to her waist.'

Ryan told us his widowed mother was very brave, but he was uneasy about his delicate sister. He was their sole support.

We spoke a little about resignation to God's Holy Will and the care Divine Providence would have over those left behind. All then reverently knelt down and joined in prayer … After this the men's spirits seemed to rise and peals of laughter were heard in the cell. They said we had brought them great comfort and that they would long to see us on the morrow.

During the same visit the nuns found Frank Flood and Thomas Bryan similarly 'low spirited. Bryan spoke of his young wife whom he had loved for years, but only married lately when he was in a position to keep her,' possibly thanks to his wages as a member of the ASU. Flood talked about his 'great chum' Kevin Barry, and 'it was with difficulty we tore ourselves away. … All were strong in the conviction that the fight for our country is a fight for the Faith.'

Paddy Moran's visitors included relatives and his girlfriend Bea Farrell. His last visit was from his parish priest in Crossna. Moran told him he was 'perfectly reconciled' to his fate. He signed a number of religious cards, including one with a personal message for Constance Markievicz.

Thomas Whelan's mother came up from Galway for his last visit and said afterwards: 'You would imagine he was going to see a football match.' He told her he was completely innocent. Frank Flood's father told him they were still working on a reprieve. Flood replied, 'We asked not for a reprieve but for justice.'

Both the married men were visited by their wives. Bryan's wife was pregnant with their first child and would die in childbirth six months later, but that day the talk was of a hopeful future, and he told his sister to tell his comrades: 'Carry on. No surrender.'

Patrick Doyle's wife, Louisa, brought their daughter, Kathleen, with her and the twins, who had been born while he was in prison. On her way home one of the twins, who was ill, would die in her mother's arms in Berkeley Road.

The families were in the waiting crowd next morning. At 8:25 a.m. the main gates of Mountjoy opened partially, revealing an armoured car, as the official notice was pinned up to announce that the six executions had taken place. Whelan's mother,

dressed in her striking western attire, who occupied a chair beside the gate, gave way to heart rending sobs, but she soon regained her courage and composure, and later, with the relatives of the other executed young men, left the precincts of the prison.

The crowd recited the Rosary, and some hung on in the hope of hearing of the men's last hours from the priests, but these were taken out by another exit, while soldiers dispersed the remaining spectators peacefully.

The *Irish Times* confined its comment on the proceedings to recording that 'nothing unbecoming of the occasion occurred'; but the *Irish Independent* printed a blistering editorial.

The British Government began the celebration of St Patrick's Week by hanging six young Irishmen in Mountjoy Prison yesterday morning. Two of them protested their innocence to the last, and the public believed them. The others, of whom two were under twenty years of age, were launched into eternity on the charge that they had taken part in an ambush in which none of those attacked was even wounded.

It predicted that 'the Irishmen executed yesterday will be regarded as martyrs.' The official notice of the executions

states that they were carried out under sentence of the law. The prisoners, although civilians, were not tried by the ordinary courts, but by courts martial. So little regard was shown for the mere form of law at the executions that the Sheriff was, apparently, not present, nor was there a Coroner's inquest held afterwards, although both are prescribed by law as necessary ... This is not the way to settle the Irish problem ... Rather will it help to make extremists of moderates and to still further embitter the extremists.

The *Independent* quoted Sir Horace Plunkett, liberal unionist and founder of the co-operative movement, who was visiting the United States, as warning that indignation over what was happening in Ireland

is wider and deeper than I have known it for forty years. The British Government and the military rulers it has set up in Ireland may ignore this fact but the verdict not of America alone but of the whole world is given against it.[26]

On the evening of the Mountjoy executions there was a major gun battle in Pearse Street. It arose out of the increasingly aggressive patrolling tactics of combatants on both sides. In this instance a local IRA company began to patrol the area as soon as it grew dark. Frustrated in an attempt to ambush a military vehicle in Tara Street and Burgh Quay, it mounted an attack on the DMP station in Pearse Street in the hope of drawing the enemy into the area. This resulted in one Volunteer being seriously wounded when a grenade he threw rebounded, blowing him into the roadway, where he suffered the added misfortune of being hit by a passing tram.

The explosion attracted two Auxiliary lorries, supported by an armoured car, which clashed with IRA patrols towards the far end of the street, outside St Andrew's Catholic Club, a regular IRA meeting-place. Although the British claimed later to have been acting on information that a hundred senior IRA figures were congregating at the club, this hardly squares with the despatch of a patrol of only sixteen Auxiliaries. Nevertheless the fighting escalated and lasted until three o'clock in the morning, by which time it had declined into desultory sniping. Once they entered the club the Auxiliaries carried out the usual ritual destruction of furniture and fittings. The billiard table was smashed, billiard balls thrown through the windows and photographs of executed 1916 leaders and local priests defaced. If nothing else, they had ensured the continued disaffection of the local people, which helps explain why so many residents, especially in the Erne Street area, took risks in the skirmishes that ensued to pull wounded Volunteers into their homes and help others slip away.

By the end of the engagement three Volunteers had been killed and two captured, along with the badly wounded man injured in the attack on the police station earlier that evening. Two Auxiliaries were killed and three were wounded. One of the dead Auxiliaries was the English section-leader, James Beard, but the other, James O'Farrell, was a Dubliner. A single man, twenty-eight years old, he was a fitter by trade but had served in the Royal Dublin Fusiliers during the Great War, had been commissioned as a lieutenant in the Tank Corps and mentioned in despatches. He had joined the RIC as a special reserve constable—literally a Black and Tan, who was on secondment to the Auxiliaries as a driver.

The two dead Volunteers were very young. One was sixteen-year-old Bernard O'Hanlon, who had come from Dundalk to work as a pawnbroker's assistant. He had been detained in Portobello Barracks after Bloody Sunday, but his captors were persuaded he was not old enough to be involved in any serious activities. The other was eighteen-year-old Leo Fitzgerald, a local youth who had served in Fianna Éireann in 1916 and been on active service with the IRA.

As usual, there were also fatal civilian casualties. They were Thomas Asquith, a caretaker at a local foundry, and David Kelly, manager of the Sinn Féin Bank and brother of Alderman Tom Kelly. A seventy-year-old local woman, Mary Morgan, was shot in the hip, by which side it was impossible to ascertain.

In some respects the most unfortunate casualty of the night was Thomas Traynor. At thirty-nine he was relatively old for a Volunteer. He was a cobbler by trade, married with ten children. His wife, Elizabeth, was a Protestant, and the couple had had to elope to overcome family objections to a mixed marriage. Traynor had served in Boland's Mill in 1916 and had been 'master shoemaker' in Fron Goch internment camp in Wales. He lived in Mount Brown and had a shop in Crown Alley. Like most of the older, settled Volunteers with families who had been 'out' in 1916, Traynor was not asked to become heavily involved in IRA activity during the War of Independence but was entrusted with vital and sometimes dangerous tasks. On that particular night he had been told to deliver a pistol to St Andrew's Club for collection. Caught unprepared in the middle of the gun battle, he tried to escape but was brought down in a rugby tackle by an Auxiliary. Although he had not fired the weapon in his possession he was charged with the murder of the Dublin Black and Tan, James O'Farrell, and was hanged three weeks later.[27]

Given the mayhem, with raids and ambushes taking place every night, it was not surprising that St Patrick's Day celebrations were muted in 1921. Masses for peace were said in all the Catholic churches in the city, and the Companions of St Patrick held their annual dinner in the Shelbourne Hotel, where the former Chief Commissioner of the DMP Sir John Ross gave the toast. Ross epitomised the old Ascendancy. A Northern Protestant, former officer in the Coldstream Guards and brother-in-law of Viscount Masserene, he had won the grudging respect of opponents when he resigned in 1914 over the dismissal of his Assistant Commissioner, William Harrel, whom he felt had been made a scapegoat for the Bachelor's Walk shootings. Yet Ross's theme that day was peace. He told his Companions that 'Irishmen could hardly find themselves celebrating St Patrick's Day in more depressing circumstances.' But 'I do not agree with the pessimists ... We are all longing for peace [Hear, hear], and if there were a truce for a month, or even for a week, I doubt if hostilities would be renewed.' (Applause.) In an admission he would probably not have made even a few months before, he added, 'Indiscriminate force will never solve anything.'

The gathering decided to send a message to the Prime Minister, 'asking him to make a definite, generous and open offer to the Irish People for a peace and settlement, believing, as we do, that it would meet with a generous response.' Probably not all the Companions shared Ross's optimism, but there was no doubting the desire for peace in a body that embraced a broad spectrum of what might be described as the old regime. It included members of the Ascendancy and its putative successors, leading lights in the displaced Home

Rule movement. These were people with few prospects of sharing in the spoils of any new political settlement but who still hoped to hang on to what they had if the chaos would end.

Some seemed to spend most of their time out of the country, including the society's President, the Earl of Granard, who sent his apologies from California. Another absentee was the Lord Chancellor, Sir James Campbell, a former MP for Dublin University. His message to the gathering was representative of the rest. He expressed the wish for 'a speedy and honourable deliverance from the troubles and tragedies ... which threaten to submerge the instinctive chivalry and generosity of our race.' Sir John Irwin, a paper manufacturer and former unionist who had been an unsuccessful MRA candidate in the corporation elections, took the chair in the absence of more prominent luminaries. Despite these absent members the room was still full of his fellow-businessmen, such as the shipbuilder John Smellie and a flock of Findlaters and Hewitts, and fugitives from the United Irish League, such as the former Lord Mayor Sir James Gallagher.

If Sir John Ross did not get his week's truce, the saint's day was at least marked by a sharp reduction in military activity. Government offices closed, most of the garrison was confined to barracks, and the irrepressible Auxiliaries strutted the streets sporting shamrock in the muzzles of their rifles.

One important death passed almost unremarked in the shambles that was Dublin in early 1921. It was that of Dr Charles Cameron, who had been the city's Public Analyst since 1862, Medical Officer of Health since 1874, Medical Superintendent Officer of Health since 1879 and Secretary of the Public Health Committee from 1881. Eventually all these posts were subsumed in the title Chief Medical Officer. He died on 27 February 1921 and was buried at Mount Jerome Cemetery in Harold's Cross on 3 March. He had been on extended sickness leave since the previous October and had surrendered most of his duties to his deputy, M. J. Russell FRCS, after the Great War. Although he never recovered from the death of his son, Ewan, an officer in the Royal Dublin Fusiliers who shot himself in 1915, he had continued to perform his public duties and serve as Deputy Grand Master of the Freemasons in Ireland, effectually running the organisation, as the Grand Master, the Earl of Donoughmore, was abroad on military service for most of the war years.

The funeral procession from St Bartholomew's in Clyde Road included representatives of the Royal College of Surgeons, the Royal Dublin Society, academics, the Masonic Order, the judiciary, senior military officers, serving and retired, family friends, members of the business community, theatrical and musical societies and, above all, members of the medical profession. All the serving councillors from the Municipal Reform Association attended, as did some former nationalist members. But the Lord Mayor, and the Sinn Féin and Labour members of the city council, did not attend. Nor did that body adjourn as a mark of respect for the city's longest-serving public servant. Ironically, it was a far less ecumenical affair, both religiously and politically, than his son's funeral six years earlier. There was a vote of sympathy for Cameron's family at the next meeting of the corporation, and Jennie Wyse Power of Sinn Féin used the opportunity to point out that Cameron's sixty years of

> doing work in connection with the sanitary affairs of the city ... was an example of the wonderful tolerance of the Irish people, and is a complete answer at this time, when the North will not come in with the rest of Ireland, to any fears expressed on the grounds of toleration. [Hear, hear.]

The executions of six men in Mountjoy, further executions in Cork and the prospect of more in Dublin must have soured the temper of many nationalists. For them Sir Charles Cameron and his procession of mourners belonged to a different world and one indifferent to the nation's suffering.[28] In many ways he was the victim of his own longevity. A leading figure in public health reform in his youth and middle age, he had become indelibly identified in old age with the failings of the system he had helped create and the values of a regime that a younger generation of political activists wished to sweep away.

The passing of Sir Charles Cameron and Surgeon-Captain James McWalter coincided with a crisis in the treatment of TB in the city. This was in large part brought about by the deadlock over finance between the rebel corporation and the Local Government Board. The problem was aggravated by the significant if uncharted numbers of soldiers returning with the disease and with rising poverty as the wartime boom finally ran out of steam. The number of workers on the live register of unemployment rose from 8,964 in December 1920 to 13,313 by December 1921. Kingstown had the distinction of having the sharpest rise in the number unemployed of any town, with an increase from 15 to 816 over this period.[29]

Dublin Corporation tried to address the problem by establishing an Unemployment Committee in February. This prepared several projects for those on the dole, including work on preparing Fairbrother's Fields for housing.[30] Like other local authorities, Dublin could approach the British government's Unemployment Grants Committee for assistance, but there were a number of caveats, ranging from the merely objectionable, such as the requirement to give first preference on schemes to unemployed ex-servicemen, to the insurmountable, namely the requirement that the corporation's accounts be submitted to the Unemployment Grants Committee for audit. In a move of which Dr McWalter would have approved, P. T. Daly and John Lawlor of the Trades Council Labour group proposed that the Lord Mayor be empowered to approach the committee with a view to seeking a variation of the conditions attaching to grants. It proved a futile exercise.

TB posed an even bigger problem than unemployment. At any time there were estimated to be 10,000 people with the disease in the city, for whom there were 76 places at the Allan A. Ryan Home Hospital for Consumption in Pigeon House Road, another 130 at Crooksling Sanatorium and between 35 and 40 in the smaller Peamount and Newcastle Sanatoriums. The city's hospitals and hospices never took more than a handful of cases each, for fear of spreading the infection to other patients. There was also a specialist health centre for TB outpatients at the P. F. Collier Memorial Dispensary for the Prevention of Tuberculosis in West Charles Street, off the north quays.

The workhorse of the system was the Pigeon House hospital, which dealt with patients at an advanced stage in the hope of saving their lives and sending them to sanatoriums for recovery. But these institutions were heavily dependent on central government funding, and in September 1920 the corporation instructed the Tuberculosis Committee to shut the hospital at Pigeon House Road, the Crooksling sanatorium and the Charles Street dispensary as part of its economy drive. Most patients had already been discharged when these institutions closed their doors from October for the rest of 1920.

There were few working-class or lower-middle-class families in Dublin not affected by TB, and fear of contagion permeated every class. This was reflected in the corporation debate on the crisis. The issue crossed party lines. Sinn Féin members were acutely aware of the political dangers of being blamed for the cuts. At the first meeting of the corporation in January 1921 Kathleen Clarke and P. T. Daly asked that standing orders be suspended to allow the council to discuss reopening the Pigeon House Road hospital. Clarke said there was an urgent need to act, 'isolating at the earliest possible moment as many as can be accommodated of the advanced—and consequently highly infectious—cases of pulmonary TB.' The urgency was all the greater because the Crooksling complex was in very poor condition and could not reopen before June 1921 without extensive renovation.[31]

The campaign against TB and the promotion of public health generally had always been close to P. T. Daly's heart. He argued that if contributions from patients who were insured—such as trade union members and their dependants—were factored into the cost of running these institutions it should be possible to keep both open. But the Insurance Commissioners, who controlled the funds, were reluctant to engage with the rebel authority, effectually withholding almost £32,000 by March 1921.[32] Unlike some of the Republican Labour newcomers to the corporation, Daly had developed a good working relationship with many of the old guard in the system, including Sir Charles Cameron. When the corporation met again on 14 February, Daly's colleague Tom Lawlor and Councillor Michael Brohoon (Republican Labour), fellow-veterans of the 1913 Lockout, joined him in urging that Crooksling reopen at the earliest opportunity.

John Forrestal and William Paul (Sinn Féin) proposed that the limited scheme in operation at Pigeon House Road be continued instead. Forrestal and Paul tended to veer to the conservative side of most social and economic issues, but there was sense in their proposal if the corporation was to keep within the financial constraints imposed by the stalemate with the Local Government Board. The debate resulted in a tied vote, 11 to 11. In a rare use of his casting vote, the Lord Mayor, Laurence O'Neill, cast it in favour of the Forrestal-Paul proposition, as this upheld the existing position.

The matter was not allowed to rest there. It had been a poorly attended meeting, and those maintaining the minimalist position of containment consisted of a rare combination of the MRA group with a handful of conservative Sinn Féin and independent nationalist councillors. The eleven votes for reopening the Pigeon House and Crooksling hospitals came from an equally rare alliance of Trades Council and Republican Labour members, who could have outvoted their opponents with a better turn-out. One reason for this new-found, if brief, unity was that not only were working-class districts most at risk from TB but both groups of councillors had union members in the institutions affected, particularly Crooksling. Seeing which way the vote had gone and the low attendance, some Labour councillors left the chamber, so depriving the meeting of a quorum. This was the same tactic the MRA had employed previously to block the blanket payment of wages lost by members of the corporation in prison or interned for IRA activities.

The issue was returned to on 21 March 1921 when the champions of Crooksling used a report on the sanatorium to show that its farm was making a profit of more than a thousand pounds a year, and could make more. The farm had the added attraction, from the ratepayers' viewpoint, that patients supplied free labour, cutting running costs by a third. This appeared to clinch the debate. It was then decided to close the Pigeon House hospital and reopen

Crooksling; however, as Crooksling would not be fit to receive patients until June 1921 it was agreed that the Pigeon House hospital would remain open until the autumn. The total saving on this alternative plan would be £3,000, just under 10 per cent of the budget for combating TB.[33]

At the March meeting the Labour councillors secured the support of Councillor Michael J. Moran (MRA) and Councillor John Grace (Sinn Féin), ensuring the reopening of Crooksling by 14 votes to 11. The vote is of interest because it was one of the few occasions on which the MRA members split, albeit only two were present. In many ways it was the most consistent party on the corporation, in that its imperative was to vote for measures that kept the rates low. However, members also realised that saving on health services did not always make good economic or social sense.

One of the unfortunate consequences of Sir Charles Cameron's departure was that Dublin Corporation ceased issuing its quarterly breviates (short reports) on the health of its citizens. While these were far from adequate—for instance, influenza did not become a notifiable disease until 25 February 1919, shortly before the flu pandemic began to abate—they at least provided an indication of trends in the city. One thing that clearly emerges from the mortality rates was that, apart from a sudden surge of deaths in the first quarter of 1915, the Great War had been good for the health and life expectancy of the average Dubliner, whereas the return of 'peace' saw the risk of illness rise and life expectancy fall. Undoubtedly part of the reason was the fall in living standards, especially for women who lost relatively well-paid jobs in war industries. The money that had flowed to 'separation women' in the tenements also dried up, adding to the suffering that peace inflicted on the city.

The shortfall in funding for the city's hospitals (see chapter 5) arose out of cuts in payments by the British exchequer, even before the stalemate between the corporation and Local Government Board. Such health returns as survive show that deaths from infectious diseases reached their lowest point in late 1918 and early 1919, after which they began to rise again. Tuberculosis consistently topped the list of notifiable diseases in the city from well before the outbreak of the Great War. The only potential rivals were sexually transmitted diseases, but these were never included in the list of notifiable infectious diseases.

The corporation showed inconsistency not only in how it collated statistics but in how it financed essential services. This in turn made planning almost impossible. For instance, when the Improvements Committee showed a surplus of more than £4,000 in the estimates for sanitary services for the coming year, one of Sinn Féin's most left-wing councillors, Hanna Sheehy Skeffington, proposed successfully that £5,000 be invested 'to permit of the erection of a suitable ladies' lavatory in the city.' The motion was strongly supported by the MRA, always supporters of women's rights, and was easily carried. Yet at the same meeting an amendment from Councillor Peter Doyle of Sinn Féin proposing that £1,500 of the Paving Committee's surplus of more than £128,000 be given to the Dangerous Buildings Department was narrowly defeated. The decision, in a city full of unsafe tenements, suggests that the slum landlords' lobby was still a greater political force in the council chamber than that of their tenants.[34]

Fortunate indeed were the patients of the Richmond Asylum to have officials prepared to put their careers on the line to maintain an adequate level of care and to seek British exchequer funds in defiance of corporation policy and 'high-falutin' political theatrics.

Chapter 9 ～

'PROBABLY THE STUPIDEST THING THE SINN FEIN EVER DID'

Violent death was ubiquitous in Dublin in early 1921, but the natural passing of one particular corporation official drew unaccustomed attention to a business that was so commonplace that its existence was taken to be as immutable as the weather. It was that of Michael Losty, the city's Sword-Bearer, who died on 25 March. The new Town Clerk, John F. Murphy, asked if the corporation wished to maintain the position, as the duties were largely ceremonial, namely attendance on the Lord Mayor and the council with the Lord Mayor's Sword and keeping order in the public gallery. Even the sword was redundant, as it was now consigned to the muniment room.

What was more, it was an unpaid position. But the Sword-Bearer was also one of Dublin's four divisional auctioneers, charged with administering the Pawnbroking Laws. Two of these posts were filled by the Lord Lieutenant and two by the Lord Mayor. General auctioneers were usually appointed by the Lord Lieutenant and conducted the business from their own premises, where forfeited items were sold off. By tradition and right immemorial the other two divisions went to the City Marshal, who was also the Registrar of Pawnbrokers, and to the Sword-Bearer.

Losty's income had come from renting out his auctioneering franchise. The position had once commanded as much as £5 a week, but it was now impossible to secure more than £3 from a general auctioneer for the practice. While the volume of business rose with the poverty of the slums, its real value appears to have fallen. According to Thomas Lyng, who came to the business as a fourteen-year-old fugitive from school, there were about fifty pawnshops in the city at the time. 'It was really a weekly business—in on Monday and out on Saturday.' While Lyng would describe such shops as 'the people's bank', the reality was somewhat different. Pawnbrokers were a less voracious breed of moneylender. The business pattern was dictated by the vagaries of the labour market and the size of the weekly pay packet. The great majority of clients were women—wives, mothers and daughters—who brought in whatever valuables they possessed to pledge against a loan that would support the family until the following Friday, especially if the breadwinner, generally a man, was out of work, had earned less than the family needed to survive for the week, or had drunk more of the household budget than he ought.

Although there was a great deal of competition among pawnbrokers, it was for customers rather than for goods. The goods pawned included such varied items as wedding rings, jewellery, bedclothes, shoes, crockery and open razors. What mattered more than the intrinsic value of the possessions was the reliability of the owner in redeeming the pledge, with interest, at the end of the week. Pawnbrokers learnt the hard way to discern the honest pledge from those made by customers depositing goods 'borrowed' from relatives or fellow-tenants.

> All that was taken in was old and smelled, and the sheets and clothes would have fleas and everything in them. They just threw their clothes on the counter and the pawnbroker would just have to try and sort it out and take in whatever he could.

Despite the relatively low value of the goods, customers would redeem them because they could not afford to replace what were often essential items. Lyng recalled some men leaving their shoes on the counter and walking out in their bare feet. The pledges were often piled up to the ceiling, and this 'chaotic hell' was bearable only because

> most of the managers of pawn offices were all very easy-going, had a jolly kind of air so that they were able to have a great rapport with the customer ... A pawn office was never as strict as you'd get in other businesses.

Nevertheless, as the business was built on poverty, defaults were common, and Losty's death allowed concerns to be voiced in the city council about the behaviour of many pawnbrokers. Under two statutes passed by the Irish Parliament in 1786 and 1788 a pawnbroker was obliged to provide two weeks' notice to a client that their goods were forfeit and would be auctioned off. There was an auctioneer's commission on each of the items sold: this was 1d on the first 20s worth of goods, 1s 4d on the next 20s to 40s worth and 1s per £1 on all goods over 40s sold per individual.

At the beginning of May 1921 the Town Clerk suggested that the corporation might dispense with the services of a Sword-Bearer. The City Marshal, perhaps fearful that his own office and paraphernalia might be consigned to the muniment room with other relics of foreign subjugation, wrote to the Town Clerk on 14 May defending the system and assuring him that in his own capacity as Registrar he could confirm that it was strongly supported by the pawnbrokers—all of whom kept the law scrupulously. This evoked a strong reaction from the Trades Council Labour group. In a letter to the City Marshal, Alderman Tom Lawlor told the Town Clerk that, far from pawnbrokers notifying clients when their goods were sent for auction, most did not bother keeping clients' addresses. Nor were many clients aware that they were entitled to any surplus that might arise from the sale of their goods after the debt to the pawnbroker and the auctioneer's commission had been deducted.

The leader of the Trades Council Labour group, P. T. Daly, went further and denounced 'the rapacity of the pawnbrokers in Dublin.' He told a corporation meeting that the acts passed by the old Irish Parliament were 'a measure for the relief of the necessitous pawnbrokers by the poor,' and he accused the City Registrar, J. H. Parnell, of farming out his business, just like Losty, while the legal work was done on his behalf by a Belfast solicitor.

The controversy continued to rage for months; but Daly and his group seem to have undergone a change of mind when they realised that, for all their faults, the Sword-Bearer and City Marshal were at least answerable to the corporation. 'If the appointment were not made, the very poor of the city would be at the mercy of unscrupulous pawnbrokers, as against scrupulous traders. And,' Daly conceded, 'there are many honourable men in the business.' A successor to Losty, Christopher Andrews, was eventually elected in November 1921.[1]

Meanwhile a far more distinguished son of Dublin had died. Dr William Walsh had been in relatively good health, considering his eighty-two years, until February 1921. His last major public outing had been to lay the foundation stone for the new Catholic parish church in Finglas. It had been overshadowed by Bloody Sunday, but the congregation had been oblivious to events in the city that morning as the Lord Mayor, Laurence O'Neill, paid a tribute to the archbishop, whose fragile heath was already apparent but who continued to soldier on in the national cause. As late as the beginning of February he wrote to the Lord Mayor: 'Don't spare me any work for the White Cross movement, provided ... it does not involve attending public meetings.' He was, as always, particularly concerned to counter the activities of apologists for British policy within the Catholic Church. In the process he inevitably attracted criticism that he was defending men 'who have been ... bound and sworn to the immoral principles of Bolshevism, in the desecrated name of nationalism,' as Cardinal Bourne's *Westminster Cathedral Chronicle* put it. A shrewd propagandist and political infighter himself, Walsh had the satisfaction of seeing Bourne's pastoral letter condemning Sinn Féin publicly denounced at a large gathering of Irish Catholics in King's Hall, London, a few weeks before his death.

The archbishop also used contacts in the North American church to promote Sinn Féin's objectives. In a letter to Cardinal William Henry O'Connell of Boston he asked him to endorse the Dáil Éireann loan.

I cannot bear but think that, as far as the people of our Irish race are concerned, their knowledge of the fund ... would be of at least as much help as any money subscription of mine could be ... But as matters now stand in Ireland, none of our newspapers dare publish the fact that I had subscribed. We are living under martial law ... Freedom of the Press, the right to public meetings, the right of personal liberty, the right of trial by jury no longer exist in this country except in so far as they can exist subject to the absolutely uncontrolled discretion of some military ruler designated the 'competent military authority.'[2]

The Archbishop's last overt political act was to seek an urgent meeting with Lord French and General Macready in March 1921, despite his poor health, to plead for clemency for the six men waiting to be hanged in Mountjoy, as he had for Kevin Barry. The request was refused.

Walsh's clerical opponents at home and abroad believed his support for Sinn Féin was 'in opposition to the law and to the Catholic Church.' But Walsh's policy was, and always had been, more subtle than his critics, lay or clerical, appreciated. His father, a Dublin watchmaker and devoted follower of Daniel O'Connell, had enrolled him in the Repeal Association at the age of twenty-one months, presented him to the Liberator at five years of age and bequeathed him an abiding love of his native country. Walsh's own political evolution led him to seek as much freedom as possible for Ireland as political conditions allowed. His acute political antennae told him that in doing so he was also safeguarding and strengthening the influence of the Catholic Church. If James Connolly believed 'the cause of Labour is the cause of Ireland,'[3] Walsh's credo was that the cause of the Catholic Church was the cause of Ireland, and he proved by far the more effective practitioner of the two.

A strong supporter of Parnell, Walsh did not hesitate to move against him when it was obvious that the O'Shea divorce case would destroy the Liberal alliance. If William Martin Murphy bankrolled the anti-Parnellite movement, Walsh provided much of the political strategy. It was something for which many Dublin Parnellites never forgave him, just as many of the city's Larkinites had bitter memories of his condemnation of the controversial scheme to send strikers' children to English foster-homes during the 1913 Lockout. On the other hand it was Walsh who negotiated the establishment of a National University for Ireland with the British government, who promoted the establishment of hostels for migrant workers in the city and built the country's first and regrettably only industrial day school to keep young offenders in the home.[4] But it was his strategic positioning of the Catholic Church at the head rather than the rear of the movement to secure home rule, and then independence, that made him such an important figure. Without him there would have been no Sinn Féin victory in the crucial South Longford by-election of 1917 and no united front of bishops, Irish Party MPs, Sinn Féin, Irish Volunteers and Labour leaders against conscription in 1918. He also worked tirelessly to improve industrial relations throughout the country, spending many hours in conflict resolution. He came tantalisingly close to creating a fully fledged mediation and conciliation system for Dublin before the 1913 Lockout erupted. Many of its features were later incorporated in the Labour Court, created a quarter of a century after his death.

It was inevitable that his funeral on 14 April would not only be enormous but would require such complex organisation that it is probable that Walsh, with his usual foresight, had planned it himself. Not only was Dublin Corporation represented but most of the other large corporations and county councils in the country as well. Delegations from the National University and other educational institutions, religious and secular, were there, together with representatives of the city's hospitals and charitable bodies. Special provision was made for representatives of Dáil Éireann, the Lord Chief Justice of Ireland and senior British law officers, of the Protestant churches, the Jewish community in the city, the trade unions and Cumann na mBan. Places were reserved in front of the hearse for schoolchildren, including the boys and girls of the St Vincent de Paul orphanage, the Christian Brothers, students and staff of Holy Cross College and senior Catholic clergy. Cardinal Logue's carriage brought up the rear of this section, immediately in front of Dr Walsh's remains. The Irish Volunteers provided stewards for the crowds but had no formal presence at the funeral.

The only individuals explicitly refused permission to attend were the Lord Lieutenant, Lord French, and the British army commander, General Macready, or anyone seeking to represent them. French took it in good spirit. When told that his letter of condolence arrived at the Archbishop's Palace in the same post as Richard Mulcahy's, he said that Smuts, the Boer commander he fought in South Africa twenty years earlier, 'was described as a bloodthirsty murderer ... just as Mulcahy is today.' Macready ordered all flags to be flown at half-mast and all soldiers to be confined to barracks for the duration of the funeral. Dublin Corporation closed its offices from noon until 3 p.m. to allow employees to attend.

Thursday 14 April 1921 was a typical spring day in Dublin. Sunshine alternated with showers, and there was a sharp, contrary wind. According to press reports, 200,000 people attended the funeral or lined the route, equivalent to two-thirds of the city's population and making it even larger than that of the rebel leader Thomas Ashe in 1917. One unusual feature was that there were no flowers. However, there was music at the Requiem High Mass in the Pro-Cathedral, provided by the Palestrina Choir and Dublin Priests' Choir. Dr Walsh had been a music-lover and left his piano and pianola to the Merrion Blind Asylum.

There was a final and fitting tribute for a champion of workers' rights when the Glasnevin Cemetery gravediggers suspended their strike for the day to bury the archbishop. During the dispute families had to dig the graves themselves.[5] So frequent were disputes at Glasnevin, because the committee consistently refused to pay the same rates as the city's other cemeteries, that the councillors asked their Law Agent to examine whether the corporation would be legally empowered to open its own cemetery. He said they could, but it was impractical without the co-operation of the Local Government Board.[6]

On the same day that the archbishop was being buried, Captain William King went on trial for murder before a field court-martial in the council chamber of City Hall, where he had made such a dramatic entrance on 6 December 1920. Along with two Auxiliary cadets, Frederick Walsh and Herbert Hinchcliffe, he was charged with the murder of 27-year-old James Murphy and eighteen-year-old Patrick Kennedy. The dead men were not members of the IRA but appear to have been lifted in a routine trawl in Talbot Street on 9 February. They were then taken to Clonturk Park, where Frank Flood's unit had been taken prisoner after the disastrous January ambush. Both men may have been tortured before being shot. An official communiqué stated that Murphy and Kennedy were killed 'attempting to escape.' Unfortunately for King, Murphy was still alive when he was found by two DMP members shortly afterwards. They were patrolling in Drumcondra when they heard shooting. Murphy was able to make a full statement implicating King and his subordinates in what had happened before he died at the Mater Hospital.

There were several witnesses, one of them a British officer, to corroborate Murphy's statement that the men were beaten and ill-treated at Dublin Castle before leaving in the company of King and his associates on the night of 9 February in a Ford car. The DMP witnesses also saw a Ford car, the same model as Captain King's, driving towards the city centre while on their way to investigate the shots.[7] However, Murphy's deathbed statement was disallowed, and several Auxiliaries gave evidence that Murphy and Kennedy had been released unharmed after questioning. They explained the evidence of other witnesses that the prisoners had been ill-treated in the Castle Yard by saying they must have witnessed a fight between two members of the Auxiliary Division that night, whose names no-one could now recall.

This evidence is far more interesting for the picture it reveals of garrison life in Dublin Castle for members of F Company than for its veracity. According to defence witnesses, King had gone to a Masonic meeting in Molesworth Street that evening and his car broke down on the way back to the Castle. In the meantime two Auxiliaries had gone out in civilian clothes to gather intelligence in a nearby pub, where they 'picked up with two women and ... became very drunk.' On their return they had a row and began fighting outside the YMCA club. They were eventually parted, and one of them was so bloodied that he had to be washed down at the pump in the Castle Yard. Both men were then taken to hospital for examination in an unidentified car driven by unidentifiable colleagues. During this time King's co-accused, Hinchcliffe and Walsh, were supposed to be playing cards in a room behind the pump.

Asked by the prosecution if there were 'fights going on there every night,' a defence witness said, 'Not every night; there may be a fight on pay night.'

'Do they all get on the "rampage" when it comes near pay night?' the witness was asked.

'Not necessarily; there might be a fight on a Monday night.'

When the platoon commander was asked why he had not put the men on report, he answered: 'These men are risking their lives in carrying out dangerous duties ... I am not going to push them off, because I could not get other men to do it.'

King and his co-defendants were acquitted.

In a blistering editorial, the *Irish Independent* itemised the evidence against the accused and compared it with the very different way in which a field court-martial had treated much weaker evidence against Paddy Moran and Thomas Whelan, who were hanged for their alleged part in the Bloody Sunday shootings. In many ways the silence of the *Irish Times* on the verdicts was worse.

Ironically, King had spent some of his time in prison while awaiting trial discussing his case with Éamonn Broy, one of Collins's agents in the DMP, whose cover had been compromised by the seizure of an IRA intelligence cache in the city.[8] Because the British state was their employer, the men were exercised separately from other prisoners. Broy recalled:

> King was full of his own grievances ... and, of course, I duly enlarged on mine. King said, 'All governments are the same. They utilise the services of people like you and me and are then quite prepared to hang us if it suits their purpose.' He appeared to be afraid that the 'politicians' would have him executed 'just to show how "fair minded" they were.'

King's sidekick, Captain Jocelyn Hardy, drummed up witnesses for the defence. It cannot have been hard: after all, King had given evidence on behalf of the Auxiliaries who shot McKee, Clancy and Clune while they were 'attempting to escape' from Dublin Castle in November. Collins's agents were equally successful in suborning Joe Supple, the DMP inspector in charge of the Broy investigation.[9]

The *Irish Bulletin* outed King and Hardy as 'inhuman brutes' a week later, itemising the treatment they had meted out to various prisoners. Both survived all attempts by the IRA to kill them.[10]

Ironically, as King had pointed out to Broy, the more successful such men were the less essential they became. Just like the excesses of the IRA, those of the British forces were promoting the war-weariness that Sir John Ross and his Companions of St Patrick saw as the best hope of peace.

Indeed nowhere was the urge for peace stronger than among southern Unionists, such as Sir John Ross. The mood at the annual meeting of the City of Dublin and Pembroke Unionist Association on 1 April 1921 was very different from the pre-war years. In 1914 the new president, Captain Sidney Herbert, Earl of Pembroke, had pledged himself as a young army officer to win back the parliamentary seat in the St Stephen's Green division from the Irish Party in the next general election. Now a grizzled veteran, Lieutenant-Colonel Herbert sent his apologies as president that he could not attend. Neither could the vice-president, Andrew Jameson, recently appointed to the Irish Privy Council; nor

254 A CITY IN TURMOIL

could Fane Vernon of Guinness's and the Great Northern Railway and other senior members of the unionist community in the city. Several leading lights of the association from the pre-war era had died, such as Sir Robert Gardner of Craig Gardner, a former chairman of Pembroke Urban District Council, philanthropist and High Sheriff of the city.

The task of chairing the meeting fell on the remaining vice-president, William Ireland. A former unionist member of Dublin Corporation, he had to retreat to Rathmines to secure a council seat in the 1920 municipal elections in the party's interest. Although a substantial businessman in the city, Ireland was very much in the second tier of the traditional leadership.

William Jellett, one of the MPs for Dublin University, gave the main speech of the day. Speaking almost with fondness of the old enemy, the Irish Party, he warned members that they now faced 'a movement much more combined, much more dangerous, much more outspoken and much more determined than anything that we have met with before.' Its object was 'the destruction of the British Empire.' Unionists must either 'smash the conspiracy' or 'surrender to it.'[11]

It was a speech that reflected the increasingly contradictory attitudes of many Southern unionists to the crisis. Unlike the Anti-Partition League, headed by Lord Midleton, the rump of unionist associations in the South clung blindly to assurances by Ulster unionists that the threat of partition was ultimately the best defence of the Union with Britain. The Midletonians, on the other hand, were gradually feeling their way towards a political settlement based on dominion status. Following a speech Midleton gave to the Rotary Club in Dublin on 7 March 1921 on commercial aspects of dominion home rule, an Irish Business Men's Conciliation Committee was established. Among the members were Sir William Goulding, probably Dublin's wealthiest businessman, Sir Walter Nugent, a director of the Bank of Ireland and the Midland Great Western Railway, and Sir Andrew Jameson, another Bank of Ireland director and current president of Dublin Chamber of Commerce. Some of these men could not be bothered to attend the AGM of the Dublin Branch of the Irish Unionist Alliance the following month but worked assiduously to provide a reliable information conduit between the British and Dáil Éireann cabinets in the months leading up to the Truce. The committee's purpose was not only to ascertain if peace could be negotiated on the basis of dominion home rule but what safeguards would be created for the unionist minority in the South —for Midleton, like Sir John Ross, was convinced that once a Truce was achieved it would be difficult, if not impossible, for either side to resume hostilities.

When talks eventually took place between de Valera and Griffith on one side and the Southern unionists on the other, Jellett and the Irish Unionist Alliance were sidelined. The unionist community in the South was represented by Midleton and his allies. These included Jellett's fellow-MP for Dublin University, Sir Robert Woods, and Dublin's only other unionist MP, Sir Maurice Dockrell. Both men had adopted the Ulster Unionist whip in the House of Commons only for lack of an alternative.

Another prominent Dublin unionist, William E. Wylie, also adopted a more realistic appreciation of the situation than Jellett. Wylie's loyalist credentials were impeccable. Like Jellett, he was a barrister. He had prosecuted the 1916 leaders, and he continued prosecuting rebels for a living throughout the War of Independence. Yet as early as September 1920 he had come to the conclusion that the British government had made the 'cardinal error' of conceding partition to the 'vocal minority in North-East Ireland.' In a memorandum he asked, 'What should the government do now? They should either make peace or declare war. There is no middle course, such as they are now trying to pursue.'[12]

Wylie's involvement in the machinery of repression and his travels around the country meant he was not insulated from the realities of Irish life outside the capital, like some of his contemporaries. Although Dublin was hardly a backwater of military activity—a mobile army patrol was ambushed in York Street on the day the Irish Unionist Alliance met in nearby South Frederick Street—there was not the sense of physical isolation and vulnerability experienced by unionists in rural areas.

'It was difficult to say who really was safe in those days,' Sir Henry Robinson, vice-president of the Local Government Board, recalled. Like Wylie, he spent most of his time in Dublin but had to make regular excursions into the countryside. He refused to move into Dublin Castle and commuted daily from his home in Foxrock to his offices in the Custom House. He regularly called to the Castle on business, as he did to the Viceregal Lodge, and was an habitué of the Kildare Street Club. On one occasion he asked 'a legal friend, who I knew was in touch with militant Sinn Féin, to find out if they intended to wipe me out.' The word back was ambiguous. Robinson's legal friend felt he was safe 'so long as I was not appointed Under-Secretary but that circumstances changed very rapidly.'

After a death notice was pinned on the door of the Custom House, Robinson was assigned two DMP bodyguards. 'Splendid creatures they were, about six foot two in height, each of them so straight and well set up that no-one could have suspected them of being anything but military or police.' On occasion they could prove an embarrassment, as when one day in Dawson Street the secretary of a county council approached Robinson from behind, only to find himself 'caught by the throat looking down the barrel of a revolver.' Robinson strode on, oblivious of the drama behind him, to the Kildare Street Club. It was only when the secretary appeared in the club a few minutes later, 'shaking like an aspen leaf,' that Robinson discovered what had happened. After a while he dispensed with his protectors, 'convinced that they were a challenge rather than a protection.'[13]

The young clerk Wilmot Irwin felt as threatened by the British forces as by the IRA.

> Since 'Bloody Sunday' the Auxiliaries … began to adopt more provocative tactics. They picked up a couple of 'hostages' daily and forced them to sit in the front of an open Crossley, the back axles of which were decorated with tricolour flags, which trailed the mud behind.

The hostages were usually Sinn Féin councillors or other notables; but perhaps the most infamous case was that of Colonel Maurice Moore, former commanding officer of the 1st Battalion of the Connaught Rangers. The 66-year-old veteran soldier came from a prominent landowning family in the west of Ireland, which was unusual for having converted to Catholicism as well as for its involvement in the constitutional nationalist cause.[14] Moore had pursued a distinguished military career but became a thorn in the side of the authorities for exposing human rights abuses in the Anglo-Boer War, including the use of hostages. He had helped found the Irish Volunteers in 1913 and served as Inspector-General of John Redmond's National Volunteers when they split with the more radical leaders of the Provisional Committee in 1914. After 1916 Moore persuaded the rump of Redmondites to reunite with their militant brethren, although he did not engage in any paramilitary activity himself.

On 5 January 1921 a letter appeared in the *Irish Independent* from Colonel Moore, condemning the use of hostages on military trains, motor convoys and patrols. He cited the British army's own Manual of Military Law as censuring the practice and pointed out that the order permitting the use of hostages in South Africa had been withdrawn after eight days.

Not only did the military authorities ignore Moore's strictures but in some areas they increased their use of hostages. On 30 January 1921 a patrol raided Colonel Moore's house at Seaview Terrace, Donnybrook, found a copy of the *Irish Bulletin* in his mail, and promptly arrested him. He was taken to the military post in the RDS grounds in Merrion Road, held overnight and then used as a hostage on an extended tour of the Dublin military district next morning. He was eventually released 'as an act of clemency and on account of his age and position.'

The following week Seán Ó hUadhaigh, a well-known Sinn Féin solicitor and member of Kingstown Urban District Council, was similarly paraded through the streets in a military lorry.

Whatever success such activities had in discouraging attacks was more than offset by the hostility they generated, not only in Ireland but in Britain. Colonel Moore's treatment was singled out for special mention in a general attack on the government's Irish policy from the opposition benches in the House of Commons on 21 February.[15]

The speed at which military vehicles raced through the streets was also resented. They seem to have caused remarkably few casualties, despite frequent collisions, especially with trams. In such instances the bill for the repair of both vehicles would be presented to the courts for deduction from the LGB contribution to the city's rates.

Another activity that appears to have had little military effect but further heightened public apprehension was the tactic of deploying Auxiliaries in plain clothes along the routes that military patrols would take in the hope of ambushing the IRA ambushers. The Auxiliaries carried their distinctive Tam o' Shanter caps in their pockets to don if action ensued, but there are no instances of this tactic ever working. By contrast, routine foot patrols and military cordons caused constant disruption to IRA operations and frequent losses of men and materials. Internment also continued to take its toll. By 7 May 1921, 3,594 suspects from Dublin had been interned at Ballykinler, the largest number from any British military district.[16]

Systematic raiding also yielded intelligence dividends. On New Year's Eve a raid on Eileen McGrane's home at 21 Dawson Street yielded a large cache of IRA intelligence material. She was a university lecturer in nearby Earlsfort Terrace and a senior officer in Cumann na mBan who had been imprisoned for Republican activities. While much of the material was old, it contained personal details of many Volunteers and the carbon copies of Broy's notes, which led to his arrest. The days when such material could be safely held by such people as McGrane were fast disappearing. In April, Colonel Winter's men found Collins's office at 5 Mespil Road. He narrowly escaped capture, and the material seized included some of his personal papers.[17]

The scale of military operations in the city was an indication of how seriously the British took all manifestations of rebel activity. An important British initiative in early 1921 was the formation of a unit made up of experienced and committed Irish members of the RIC under Temporary Head

Constable Eugene Igoe. From a Mayo farming family, Igoe believed in taking the war to the enemy, and his men patrolled the streets using the same tactical formation as the Squad. This consisted of an extended formation of pairs close enough to provide mutual support but dispersed enough to make it difficult for them to be ambushed. Because Igoe's team was drawn from the provinces, they posed a particular danger to Volunteers from rural areas reporting to GHQ in Dublin. As a result, the railway stations were a frequent haunt of the 'Igoe Gang', as the IRA called them, or 'Tudor's Tigers', as they were admiringly referred to in Dublin Castle.[18]

One of the few organisations that sought to bridge the widening gap in Southern society was the United Irishwomen. Like the Anti-Partition League, its name was somewhat misleading.[19] It had been established in 1910 on the initiative of the South's most distinguished champion of liberal unionism, Sir Horace Plunkett, founder of the co-operative movement and a proto-feminist. Its aim was to provide a forum 'for Irish women to take up their rightful part in the building up of a rural civilisation in Ireland.' Plunkett recruited a number of women collaborators in the co-operative movement to this new endeavour, and one of these, Elizabeth, Countess of Fingall, was president in 1921. She told delegates to the annual conference that while significant progress had been made in some areas, such as the extension of the 'village nurse' system, providing maternity, general nursing and some elements of public-health nursing to local communities, the past two years had been difficult. No annual meeting had been possible in 1920, and new recruits could not compensate for resignations. Total membership in the branches had fallen from 1,985 in 1920 to 1,871 in 1921.

The female membership of the Irish Unionist Alliance increased in Dublin, but declined in rural Ireland, in line with the experience of the United Irishwomen. However, it was much less affected by the Troubles than social projects that emanated from Protestant and unionist sources that had a proselytising edge to them.[20] By contrast, Countess Fingall was able to put a brave face on the figures, giving the disturbed state of the country and the dislocation of transport services as the main reasons for resignations rather than political polarisation. She concluded her address on the optimistic note that when peace came there would be

fresh opportunities for the exercise of their usefulness ... in the rebuilding of the home life of rural Ireland. It would be a changed Ireland they would see, whatever the issue; and life would be ... very hard. They should widen their work for home life, going deeply into the milk question, and no child should ever again be fed with the vile milk that decimated their city slums.[21]

The state of the milk supply in Dublin had been a source of concern from time immemorial. Wartime price controls from 1916 onwards and a crack-down on the sale of contaminated and adulterated milk from 1917, spearheaded by Councillor P. T. Daly, meant that it was cheaper, after inflation was taken into account, and purer than ever before. Nevertheless the average retail price was 35 per cent more than in British cities and the quality was uneven, as reflected in continuing high rates of infant mortality and the prevalence of TB.

In June 1921 the corporation set up a special subcommittee to work with the Public Health Committee in tackling what the *Irish Times* described as a 'price ring' that exploited citizens in 'a most unmerciful manner.' It was a cross-party group comprising Sir Andrew Beattie (MRA) and Hanna Sheehy Skeffington (Sinn Féin) as well as Daly. They had some futile meetings with the Dublin Cowkeepers' and Dairymen's Association, whose five hundred members supplied between 60 and 65 per cent of the city's milk from herds kept in the city or on nearby farms. Prices varied enormously, from 1s 2d to 2s 8d a gallon. The Dublin Union paid no less than ten tariffs to suppliers. Milk brought into the city by railway from large rural producers was significantly cheaper than that produced in the city, but it often had a bitter taste and soured quickly. Dubliners who could afford it preferred local produce. The best milk was produced by the Richmond and Portrane Asylums at their farms and sold for a mere 6d a gallon, the labour being supplied by patients. High-quality milk was also produced for 1s 6d a gallon by the state-owned Model Farm in Glasnevin, where much of the labour was provided by agricultural students. This was earmarked for the Infant Aid Society and Babies' Clubs in the city— part of the health and welfare legacy from the war.

The commercial milk producers pleaded poverty and pointed out that wages had risen by 315 per cent since 1914 while prices had risen by only 154 per cent. The figures presented to justify their claims were highly suspect, and they refused to co-operate with any investigation that was not 'impartial', in other words composed of experts nominated by or acceptable to themselves. In the absence of progress the corporation examined operations in Britain, America and elsewhere and concluded that the establishment of a municipal dairy was the best option. Meanwhile it could promote better standards only through prosecutions. Nineteen of the 194 distributors of milk in the city were convicted for breaches of the Public Health Acts in the year ending June 1921 and a further ten between then and 23 August, when the committee reported. However, fines as low as £1 were imposed by magistrates. These were no deterrent to unscrupulous operators.

The matter was considered serious enough to be investigated by the Dáil Éireann Commission of Inquiry into the Resources and Industries of Ireland. The Lord Mayor, Laurence O'Neill, told the commission that, while some progress had been made in ensuring that better-quality milk was produced in the city, the corporation had no supervisory powers regarding milk brought in from the countryside. Dr Russell, the new medical officer for the city, said that 4,000 gallons a day arrived at railway stations to add to the 10,200 produced locally. He favoured stronger controls on milk supply and production, similar to those in large British cities. 'Vendors should be compelled to have veterinary certificates as to the health of their cattle' to ensure that TB and other diseases were not transmitted to consumers. He called for stiffer fines and said that on a second conviction a man should be 'put out of business.'

The head of St Ultan's Hospital for Mothers and Infants, Dr Kathleen Lynn, told the commission that 'much of the milk … sold was absolute poison to babies.' She recommended that the milk be bottled in sealed, sterilised jars. However, she acknowledged that a lot of people could not afford to pay for milk supplied in open cans, let alone the bottled product. 'Many mothers were living on bread and tea—a most insufficient diet, but they complained that the price of milk was too high.' Thomas Johnson, Secretary of the Labour Party and a member of the commission, estimated that it would cost 10s 6d a week to provide a child with an adequate supply of milk, a price Dr Lynn declared 'absolutely prohibitive' for many mothers. Even where dairies offered bottled milk, such as that at Lucan, the manager said that customers were not prepared to pay the extra 1d a quart, and the bottles 'disappeared.'

The notion of establishing a municipal dairy in Dublin was even more intractable. As well as meeting scepticism among members of the business community and outright hostility from the city's cowkeepers, it would require legislation.

The controversy underlined the ambivalent nature of local government in Ireland. The corporation had established an Anti-Profiteering Committee at the outbreak of the war but it had no real power. In the motion establishing the cross-party investigation into the city's milk supply it requested 'the Government of Ireland … to give us the power to establish a genuine Anti-Profiteering Committee.' The very ambiguity of the term 'Government of Ireland' was necessary to secure consensus on a critical issue affecting the health of Dubliners.[22] The advent of the Truce in early July would plunge Dublin, and the rest of Ireland, into a political limbo, neither republic nor kingdom. Like the lack of progress on slum clearance,[23] the powerlessness of anyone to impose real controls on the milk supply took a heavier daily toll on the urban poor and their young than on any other section of the community.

The biggest problem of all in this political limbo was that of finance. Dublin Corporation remained in deadlock with the Local Government Board over grants in aid. The board had at first applied pressure very slowly, allowing funds already approved before the corporation had formally declared its allegiance to Dáil Éireann to be drawn down. The vice-president of the board, Sir Henry Robinson, observed of Dublin and the other eighty dissident local authorities:

> We made no counter measures at first, hoping that, as the councils were still corresponding with us and could not legally borrow money without our consent or make any valid appointments, this attitude ... was only a passing phase, which would end when Treasury advances were required for housing of the working classes or feeding children, or the relief of unemployment.

It was pressure from London that forced the pace as government backbenchers expressed outrage that Irish local authorities refusing to recognise the Crown were still receiving funds from the exchequer.[24]

As we have seen, a good deal of ingenuity was employed by the corporation in extracting funds from the LGB, and considerable flexibility was exercised in the submission of accounts. The willingness of the banks, led by the Bank of Ireland, to finance the rebel municipality without the approval of the LGB was an important additional source of income, and in April 1921 the municipality received an important psychological boost when the City Treasurer, Edmund Eyre, was approached by Butler and Briscoe, stockbrokers, with a proposal for an investment of £50,000 in Dublin securities at the standard 6 per cent return. Eyre was told that the investors would prefer to see it invested in housing or reconstruction but laid down no conditions. It subsequently emerged that the interested party was the Irish National Foresters' Approved Society, which wanted to transfer its National Insurance Commission funds from British investments to investments at home.[25]

While business confidence in the long-term solvency of the corporation rose, the British tightened the financial noose by rigorously applying the malicious damages legislation. This made local authorities liable for all claims for personal and property loss in their jurisdiction. In March 1921 Dublin and its suburbs were presented with a bill for £117,618, based on awards made in the courts, and

Dublin County Council was given a bill for £159,834, primarily the result of claims arising from the sack of Balbriggan by Crown forces.

Not only did members of the Crown forces cause most of the damage in Dublin city and county but they tended to lodge the largest claims. For instance, Mary O'Farrell, a teacher in Birmingham, received £1,000 for the death of her brother, the Dublin police cadet shot in the Pearse Street gun battle on 14 March 1921. Ellen Clarke received only £500 for her husband, killed in the crossfire that day. Like Farrell, Stephen Clarke had served in the British army in the Great War and had since been employed as a labourer with the Gas Company. The amounts were based on potential earnings and pension entitlements rather than the number of dependants they left behind. On the same basis Richard Dentith, a cadet wounded in the same incident, who required fifteen days' treatment in hospital, received £150 for his injury. Alice Beard, whose husband, James Beard, a former brigade major, had been the Auxiliaries' section-leader killed that night, was seeking £15,000 on the grounds not alone of current earnings but of potential earnings from his business interests in England. This claim was condemned as 'perfectly monstrous' by the Recorder of Dublin and reduced to £2,000, because Mrs Beard's father was a wealthy lace manufacturer on whose generosity her late husband's future career prospects had largely depended.

Wounded servicemen and ex-servicemen did relatively well in the compensation stakes. Colour-Sergeant Francis Christian, sole survivor of the affray between Seán Treacy and British intelligence officers in Talbot Street the previous October (see chapter 6), received £1,250 for being wounded in the arm, although he would also receive a full service pension. The size of the award was explained by the fact that he had been a boxing champion in the army in India and now suffered from lameness. Former Sergeant D. Lenehan, who was shot on his way home from his civilian job at Islandbridge Barracks, received £2,000 after losing the use of his right arm.

Property-owners could also claim. Lord Talbot de Malahide received £1,700 for the destruction of Malahide police barracks, one of the few police posts that had been evacuated in the greater Dublin area and had been burnt out by Volunteers.[26]

Not alone individuals but the armed forces presented claims. The Air Council was awarded £1,700 for the destruction of two Crossley tenders and a touring car in an ambush of RAF personnel at the Half-Way House in Crumlin in April 1921. The War Department secured many more awards, ranging from relatively small amounts of £15 to £17 for damage to military vehicles when drivers ran into unspecified 'obstructions' in the road to as much as £240 for the destruction of a motor car. A surprisingly high number of claims were for the execution of military mules (£40 a head) and horses (£80 a head).[27]

The shooting of animals caused considerable public revulsion and seemed senseless to civilians. Wilmot Irwin's brother came home shocked after seeing a mule shot through the head by a Volunteer in Berkeley Road. 'The bloody swine; if I had a revolver I would shoot him dead!' he said. Irwin felt that his brother 'would not have been half so indignant if the Sinn Feiner had shot the soldier and left the mule alone.'[28] However, there was an impeccable military rationale for these attacks. The animals were involved in the essential if lowly task of transporting rations to military posts, and the attacks meant that soldiers had to be employed to protect the mules and horses. Attacks on army despatch-riders failed to elicit any similar public sympathy but were very effective in forcing the British army to use its handful of armoured cars to carry despatches.[29]

Concern for animal welfare did not outweigh the fundamental injustice, in Irish eyes, of being made to pay for the transgressions and accidents of the police and military, on top of everything else. The refusal of the corporation to pay these awards drew support from across the political and economic spectrum, from the MRA and the chamber of commerce to Sinn Féin and the Dublin Trades Council. In line with its policy of refusing to adopt a rate to pay such claims, Dublin Corporation decided not to contest the cases in the British courts. While this delayed awards it did not prevent them being granted. Once an award was made, solicitors for the successful claimant could apply for a garnishee order and the amount was deducted by the LGB from the grant in aid to the corporation. To counter this move the corporation's Estates and Finance Committee proposed

> that the name and address of every person who secures garnishee orders against the rates, or of any company which adopts this method of seizing civic funds should be published and circulated throughout the city, so that the citizens will be at least acquainted with those who are directly responsible for seizing monies collected for the supply of water, the operation of the Public Health Department, the provision of Poor Relief and medical attendance, and the treatment of the insane.

This had an inhibiting effect on local firms, as had warnings from the IRA against individual claimants and their solicitors, but British claimants were largely impervious to such threats and often had their cases heard in Britain.

The dispute over garnishee orders dragged on until the Truce, when Dáil Éireann became embroiled on behalf of all the local authorities. By then the total of awards amounted to £6½ million, of which more than £2 million was in relation to the burning of Cork city centre by Auxiliaries, in retaliation for an ambush at Dillon's Cross in which one Auxiliary was killed and several wounded. The issue would finally be resolved as part of the Treaty settlement; in the meantime it added to the apprehensiveness of business people and ratepayers of all complexions, not knowing what new calamity would be visited on them by the combatants.

Even without the looming burden of the criminal and malicious damages bill, Dublin Corporation faced an inevitable increase in the rates, not to mention problems with collecting them. After the raids on some collectors by the Republican Police in January 1921, half the remainder resigned. This provoked a debate on the need to reform the collection system. By 1921 two-thirds of the rates were paid over the counter at the Rates Office, raising the question whether external appointments were needed at all. Collectors were paid by commission, and these appointments had become very lucrative since 1914, as the exigencies of war and the onset of the independence struggle had seen the rates bill soar.

There was general agreement that the post of rate-collector should be made a promotional outlet for corporation staff, and that collectors be paid on an incremental scale rather than by commission. It was at this point that disagreement arose over the number of appointments. Councillor John Forrestal (Sinn Féin) advocated that the six collection districts be increased to ten, while J. Hubbard Clark (MRA) and P. T. Daly (Trades Council Labour) objected that this would simply increase the collection costs for no extra gain. The dominant Sinn Féin-Republican Labour alliance pushed through the increase. The whole exercise smacked of patronage. At least three of the five staff members promoted were Volunteers, including Harry Colley (clerk, first class), Adjutant of the Dublin Brigade. The fact that all these internal promotions continued to be by election in the council chamber rather than by competition meant that appointments remained highly politicised. On this occasion it was even worse than usual, because of voting irregularities that meant the election had to be repeated a month later—with the same outcome.

The meeting that debated reform of the rate-collection system also saw the corporation threatened with a legal challenge by a deputation from the Citizens' Association. Its secretary, M. Sidney Orr, said the association had 'a strong opinion from a well-known member of the Bar' that the rates could not be increased above 20s in the pound, as it would amount to double taxation of property and would be quashed in the courts. Orr suggested that this could easily be avoided by cutting the budget for the construction of working men's dwellings and staff salaries. Otherwise, he warned, ratepayers might decide not to pay their bills and to await the outcome of a test case. However, he drew short of advocating a rates strike.[30] There was little support for the association in the council, and its strongest ally, Sir Andrew Beattie, was indisposed, having undergone major surgery the previous day.

Whatever the merits of Orr's legal advice, the fundamental flaw in his position was that the only court the corporation would pay any attention to would be a Republican court, which was unlikely to uphold a challenge by the Citizens' Association. The underlying reality was that the great majority of ratepayers accepted—as the banks and stockbrokers did—that maintaining Dublin Corporation in a time of violent turmoil was a far safer bet for the security of businesses and property-owners than the alternative of seeing the administration of the city collapse.

The new leader of the MRA group, Alderman J. Hubbard Clark, took a far less assertive stance on such issues than his predecessor, Dr McWalter.[31] When the rate was eventually struck at 22s 6d in the pound on 17 May 1921 the main reaction of the business community was one of relief that it had not been set higher. The reason was that rebel councillors refused to make provision for the mounting criminal injury claims.[32]

On the military front, the IRA managed to sustain operations in the city. The activities of the Igoe gang and other British intelligence operatives continued to pose a threat to the leadership of the Republic's army, and therefore they have tended to feature in the recollections of prominent participants in the struggle, with concomitant attention from historians.[33] But at the local level the Dublin Brigade retained a capacity to maintain psychological pressure on the enemy, inflict casualties and prevent anything approaching normality returning to the city.

Vivid images of military repression on the streets provided vital propaganda for the Republican cause at home, in Britain and internationally. Despite the debilitating effects of internment, Traynor organised weekly meetings of battalion OCs with the brigade staff to discuss forthcoming operations. These imposed the discipline of planning on units, encouraged a sense of competitiveness and provided an opportunity for the joint discussion of problems. Above all, such meetings ensured that enemy pressure did not lead to demoralisation and inactivity. The number of IRA operations in Dublin rose from 53 in March to 67 in April and to 117 in May.

The brigade was also reorganised and expanded. In early 1921 the four city battalions had an aggregate of just over a thousand men. There was a fifth, engineering battalion that concentrated on munitions, under Vice-Brigadier

Seán Russell. He developed the production of hand grenades and land mines on a large scale. The grenades were passed to the Quartermaster-General for distribution throughout the country, while the production of land mines was decentralised, with local engineering units being taught how to make and lay them. Russell was so efficient that he was transferred to GHQ, his place as vice-brigadier being taken by Seán Mooney.

The improved reliability of grenades boosted morale among Dublin Volunteers, as these became the most effective weapon against British mobile patrols. Other armaments consisted mainly of automatic pistols and a limited number of Thompson sub-machine guns, which were smuggled into the country in May. There were some rifles, but most were despatched to rural units. There were also some shotguns in the city, but there was a reluctance to use them, as they were inaccurate at anything other than point-blank range and as awkward to carry concealed as rifles.

Units providing such services as signalling, first aid, transport and specialist training were reorganised, as was intelligence, and an armourers' section was established to repair damaged weapons. J. J. Doyle, a senior officer in the St John Ambulance Brigade, was appointed First Aid Officer. The fact that some St John Ambulance personnel were Volunteers was invaluable in helping to spirit away injured men. Ambush parties normally included Volunteers who had undergone first-aid training and could act as medical orderlies.

The paucity of weapons meant they often had to be carried across the city from one battalion area to another for operations. A specialist Transport Section was set up, and the most common mode of conveyance was the humble horse and cart. Handcarts were another favourite form of transport and attracted less attention from the military or Auxiliaries than motor vehicles or suspect pedestrians. However, losses were inevitable and were often accompanied by the arrest of the couriers, sometimes with tragic consequences, as with Thomas Traynor during the Pearse Street battle.

Organising safe houses for men on the run was a growing problem as the number of wanted Volunteers increased and the British identified the homes of Sinn Féin activists and sympathisers. Empty premises were used where possible, as there were no repercussions, and some religious communities provided a refuge for Volunteers on the run. In 1920 Cumann na mBan held its convention in the house of the Carmelite Fathers in Whitefriars' Street under the guise of a women's sodality.[34]

In March 1921 two new battalions were set up. The 6th covered the east coast as far south as Bray and as far west as the Dublin Mountains, Dundrum and Stepaside. Its commandant was Andy McDonnell. The 7th Battalion covered the area from Templeogue to Hollywood and Ballyknocan, Co. Wicklow. Its commandant was Gerry Boland.

It was not until April that the British became aware of the existence of active-service units in the city, and, curiously, they interpreted this development as a sign of weakness. This may have been in part because the men were paid. The rate of £4 10s a week was the same as for members of the Squad. It was also more than the £3 10s a week paid to the Black and Tans but significantly less than the Auxiliaries, who were paid £7 a week. Both groups of RIC men also received significant extra payments in allowances. The ASU rate was based on the weekly wage of a skilled worker in the city and was a statement about the social status of soldiers of the Republic. Any comparison with mercenaries of the Crown would have been as distasteful as it would have been inconceivable to the average Volunteer.

The performance of IRA units remained uneven, and the Dublin Brigade generally lacked the capacity to carry out major ambushes, as typified by an attempt by F Company of the 4th Battalion to ambush an RAF group returning to their base in Baldonnel after a night on the town. The attack, near the Red Cow Inn on the Naas Road in May, was planned as a textbook operation, with three sections pouring enfilading fire into the enemy after carts had been wheeled out of a farmer's shed to block the road. However, the gates of the shed were found to be locked at the critical moment—which was probably just as well, because two of the three firing parties had failed to reach their positions in time. The third opened fire as the lorries passed and claimed to have hit five of the enemy. One Volunteer was injured, shot in the thigh by friendly fire.[35]

Shortly before this attack Thomas Traynor was hanged. Again crowds began assembling at an early hour outside Mountjoy, with a clear sunlit early-summer sky overhead. The Rosary was recited by members of Cumann na mBan, the *Freeman's Journal* reported,

> followed by the singing of 'Hail, Queen of Heaven,' in which all the people joined till the strains of the hymn rose triumphantly in the morning air.
>
> Yesterday morning it was no youth whose bright spirit was to be quenched, it was no young man in the first flush of life's hope and strength that had to make the supreme sacrifice, but a man of riper years, the responsible head of a family, and the father of ten children, most of them little ones, mere babes.

At 8 a.m., as the hour of execution approached,

all within the prison seemed as silent as the grave. The shrill scream of a steam siren in the distance was the first herald that the fatal hour had struck … The wicket gate in the main door was slightly opened and the arm of the warder stretched forth with the brief notice that 'sentence of the law' had been carried out. For the first time at scenes of this character a burst of indignation arose from the assembled people … The notice was literally torn from the warder's hand. But in a flash the storm was over and a woman's voice rang out: 'May the Lord have mercy on that man's soul.' Responses of 'Amen' and prayers again arose, mingled with loud sobbing of the little boy, one of the executed man's sons.

Traynor's wife,

who had spent all morning at the jail gate, collapsed and lay for minutes limp … in the arms of her friends … She was soon taken to a cab and escorted by kind friends from the scene of her husband's sacrifice and of her own great trial and sorrow.

Once more the Sisters of Charity were the executed man's last visitors. As on previous occasions, they reported the prisoner's brave demeanour. He was described by them as an

ideal husband and father, devoted to his home and family. His wife is a convert. He left her his Rosary beads and asked her to say it every day that Our Lady might make her strong in the Faith. 'I laid no commands on her,' he said, 'but I requested that she should not live with her mother, who is still a Protestant, for fear there might be danger to the Children's Faith.'

Strong religious faith was a powerful asset for Volunteers going out to take on the forces of an empire. Even the Citizen Army leader James Connolly, a Marxist, shared it, and while awaiting execution asked his Protestant wife, Lillie, to convert to Catholicism. Traynor appears to have been a remarkable character. He used his shoemaker's skill to make toys for his children, taught the oldest boys his trade so that they could keep the little family business going, and invested in two violins to teach his children to play. 'If my home was not happy I would not stay in it,' he used to say.[36]

There was a sad inevitability in the way in which religious communities such as the Sisters of Charity would embrace the independence struggle and hold up the example of national martyrs for emulation so that the marriage of Faith and

Motherland would be cemented in the blood of Mountjoy, even in the case of a mixed marriage such as that of the Traynors. It was probably this emotional magnet that drew several prominent Protestant nationalist women, such as Constance Markievicz, to the Catholic Church. She herself cited the example of Citizen Army men in the Easter Rising saying the Rosary each evening as a factor leading her towards her conversion. Oonagh Walsh points out that it reinforced their claim to political legitimacy in the eyes of other nationalists. As Maud Gonne put it in her own inimitable egomaniacal way, in a letter to W. B. Yeats,

> I prefer to look at truth through the same prism as my country people ... You say I leave the few to mix with the crowd while Willie I have always told you I am the voice, the soul of the crowd.[37]

More reflective converts sometimes found that religious conversion repelled friends and relations more than changed political allegiances.

Side by side with the dignified protests outside Mountjoy, the campaign of violence continued to cause mayhem on the city's streets. The DMP log for 10 May 1921 is fairly typical.

> 8.20 a.m.—Tank Corps Sgt. from Marlborough Barracks ... held up in Vegetable Market, Halston Street and robbed of his revolver and £6.
>
> 9 a.m. to 10 a.m.—Trench cut in Bray Road near Deans Grange. Pick axes and shovels worth £3 stolen from cemetery shed.
>
> 9.30 a.m.—Military Guard leaving the Richmond Barracks is fired upon from the direction of Inchicore Road. No casualties reported.
>
> 12.15 p.m.—Two men attempt to rob Post Office at 38 Upper Kevin Street but run away when the post mistress, Miss Dowling, shouts for help.
>
> 12.40 p.m.—Two men entered the chemists shop of Robert Duggan, 49 Summerhill Parade, and ordered 17 tins of bicycle enamel, which was given to them by the owner's son, James Duggan. The men then said they were commandeering the enamel for I.R.A. and on the owner coming from behind the counter to take it back he was fired on by the men and shot dead.
>
> 4 p.m.—Two men enter the shop of Mr. Finnegan, 8 George's Quay, and carry away Belfast tobacco, cigarettes, value £16 19s. od. They leave a receipt as follows: "Confiscated by I.R.A."
>
> 4.10 p.m.—Postal engineers Thomas Walsh and George McMullen have 'telephone instrument' stolen while repairing telephone wires at Hardwicke Lane.

5.27 p.m.—Two bombs thrown at three Crossley tenders in North Frederick Street as they brought soldiers and workmen from Collinstown aerodrome back to city.

8.30 p.m.—Bomb thrown at Auxiliaries mobile patrol n Haddington Road—no casualties reported.

10 p.m.—Large quantity of sacks in Paul and Vincent's on Sir John Rogerson's Quay, burnt with petrol. The sacks arrived from Belfast on same date.[38]

The IRA's use of crowds as cover for attacks resulted in a particularly high number of casualties two days later, on 12 May, in Dublin's premier shopping district. A bomb was thrown at a semi-armoured Crossley tender carrying an Auxiliary patrol in Johnson's Place, between Clarendon Street and South William Street. It exploded but, miraculously, caused no casualties. The vehicle continued into Grafton Street, where two more bombs were thrown; both fell short. Shots were fired at the tender as well, but it was the bombs exploding on the street that caused the main damage. A DMP constable and fourteen civilians were seriously injured, including three newsboys and a small child.

'Scenes of indescribable panic followed,' the *Freeman's Journal* reported. 'Men, women and children dashed for cover, and above the shots and explosions could be heard the terrified shrieks of the women and children.' Some civilians, 'overcome by terror, lay prone on the roadway and pathways in a fainting condition.' The attackers fled the scene. The Auxiliaries used their first-aid kits to tend the wounded, some of whom were carried into the porch of St Teresa's Church in Clarendon Street and the vestibule of the Grafton Picture House until the ambulances arrived. Some of the walking wounded made their own way to Mercer's Hospital nearby, where the floor of the accident ward was 'covered in blood,' according to the *Irish Independent*.[39]

On the next day, 13 May, Ireland experienced its most extraordinary general election, the result of the final enactment of the Government of Ireland Bill. It provided for two home-rule parliaments, one in Belfast for the six north-eastern counties and the other in Dublin for the remaining twenty-six counties. Both provided for an extension of the PR system used in the local elections, and for the same reason: to protect the rights of minorities—nationalists in the North and unionists in the South. While the North would have a contest that the Ulster unionists comfortably won, in the South 124 of the 128 seats were secured by Sinn Féin without opposition. The other four seats, those for Dublin University, were secured by unionist candidates, again without a contest. Nowhere else in the South did unionists put up candidates, not even in the Dublin townships, where Sir Maurice Dockrell had won the Rathmines seat in the 1918 general election, nor in Pembroke and South County Dublin, where they had performed well that year. The leader of the Irish Party, John Dillon, remained opposed to the policies and methods of Sinn Féin but openly acknowledged its hegemony. As he wrote in a letter published by most newspapers in the week before the election, 'to oppose and condemn Sinn Féin in this election would leave one open to the charge, however unjust that charge might be, of supporting the Black and Tans.'[40]

While the *Irish Times*, the voice of liberal unionism, paid tribute to the University of Dublin and the 'four gentlemen' it had chosen[41] to speak for 'some hundreds of thousands of Southern Irishmen and Irishwomen,' it acknowledged that 'they are not politicians; they are not even Unionists in the old sense, for the old Unionism has vanished with the Act of Union'. It also accepted that 'the Southern elections have put Sinn Féin in a position of indisputable strength as the spokesman of a large majority of the people' and expressed the hope that the way had been cleared for the negotiation of a settlement between the British government and the two dominant forces in Ireland, North and South. Like most Irish nationalists, Southern unionists still refused to accept the reality of partition.

The successful Sinn Féin candidates constituted themselves the second Dáil Éireann. Some of the Dublin TDs had previously won seats in the British House of Commons and most were national figures, such as Joe McGrath, Richard Mulcahy, Michael Staines, Constance Markievicz, Tom Kelly, Phil Shanahan, Kathleen Clarke and Seán T. Ó Ceallaigh. The others were Philip Cosgrave, a brother of W. T. Cosgrave, and two IRA officers, Alderman Charles Murphy, a newspaper manager, and Daniel McCarthy, a clerk. There was a similar pattern in the county, where the Ashbourne veteran Frank Lawless, Desmond Fitzgerald and Charles Gavan Duffy were joined by Patrick Pearse's mother, Margaret Pearse, Michael Derham from Balbriggan and James Dwyer from Rathmines. McGrath, Cosgrave, Staines, Fitzgerald, Markievicz and Derham were all in prison; Mulcahy and McGarry were on the run; Gavan Duffy and Ó Ceallaigh were working abroad; and 'the Alderman', Tom Kelly, was still recuperating from his breakdown while in prison.[42] A similar pattern emerged around the country, with many new TDs in prison, interned or on the run.

If the political victory was therefore largely symbolic it was balanced within a fortnight in Dublin by an almost equally symbolic military action, the burning of the Custom House. Whether this was a victory or a defeat has been disputed ever since. It was certainly the most ambitious IRA operation in Dublin since the Rising and followed a spectacular attempt to rescue the Longford IRA leader Seán Mac Eoin from Mountjoy on 14 May. IRA Volunteers had hijacked an armoured car and, wearing British uniforms, bluffed their way into the prison but failed to reach Mac Eoin. They had to fight their way out, and the vehicle was subsequently abandoned after breaking down. The Volunteers took its two Hotchkiss machine guns with them.[43]

De Valera, who had returned to Dublin from America just before Christmas, 1920, was involved in informal talks on a peace settlement by May 1921, and at first sight it seems ironic that he should be the prime advocate of the Custom House operation. It was unnecessary, because, as the *Irish Times* had pointed out, the election result had given an unequivocal answer to the question of who represented the Irish people. But what the President of the Irish Republic was looking for was a demonstration of strength in the capital to underpin victory at the polls. Such a protest in arms would carry far more weight in the period before peace negotiations than a multitude of minor actions.

The attack on the Custom House was in fact a relatively poor second choice to de Valera's preferred option of seizing a major military post, such as Beggarsbush Barracks, which housed the Depot Company of the Auxiliaries. As it turned out, even the destruction of the Custom House proved dangerously ambitious for the infant Irish army. Collins and Mulcahy knew that the Dublin Brigade lacked the training and experience to conduct a major military operation, let alone adequate weapons and ammunition. Collins tried to insist that members of the Squad be restricted to a supporting role, to minimise casualties among his most experienced and reliable operatives. In fact several members were roped in, including Tom Ennis, who played a critical role as the new OC of the 2nd Battalion.

All five city battalions were mobilised for the attack, which was meticulously planned and took place on 25 May. Oscar Traynor had overall responsibility, and he recalled later carrying out a thorough reconnaissance of the building, 'armed with a large envelope, inscribed with OHMS' ('On His Majesty's Service,' the mark of official postal items). Tom Ennis was given operational responsibility for the destruction of the building and carried out a similar examination before both men pored over plans supplied by Volunteers working in the LGB. It was the largest office complex in the city, sturdily built, and was between the two main fire stations. The only point in favour of the attackers was that it contained enormous amounts of highly combustible documents and wooden furnishings.

The main task of destruction lay with the 2nd Battalion, in whose area the Custom House was, while the adjoining north-side battalion, the 1st, was to provide what outer protection it could. The 5th (Engineering) Battalion was to cut telephone communications between the Custom House and the outside world, including the direct line to Dublin Castle. The 1st, 3rd and 4th Battalions were to raid the Central Fire Station in Tara Street and the sub-stations to disable vehicles. At Thomas Street the Leyland pump was driven all the way to Crumlin and held for an hour to make sure it was kept out of action. Meanwhile a lorry brought cans of kerosene to the bottom of Gardiner Street, whence Volunteers carried them across Beresford Place and through the rear entrance of the Custom House in preparation for the conflagration.[44]

Surprisingly, the Custom House was one of the few major government facilities in the capital without a permanent military guard. The main problem was the large staff and the public traffic in and out. The attack was therefore made at 1 p.m., to coincide with the lunch hour. Some staff members still on the premises resisted the invaders until the caretaker and a temporary clerk were shot dead. Each floor was secured and whistles used to synchronise the ignition of fires in each section of the building.

The sequence of fires went almost according to plan, with each unit retreating to the main hall after igniting its section of the building. Then, as Ennis prepared to evacuate, word came back that one area had still to be lit. Ennis sent men back to complete the job. 'The few minutes lost here, not quite five, was the difference between the successful retirement of all the participants and the arrival of large numbers of enemy forces in lorries and armoured cars,' Traynor said afterwards. He soon found himself trapped with other Volunteers under the arches of the railway bridge that crosses the Liffey beside the Custom House. The few stray shots of poorly armed and ill-trained part-time soldiers of the 1st Battalion failed to slow the enemy.

It was a young Volunteer of the 2nd Battalion who enabled Traynor and many others to escape. Seventeen-year-old Daniel Head from Seville Place, an unemployed apprentice carpenter, ran forward from under the arches and hurled a grenade into a lorry full of Auxiliaries. He probably caused most of the Crown casualties that day and certainly distracted them as he was mown down in a hail of bullets. His heroism provided valuable seconds that allowed other Volunteers to flee.

Ennis and experienced members of the Squad also managed to escape in the mayhem, either fighting their way out, and being severely wounded in Ennis's case, or using the street craft that kept them alive through the Tan War. Vinnie Byrne discarded his gun and furiously puffed on a cigarette to mask the kerosene fumes from his hands before satisfying the military that he was a carpenter on his way to Brooks Thomas for supplies when he was caught up in the affray. A body search revealed a carpenter's rule and sheets of paper with measurements of wood, which convinced the enemy he was telling the truth. Meanwhile, like Dan Breen before him, Collins had Ennis removed to the Sisters of Mercy's private nursing home in Eccles Street. Volunteers trapped in Tara Street fire station were given spare uniforms by comrades in the Fire Brigade, enabling them to escape on the back of the tenders that rushed, belatedly, to put out the fire. By contrast, some members of the LGB staff in the Custom House were at pains to point out Volunteers trying to hide in their midst.

Meanwhile the insatiable curiosity of Dubliners drew them to the Custom House flames, even while the sound of gunfire and grenades reverberated. Among the witnesses was the leader of the lost cause of constitutional nationalism, John Dillon. He strolled down from his house in North Great George's Street with his daughter Nano

> and from O'Connell Bridge, on which a great crowd had collected, looked on at a most tragic and awful sight—the most beautiful building in Ireland a mass of flame and awful clouds of black smoke … A lovely summer afternoon, the crowds of silent people, afraid to express any opinion, and the appalling sight of the most beautiful [building] of Ireland … deliberately destroyed by the youth of Ireland as the latest and greatest expression of idealism and patriotism.[45]

The Custom House had no military significance, and Sir Henry Robinson, Vice-President of the LGB, described its burning as 'probably the stupidest thing the Sinn Fein ever did.' Although he played down the loss of his head office and all the documents inside, he admitted that the 'Inland Revenue [tax] Department were put to a good deal of inconvenience.' The reality was that Ireland had already become ungovernable; the loss of so much official data simply ensured it would remain ungovernable for the foreseeable future.

Robinson himself, who had left the office at five to one to award the LGB Silver Cup for golf to the finalists at Dollymount, continued to lead a charmed life. Another important member of the LGB staff had an even narrower escape. Sir George Vanston, senior legal adviser to the board, was quite deaf,

> so he never heard the firing going on, and he was working away while the place was burning fiercely and bombs and machine guns keeping up a fearful din outside … At 1.30 he rang for a messenger to bring him up some lunch; getting no reply … once more he rang, and this time, getting very angry, seized his hat and went down the corridor to look for a messenger.

He ran into a British officer searching for 'hidden Sinn Féiners', who promptly arrested him. The officer was taking him to join other prisoners lined up outside Brooks Thomas when Vanston turned to him, bewildered, and asked, 'Has there been any firing going on?' The officer decided that his prisoner was having a mental breakdown and threw him out of the building, as he did not want to be 'saddled with a lunatic.'

Others were less fortunate. Five civilians had been killed, including the caretaker of the Custom House, F. Davies, and a temporary clerk, M. J. Lawless, both shot by the IRA. Two dockers and an East Wall resident were caught in the crossfire, almost certainly killed by Crown forces. The IRA fatalities, besides Daniel Head, included Seán Doyle (see chapter 1 above) and twenty-year-old Captain Stephen O'Reilly, variously described as a draper's assistant and a commercial traveller, from Wesley Place, off Russell Street, beside Croke Park. He had taken an early lunch break from Arnott's to play his part in the attack on the Custom House.[46]

The British forces arrested more than a hundred suspects at the scene and claimed to have suffered only four casualties. While this figure appears extremely low, there can be no question that in purely military terms the encounter had been an unqualified success for them. It also resulted in another massive bill of £35,000 for the Dublin ratepayers, later reduced to a charge of £5,151 19s 4d against the Irish Free State as part of the Treaty settlement.

The 2nd Battalion had been the workhorse of the War of Independence in Dublin, and it never recovered from the Custom House debacle, which also saw most of the city's ASU arrested. Anxious to disguise the impact, Traynor ordered other city battalions to increase activity and ensure that the scale of the setback did not register with the enemy, or the public.[47] The most spectacular operation carried out in response to this order was the destruction of the National Shell Factory in Parkgate Street. It had been converted into a repair depot for military vehicles after the Great War, and most of the two hundred employees were ex-servicemen. On 3 June it was set alight about an hour after work finished. Again large crowds gathered to watch the spectacle from Kingsbridge station, as the factory backed onto the Liffey opposite. On this occasion armoured cars were despatched to fire stations to make sure that crews were not held up, and soldiers helped put out the fire. It made little difference. Much of the structure was wooden, and it was full of tyres, petrol and other combustibles that flared into the night skies, making it a greater spectacle than the Custom House. Many Dubliners stayed to watch almost until the curfew at 10:30 p.m.

The same day saw Volunteers snipe at a cricket match between the Gentlemen of Ireland and the Military of Ireland in Trinity College. The *Irish Times* reported:

The event attracted a very large and fashionable crowd. The weather was delightfully fine, and the hot sun induced many to seek the shade of the trees bordering the beautiful grounds. Interest in the match was very keen, and the play had reached, perhaps, its most attractive stage at 5.30 when suddenly the spectators were startled by a rapid fusillade of revolver fire from the direction of the railings on the Nassau street side of the ground.

Seven shots rang out in rapid succession and the spectators rushed for shelter. When the military, who were fielding at the time, were seen lying prone on the ground it was feared that the shots … had taken effect. But soon after the firing ceased the players resumed their places.

The only fatality was twenty-year-old Kathleen Alexanderson Wright, a student from London whose father was Vicar of All Saints' Parish in Clapham. She had become engaged to the son of a Church of Ireland clergyman shortly beforehand. Another woman student was shot in the arm. The two young gunmen escaped on bicycles.

On 7 June, on the opposite side of the Trinity College grounds, five Auxiliaries were wounded when a grenade landed in their lorry. They raced to the end of the street and then opened up indiscriminately on the crowd, killing a sixty-year-old man and wounding five other civilians, including three women. It was one of many such incidents in which standing orders in the Dublin Military District covering the circumstances in which mobile patrols could open fire were blatantly disregarded. There was a certain savagery entering the war in the city on both sides in its closing stages.

A Dublin Guard was formed from members of the Squad and ASU veterans to put some steel into the remnants of the Dublin Brigade. It certainly lived up to the Squad's tradition for brutality. Two off-duty Auxiliaries were shot in front of their families in the Mayfair Hotel in Lower Baggot Street,[48] and a suspected informer was dragged from his bed in Jervis Street Hospital and shot in the courtyard below. It took all Collins's diplomatic skills to assuage the anger of the medical profession and persuade the Sisters of Mercy to continue treating wounded Volunteers in the Mater nursing home, although the fact that the IRA provided such a steady source of income must have helped.

Some of the last attempts at a major military operation by the Dublin Brigade were attacks on trains bringing troops into the city. On 16 June an attempt to derail a military train failed only because a goods train ran into the ambush position first. Relatively few casualties were inflicted in these attacks, even when Thompson sub-machine guns smuggled into Dublin in May were used, probably because of a combination of poor maintenance of the weapons in transit, causing them to jam, the inexperience of the operators and the weapon's inaccuracy at long range.[49] Nevertheless the military were acutely aware of the danger, and of the fact that IRA intelligence had access to information on troop movements. The British army's own historical record of operations stated:

> They were anxious times for us, and several narrow escapes occurred. As a result of these experiences the use of troop trains was stopped. Troops marched or travelled by motor transport in tactical formation, while their heavier baggage, with escort, used the ordinary trains.
>
> The final procedure adopted in the city for the protection of these troops during their move through it, by route march was to picquet certain commanding roofs of houses and patrol the flanks of the route with Crown forces in motor transport. Of the 14 units passed into or through Dublin between May and July, our total casualties were two wounded.

The failure of the Dublin Brigade to attack these detachments or even to snipe effectively at such large targets was testimony to its debilitated state, and it had reached the end of the line by the time the Truce came into force on 11 July. Besides internment and the relentless pressure of military cordons, raids and patrols, a shortage of ammunition was crippling operations. After shooting the two Auxiliaries in the Mayfair Hotel on 26 June two of the Volunteers involved remained on the scene long enough to move a sideboard out from the wall to retrieve two rounds of ammunition one of them had dropped.

IRA operations in the city fell from a record of 117 in May 1921 to 93 in June, the last full month of the struggle. It was clear by the beginning of July that a truce was on the way and units would earn a vital reprieve.[50]

Whatever the effect of the War of Independence on participants and spectators in the city, a far more mundane problem confronted all Dubliners from March 1921 until June. This was the threat of a national coalminers' strike in Britain. Coal shortages and the fear of coal shortages had hung like a cloud over Dublin almost continuously since the outbreak of the Great War. The diversion of supplies to Britain's war industries, high shipping charges because of the submarine menace and profiteering had made coal both scarce and expensive. Coping with the shortages was a constant preoccupation for hospitals, industries, businesses, public utilities and consumers alike. In the aftermath of the war British government policy remained antithetical to Irish interests. Priority was given to export markets, because record prices internationally were helping to restore the public finances and the balance of payments. Coal was 53s a ton in early 1921, more than double its pre-war price.

When prices began to fall the British government divested itself of its wartime control of the industry, and the employers cut wages by as much as half in major coalfields, such as those of south Wales, from which Dublin obtained most of its supplies. When the miners refused to accept the terms and threatened to strike, the employers introduced a pre-emptive lockout from 1 April. The miners, who also wanted the mines to be nationalised, invoked the support of dockers and railway workers in the Triple Alliance and called for what was in effect a general strike. The government responded by declaring a state of emergency, but it also offered the olive branch of a temporary price subsidy for the industry to curb wage cuts and encourage further talks. When the miners rejected the offer of talks the other unions in the Triple Alliance withdrew support for the strike. 'Black Friday', as 15 April 1921 was dubbed, 'was branded on the souls of all good trade unionists as the moment when timid leadership sacrificed the miners and, with them, the supreme virtue of solidarity.'[51]

Black Friday would also have serious consequences for the trade union movement in Dublin during the summer of 1921; but for the moment the principal concern of Dubliners was the fact that the miners were now involved in a protracted dispute that would see the return of coal shortages. The city needed between 23,000 and 25,000 tons a week in 1921, but from 3 April until the end of the miners' unsuccessful battle to avoid pay cuts there were only two shipments from Britain, both of which were for the military. Turf made up some of the shortfall in domestic fuel deliveries, but most industrial and public utilities needed coal for their boilers.

The United States was the source that these enterprises turned to, and in early May the corporation established a subcommittee to explore the possibility of securing American supplies for its own purposes and for offering emergency supplies to householders. The subcommittee included the leaders of the two Labour factions, William O'Brien (Republican Labour) and P. T. Daly (Trades Council). Daly had been heavily involved in efforts to tackle coal shortages during the Great War, with varying degrees of success. The subcommittee worked hard to find a supplier and establish lines of credit. In mid-May it accepted a quote from the Irish representative of Emil Franck Ltd of New York for five thousand tons of screened coal (of a standard size and with foreign substances removed) at $12 a ton, only to be told that because of demand Dublin would have to settle for unscreened coal at $11.50 a ton. The subcommittee placed the order nevertheless; and it appears that it was only at this point that it bothered to contact the Dáil Éireann consul in New York, Diarmuid Fawsitt. A Corkman widely respected for his business acumen, Fawsitt reported back that the documents from Franck's were very unsatisfactory. He suggested that the order be cancelled, as he could get better-quality coal elsewhere for the same price. However, Franck's Dublin agent, Thomas Keating, refused to cancel the shipment, because, he said, the consignment was already *en route*. He was probably bluffing, because it arrived two weeks late, on 11 July, the day the truce was declared in the War of Independence. It was found to consist of 50 per cent slack. The Richmond Asylum and Portrane Hospital took five hundred tons each, but there was no demand for the rest, because of its poor quality.

The decision by the councillors to buy so recklessly in a market of which they had no knowledge or experience had been driven by fear that the British coal dispute would drag on indefinitely, and because past experience suggested it would take at least a month from its settlement to secure regular supplies for Dublin. Commercial firms, however, such as Heiton's, Guinness and the DUTC, had organised their own supplies from America at far more competitive prices. The subcommittee ended up paying 80s a ton. The corporation's Electricity Supply Committee, which made its own arrangements for the power station, paid only 45s a ton.

To rub salt in the wounds, British supplies began arriving the following week, and by 1922 the price of coal would fall to 25s a ton. Shaken by the experience, the corporation decided to reactivate a plan to assess the capacity of the Liffey to generate hydro-electric power and end the city's dependence on coal imports.[52]

If the decision to explore hydro-electric power was a look to the future, the same meeting of the corporation on 6 June 1921 also cast a glance backwards. Not satisfied with the fairly modest decision to name streets in the new corporation housing estates after Volunteers who died in the Easter Rising, the corporation proposed renaming some of the city's main thoroughfares. A report prepared for the city council showed that 19 streets and public places were named after kings or queens and their relatives, a further 49 were named after Lord Lieutenants and their relatives, and 120 were attributed to former Lord Mayors, noblemen, merchants, property developers, officials and others who 'may be said to have represented English influence, were hostile to the national spirit and development of the people.' This was not the first attempt by nationalists on the city council to rename various streets and squares, but it was certainly the most comprehensive. No fewer than seventy-six would be renamed or melded into new composite identities.

Proposing the changes, Councillor Peter Doyle said that 'the object was to bring the names of the streets more into harmony with the spirit of the race.' Nevertheless, in a concession to the realities of the situation, he suggested that the changes be introduced incrementally, at the rate of six a year.

Among the changes proposed were some relatively minor obliterations, such as subsuming Cavendish Row in Rutland Square. This would now be renamed Parnell Square, while Sackville Street would be renamed O'Connell Street. Other changes proposed included:

— North Earl Street and Talbot Street would become Brian Boru Street.
— Grafton Street would become Grattan Street (the existing Grattan Street would become Little Grattan Street).
— Capel Street, Bolton Street and the adjoining portion of Lower Dorset Street as far as the junction with North Frederick Street would become Silken Thomas Street.
— Gardiner Row, Great Denmark Street and Gardiner Place would become Thomas Ashe Street.
— South Great George's Street, Aungier Street, Redmond's Hill, Wexford Street, Camden Street and South Richmond Street would become Cahirmore Road, in honour of the apocryphal founder of the ancient dynasty of Leinster.
— Fitzwilliam Square would become Oliver Plunkett Square.
— Mountjoy Square would become Tom Clarke Square.
— Henrietta Street would become Primate's Hill.

There were some concessions. For instance, Merrion Square could keep its name, as it was considered to be associated primarily with a district rather than a person. The saintly prefix (unofficially dropped) would be restored to St James's Street and St Stephen's Green, acknowledging their roots and the link between Faith and Nation.

But immediately the project encountered opposition, even from intended beneficiaries. The Blessed Oliver Plunkett Memorial Association was unhappy about the choice of Fitzwilliam Square. Its vice-president, J. Dunne, wrote to the corporation expressing concern that 'the majority of the residents of that district, being out of sympathy with national views, would oppose the change by all legal powers available.' Even moderate nationalists might 'object at the change in nomenclature as it was believed [correctly] to derive from the Earl of Fitzwilliam of pre-Union days, who had supported the policy of Grattan and the independence of the Irish Parliament.' Dunne suggested that renaming 'a prominent thoroughfare, adjacent to Dublin Castle, in whose dungeons the martyr underwent the first imprisonment,' would be more appropriate.

The secretary of the Dublin Citizens' Association, Howard H. Hely, in a personal capacity, objected to the imposition of widespread changes as undemocratic and said they would cause confusion. He was certainly acting in a very public-spirited way: as a printer and supplier of stationery he could look forward to much extra business from the new corporation policy. Nevertheless, he argued that it was important to maintain continuity of place-names, and that the erection of statues in public places to commemorate important national figures would be a preferable way to honour the dead.

Some of the changes proposed made little sense, even within the terms of advanced nationalism, such as Henrietta Street reverting to its supposed previous name of Primate's Hill. The Henrietta concerned may well have been the Duchess of Grafton, but the primates referred to would have been Archbishops of Armagh, who had been at least as loyal to the Crown and 'hostile to the national spirit' as the duchess. It was perhaps not surprising that the matter of street names was referred back for further consideration.[53]

Chapter 10 ～

'IN THE EVENING THE TRICOLOUR WAS EVERYWHERE ... NOT IN THE MEAN STREETS ONLY BUT ON PROUD HOUSES IN PROFESSIONAL QUARTERS'

The large-scale troop movements through Dublin in May and June represented part of a plan to ramp up military operations throughout the country. The continuing dry weather, which amounted in many places to a drought, provided ideal conditions for a major offensive. Simultaneously, peace initiatives were taking place in the capital through various intermediaries, including Dr Patrick Clune, Archbishop of Perth, whose nephew Conor Clune had been killed in Dublin Castle; the unionist banker Andrew Jameson; Lloyd George's special emissary in the Castle, Andy Cope; and the Lord Mayor of the city, Laurence O'Neill. Arthur Griffith, perceived as the leading moderate in Sinn Féin ranks, was released from custody; and when de Valera was arrested on 22 June in Blackrock, Co. Dublin, he was released at the insistence of Cope, who wanted to maintain the peace momentum. On the same day as de Valera's arrest King George v made a conciliatory speech at the opening of the Northern Ireland Parliament, much of it written by Jan Smuts, the Prime Minister of South Africa and former Anglo-Boer War commander, who travelled to Dublin to meet de Valera.

For all the talk of peace, Dublin remained a city at war, albeit a war that was sputtering to a standstill. The last fatal casualty of the curfew was Daniel Duffy, a 45-year-old fitter in Guinness's brewery. On 3 July he was on his way home with a bunch of flowers at 10:45 p.m. when, according to eye-witnesses, he was called upon to halt. He dropped the bouquet, and when he bent down to pick it up he was shot.[1]

The next day crowds gathered outside the Mansion House, where the Lord Mayor hosted the first public peace initiative in the city. De Valera had invited members of the unionist minority to meet him there so that he could ascertain their feelings before meeting Lloyd George. Sir James Craig, the new Prime Minister of Northern Ireland, declined the invitation, as expected, but the Southern unionist leaders attended. Shortly after de Valera arrived in a taxi the unionist MP for Rathmines, Sir Maurice Dockrell, made his way 'with difficulty ... through a mass of cheering enthusiasts,' many of whom wanted to shake his hand. Similar welcomes awaited Sir Robert Woods, Lord Midleton and Andrew Jameson. The *Irish Times* and *Irish Independent* were equally at pains to emphasise the popular greeting given to the Southern unionist leaders. By contrast, the arrival of de Valera's fellow-negotiator Arthur Griffith was barely mentioned. 'All Ireland is longing for peace, provided it can be secured upon honourable and satisfactory terms,' the *Independent* wrote in an editorial. 'While the will for peace is so strong full advantage should be taken of it.'

The round table O'Neill had used to avoid issues of precedence at the meeting to launch the anti-conscription campaign three years earlier was once more called into service in the Lord Mayor's drawing-room. Outside, the crowd enjoyed the brilliant sunshine, and the Stars and Stripes vied with the Tricolour in popularity. After three hours the conference concluded with an announcement that it would meet again on Friday.

At the monthly meeting of Dublin Corporation later that afternoon in the Oak Room, O'Neill gave a brief report on the proceedings and declared it to be 'the happiest day of my life.' He told his fellow-councillors:

Peace is in the air. I am breaking no confidence in telling you that during the past three or four hours in the drawing-room close by ... one of the most delicate and one of the most momentous conferences that has ever been held in this country has taken place.

Otherwise it was a fairly routine corporation meeting, with such matters as final approval for the Fairbrother's Fields housing development being secured and complaints being aired about the Commissioners of Irish Lights sending vessels for repair to British yards.

The city itself was in festive mood. The soldiers, armoured cars and barbed-wire cordons that had enmeshed the Mansion House for months were absent, and the good-humoured crowd enjoyed the magnificent weather. DMP members resumed their old role of directing traffic and keeping the crowds under control. But there was a sour note to the day's end in Lower Dominick

Street when a patrol of Auxiliaries removed a Tricolour flown from a chimney-top and then fired into the jeering crowd, wounding nineteen-year-old Lily Douglas.[2]

Far more serious incidents were occurring in the provinces and Belfast, but the momentum for peace proved unstoppable. Behind-the-scenes diplomacy continued, and at the second Mansion House meeting, on Friday 8 July, a firm offer of a truce was made to de Valera by Lloyd George through the offices of Lord Midleton. The crowds were as large as on Monday, but the newspapers reported the mood as more subdued and anxious. Many of the women were reciting the Rosary. Nevertheless, the unionist delegates once more received a particularly warm reception.

At 1 p.m. Midleton and his colleagues left the Mansion House for military headquarters to seek Macready's sanction for a truce. Macready, who expected that 'something of the sort might result from Cope's subterranean activities,' consulted Major-General Tudor, *de facto* commander of the RIC, and Major-General Boyd, the British army commander in Dublin, before drafting proposed terms for a ceasefire.

The unionist delegation returned to the Mansion House at 4:15 p.m., accompanied by Macready's aide-de-camp, whose task it was to explain the proposed terms. The crowds still waited, entertained by 'two juvenile street singers whose services were in great request,' and the mood lightened with an expectation of some sort of dramatic announcement.

But they were to be disappointed. De Valera insisted on some minor changes in the ceasefire terms, and Midleton travelled once more to military headquarters in Parkgate Street shortly after 5 p.m. On this occasion Macready, knowing Midleton was anxious to catch the night boat to London to report on developments, decided to go down to the Mansion House himself with Boyd. Despite all the talk of peace, Macready carried an automatic pistol in his pocket. In Dawson Street he made his way through the masses of people gathered outside the Mansion House, 'mostly composed of women and boys,' to be greeted by the Lord Mayor 'as a long-lost brother.'

> The crowd began to shout and cheer, one excited and unwashed old dame seized my hand and kissed it, others commending me to the saints. It was a vivid picture of the unstable excitability of a populace who, with tears running down their cheeks, could cheer to the echo a man who, a few hours before, and indeed afterwards, they would have rejoiced to hear had met his death at the hands of the gunmen.

Macready's caution was justified. It took another day to complete the terms of the Truce, and the IRA mounted a series of attacks around the country before the ceasefire deadline of noon on Monday 11 July. The last serious incident in Dublin occurred on Friday 8 July while the Mansion House talks were still under way. With Macready's approval, the military authorities were now putting soldiers on civilian trains to discourage attacks. In this instance Volunteers opened fire on a large detachment of Gordon Highlanders as their train headed south under Ballyfermot Bridge. Petrol was poured on carriage roofs in an unsuccessful attempt to set them on fire. Civilians found what cover they could, crouching on the floor as the soldiers returned fire. The only casualties were four civilians, one of whom had to have a leg amputated after the train reached the safety of Clondalkin station.[3]

The only fatality in Dublin was Andrew Knight, a tram inspector from Clarinda Park, Kingstown, whose body was discovered in Dalkey. He was a founder-member of Kingstown Unionist Club. By contrast, eight soldiers, two RIC men, three Volunteers and two civilians were killed in the provinces in the last hours of the conflict, including the fifteen-year-old daughter of a former RIC man, shot as she tried to protect her father from his attackers, who suspected him of being an informer.

In Belfast news of the Truce provoked widespread violence, resulting in 14 civilians killed, 120 wounded and 82 families being burnt out of their homes. The number of dead in Belfast would continue to rise until the pogrom subsided on 15 July.

A sharper contrast with Dublin on Monday 11 July would be hard to find. As Belfast smouldered, Dublin came to life. At noon ships in the port sounded their steam sirens and barges on the Liffey blew their whistles. Many large employers gave their workers the half day off to celebrate the Truce. Crowds flooded the streets, and overladen trams took tens of thousands of day trippers to the seaside in temperatures of 105 degrees Fahrenheit in the shade. Members of the Auxiliary Division commandeered military vehicles to join them. Ice cream vans sold 'Gaelic ice cream', and the city's dealers laid out the fruit and vegetables on their handcarts in patriotic displays. Bands played rebel airs, 'A Nation Once Again' being a particular favourite, and bonfires blazed into the night.

The most striking feature of all was the flags. 'In the evening the Tricolour was everywhere,' the *Irish Independent* reported—'not in the mean streets only, but on proud houses in professional quarters and big places of business.'[4]

Once the Truce came into force several units of the Dublin garrison were sent for badly needed musketry training in case hostilities resumed. The IRA also began training openly, 'but not on the whole provocatively.' The British government ordered the immediate cessation of all intelligence activities in Dublin, much to the chagrin of the military, who complained that 'rebel Intelligence abated not at all.' Despite the strictures, the British army kept a discreet watch on IRA training camps, which was surely easier in Dublin than in many parts of the country. There were seven around the capital, each consisting of

> a few tents with a permanent staff in occupation. At the weekends the numbers would swell up to a few hundred ... Drill, skirmishing, revolver practise, and musketry were carried out. The initial object of this intensive training was probably to keep the IRA occupied and out of trouble. The final object was to have an armed force, with some idea of discipline, available when the peace was ratified.[5]

For Dublin Corporation the Truce was an opportunity to plan for the future. In May a Re-organisation Committee, first proposed a year earlier, had finally been established, and it produced a report in July. All parties were represented, and it concentrated on procedural and organisational issues, such as holding two regular meetings each month instead of one, to expedite business; having proposals costed before being debated; sharpening guillotine procedures on debates; reducing and rationalising the number of committees, to avoid situations where some functions, such as drain-testing, were under the remit of up to three committees, and the staff working for one committee were formally employed by another; synchronising committee meetings to avoid clashes; bringing all employee posts under a unified appointments system, including the regulation of casual workers on the Labour Bureau list (see chapter 8); and making the Town Clerk responsible for overseeing the records of all committees to ensure uniformity and consistency in recording minutes, policy decisions and correspondence.

Centralising the secretariat under the Town Clerk made sound organisational and financial sense. The decision stemmed partly from impatience at the old regime, where the secretary of each committee acted as if he was Town Clerk of his own bailiwick, but also from the bitter pay dispute of 1920, when senior staff members brought administration to a halt. The collaboration of Henry Campbell and his deputy, John J. Flood, with the British military regime added to resentment against the incumbent bureaucracy. By early 1921 there was a vacuum at the top in City Hall. Not alone had Campbell and Flood been dismissed but the City Secretary, the veteran IRB man Fred Allan, had been interned following the completion of his prison sentences. When the Deputy City Treasurer, John J. Murphy, was appointed as the new Town Clerk his replacement, Thomas Lawlor, acted as temporary head of the Finance Department. He proved surprisingly willing to help councillors identify the duplication and featherbedding at the top.[6] He had a ready audience. Both Labour groups on the corporation represented mainly manual workers and had little sympathy with the white-collar staff. The MRA had made municipal reform the main plank of its political platform, while Sinn Féin representatives were acutely aware that they had to put the ratepayers' interests first if they wished to be re-elected.

By subsuming the secretariats of the various committees in the Town Clerk's office the corporation could suppress eight senior posts. Amalgamating the City Treasurer's office with the Rates and Accountant's offices was also proposed, and the City Architect's office would take over those of the Chief Building Surveyor and the Clerk of Works. Finally it was proposed that the pensions of retired employees be reduced to reflect general wage trends in the deepening economic crisis. The proposals provoked a furious reaction from the Local Government Officials (Ireland) Trade Union, which argued that the abolition of long-standing promotional opportunities would lead to members of the staff seeking better positions elsewhere. The protests evoked little sympathy. Even the argument about promotional outlets held little water, as some senior officials already held more than one position, and unemployment was soaring. Furthermore, no pay cuts were proposed.

The person with most positions was the veteran Fenian Fred Allan. As well as being Secretary to the Corporation he had alternated as City Treasurer, Commercial Manager and Secretary of the Electricity Supply Committee as well as Secretary of both the Public Lighting Committee and the Cleansing Committee. As an active member of the IRB and former member of its Supreme Council he not alone had strong allies on the corporation but had friends in the government of the Irish Republic, including Harry Boland and Michael Collins. Above all, he enjoyed a new halo of martyrdom for his present status as internee no. 1580F at Ballykinler. Nevertheless, Allan found himself divested of his duties *in absentia*. An attempt by P. T. Daly to have the reorganisation report referred back to the Law Agent for review on Allan's behalf was defeated by 25 votes to 4. As George Lyons (Sinn Féin) put it, councillors 'have to consider the citizens before the officials.'

By early 1922 Fred Allan would find himself a free man but redundant. As consolation he was awarded a pension worth almost twice what he was entitled to, and new public-service career opportunities would soon beckon.[7] The new broom was proving not so different from the old Redmondite model.

At the same time there had been significant progress in other areas. Perhaps the most progressive move of all was the adoption of a proposal by Hanna Sheehy Skeffington in June 1920:

> That this Council declares (and that committees be instructed accordingly) that in future no woman should be disqualified by reason of her sex from holding any appointment under the council, and, that, women be eligible to compete at all future examinations on the same terms and conditions as men.

In December 1921 the corporation built on that initiative, passing a motion that 'no woman employee should, by reason of her sex, receive less remuneration than a male employee performing work of equal value.'

What was almost as significant as the motions themselves was the fact that the corporation's most populist member, Alderman Alfie Byrne, seconded Sheehy Skeffington's motion, and the surprisingly modern-worded equal-pay proposal was made by Alderman Tom Lawlor (Trades Council) and seconded by Alderman Bernard Shields (MRA).[8] It was further proof of the MRA's progressive stance on many social issues while it remained deeply attached to fiscal rectitude, the rights of property and the rule of law.

The move towards greater equality would prove illusory in the decades ahead, but another important initiative fared better. This was the reintegration of the old unionist interest in the city's governance. Unlike rural dwellers, Dubliners were not cursed with long peasant memories or animosities over land, compounded by sectarian differences. Dr Miriam Moffitt has made a strong case for persistent low-intensity activity against Protestant farmers being the norm, rather than 'ethnic cleansing'. Catholic neighbours wanted land rather than blood.[9] Nor was Dublin afflicted, like Belfast, with a political geography that allowed for the development of ghettoes based on religious and political affiliations. In Dublin the sprinkling of poor Protestants shared the slums with poor Catholics, just as the more numerous Protestant middle class cohabited with Catholic neighbours in the suburbs. The different denominations rarely socialised, but there had been no sectarian riots in Dublin since the 1880s. Ironically, Dublin's traditionally militant skilled Protestant working class had largely emigrated in the nineteenth century when the industries it relied upon for employment were destroyed by British competition following the Act of Union.

Anticipating their own demise, the majority of politically attuned unionists and home-rulers alike had regrouped in the Municipal Reform Association. In many ways its first leader, the ex-nationalist Dr James McWalter, had proved less willing to accept the new dispensation than his ex-unionist successor, J. Hubbard Clark. Under Clark's stewardship the MRA repositioned itself as the leading champion of the ratepayers and the business community. It found some of the more conservative Sinn Féin councillors ready to vote with it against measures that increased the burden on the ratepayer. Dublin unionists, and the business community of which they still constituted a very large part, felt therefore that they could look to the future with some modest measure of confidence.

Dáil Éireann's new civil service members looked to the future with even greater confidence. It just happened to be misplaced. One of the ironies of the funding crisis in local authorities was that it resulted in extra work for the Dáil's Department of Local Government. It had to recruit extra personnel, employing 60 people out of a total staff of 300 employed by the Irish Republic. This made it by far the largest department and probably the most effective after Finance. It even helped the latter implement the Belfast boycott and related economic activities, such as the 'Buy Irish' campaign. In contrast, the British civil administration employed 12,000 people. Even allowing for the estimated 2,000 volunteers who supplemented the full-time staff of the Republic's civil service,[10] it was a remarkable achievement that such a small staff provided at least a semblance of dual power in the civil sphere.

The Department of Local Government operated out of the offices of Dublin County Council and the General Council of County Councils in Rutland Square, now Parnell Square. It had the Grand Orange Lodge of Ireland among its neighbours. But then Rutland Square was something of a cockpit, with bodies as varied as the Orange Order, the Ancient Order of Hibernians, the Irish National Foresters, the Gaelic League, the Registrar-General and the Congested Districts Board having their head offices there, not to mention more surreptitious centres of power, such as Vaughan's Hotel and Kirwan's pub around the corner, which played host to Collins and his coterie.

The Department of Labour had its offices just up the road at 14 North Frederick Street. One of its employees was Jeremiah Mee, the former RIC constable who had led the mutiny at Listowel barracks. Mee described his minister, Constance Markievicz, as a 'martinet' but 'still beautiful and every inch a lady.' The department operated on the second floor of the building, under the auspices of 'Miss Annie Higgins, Music Teacher'. Mee lived on the premises as a caretaker, and one of his jobs was ensuring that if anyone called to enquire about the 'Apartments to let' sign in the window the rent he demanded was extortionate enough to make sure the prospective tenant could not afford them. The pianos provided a hiding-place for any compromising files in the event of a raid, and there were two strong planks that could be lowered out the rear window to provide an escape chute into the back garden.[11] Markievicz attracted some derision for her sense of the dramatic, but the fact remains that her department was never raided, and its records are among the most complete to have survived the War of Independence.

The Department of Finance had relatively modest offices in Abbey Street, while the Department of Agriculture, which might have been expected to be one of the largest departments, occupied 'a couple of rooms over a tailor's shop in North Earl Street, a few yards from Nelson's Pillar, and the staff was correspondingly tiny,' Leon Ó Broin recalled many decades later.

> When I joined, there was the minister or director of Agriculture, the chubby … and good humoured TD Art O'Connor, who dealt personally with the strictly agricultural correspondence that had to be done, aided surreptitiously I suspect, by Dan Twomey of the [British] Government Department of Agriculture's inspectorate.

Most of the other business of the department was with the British-controlled Land Settlement Commission, handling disputes arising out of tenant-farmer purchase schemes. To deal with this business

> there were two legal commissioners, a registrar and two typists—one of them a sister of Kevin Barry—and a messenger whose father had died in the Rising. My £3 a week job was not defined. I assumed I was to act as a private clerk or secretary to the minister/director as well as a general dogsbody. And that was how I functioned anyway.

In fact Art O'Connor appears to have felt keenly the need for more than 'a general dogsbody' to deal with the intricate and vital areas of land reform and land purchase. In May 1921 he secured the agreement of Michael Collins and the now-returned President, Éamon de Valera, to the employment of Crompton Llewellyn Davies, 'an expert in all matters concerning Irish land tenure,' at the unprecedented salary of £1,000 a year. This made Davies the highest-paid official in the Dáil administration.[12] Davies had in fact been a close associate of Lloyd George and was a former Solicitor-General who had been forced to resign because of the activities of his wife, Moya, on behalf of the Irish cause. And there may have been a sense of obligation to do the right thing by him, as Collins was rumoured to be the father of Moya Llewellyn Davies's son.[13]

The experience of this shadow administration was of limited value to the Republic during the Truce. Its members would face a difficult choice in the spring of 1922 over whether to adhere to the Republic or join the new Free State administration that sprang from the Treaty settlement.

No such dilemma confronted the employees of Dublin Corporation, nor indeed its elected representatives. Only individuals such as the former Town Clerk, Henry Campbell, or the unionist councillor William McCarthy, who insisted on cleaving to old allegiances, were left stranded by the rapidly changing political current. A majority of corporation members had been elected by the citizens to stand by the Republic and did so, as did the majority of employees. Both groups tended to reflect the views of the communities whence they came. Nationalist and MRA councillors accepted that their first duty was to the city, and they performed that duty despite increasing harassment by the British forces.

Inevitably, the retreat of the DMP from the streets left a vacuum that could only partially be filled by the Republican Police. The British courts, whether those of the Dublin Police Magistrates or the Lord Chancellor, impinged even less on the lives of the ordinary man or woman in the street during these years than in normal times. The British government's decision to restore law and order by introducing its own paramilitary forces, the Black and Tans and, more especially, the Auxiliaries, had precisely the opposite effect to that intended. While the lawlessness of those groups never achieved the scale in Dublin that it did in some parts of the country, it was still sufficient to ensure that the majority of Dubliners would opt for the Republic as the lesser of two evils by the time of the Truce.

Attempts at collective punishment, such as imposing the bill for malicious damage and injuries inflicted by Crown forces as well as the IRA on the community, only reinforced alienation from the old regime. By July 1921 the Local Government Board was deducting more than £2,000 a month from the frozen funds due to the corporation to pay compensation. It made little difference to the day-to-day running of the city, so long as banks were willing to advance credit.

Where Dubliners of even the most determined republican stripe blanched was when it came to the personal monetary and economic consequences of rebellion. Going to prison or dying for their country was one thing, losing their livelihood was another. Employment by the corporation at least ensured that this did not happen to Volunteers interned or sentenced to terms of imprisonment. But Volunteers in private employment were in a more precarious situation, especially once unemployment began to rise sharply in 1921. Among the self-employed it tended only to be those with family or professional networks to sustain them that risked active involvement in the independence movement. In contrast, Dáil Éireann employees received half pay if they were sentenced or interned, or two-thirds if they had dependants. Favouritism even saw some individuals granted full pay by their departments, despite the fulminations of the Republic's Minister for Finance, Michael Collins.[14]

One feature of the military occupation that affected every citizen was the curfew. The city was still dealing with the problems posed by coal shortages and wartime inflation when the military first imposed a curfew from midnight to 5 a.m. in February 1920. The corporation refused to seek military permits for public-lighting workers to be out during the curfew, which meant that all hand-lit lamps had to be lit at least an hour and 45 minutes before the curfew began to make sure that lamplighters could complete their rounds and return home in safety. Similarly, they could not begin extinguishing the lamps until after the curfew ended. This was not a particular problem during the long winter nights, but as the military extended the curfew and the nights shortened it imposed excessive expenditure on the straitened corporation finances. From 4 June the Lord Mayor ordered all hand-lit public lights to be shut down until 26 July. Dubliners were far from happy negotiating the darkened streets, running the gauntlet of trigger-happy soldiers and Auxiliaries, who enjoyed a freedom of action not possible in the daytime when there were witnesses around.

After Bloody Sunday public fear was so great that all-night lighting was resumed, although it meant that lamps had to be lit almost perpetually in some districts. Despite the cost, councillors

> generally admitted that the arrangements carried out by the Lighting Committee since November last have relieved the tension and anxiety which existed not alone on the part of members of the public who have to carry out night duties, but also on the part of the residents generally in the city and outlying districts.

However, in June 1921, with the need for major cuts in the corporation budget, the Lighting Committee sought guidance from the council on whether the lights should be switched off again or a special levy should be imposed on the rates. The proposal to review its options came from Councillor John Forrestal (Sinn Féin), seconded by Councillor Richard White (MRA). It was passed by thirty-five votes to five. All those opposing the motion were members of the Trades Council Labour group, probably mindful of the loss of earnings to lamplighters. Fortunately for the ratepayers, lamplighters and the general public, the military resolved the problem for all concerned by ending the curfew on the day of the truce, 11 July.[15]

Corporation pensions were another issue on which employees had conflicting views. Traditionally the corporation paid for the pensions and the LGB approved them. Some employees, including Henry Campbell and his deputy, John J. Flood, refused to deal with their former employer: they would treat only with the LGB, eventually ending up in the courts. All other pensioners applied to the corporation, which referred applications for approval to Dáil Éireann's Department of Local Government. Some pensioners, to play safe, applied to both the corporation and the LGB. In those cases the corporation simply 'noted' the correspondence. Again, the Truce cut the Gordian knot for many.

Various efforts were made to enlist the Republic's citizens in the independence struggle. Apart from the Dáil loan the most effective way of mobilising public support was probably the boycott of imports from early 1921. Dáil Éireann requested Dublin Corporation to enforce a ban on the importation and sale of British-made goods from 31 March 1921. The first order concerned agricultural implements and machinery, such as 'Binders, Mowing Machines, Horse Rakes, Ploughs, Swathe Turners, Hay Trolleys ... Harrows, Corn, Drills, Root Cutters.' A similar ban followed on 'British Biscuits, Boot polishes, and Soap' from 14 May, and on 26 May it was the turn of British-made margarine. In this order councillors were reminded that 'every loyal citizen of the Republic is expected to give active support to the Government in making this Order absolute.' It was signed by Earnán de Blaghd (Ernest Blythe), Minister of Trade.[16]

Another feature of the struggle in the city was the increasingly conspicuous religiosity of the crowds attending public events. This began with the recitation of prayers, and the Rosary in particular, outside Mountjoy Prison during the 1919 hunger strike and then at the executions of 1920 and 1921. By the time talks leading to the Truce began, reciting the Rosary had become a central feature of such events.

There were no fresh decrees on the Belfast boycott in 1921, but the bloody events of July and the refugees arriving in Dublin reinforced the feeling of animosity against Ulster unionists and the Orange Order in particular. The actual numbers reaching Dublin were relatively small, but the queues outside the White Cross seeking aid had an enormous effect on popular feeling. Efforts by some Sinn Féin leaders to avoid charges of sectarianism where the Belfast boycott was concerned were of little avail. Inevitably, leaflets and advertisements, such as the following notice on the front page of the *Irish Independent* on 4 June 1921, emphasised the religious aspect of the campaign. It posed fourteen questions to readers:

- DO YOU APPROVE of the STARVATION of Men, Women, and Children because they are CATHOLICS
- DO YOU APPROVE OF POURING PETROL OVER A CHILD OF SIX and of attempting to SET FIRE TO HER BECAUSE HER MOTHER IS A CATHOLIC
- DO YOU APPROVE OF THE BURNING OF THE CATHOLIC PRESBYTERY and the DESECRATION OF THE CATHOLIC GRAVEYARD AT LISBURN
- DO YOU APPROVE OF THE ORANGE MOB which FORCED THE NUNS of Lisburn TO FLEE FOR THEIR LIVES
- DO YOU APPROVE OF THE EXPULSION OF THE CATHOLIC RELIGION FROM EVERY SCHOOL IN THE SIX COUNTIES
- DO YOU APPROVE of the Orange doctrine that NO CATHOLIC HAS A RIGHT TO LIVE IN THE SIX COUNTIES
- DO YOU APPROVE OF THE ATTEMPTED MURDER OF A PROTESTANT IN BELFAST on 24th May because he was SUSPECTED OF BEING A SINN FÉINER
- DO YOU APPROVE OF THE MURDEROUS ORANGE ATTACKS ON HELPLESS PRISONERS while under armed escort
- DO YOU APPROVE OF THE EXPULSION OF THE SINN FÉIN PERSONATING AGENTS BY ORANGEMEN from the Polling Booths during the PARTITION ELECTION on 24th May 1921
- DO YOU APPROVE OF THE BURNING OF DE VALERA'S EFFIGY ...
- DO YOU APPROVE OF THE BELFAST CORPORATION'S 'TOLERANCE' in DENYING the use of the Ulster Hall for Election meetings TO ALL BUT ORANGEMEN
- DO YOU APPROVE OF ORANGE BARBARITIES AND ATROCITIES
- DO YOU APPROVE OF PARTITION
- DO YOU APPROVE OF ORANGE TACTICS generally in its FIGHT AGAINST CHRISTIANITY AND IRELAND

IF SO BUY BELFAST GOODS
IF NOT YOUR DUTY IS CLEAR
BOYCOTT ALL BELFAST GOODS

The explicit references to attacks on Catholics and Catholicism in six of the points, the emphasising of discrimination against Catholics and Sinn Féin by Orangemen and murderous Orange mobs and, finally, the equation of the Belfast boycott with the defence of Christianity and Ireland helped create an atmosphere in which dissent by Protestants in Republican ranks, let alone outside them, was virtually impossible. Even within the Dáil cabinet those who questioned the wisdom of the boycott and its extension, including the Northern Protestant Ernest Blythe, had to be cautious in advancing their case, especially as some of their fellow-Ulstermen, such as Seán MacEntee and Eoin O'Duffy, were strong advocates of it as a weapon.[17] That Catholics were indeed the targets of murderous Orange mobs only made the challenge posed by sectarianism all the more urgent and insurmountable.

Ironically, the firms most affected by the boycott were those that had business with the South and tended to be owned by Catholics or employed significant numbers of Catholics. As several historians have noted, the boycott, like the pogroms, helped instil a partitionist mentality in both parts of Ireland.

In the days immediately before the Truce a 'Solemn Seven-Fold Novena of Masses and Prayers' was launched in honour of 'Our Lady of Victories' by the Society of the Little Flower. The Masses were to be celebrated in Rome, Lourdes and Lisieux, the Norman town that was home to the Carmelite convent where Thérèse Martin, 'the Little Flower', had died in 1897, aged twenty-four. She would not be canonised for another twenty-eight years but already she had an immense following in Ireland. She proved a special influence on the young. Kevin Barry and Frank Flood, the two youngest Volunteers executed in the War of Independence, told family, friends and the Sisters of Charity who visited them of the courage they drew from her as they awaited execution.

Father Thomas Newsome, who had organised a novena campaign for peace, proclaimed: 'This glorious news of a Truce seems like the first fruits of our campaign of prayer. We must not slacken our devotion ... Let us wax yet more earnest in prayer, while the issue is still doubtful.'[18] After witnessing two-and-a-half years of violent revolutionary struggle on the streets of the capital, many Dubliners turned increasingly to belief in the power of prayer rather than that of the gun.

Nevertheless, the IRA and Dáil Éireann administration had achieved a considerable degree of acceptance in the city since 1919. The relatively tight control exercised by GHQ on Volunteers, especially those in the Squad and the ASUs, ensured that Dubliners were spared the excesses that took place in some parts of the country. It was also due in no small measure because of the assistance of Dublin Corporation and the labour movement. The role of the former was very publicly acknowledged by the inclusion of the Lord Mayor, Laurence O'Neill, in de Valera's first peace delegation to London. The role of the labour movement in the new phase of the struggle for independence remained unclear, but it had undoubtedly grown in size and influence—not least with the emergence of a major Irish engineering union, the IESFTU, to complement the ITGWU.

Ironically, during the Truce a heady peace of sorts heralded the increasing militarisation of Irish society. North and South, armed formations would proliferate. Nor would Dublin, which had been the cockpit of revolution since 1913, be spared the experience of increased lawlessness that flourished in a climate of mounting political uncertainty. Most Dubliners yearned for peace and a respite from terror. The crowds reciting the Rosary outside the Mansion House in July 1921 provided a better clue to the nature of the emerging independent state than the violent rhetoric of politicians and military men. But more blood would have to be shed first. Within a year, Dubliners would witness the outbreak of Civil War.

NOTES

Chapter 1: A Victory Ball, 'a regular little arsenal' and a midnight visit to detective headquarters (p. 1–31)

1. *Weekly Irish Times*, 4 January 1919.
2. *Irish Independent*, 2 January 1919; *Weekly Irish Times*, 11 January 1919; Dublin Corporation Minutes, 18 October 1918, item 646; *Irish Times*, 12 November 1918; Dublin Corporation Minutes, 2 January 1919, item 666; *Irish Times*, 18 January and 8 April 1919.
3. *Irish Times* and *Irish Independent*, 22 January 1919; *Weekly Irish Times*, 25 January 1919.
4. There may have been thirty-two, as Michael Collins and Harry Boland were seen in the Mansion House but they did not answer the roll call. See Comerford, *The First Dáil*, p. 11–12.
5. The constituencies were Pembroke, South County Dublin and Harbour Division.
6. Mitchell, *Labour in Irish Politics*, p. 107–10; Farrell, *The Founding of Dáil Éireann*, p. 59–60 (contains the original draft of the Democratic Programme); Fitzpatrick, *Harry Boland's Irish Revolution*, p. 106–8.
7. Dáil Éireann, Minutes of Proceedings, 21 January 1919, p. 22–4; Gaughan, *Thomas Johnson*, p. 157; Morrisey, *William O'Brien*, p. 162.
8. See, for example, Collins's contributions to Dáil Éireann debates, June and August 1921; also Mitchell, *Revolutionary Government in Ireland*, p. 46–9.
9. *Irish Times*, 25 January 1918.
10. McDowell, *Crisis and Decline*, p. 65.
11. *Evening Telegraph*, 24 January 1919; *Irish Times*, 25 and 27 January 1919; Buckland, *Irish Unionism*, 1, chap. 6.
12. Wolfe, *Labour Supply and Regulation*, p. 304–7. In Scotland some shipyard workers demanded a thirty-hour week: Lysaght, *The Making of Northern Ireland*, p. 29–9.
13. *Irish Times*, 28 January to 2 February 1919.
14. Milk was one of the few commodities subject to effective price control.
15. Eagar, *The Inception and Early History of the Irish Bank Officials' Association*.
16. *Weekly Irish Times*, 15 February 1919.
17. *Irish Times*, 15 March 1919.
18. Shane Leslie, in Cruise O'Brien, *The Shaping of Modern Ireland*, p. 101; Morrissey, *William J. Walsh*, p. 320–21.
19. Mitchell, *Revolutionary Government in Ireland*, p. 33–4: he estimates that 22 out of the 73 people he considers most influential in the struggle for independence came from Dublin; Laurence O'Neill Papers, National Library of Ireland, ms. 35,294/4.

20. *Irish Times*, 2 April 1919; Kissane, *The Politics of the Irish Civil War*, p. 40; Laurence O'Neill Papers, National Library of Ireland, ms. 35,294/3/5.

21. Mitchell, *Revolutionary Government in Ireland*, p. 42; *Irish Times*, 2 April 1919. Gavan Duffy would go on to promote Sinn Féin's cause in South Africa and South America.

22. *Irish Times*, 13 and 14 March 1919; Bureau of Military History, Witness Statements, ws 1687 (Harry Colley).

23. *Irish Times*, 22, 24 and 25 March 1919; *Weekly Irish Times*, 29 March 1919; *Dublin's Fighting Story*, p. 126–8; Carey, *Hanged for Ireland*, p. 100–101.

24. *Irish Independent*, 18 and 31 March 1919; *Irish Times*; Hogan, *The Four Glorious Years*, p. 65; Carey, *Mountjoy*, p. 189.

25. Hogan, *The Four Glorious Years*, p. 228–31.

26. *Irish Independent*, 4 October 1916; *Irish Times*, 18 November 1916; *Irish Independent*, 21 October 1916; *Irish Times*, 27 November 1916.

27. O'Neill Papers, National Library of Ireland, ms. 35,294/4; Archbishop Walsh Papers, 1913.

28. Archbishop Walsh Papers, 1913; O'Neill Papers, National Library of Ireland, ms. 35,294/4; Neligan, *The Spy in the Castle*, p. 55; Foy, *Michael Collins's Intelligence War*, p. 18–22; Dwyer, *The Squad and the Intelligence Operations of Michael Collins*, chap. 1 and 3; Ryan, *Comrades*, chap. 6.

29. Bureau of Military History, Witness Statements, ws 357 (Dr Kathleen Lynn).

30. *Irish Times*, 22 and 24 February 1919.

31. *Irish Times*, 26 February and 27 March 1919.

32. *Irish Times*, 11 March 1919.

33. *Irish Times*, 15 February 1919. By comparison, the modern DART service carries 88 million passengers a year.

34. Morrissey, *William Martin Murphy*, p. 32, 72–5; Yeates, *Lockout*, p. 2–5.

35. Reigh had been a substantial shareholder in many companies, including the Dublin United Tramways Company. He began his political life as an alderman; his relegation to mere councillor probably reflected the general decline in social deference, where prosperous businessmen could no longer expect to command automatic political success.

36. *Irish Times*, 28 February 1919. McGarry succeeded Thomas Ashe as president of the IRB and was in turn succeeded by Michael Collins.

37. Dublin Corporation Minutes, 7 August 1916; *Irish Times*, 4 December 1917 and 25 February and 22 March 1919.

38. *Irish Times*, 22 and 27 February 1919.

39. Dublin Corporation Minutes, 2 April 1919; *Irish Independent*, 14 June 1919; *Irish Times*, 3 April 1919.

40. Kelly was known for his memorable if sometimes parochial comments on local controversies. In 1913, when the debate over the proposal to have Edwin Lutyens design an art gallery spanning the River Liffey to house the Hugh Lane pictures was in full flood, Kelly told his colleagues: 'We don't need a Dutchman building bridges for us.'

41. *Weekly Irish Times*, 15 February and 2 April 1919.

42. *Irish Times*, 24 February 1919; Geraghty and Whitehead, *The Dublin Fire Brigade*, p. 130–36.

Chapter 2: 'I had no revolver myself and I am glad now ... as I might have shot some of them' (p. 32–62)

1. Lynn herself appears to have been embarrassed in later years by her propagandising efforts and made no mention of them in her statement to the Bureau of Military History.

2. Bureau of Military History, Witness Statements, ws 357 (Dr Kathleen Lynn); Mulholland, *The Politics and Relationships of Kathleen Lynn*, p. 66; Luddy, *Women and Philanthropy in Nineteenth-Century Ireland*, p. 84; Shaw, *New City Pictorial Directory, 1850;* Matthews, *Renegades*, p. 210–23. See also Yeates, *Dublin in the First World War*, chap. 14.

3. Ó hÓgartaigh, *Kathleen Lynn*, p. 42; O'Brien, *Dear Dirty Dublin*, p. 120; Dublin Corporation Public Health Committee Breviates.

4. *Irish Independent*, 27 and 30 May, 13 and 30 August and 17 September 1919; *Irish Times*, 26 May and 22 December 1919.

5. Ó hÓgartaigh, *Kathleen Lynn*, chap. 3.

6. Luddy, *Women and Philanthropy in Nineteenth-Century Ireland*, p. 191; Ó hÓgartaigh, *Kathleen Lynn*, p. 39.

7. Luddy, *Women and Philanthropy in Nineteenth-Century Ireland*, p. 204–5. Treatment was also provided to 'fallen women' who entered the Magdalen laundry network: O'Brien, *Dear Dirty Dublin*, p. 119–20.

8. For a detailed debate on the issues raised by the 1926 interdepartmental report see Howell, 'Venereal disease and the politics of prostitution in the Irish Free State,' Riordan, 'Venereal disease in the Irish Free State,' and Howell, 'The politics of prostitution and the politics of public health in the Irish Free State.'

9. *Irish Times*, 2 August 1919. His brother, J. W. Jellett, was elected to succeed A. W. Samuels as one of the two MPs for Dublin University after the latter's elevation to the Bench in July 1919.

10. *Irish Independent*, 5 August 1919.

11. *Irish Times*, 20 September 1919.

12. *Irish Independent*, 20 September 1919.

13. Sir Maurice Dockrell was senior grand deacon of the Freemasons in Ireland; Sir Charles Cameron was deputy grand master.

14. *Irish Times*, 25 March and 3 April 1919.

15. McManus, *Dublin, 1910–1940*, p. 41.

16. *Irish Times*, 2 and 8 July 1919.

17. *Irish Independent*, 15 June 1919; *Irish Times*, 2 April 1919.

18. Mitchell, *Revolutionary Government in Ireland*, p. 121.

19. *Irish Times*, 25 March and 20 September 1919. Dockrell was exaggerating the probable effects of PR in the Dublin constituencies. It was unlikely to have altered the outcome in any of them. On the other hand, if Labour had run candidates this might have robbed Sinn Féin of a couple of seats under the 'first past the post'

system, by splitting the radical vote rather than enhancing the value of Unionist votes.

20. Yeates, *Dublin in the First World War*, chap. 11.

21. Laffan, *The Resurrection of Ireland*, chap. 5 and 6.

22. Laffan, *The Resurrection of Ireland*, p. 80–84. The *Statist* (London) gave particularly close coverage to the Commission's activities. Its editor was J. J. McElligott, who had emigrated to pursue a career in journalism after being sacked as a clerk, first class, in the Irish civil service for his participation in the Easter Rising.

23. O'Neill Papers, National Library of Ireland, ms. 35,294/5; Mitchell, *Revolutionary Government in Ireland*, p. 53–4.

24. Hogan, *The Four Glorious Years*, p. 84–5, 118–19, 271–2.

25. Yeates, 'Craft workers during the Irish revolution'; Bureau of Military History, Witness Statements, ws 1687 (Harry Colley); Dwyer, *The Squad and the Intelligence Operations of Michael Collins*, p. 14.

26. *Minutes of Proceedings of Dáil Éireann*, 10 April 1919.

27. George Willoughby was one of the most respected senior officers in the DMP and a veteran of the 1913 Lockout, when he saved his fellow-parishioner Seán O'Casey from a beating on Bloody Sunday (1913). He was later a chief superintendent in the Garda Síochána.

28. *Irish Times*, 30 June, 2 August and 3 October 1919.

29. *Irish Times*, 17 July 1919. Most of the speakers at the meeting stressed that in refusing to participate in the parade they intended no personal slight to Field-Marshal French.

30. O'Neill Papers, National Library of Ireland, ms. 35,294/9; *Irish Times*, 19 July 1919.

31. *Irish Times* and *Irish Independent*, 21 July 1919.

32. Sergeant Roche and Constable Keogh, who was shot in Cork, both recovered from their injuries.

33. Dwyer, *The Squad and the Intelligence Operations of Michael Collins*, p. 46–8; Foy, *Michael Collins's Intelligence War*, p. 25–6; Abbot, *Police Casualties in Ireland*, p. 40–43.

34. O'Donoghue, *No Other Law*, p. 50–51. O'Donoghue claimed that the soldiers resisted, but this version was contested by Lieutenant-Colonel Hughes-Hallett, who was stationed in Fermoy at the time: Sheehan, *Hard Local War*, p. 25.

35. Dwyer, *The Squad and the Intelligence Operations of Michael Collins*, p. 51–2.

36. Foy, *Michael Collins's Intelligence War*, p. 19.

37. Dwyer, *The Squad and the Intelligence Operations of Michael Collins*, p. 48.

38. Foy, *Michael Collins's War*, p. 24, 28.

39. *Irish Times*, 20 and 22 October 1919.

40. Daly was also referred to as O'Daly.

41. Foy, *Michael Collins's War*, p. 192–3; Abbot, *Police Casualties in Ireland*, p. 46–7.

42. Dwyer, *The Squad and the Intelligence Operations of Michael Collins*, p. 60–62.

43. National Archives [London], cso 904/193/9.

44. Ferriter, *The Transformation of Ireland*, p. 209.

45. *Irish Times*, 9 and 12 July and 13 and 22 August 1919; National Archives, Department of the Taoiseach, Commission on Ex-Servicemen, 3/495, boxes 24–5.

46. Military Archives, LE 63, Handwritten note entitled 'War Service Officers—Accession of 1919–1921 Ex members of British Army who joined the IRA.'

47. See, for instance, Bureau of Military History, Witness Statements, WS 340 (Oscar Traynor), as well as GHQ Reports and Dublin Company Returns, National Library of Ireland, ms. 901, and Bartlett, 'Militarism in Ireland' in Bartlett and Jeffrey, *A Military History of Ireland.*

48. Foy, *Michael Collins's Intelligence War*, p. 61–3.

49. Ryan, *Seán Treacy and the 3rd Tipperary Brigade*, chap. 8.

50. Quoted by Kenneally in *The Paper Wall*, p. 67.

51. McBride, *The Greening of Dublin Castle*, p. 268.

52. *Irish Independent*, 20 and 24 December 1919; *Irish Times*, 22 December 1919; *Weekly Irish Times*, 20 December 1919; Morrissey, *William J. Walsh*, p. 326–7.

53. The county council elections would not take place until June 1920.

Chapter 3: 'One half of the population is wrong and the other isn't' (p. 63–89)

1. *Irish Independent*, 7 and 15 January 1920.

2. *Irish Times* and *Irish Independent*, 3 January 1920.

3. *Irish Independent*, 2 and 3 January 1919.

4. *Irish Independent*, 6 January 1919; *Rebel Cork's Fighting Story*, p. 179–81.

5. *Irish Independent*, 6 January 1920.

6. *Irish Times*, 1 December 1919.

7. *Irish Independent*, 8 December 1919.

8. Dublin Corporation, Report No. 36, 1920. The numbers rose to 265 newly registered vehicles and 116 transfers in the following year.

9. *Irish Times* and *Irish Independent*, 9 December 1919. William Archer Redmond was the son of the former leader of the Irish Party, John Redmond, and represented Waterford. It was one of two Irish Party seats outside Ulster; the other was T. P. O'Connor's seat in the Scotland division of Liverpool.

10. *Irish Times* and *Irish Independent*, 16 January 1920.

11. *Irish Independent*, 27 January 1920.

12. *Irish Independent*, 24 January and 5 February 1920.

13. Ministry of Labour Report on Disputes, Dáil Éireann, June 1920, National Archives, DE2/5.

14. *Irish Independent*, 10 February 1920; *Irish Times*, 14 February 1920; ILP&TUC Report 1920, p. 11–17.

15. *Irish Independent*, 6 January 1920.

16. Moran, *Executed for Ireland*, p. 52–4.

17. Bi-Weekly Precis of Reports of Important Occurrences in DMP Area, 3 February 1920, Bureau of Military History; *Irish Independent*, 14 and 15 January 1920.

18. *Irish Times*, 8 March 1920.

19. Walter Carpenter had been a Socialist candidate in 1914 as well and was equally unsuccessful in 1918.

20. One of the 'unofficial' candidates, Owen Hynes of the Brick and Stonelayers' Union, ran as an independent but served as a member of Republican Labour once elected.

21. Ironically, the founder of the ITGWU, Jim Larkin, had been sacked for a similar offence from the National Union of Dock Labourers in Britain. It was following this that he established the ITGWU.

22. Cody, O'Dowd and Rigney, *The Parliament of Labour*, p. 126–33; Morrissey, *William O'Brien*, p. 170–77.

23. Dublin Corporation Minutes, 12 January 1920.

24. *Irish Independent* and *Irish Times*, 3–14 January 1920. More than 30 candidates withdrew their nominations, but these included a number of Sinn Féin candidates nominated for more than one constituency. The figure of 25 is a net total.

25. Buckland, *Irish Unionism, 1*, p. 195–203; *Irish Times*, 16 January 1920.

26. McBride, *The Greening of Dublin Castle*, p. 268–9; O'Halpin, *The Decline of the Union*, p. 166–7, 194–5; Townshend, *The British Campaign in Ireland*, p. 44–5; *Irish Independent*, 10 January 1920. See O'Neill Papers, National Library of Ireland, ms. 35,294, for the warm personal relationship that existed between O'Neill and Mahon over many years.

27. *Irish Times* and *Irish Independent*, 9–14 January 1920.

28. *Cuala News*, 11 January 1920.

29. This includes Owen Hynes, a close associate of William O'Brien, who would be one of his allies in the ITUC split in 1945 that led to the formation of the Congress of Irish Unions.

30. *Irish Times* and *Irish Independent*, 10–31 January 1920.

31. Dublin Corporation Minutes, 12 January 1920.

32. Dublin Corporation Minutes, 30 January 1920.

33. Dublin Corporation Minutes, 30 January 1920; *Irish Times*, 31 January 1920.

34. Carden, *The Alderman*, p. 169–72. On the English leg of his trip home Kelly jumped out of the train when it stopped and tried to run away.

35. Dublin Corporation Minutes, 2 February 1910.

36. *Irish Times*, 31 January 1920.

37. *Irish Independent*, 7 January and 4 February 1920.

38. Walsh, *Anglican Women in Dublin*, p. 200.

39. War wives and widows could lose their allowance if they were found to be 'cohabiting' or having a casual relationship with a man. This performed the double function of reassuring men at the front that their wives were being morally policed and saving the exchequer money.

40. Ó Móráin, *Irish Association of Directors of Nursing and Midwifery*, p. 27.

41. *Irish Times*, 14 February 1920.

Chapter 4: 'On Friday evenings God Save the King will NOT be played' (p. 90–115)

1. Bi-Weekly Precis of Reports of Important Occurrences in DMP Area, Bureau of Military History; Abbot, *Police Casualties in Ireland*, p. 62; Herlihy, *The Metropolitan Police*, p. 180–81; Bureau of Military History, Witness Statement, WS 819 (Liam Archer).

2. Leeson, *The Black and Tans*, p. 234, n. 81.

3. *Irish Times*, 24 February 1920.

4. *Irish Independent*, 23 February 1920.
5. *Irish Times*, 24 February 1920.
6. *Irish Times* and *Irish Independent*, 23–8 February 1920.
7. *Irish Independent*, 28 February 1920.
8. Dublin Corporation, Report No. 265, 1919.
9. Dublin Corporation, Report No. 265, 1919.
10. Irwin, *Betrayal in Ireland*, p. 49–50.
11. Woodcock, *Experiences of an Officer's Wife in Ireland*, p. 31.
12. Dublin Corporation Minutes, 2 March 1920; *Irish Independent* and *Irish Times*, 2 March 1920.
13. Dublin Corporation Minutes, 8 March 1920; *Irish Times*, 9 March 1920.
14. Morrissey, *William O'Brien*, p. 184–9.
15. *Irish Times*, 9 March 1920.
16. Buckland, *Irish Unionism*, I, p. 198.
17. *Irish Times*, 24 February and 9 March 1920.
18. *Irish Times*, 28 February and 3 March 1920.
19. Church of Ireland, 'Stained glass in the Church of Ireland', at www.gloine.ie, images 110280, 110140, 110750.
20. *Irish Times*, 25 March 1920.
21. *Irish Times*, 24 February 1920.
22. *Irish Times*, 26 March 1920.
23. Abbott, *Police Casualties in Ireland*, p. 67–8. The relationship between the Irish Volunteers and Dáil Éireann was complex, and it was not until June 1920 that the long process by which the Dáil recognised the Volunteers as the army of the Irish Republic, and the Volunteers recognised Dáil Éireann as the government of the Irish Republic and swore allegiance to it, was completed. As a democratic organisation, the Volunteers conducted a poll at unit meetings, and postal ballots where that was not possible, to secure the agreement of members to their subordination to the Dáil.
24. Bureau of Military History, Witness Statements, WS 538 (Father Michael Browne, secretary to Archbishop Walsh).
25. Mitchell, *Revolutionary Government in Ireland*, p. 57–65; Kenneally, *The Paper Wall*, p. 7; *Irish Independent*, 2 and 3 January 1920; Bureau of Military History, Witness Statements, WS 660 (Thomas Leahy).
26. *Irish Independent, Freeman's Journal* and *Irish Times*, 9–30 March 1920; Dwyer, *The Squad and the Intelligence Operations of Michael Collins*, p. 96–101; Foy, *Michael Collins's Intelligence War*, p. 81–3; Kenneally, *The Paper Wall*, p. 104.
27. *Freeman's Journal*, 29 March 1920.
28. National Archives [London], CO 904/193/10; Dwyer, *The Squad and the Intelligence Operations of Michael Collins*, p. 98–102.
29. *Irish Times*, 4 February 1920; Woodcock, *An Officer's Wife in Ireland*, p. 38–9.
30. The White Cross was established at the instigation of Éamon de Valera as an alternative source of relief to that provided by the British Red Cross Society.
31. Mitchell, *Revolutionary Government in Ireland*, p. 55.

32. Griffith and O'Grady, *Curious Journey*, p. 208.
33. Bureau of Military History, Bi-Weekly Précis of Reports of Important Occurrences in the DMP Area, 16 April 1920.
34. Kee, *The Green Flag*, p. 676; Dalton, *With the Dublin Brigade*, p. 70–72; *Irish Times*, 5 April 1920.
35. *Irish Independent* and *Irish Times*, 13–15 April 1920.
36. Sheehan, *Fighting for Dublin*, p. 12–13.
37. Hogan, *The Four Glorious Years*, p. 181.
38. Macready played the hypocrite well. Congratulating O'Neill on his re-election as Lord Mayor, Macready assured him in a private letter that he would 'always retain a pleasant remembrance of the occasions on which we have met': National Library of Ireland, O'Neill Papers, ms. 35,294/13; *Irish Times* and *Irish Independent*, 15 April 1920; Macready, *Annals of an Active Life*, vol. 2, p. 446–9; Bureau of Military History, Witness Statements, ws 465 (Mary O'Sullivan, private secretary to the Lord Mayor).
39. *Irish Independent* and *Irish Times*, 15 April 1920; Sheehan, *Fighting for Dublin*, p. 15. A 'buckshee' detective was a member of the uniformed branch who worked in a temporary capacity in plain clothes without extra pay, usually in the hope of boosting his promotion prospects.
40. Abbott, *Police Casualties in Ireland*, p. 72–3. Dalton's companion, Constable John Spencer, was wounded: Herlihy, *The Dublin Metropolitan Police*, p. 181. There was one indirect Republican fatality of the hunger strike, Frank Gleeson. A 1916 veteran, Gleeson suffered an acute attack of appendicitis and died during the operation to remove it while still recovering from the effects of the hunger strike. Thousands attended the funeral.

Chapter 5: 'Not the Empire but the Irish Republic' (p. 116–45)

1. Mitchell, *Revolutionary Government in Ireland*, p. 157–9.
2. Carden, *The Alderman*, p. 178–9.
3. Dublin Corporation Minutes, 3 May 1920; *Irish Times* and *Irish Independent*, 4 May 1920; Mitchell, *Revolutionary Government in Ireland*, p. 158–9; Carden, *The Alderman*, p. 178–9. Ironically, the only rate for which the Corporation could distrain goods without the co-operation of the Sheriff was the police rate.
4. Dublin Corporation Minutes, 3 May 1920; *Irish Times* and *Irish Independent*, 4 May 1920. Legal advice from Ignatius Rice, Corporation Minutes, item 266–7, June 1910.
5. Bureau of Military History, Witness Statements, ws 449 (W. T. Cosgrave), note 1. Cosgrave later appointed both Bank of Ireland directors to the Free State Senate in recognition of their help at this and other critical junctures over the next two years.
6. *Irish Independent* and *Irish Times*, 4 May 1920; Dublin Corporation Minutes, 3 May 1920. Forrestal also used an Irish form of his name, Seán Mac Coillte, on occasion.
7. Dublin Corporation Minutes, 7 June 1920. Another motion calling for his release was passed in August after Larkin's sister, Delia, wrote requesting the Corporation's assistance.
8. *Irish Times*, 4 May 1920; *Irish Independent*, 12 June 1920.
9. Dublin Corporation, Report No. 62, 1920.

10. Dublin Corporation Minutes, 21 June 1920.
11. These figures were in line with the increases that had been agreed for British public servants through the Whitley Committees in March 1920.
12. *Irish Independent* and *Irish Times*, 1–29 June 1920; Dublin Corporation Minutes, 7 and 28 June and 6 September 1920; Maguire, *Servants to the Public*, p. 46–7.
13. *Irish Independent* and *Irish Times*, 1 June 1920 to 11 March 1921. If mortality rates in Dublin are anything to go by, the number of patients who died after being referred to Dublin institutions from outside the capital accounted for approximately 3½ per cent of all deaths per year.
14. National Library of Ireland, ms. 901/5.
15. *Freeman's Journal* and *Irish Independent*, 10 May 1920.
16. Irwin, *Betrayal in Ireland*, p. 81.
17. Wolfe, *Labour Supply and Regulation*, part 2.
18. Dáil Éireann Report, National Archives, 2/116.
19. Family memoir by Seán Redmond (grandson of Jack Redmond), sent to Archives of the TEEU, 17 December 2007.
20. Bureau of Military History, Witness Statements, ws 660 (Thomas Leahy); *Irish Times*, 4 and 19 January 1920.
21. Bureau of Military History, Witness Statements, ws 660 (Thomas Leahy). Thomas Maguire, submission for military service pension, 13 May 1938; *Comment*.
22. The Technical, Engineering and Electrical Union can trace its origins to the meeting of 9 May 1920 and still holds the minute-books from the period.
23. Dáil Éireann, Minutes of Proceedings, p. 120.
24. Letter to Alderman J. MacDonagh TD on behalf of Joint Committee, National Archives, Dáil Éireann, 2/116. 'Amalgamated unions' was a generic term used to describe British unions.
25. This figure may have been artificially low, as there was full employment during the First World War and the post-war boom.
26. Letter to Alderman J. MacDonagh TD on behalf of Joint Committee, National Archives, Dáil Éireann, 2/116.
27. These included mediation structures for dealing with land disputes as well as industry.
28. Ministry of Labour Report on Disputes, Dáil Éireann, June 1920, National Archives, DE2/5.
29. Ministry of Labour Report on Disputes, Dáil Éireann, June 1920, National Archives, DE2/5; Memorandum of Discussion at Conference of Representatives of Joint Committee re Scheme for the Formation of One Irish Union Comprising all Branches of Engineering Trades in Ireland, National Archives, DE2/116.
30. Morrissey, *William O'Brien*, chap. 9–11.
31. *Irish Times*, 1 December 1919. See minutes of the Provisional Committee of the IES&FTU for numerous references to consultations with Foran on various disputes.
32. Memorandum of Discussion at Conference of Representatives of Joint Committee re Scheme for the Formation of One Irish Union Comprising all Branches of Engineering Trades in Ireland, Dáil Éireann, National Archives, DE2/116.
33. Memorandum of Meeting, Report to Dáil Éireann, National Archives, DE2/116.

34. Gallacher was an engineer and the son of Irish immigrants. He had been chairman of the Clyde Workers' Committee during the First World War and led the campaign against conscription in Scotland. He supported the Republican side in the Civil War and later became Britain's first communist MP.

35. The union was given various names in its first couple of years, but the full title is inscribed in the first Minute Book, containing the proceedings of the Provisional and Executive Committees.

36. Minutes of the Provisional Committee of the IES&FTU, 19 May 1920, Archives of the TEEU. For the use of the Foresters' Hall see Connell, *Where's Where in Dublin,* p. 101.

37. Minutes of the Provisional Committee of the IES&FTU, 11 May 1920, Archives of the TEEU.

38. Connell, *Where's Where in Dublin,* p. 15; Minutes of the Provisional Committee of the IES&FTU, 11 May and 1 and 17 June 1920, Archives of the TEEU.

39. Dáil Éireann, Note on Irish Union for Engineering Trades, National Archives, DE2/116.

40. Dáil Éireann, Correspondence from Jack Redmond to Countess Markievicz, 18 May 1920, DE2/116.

41. Ministry of Labour Report on Disputes, Dáil Éireann, June 1920, National Archives, DE2/5; Minutes of the Provisional Committee of the IES&FTU, 17 May and 18 June 1920, Archives of the TEEU.

42. Minutes of the Provisional Committee of the IES&FTU, 10 November 1920, Archives of the TEEU.

43. *Irish Independent,* 7 June 1920.

44. Amalgamated Society of Engineers, Annual Report for 1920. This was the last annual report of the union, which amalgamated with other craft unions to form the Amalgamated Engineering Union.

45. Bureau of Military History, Witness Statements, WS 660 (Thomas Leahy); Ministry of Labour Report on Disputes, Dáil Éireann, June 1920, National Archives, DE2/5; Clarkson, *Labour and Nationalism in Ireland,* p. 323.

46. Minutes of the Provisional Committee of the IES&FTU, 29 May, 18 and 21 June, 12 July, 17 August and 11 September 1920; minutes of the Executive Committee of the IES&FTU, 6 and 17 November 1920.

47. When Clydeside rates began to fall at the end of 1920, because of the post-war recession, this led to a series of disputes in Dublin, where workers resisted the pay cuts, leading to the ultimate closure of the yard. See Smellie, *Shipbuilding and Repairing in Dublin.*

48. Minutes of the Provisional Committee of the IES&FTU, 16 and 25 September 1920.

49. At the time of writing, the wage structures for employment rights orders and registered employment agreements (including the ENJIC) are facing legal challenges from a number of employers and a Government review.

50. Minutes of the Provisional Committee of the IES&FTU, 26 July 1920.

51. The English Bank Officials' Guild was established at the same time. The IBOA had good relations with its English counterpart but never considered amalgamation.

52. Eagar, *The Inception and Early History of the Irish Bank Officials' Association*, chap. 2; White, *Misfit*; Maguire, *Servants to the Public*, chap. 4.
53. O'Brien, *Forth the Banners Go*, p. 194–7.
54. *Irish Independent*, 1 June 1920.
55. *Irish Times*, 1 and 2 June 1920; Kostick, *Revolution in Ireland*, p. 133.
56. *Irish Times*, 2 June 1920; Denis Holmes, 'Raid on King's Inns,' in *Dublin's Fighting Story*, p. 131–3; Sheehan, *Fighting for Dublin*, p. 19.
57. *Irish Times*, 4 June 1920.
58. *Irish Times*, 7 June 1920.
59. Townshend, *The British Campaign in Ireland*, p. 69–71; Kautt, *Ambushes and Armour*, p. 57–68.
60. Parkinson, *Belfast's Unholy War*, p. 43.
61. Farrell, *Northern Ireland*, p. 28–31; O'Connor, *A Labour History of Ireland*, p. 176. Estimates of the number of workers driven out of their jobs vary enormously. For instance, figures of between 1,000 and 1,800 are given for the number of women affected: Parkinson, *Belfast's Unholy War*, p. 37–8; Irish White Cross Report, 1922.
62. However, another Northerner, Seán MacEntee, took the opposite tack, arguing that his native Belfast had to be 'taught that it depends on Ireland': Parkinson, *Belfast's Unholy War*, p. 73.
63. Parkinson, *Belfast's Unholy War*, p. 76.
64. Mitchell, *Revolutionary Government in Ireland*, p. 166–72; Farrell, *Northern Ireland*, p. 28; O'Connor, *A Labour History of Ireland*, p. 174–80; Bureau of Military History, Witness Statements, WS 944 (Michael Staines); minutes of Bank of Ireland, Dublin Board, 14 September 1920 and 23 February 1921, Bank of Ireland Archive, V-H-00128; Parkinson, *Belfast's Unholy War*.
65. Dublin Corporation Minutes, 9 August 1920; *Irish Times*, 10 August 1920.
66. *Irish Times* and *Irish Independent*, 10 August 1920.
67. Whether this made off-duty soldiers more or less susceptible to attack is debatable; see chap. 6 below.
68. *Irish Independent*, 16 and 28 September 1920; Minutes, Bank of Ireland, Dublin Board, 27 September 1920, Bank of Ireland Archive, V-H-000128.
69. MacDonagh was a Sinn Féin alderman for Rathmines and a TD for North Tipperary as well as a member of Dublin Corporation.
70. William Sears was a radical journalist and Sinn Féin MP for South Mayo. Like MacDonagh, he lived in Rathmines and had been elected to the town council. Unlike MacDonagh, however, he was not a member of Dublin Corporation.
71. *Irish Independent*, 7 October and 11 November 1920. Some teachers did not agree, and schools had remained closed when they refused to take the oath to the Republic as a condition of resuming their duties.
72. Minutes of the Provisional Committee of the IES&FTU, 29 May, 21 June, 31 August and 11 September 1920. It was proposed that Number 1 Branch would meet in 41 Parnell Square, where the Executive Committee still sat, that premises would have to be found in Inchicore for Number 2 Branch, that Number 3 Branch would meet in the Colmcille Hall, where the office for unemployed members seeking positions

was, and that Number 4 Branch would meet in Oriel Hall and Number 5 Branch in Great Brunswick Street (Pearse Street). All these premises had strong associations with the independence movement.

73. James O'Connor also worked for Sinn Féin, collecting evidence and witnesses to testify before the American Commission on Irish Independence: Mitchell, *Revolutionary Government in Ireland*, p. 199.

74. Minutes of the Executive Committee of the IES&FTU, 1 and 5 October and 1 and 17 November 1920, Archives of the TEEU.

75. Minutes of the Executive Committee of the IES&FTU, 10, 13 and 20 November 1920, Archives of the TEEU.

76. It was also a precursor of the present-day Labour Court and Labour Relations Commission.

77. Dáil Éireann, Ministry of Labour files, National Archives, DE 2/5; Marreco, *The Rebel Countess*, p. 251–2; Mitchell, *Labour in Irish Politics*, p. 116; van Voris, *Constance de Markievicz*, p. 285; Mitchell, *Revolutionary Government in Ireland*, p. 161–2. Conciliation boards were also established to mediate between local authorities and unions. However, these proved less successful, as Sinn Féin dominated the councils and trade union militants had exaggerated expectations of each other's capacity to see the other side of the argument: Sheehan, *Fighting for Dublin*, p. 20–21.

Chapter 6: 'We cannot have a one sided war' (p. 146–83)

1. Mitchell, *Revolutionary Government in Ireland*, p. 154; Macardle, *The Irish Republic*, p. 352. Four county councils remained under Unionist control: Antrim, Armagh, Derry and Down. They also retained control of 19 rural district councils in Ulster, while Sinn Féin controlled 36.

2. Quoted by Mitchell in *Revolutionary Government in Ireland*, p. 159.

3. In this matter unionist teachers showed far more principle than their republican counterparts, such as Hanna Sheehy Skeffington, who had taken the oath to the Crown for years: Irish White Cross Report, 1922, p. 25.

4. Dublin Corporation Minutes, 13 September 1920.

5. Bank of Ireland Board Papers, Bank of Ireland Archive, 1/0655; Oliver MacDonagh, 'The Victorian bank,' in Lyons, *Bank of Ireland*, p. 48; Hall, *The Bank of Ireland*, p. 333.

6. *Irish Independent*, 27 October 1920. Another member of the judiciary accosted by the Auxiliaries and then ordered on his way was a retired police magistrate named Drury.

7. O'Flanagan, 'Dublin city in an age of war and revolution,' p. 125.

8. Dublin Corporation Minutes, 13 September 1920; Dublin Corporation, Report No. 183 f 1923. Alderman Thomas O'Reilly owned numbers 30, 32 and 35 Upper Rutland Street; the Right Honourable the Lord Mayor owned 43 and 44 Smithfield; Alderman William O'Connor owned 1 Coombe Street and Councillor James Moran owned 2 and 3 Foley Street. Two corporation officials also owned properties: John Byrne owned 73 and 74 Summer Hill and Christopher Kenny owned 108 Lower Dorset Street.

9. The St James's Walk development was renamed Ceannt Fort, in memory of the rebel commander in the south-west quadrant of the city.

10. Margaret McGarry, whose husband, Seán, represented Clontarf, voted to divert the funds to housing, but she represented Merchants' Quay ward.

11. Dublin Corporation Minutes, 15 November and 2 February 1921; Dublin Corporation, Report No. 99, 1920; *Irish Times*, 16 November 1920; Dublin Corporation Minutes, 21 February 1921.

12. *Irish Independent*, 2 November 1920.

13. Dublin Corporation Minutes, 3 May, 13 September and 15 November 1920; *Irish Times*, 14 September and 16 November 1920.

14. *Irish Times*, 3 November 1920.

15. Dublin Corporation Minutes, 4 October 1920; *Irish Independent* and *Irish Times*, 5 October 1920.

16. *Irish Times*, 15 December 1920.

17. Fingall, *Seventy Years Young*, p. 396. However, this did not save Plunkett's home in the Civil War, when it was burnt down by Irregulars: Fingall, *Seventy Years Young*, p. 416–23.

18. *Irish Independent*, 10 September 1920.

19. Kautt, *Ambushes and Armour*, p. 185–9; Sheehan, *Fighting for Dublin*, p. 33–5; Townshend, *The British Military Campaign in Ireland*, p. 52–3; West, *Horace Plunkett*, p. 189–91.

20. Hittle, *Michael Collins and the Anglo-Irish War*, p. 23–4. A former American intelligence officer, Hittle provides an interesting alternative assessment of the undercover war in Ireland to those of Irish and British historians.

21. Sheehan, *Fighting for Dublin*, p. 10–11. That it took so long for the British to uncover such an obvious place for rebel activity is an indication of their lack of background knowledge and understanding of the enemy.

22. Kautt, *Ambushes and Armour*, p. 185–9; Sheehan, *Fighting for Dublin*, p. 18–19, 35.

23. Mee, *Memoirs of Constable Jeremiah Mee*, p. 163–5.

24. Sheehan, *Fighting for Dublin*, p. 37. c Company was transferred from Cork after its losses at Kilmichael on 28 November 1920.

25. Hittle, *Michael Collins and the Anglo-Irish War*, p. 186–8. Hittle provides a critical but not unsympathetic portrait of 'O'.

26. Mark Sturgis, a senior member of Anderson's British team appointed to beef up the Dublin Castle administration, described Winter as 'clever as paint'. Winter 'looks like a little white snake and can do everything.'

27. Foy, *Michael Collins's Intelligence War*, and Dwyer, *The Squad and the Intelligence Operations of Michael Collins*, provide two of the best recent descriptions of this aspect of the War of Independence. For a worm's eye view of IRA intelligence in Dublin see Dalton, *With the Dublin Brigade*.

28. Hopkinson, *The Irish War of Independence*, p. 97; Michael Hopkinson, Introduction, in Henderson, *Frank Henderson's Easter Rising*, p. 6; Kautt, *Ambushes and Armour*, p. 190.

29. *Irish Times*, 30 July 1920.

30. Foy, *Michael Collins's Intelligence War*, p. 94; Dwyer, *The Squad and the Intelligence Operations of Michael Collins*, p. 123–4; *Irish Times*, 27 November 1919 and 2 August 1920; *Sunday Independent*, 1 August 1920. Ironically, Brooke made appeals for clemency on behalf of republican prisoners on humanitarian grounds.

31. *Irish Times*, 3 November 1920.

32. Board Minutes, 4 August 1920, Bank of Ireland Archive, V-H-000128. No debate about the shooting was recorded.

33. Indeed MacSwiney did not even consult his wife, Muriel, probably because he knew she would object. See Costello, *Enduring the Most*, p. 153.

34. Dublin Corporation Minutes, 6 September 1920. It was a significant achievement of Dublin Corporation that throughout the years of conflict, from 1914 onwards, the protocol of paying respects to the families of those who suffered loss or hardship was maintained, and was made all the more remarkable by the fact that it was the only city that experienced widespread fighting in 1916 and 1922, as well as in the War of Independence.

35. *Irish Times* and *Irish Independent*, 10 September 1920.

36. This helps to explain the excellent photographs published in the *Independent* the following day in the aftermath of the raid: Kenneally, *The Paper Wall*, p. 104. The IRA were not the only ones to benefit from sympathisers in the press: an *Irish Times* journalist tipped off British army contacts about Knightly. He was detained for seven months in Mountjoy but never convicted of an offence.

37. Family oral tradition. The IRA appears to have accepted that she acted in good faith.

38. There has been a great deal of controversy about the ages of these soldiers, especially the boy soldier Henry Washington, but it seems clear that he was younger than Barry. Although the Public Information Branch of the Dublin Castle administration tried to emphasise the youth of the soldiers killed, this secured little attention from the press. From poor working-class backgrounds, their relative obscurity made them less interesting than the handsome middle-class medical student.

39. O'Donovan, *No More Lonely Scaffolds*, chap. 9.

40. Doyle's successful nomination to the Corporation in 1917 instead of Tom Lawlor, the Trades Council nominee, was one of the seeds of the future split in the Labour Party in Dublin.

41. *Irish Times* and *Irish Independent*, 21–24 September 1920.

42. Crozier, *The Men I Killed*, p. 73.

43. *Irish Independent* and *Irish Times*, 23 September 1920; Foy, *Michael Collins's Intelligence War*, p. 131, 174.

44. Leeson, in *The Black and Tans*, p. 196, accepts at face value a claim by the Gormanston camp adjutant that it was local RIC members who sacked the town and that he had sent reinforcements to restore order. However, this self-serving letter was written in 1967 and is at variance with all contemporary eye-witness accounts. People praised Constable Magill of the local RIC for his efforts to restrain the Auxiliaries. Lesson argues more credibly that the publicity given to the sack of

Balbriggan might be responsible for the boost in recruitment figures for the RIC in the following weeks.

45. *Irish Times* and *Irish Independent*, 22 September 1920; Abbot, *Police Casualties in Ireland*, p. 122–3; Labour Party, *Report of the Labour Commission to Ireland*, p. 2, 38–9.

46. Macardle, *The Irish Republic*, p. 389–90.

47. *Irish Independent*, 6 December 1920. The best recent account is Ross O'Mahony, 'The sack of Balbriggan: Tit-for-tat terror,' in Fitzpatrick, *Terror in Ireland*.

48. *Irish Times* and *Irish Independent*, 22 September 1920; *Irish Independent*, 8 November 1920.

49. *Irish Independent*, 11 October 1920.

50. Murphy, *The Origins and Organisation of British Propaganda in Ireland*, p. 32–3. The battle over the figures continued throughout the war and long after. Murphy provides some of the best analysis of the figures from a republican viewpoint.

51. Dalton, *With the Dublin Brigade*, p. 118–20; interview with Paddy Weston, Lusk, Co. Dublin, 26 February 2012.

52. *Irish Independent*, 27 September 1920.

53. Ó Broin, *Just Like Yesterday*, p. 30.

54. Woodcock, *An Officer's Wife in Ireland*, p. 48–50.

55. Matthews, *Renegades*, chap. 10.

56. National Archives [London], CO 762/4/8. The woman was Mrs E. M. W. Biggs of Dromineer, Nenagh. She fled with her husband to England and subsequently received £6,000 in compensation—an enormous sum at the time. Remarkably, she said she did not need any more. Her mental and physical health never recovered.

57. Pike certainly paid the price for falling under suspicion as the tout who led the military to Fernside: he was shot in June 1921 outside his local pub, Fagan's in Drumcondra. He left a wife and seven children.

58. The story that five soldiers were killed at Fernside appears to stem from this comment, but it is possible that the officer was referring to the wounded corporal shot in the house and the two unidentified men in the garden as well as the dead officers.

59. Captain Jeune made his statement to the *Daily Telegraph* columnist T. E. Uttley in 1972, not long after another Irish Bloody Sunday, this time in Derry.

60. Fifty-two years later Jeune was still under the impression that Dan Breen had killed Major Smyth: Sheehan, *British Voices from the Irish War of Independence*, p. 86.

61. Neligan, *The Spy in The Castle*, p. 130–31.

62. The bodies of the officers concerned were all shipped home for burial, but no senior political or military figures attended the funerals.

63. Ryan, *Seán Treacy and the 3rd Tipperary Brigade*, p. 192.

Chapter 7: 'That night I should have understood, and forgiven, any act of reprisal by our men' (p. 184–213)

1. *Irish Independent*, 15–18 November 1920; Archbishop Walsh Papers, 1920, box 305.

2. Doherty, 'Kevin Barry and the Anglo-Irish propaganda war.'

3. *Irish Times* and *Irish Independent*, 2 November 1920.

4. Dublin Corporation, Report No. 36, 1920.
5. National Archives, DE/2/48; *Irish Times* and *Irish Independent*, 15 November and 15 December 11920; Mitchell, *Labour in Irish Politics*, p. 120–22.
6. *Irish Independent*, 10 November 1920.
7. See chap. 4. Mulcahy had an office in the chemistry corridor of the National University in Earlsfort Terrace, where he was registered as a medical student. Although its whereabouts were well known to students, staff and porters, it was never revealed to British intelligence.
8. Pinkman, *In the Legion of the Vanguard*, p. 31–2; Brady, *Ireland's Secret Service in England*, chap. 7. Although the British Department of Publicity and Public Information at Dublin Castle publicised proposals to use biological weapons, such as anthrax, they did not mention the more advanced plans for the Liverpool operation.
9. Andrews, *Dublin Made Me*, p. 153.
10. Woodcock, *An Officer's Wife in Ireland*, p. 61–9; Dalton, *With the Dublin Brigade*, p. 105–6; Foy, *Michael Collins's Intelligence War*, chap. 5.
11. Sheehan, *British Voices from the Irish War of Independence*, p. 89.
12. See chap. 3 above on the barmen's dispute. Paddy Moran and another Volunteer, Thomas Whelan, were subsequently arrested and hanged on the strength of identification evidence from British army personnel. Ironically, Teeling, against whom the strongest case existed, managed to escape from Kilmainham Gaol.
13. Sheehan, *Fighting for Dublin*, p. 144.
14. Crozier, *The Men I Killed*, p. 77.
15. Sturgis, *The Last Days of Dublin Castle*, p. 77.
16. The house subsequently became the home of the left-wing community TD Tony Gregory, who would himself be an active member of the republican movement for many years.
17. There is now a large literature on Bloody Sunday. See Jane Leonard's 'English dogs or poor devils?: The dead of Bloody Sunday morning' in Fitzpatrick, *Terror in Ireland*, for the most recent and detailed examination of the evidence. James Gleeson's *Bloody Sunday* still stands the test of time; despite some inaccuracies it gives the best feel for the period. The other sources I have used for the narrative here are the *Irish Independent* and *Irish Times*, 22–23 November 1920; Bureau of Military History, Witness Statements, ws 1687 (Harry Colley); Ernie O'Malley, 'Bloody Sunday,' in *Dublin's Fighting Story*; Foy, *Michael Collins's Intelligence War*, chap. 5; Dwyer, *The Squad and the Intelligence Operations of Michael Collins*, chap. 14 and 15; Carey, *Croke Park*, chap. 2; Woodcock, *An Officer's Wife in Ireland*, chap. 8; Andrews, *Dublin Made Me*, p. 150–57; and Hittle, *Michael Collins and the Anglo-Irish War*, chap. 9. For details about Joseph Traynor's death I am indebted to Noel Gregory.
18. Murphy, *The Origins and Organisation of British Propaganda in Ireland*, p. 32, 53; Ryan, *Michael Collins and the Women Who Spied for Ireland*, p. 46, 48; Foy, *Michael Collins's Intelligence War*, p. 48.
19. Bureau of Military History, Witness Statements, ws 1687 (Harry Colley).
20. Woodcock, *An Officer's Wife in Ireland*, p. 72–3.

21. Foy, *Michael Collins's Intelligence War*, p. 173.

22. *Irish Times*, 22 November 1920.

23. Kenneally, *The Paper Wall*, p. 92–3.

24. *Irish Independent*, 22 November 1920.

25. Mandle, *The Gaelic Athletic Association and Irish Nationalist Politics*, p. 192–4.

26. *Irish Times*, 26 November 1920; *Weekly Irish Times*, 28 November 1920; *Irish Independent*, 26 November; Gleeson, *Bloody Sunday*, chap. 12.

27. Mackay, *Michael Collins*, p. 181.

28. Bureau of Military History, Witness Statements, ws 441 (Lily Mernin), ws 715 (Frank Saurin); Ryan, *Michael Collins and the Women Who Spied for Ireland*, p. 46, 48; Foy, *Michael Collins's Intelligence War*, p. 48.

29. *Irish Independent*, 25 November 1920; Morrissey, *William O'Brien*, p. 194, 397. Among the venerable guests of honour at the reopening in 1965 were Éamon de Valera and William O'Brien.

30. *Irish Independent*, 6 December 1920; *Irish Times*, 11 December 1920.

31. Foy, *Michael Collins's Intelligence War*, p. 171–2; Woodcock, *An Officer's Wife in Ireland*, p. 77–85.

32. *Irish Independent*, 22 November 1920.

33. In his witness statement forty-four years later Alderman Michael Staines recalled the motion as, 'in effect, a vote of loyalty to the British Government': Bureau of Military History, Witness Statements, ws 943. Staines alternated with MacDonagh as director of the Belfast boycott.

34. Dublin Corporation Minutes, 6 December 1920; *Irish Independent* and *Irish Times*, 7 December 1920.

35. A graphic example of the interrogation methods of these officers is provided by Ernie O'Malley in *On Another Man's Wound*, chap. 18. He was questioned by them in January 1921. Both men were 'primarily responsible for abominable cruelties perpetrated on Irish prisoners in order to extract information … King is a degenerate; Hardy is a drunkard,' the *Irish Bulletin* wrote in April 1921 when it identified them as responsible for the 'murders, after brutal usage, of Richard McKee, Peadar Clancy and Conor Clune.' Quoted by Murphy in *The Origins and Organisation of British Propaganda in Ireland*, p. 60.

36. Lemass was released, as were P. T. Daly and John Farren. Lemass may have been arrested by mistake for his older brother, Noel, who was more senior in the Volunteers. An apprentice engineer with the Corporation, he had recently been released from Mountjoy. Dublin Corporation, Report No. 10, 1920.

37. *Weekly Irish Times*, 11 December 1920. Joe Clarke, caretaker of the Sinn Féin head office at 6 Harcourt Street and a survivor of the Battle of Mount Street Bridge in 1916, was described in the House of Commons by the Secretary of State for Ireland, Sir Hamar Greenwood, as a courier for Michael Collins. J. V. Lawlor was a captain in the Volunteers, as were Michael Lynch and James Brennan. Staines was identified, mistakenly, as a Volunteer captain.

38. Dublin Corporation Minutes, 14 December 1920; *Irish Times* and *Irish Independent*, 15 December 1920.

39. Dublin Corporation Minutes, 20 December 1920.

40. *Irish Independent,* 23 December 1920, 11 and 27 January 1921, 15 February 1921; *Irish Times,* 23 December 1920 and 8 November 1921; Clark and Fitzpatrick, *Serving the City,* p. 41–3; Ellmann, *James Joyce,* p. 34, 761 (n. 56).

Chapter 8: 'The Black and Tan guards are decent to us, and we thought we might as well order in a drink for them' (p. 214–45)

1. *Irish Independent,* 23 December 1920.

2. *Irish Times* and *Irish Independent,* 17 December 1920; Dublin Corporation Minutes, 7 June 1920.

3. Dublin Corporation Minutes, 3, 10, 17 and 26 January 1921; *Irish Times,* 18 January 1921.

4. Dublin Corporation Minutes, 10, 17 and 24 January 1921; *Irish Times,* 18 January 1921.

5. Dublin Corporation Minutes, 2 February 1920 and 14 February 1921; also Dublin Corporation, Report No. 22 and Report No. 82, 1921. See chap. 6 above regarding the attitude of the 'nationalist' banks to loans for current expenditure and for rent reviews. See O'Flanagan, 'Dublin city in an age of war and revolution,' p. 127, and O'Brien, *Dear Dirty Dublin,* chap. 5 and 9, for official British attitudes to the links between the housing problem and the political crisis.

6. Hogan, 'Payback.'

7. Dublin Corporation Minutes, 17 and 24 January 1921. The number of internees rose from 1,478 on 17 January 1921 to 4,454 by 12 July 1921, when the Truce was called.

8. The manager resigned in 1920 when the Workshops Committee reinstated an employee who had assaulted him. The unions were heavily represented on the committee, and it regularly interfered with operational activities. See Dublin Corporation Minutes, 7 June 1920 and following.

9. Dublin Corporation Minutes, 14 February 1921.

10. McManus, 'A beacon of light.'

11. Mitchell, *Revolutionary Government in Ireland,* p. 160.

12. Little was defeated in Rathmines by the Unionist candidate, Sir Maurice Dockrell.

13. Mitchell, *Revolutionary Government in Ireland,* p. 150; conversations with Larry McLoughlin; Bureau of Military History, Witness Statements, ws 1687 (Harry Colley), ws 340 (Oscar Traynor).

14. *Irish Independent,* 6 January 1921.

15. Conversations with Larry McLoughlin; see also Pinkman, *In the Legion of the Vanguard,* p. 30–32.

16. *Irish Times,* 13 January 1921.

17. Foy, *Michael Collins's Intelligence War,* p. 181. J. B. E. Hittle, in Michael Collins and the Anglo-Irish War, argues that it may have been a deliberate ploy by Collins to keep the British guessing whether Doran had been a double agent.

18. *Irish Times,* 10 May 1921.

19. *Irish Independent* and *Irish Times,* 23 February 1921.

20. Regular Minutes of the Dublin Board of the Bank of Ireland, 24 November 1921, 1 and 8 December 1921, 9 February 1921, 9 March 1921 and 14 May 1921, Bank of Ireland Archive, V-H-000128; *Irish Times*, 6, 7 and 29 July 1921; *Irish Independent*, 6 and 7 July 1921 and 16 January and 4 July 1922.

21. *Irish Times*, 15 December 1920. Captured mails were an important source of intelligence for the IRA.

22. *Irish Times* and *Irish Independent*, 13 and 14 January 1920.

23. Kautt, *Ambushes and Armour*, p. 194–9; Bureau of Military History, Witness Statements, ws 1687 (Harry Colley); Carey, *Hanged for Ireland*, chap. 3.

24. *Freeman's Journal*, 8 February 1921; *Irish Times*, 6 February 1921; see also Yeates, *Lockout*, especially chap. 7.

25. Moran was one of a number of Volunteers who took turns posing with the gun in uniform for photographs: Moran, *Executed for Ireland*, p. 54.

26. *Irish Times* and *Irish Independent*, 15 March 1921; Carey, *Hanged for Ireland*, chap. 2 and 3; Foy, *Michael Collins's Intelligence War*, chap. 5.

27. Abbott, *Police Casualties in Ireland*, p. 208–9; Carey, *Hanged for Ireland*, chap. 4; Kautt, *Ambushes and Armour*, p. 205–8; Phil Quinn, 'Battle of Brunswick Street,' in *Dublin's Fighting Story*, p. 159–61; *Irish Independent* and *Irish Times*, 14–18 March 1921. District-Inspector Gilbert Potter of the RIC, who had been taken prisoner during an ambush in Co. Tipperary, was offered in exchange for Traynor but was shot by the local IRA after Traynor's execution: Leeson, *The Black and Tans*, p. 148.

28. Dublin Corporation Minutes, 16 March 1921; Dublin Corporation, Report No. 60, 1921; *Irish Times*, 3 and 17 March 1921.

29. The biggest absolute increase was in Belfast, where unemployment rose from 12,863 to 34,226.

30. Much of this preparatory work could be carried out even with the bricklayers' strike in progress.

31. Dublin Corporation Minutes, 3 January 1921; Dublin Corporation, Report No. 165 and Report No. 219, 1921.

32. *Irish Times*, 12 March 1921. Some of these funds came from central government, but the lack of co-operation by the Commissioners added more than £14,000 to the Corporation's rates bill.

33. Dublin Corporation Minutes, 21 March 1921; Dublin Corporation, Report No. 14, 1921.

34. Dublin Corporation Minutes, 18 April 1921. One of those who voted against the extra funds was Hanna Sheehy Skeffington, one of the most left-wing Sinn Féin councillors. Her reasons are not recorded.

Chapter 9: 'Probably the stupidest thing the Sinn Fein ever did' (p. 246–81)

1. Kearns, *Dublin Tenement Life*, p. 172–3. Lyng was referring primarily to the 1930s and 40s rather than the 1920s; but little changed in the inner city before the end of the 1950s. In fact the number of pawnbrokers fell only slightly over the previous century: Dublin Corporation, Report No. 139, 1921; Dublin Corporation Minutes, 2 May and 3 October 1921; *Irish Times*, 3 May, 4 October and 8 November 1921.

2. Bureau of Military History, Witness Statements, ws 538 (Father Michael Browne, secretary to Archbishop Walsh).

3. Connolly's actual words in the *Workers' Republic* of 8 April 1916 were: 'The working class of Dublin stands for the cause of Ireland, and the cause of Ireland is the cause of a separate and distinct nationality.'

4. The school in Little Denmark Street no longer exists—nor indeed does the street. The author's father was a pupil, sent there for 'mitching'.

5. Morrissey, *William J. Walsh*, chap. 17; *Irish Times* and *Irish Independent*, 15 April 1921; Macready, *Annals of an Active Life*, vol. 2, p. 551–2; Bureau of Military History, Witness Statements, ws 538 (Father Michael Browne).

6. Dublin Corporation Minutes, 2 May and 6 June 1921.

7. There were only 514 motor vehicles registered in Dublin at the time.

8. See the raid on Eileen McGrane's home, p. 257 above.

9. Dwyer, *The Squad and the Intelligence Operations of Michael Collins*, p. 214–15.

10. *Irish Times* and *Irish Independent*, 13–16 April 1921; Dublin Corporation Minutes, 30 September 1920; Dwyer, *The Squad and the Intelligence Operations of Michael Collins*, p. 222–3; Foy, *Michael Collins's Intelligence War*, p. 180, 190; Mackay, *Michael Collins*, p. 178–81, 256; Hogan, *The Four Glorious Years*, p. 285–6; *Irish Bulletin*, vol. 4, no. 94, 23 May 1921. King returned to the army, served as a major of military police during the Second World War, and died in Gaza in November 1942. Hardy became a farmer and a successful novelist, served in the home army during the Second World War with the rank of major, and died in 1958.

11. *Irish Times*, 1 April 1921.

12. Ó Broin, *W. E. Wylie and the Irish Revolution*, p. 114–15; Buckland, *Irish Unionism, I*, p. 220–22, 238; Midleton, *Ireland—Dupe or Heroine*, p. 156–63. Both Wylie and Jellett had very successful careers in the new Irish Free State: the former became a High Court judge, the latter died as 'Father of the Bar'.

13. Robinson, *Memories*, p. 305–7.

14. Maurice Moore was the younger brother of George Moore, the novelist and joint founder of the Abbey Theatre with Lady Gregory and W. B. Yeats.

15. *Irish Independent*, 5 January and 1 and 22 February 1921; *Freeman's Journal*, 1 February 1921; *Irish Times*, 22 February 1921; Irwin, *Betrayal in Ireland*, p. 71–3.

16. Townshend, *The British Campaign in Ireland*, appendix XII, p. 223.

17. Hittle, *Michael Collins and the Anglo-Irish War*, p. 184, 204.

18. Sheehan, *Fighting for Dublin*, p. 56–7; Foy, *Michael Collins's Intelligence War*, p. 185–7.

19. In 1935 it was changed to its present title, Irish Countrywomen's Association.

20. Walsh, *Anglican Women in Dublin*, p. 101–2.

21. *Irish Times* and *Irish Independent*, 1 April 1921; West, *Horace Plunkett*, p. 102–3.

22. Dublin Corporation Minutes, 6 June; Dublin Corporation, Report No. 172, 1921; *Irish Times*, 6 and 7 June and 19 and 21 September 1921.

23. The bricklayers' strike had ended on 13 June (see chap. 8 above), which meant that this impediment to slum clearance had ended.

24. Robinson, *Memories*, p. 307–8.

25. Dublin Corporation Minutes, 18 April and 6 June 1921.
26. Other evacuated stations burnt included those at Ballybrack, Stepaside and Dean's Grange.
27. *Freeman's Journal*, 27 January 1921; *Irish Times* and *Irish Independent*, 15–18 March 1921; *Irish Times*, 9 June 1921; *Irish Independent*, 9 July 1921.
28. Irwin, *Betrayal in Ireland*, p. 49. Irwin felt that one of the worst atrocities of the Troubles was the derailing of a train carrying the 8th Hussars back from the ceremonial welcome for King George V in Belfast to the Curragh, after which dozens of injured horses had to be put down.
29. Bureau of Military History, Witness Statements, ws 1687 (Harry Colley); Sheehan, *Fighting for Dublin*, p. 50–51.
30. Dublin Corporation Minutes, 21 March and 18 April 1921; *Irish Times* and *Irish Independent*, 22 March and 19 April 1921; Sheehan, *Fighting for Dublin*, p. 49.
31. Dublin Corporation Minutes, 31 January and 21 March 1921; *Irish Times*, 22 March and 1 April 1921; *Irish Independent*, 1 April 1921.
32. Dublin Corporation Minutes, 17 May 1921; *Irish Times*, 18 May 1921.
33. It must be added that historians such as Michael Foy, T. Ryle Dwyer and J. B. E. Hittle have dramatically increased our knowledge and understanding of the intelligence war.
34. Matthews, *Renegades*, p. 260.
35. Bureau of Military History, Witness Statements, ws 340 (Oscar Traynor); IRA Papers, GHQ and 2nd Battalion, Dublin, 1921, National Library of Ireland, ms. 901; Hopkinson, *The Irish War of Independence*, p. 102; Sheehan, *Fighting for Dublin*, p. 47; Jim Donnelly, 'Attack on RAF units at Red Cow Inn,' in *Dublin's Fighting Story*, p. 161–2.
36. Quotations from *Freeman's Journal* taken from Carey, *Hanged for Ireland*, p. 150–52.
37. Walsh, *Anglican Women in Dublin*, p. 47. She provides by far the best summary of the complex relationships between Protestant nationalist women and the independence movement.
38. Bi-Weekly Precis of Reports of Important Occurrences in DMP Area, Bureau of Military History.
39. Bi-Weekly Precis of Reports of Important Occurrences in DMP Area, Bureau of Military History; *Freeman's Journal*, *Irish Independent* and *Irish Times*, 13 May 1921.
40. *Irish Times*, 9 May 1921.
41. They consisted of two fellows of Trinity College, E. H. Alton and Prof. W. E. Thrift, Gerald Fitzgibbon KC and Sir James Craig MD, who maintained the pre-eminence of the law and medicine in the university's electoral tradition.
42. *Freeman's Journal*, *Irish Independent* and *Irish Times*, 14 May 1921.
43. Kautt, *Ambushes and Armour*, p. 210–14.
44. Kerosene (at that time generally called paraffin oil) was used rather than petrol on the advice of IRA members in Dublin Fire Brigade, as it would allow more time to evacuate the staff from the building.

45. Letter from John Dillon to T. P. O'Connor, 24 May 1921, quoted by Lyons in *John Dillon*, p. 467.

46. Evidence given by relatives of the dead men before the British military inquiry tended to vary significantly from that in initial press reports. It is hard at this point in time to verify which is more accurate.

47. Bureau of Military History, Witness Statements, WS 340 (Oscar Traynor); 'The burning of the Custom House,' in *Dublin's Fighting Story*, p. 163–8; Foy, *Michael Collins's Intelligence War*, p. 214–18; Geraghty and Whitehead, *The Dublin Fire Brigade*, p. 168–70; Sheehan, *Fighting for Dublin*, p. 53–4; Robinson, *Memories*, p. 310–15; *Irish Independent* and *Irish Times*, 26–29 May 1921.

48. See Anne Dolan, 'The shadow of a great fear: Terror and revolutionary Ireland,' in Fitzpatrick, *Terror in Ireland*, for a civilian viewpoint on the Mayfair Hotel shootings. Dolan makes the point that the perpetrators of attacks were also traumatised, and that the effects could last for years.

49. More than 650 Thompson sub-machine guns acquired by Harry Boland, the Irish Republic's envoy in the United States, were impounded in New York. Some 30 were successfully shipped to Cork and 51 to Dublin before the Truce; another 158 reached the IRA after being released by the US authorities in 1925: Fitzpatrick, *Harry Boland's Irish Revolution*, p. 213–15.

50. *Irish Independent* and *Irish Times*, 4 June 1921; *Irish Bulletin*, vol. 5, no. 11; Foy, *Michael Collins's Intelligence War*, p. 219–21; Sheehan, *Fighting for Dublin*, p. 58–9, 64–5, appendix III.

51. Perkins, *A Very British Strike*, p. 18.

52. *Irish Times*, 7 June 1921; *Irish Independent*, 7 and 30 June 1921; Dublin Corporation Minutes, 6 and 27 June 1921; Dublin Corporation, Report No. 152, 1921; Rigney, *Trains, Coal and Turf*, table 2, p. 11.

53. Dublin Corporation Minutes, 6 June 1921; *Irish Times*, 7 June 1921; Craig, *Dublin*, p. 102–3. See Whelan, *Reinventing Modern Dublin*, for a full discussion of the issues and earlier efforts to rename the thoroughfare.

Chapter 10: 'In the evening the Tricolour was everywhere … not in the mean streets only but on proud houses in professional quarters' (p. 282–96)

1. *Irish Independent*, 5 July 1921.

2. Bureau of Military History, Witness Statements, WS 465 (Mary O'Sullivan); *Irish Independent* and *Irish Times*, 5 and 8 July 1921; Dublin Corporation Minutes, 4 July 1921.

3. Macready, *Annals of an Active Life*, vol. 2, p. 571–3; *Irish Times*, 9 July 1921.

4. *Irish Times* and *Irish Independent*, 8–12 July.

5. Sheehan, *Fighting for Dublin*, p. 69–70.

6. Lawlor was no relation of Alderman Tom Lawlor (Labour), a fact that both men were at pains to point out.

7. Dublin Corporation Minutes, 2 May and 29 August 1921; Dublin Corporation, Report No. 153; *Irish Times*, 30 August 1921 and 7 March 1922. P. T. Daly had been a member of the Supreme Council of the IRB in his younger days, before his

conversion to socialism. Allan was entitled to a pension of £316 a year under British legislation or £362 under the proposed reorganisation structures. The councillors voted him a pension of £603 a year.

8.   Dublin Corporation Minutes, 7 June 1920 and 6 December 1921.

9.   The scale of sectarian violence in rural Ireland is a contentious issue. See Moffitt, 'The Protestant experience of revolution.'

10. Mitchell, *Revolutionary Government in Ireland*, p. 154–66; editorial, *Irish Times*, 2 September 1920.

11. Marreco, *The Rebel Countess*, p. 249–52; Mee, *Memoirs of Constable Jeremiah Mee*, p. 156–8.

12. Ó Broin, *Just Like Yesterday*, p. 43.

13. It might help explain Collins's uncharacteristic generosity with Dáil Éireann funds. The controversy continues to rage: see, for instance, Brendan Clifford, Introduction to O'Connor, *With Michael Collins in the Fight for Irish Freedom*, p. 19–20; Ryan, *Michael Collins and the Women Who Spied for Ireland*, p. 167. Moya Llewellyn Davies was the daughter of James O'Connor, a former Fenian, journalist and Irish Party MP.

14. National Archives, DE/2/122.

15. Dublin Corporation Minutes, 4 April and 4 June 1921.

16. Dublin Corporation Minutes, 6 June 1921.

17. Mitchell, *Revolutionary Ireland*, p. 166–72; Parkinson, *Belfast's Holy War*, p. 77.

18. *Irish Independent*, 11 July 1921.

SELECT BIBLIOGRAPHY

The bibliography includes only sources cited in the text or in the notes.

Primary sources
American Commission on Conditions in Ireland, National Library of Ireland
Archbishop Walsh Papers, Laity File, Dublin Diocesan Archives
Bank of Ireland Archive
Cameron Papers, Royal College of Surgeons in Ireland, Dublin
Church of Ireland, 'Stained glass in the Church of Ireland', at www.gloine.ie
Colonial Office files
Dáil Éireann Reports, 1919–21, National Archives
Dáil Éireann, Minutes of Proceedings, 1919–1921, Dublin: Stationery Office
Department of the Taoiseach files, National Archives
Dublin Corporation Minutes and Reports, 1911–22, Dublin Civic Archives
Dublin Metropolitan Police, Bi-Weekly Precis of Reports of Important Occurrences in
DMP Area, 1921, Bureau of Military History, Dublin
Guinness Archive, Dublin
IRA GHQ and Dublin 2nd Battalion Papers, National Library of Ireland
Irish Engineering, Shipbuilding and Foundry Workers' Trade Union Archive (Technical,
Engineering and Electrical Union), Dublin
Laurence O'Neill Papers, National Library of Ireland
Masonic Grand Lodge of Free and Accepted Masons, Ireland
National Society for the Prevention of Cruelty to Children, Annual Reports, 1911–24,
National Library of Ireland
Thomas Ashe Papers, National Library of Ireland
Witness Statements, Bureau of Military History, Dublin.

Newspapers and periodicals
Comment (Dublin Bus Branch, SIPTU)
Cuala News
Evening Telegraph
Freeman's Journal
Irish Bulletin
Irish Independent
Irish Times
Weekly Irish Times

Articles in periodicals, and papers delivered at seminars and conferences

Doherty, M. A., 'Kevin Barry and the Anglo-Irish propaganda war,' *Irish Historical Studies*, November 2000.

Hogan, John, 'Payback: The Dublin bricklayers' strike, 1920–21,' *Saothar*, 35, 2010.

Howell, Philip, 'The politics of prostitution in the Irish Free State', *Irish Historical Studies*, May 2003.

Howell, Philip, 'The politics of prostitution in the Irish Free State: A response to Susannah Riordan,' *Irish Historical Studies*, November 2007.

McManus, Ruth, 'A Beacon of Light'—Canon Hall and St Barnabas PUS,' paper delivered at East Wall History Week, Dublin, 16 October 2011.

Moffitt, Miriam, 'The Protestant experience of revolution: The fate of the Unionist community in rural Ireland, 1912–27,' paper given at Centre for Contemporary Irish History, Trinity College, Dublin, 20 October 2010.

O'Flanagan, Neil, 'Dublin city in an age of war and revolution, 1914–24,' MA thesis, University College, Dublin, 1985.

Riordan, Susannah, 'Venereal disease in the Irish Free State: The politics of public health,' *Irish Historical Studies*, May 2007.

Yeates, Pádraig, 'Craft workers during the Irish revolution, 1919–1922,' *Saothar*, 33, 2008.

Books

Abbot, Richard, *Police Casualties in Ireland, 1919–1922*, Cork: Mercier Press, 2000.

Andrews, C. S., *Dublin Made Me: An Autobiography*, Dublin and Cork: Mercier Press, 1979.

Bartlett, Thomas, and Jeffrey, Keith (eds.), *A Military History of Ireland*, Cambridge: Cambridge University Press, 1996.

Brady, Edward M., *Ireland's Secret Service in England*, Dublin: Talbot Press [1928].

Buckland, Patrick, *Irish Unionism, 1: The Anglo-Irish and the New Ireland, 1885 to 1922*, Dublin, Gill & Macmillan, 1972.

Campbell, Colm, *Emergency Law in Ireland, 1918–1925*, Oxford: Clarendon Press, 1994.

Carden, Sheila, *The Alderman: Alderman Tom Kelly (1868–1942) and Dublin Corporation*, Dublin: Dublin City Council, 2007.

Carey, Tim, *Croke Park: A History*, Cork: Collins Press, 2004.

Carey, Tim, *Hanged for Ireland: 'The Forgotten Ten' Executed 1920–21*, Dublin: Blackwater Press, 2001.

Carey, Tim, *Mountjoy: The Story of a Prison*, Cork: Collins Press, 2000.

Clark, Mary, and Fitzpatrick, Hugh, *Serving the City: The Dublin City Managers and Town Clerks, 1230–2006*, Dublin: Dublin City Council, 2006.

Clarkson, J. Dunsmore, *Labour and Nationalism in Ireland*, New York: Columbia University Press, 1925, reprinted 1978.

Cody, Séamus, O'Dowd, John, and Rigney, Peter, *The Parliament of Labour: 100 Years of the Dublin Council of Trade Unions*, Dublin: Dublin Council of Trade Unions, 1986.

Comerford, Máire, *The First Dáil*, Dublin: Joe Clarke, 1969.

Connell, Joseph E. A., *Where's Where in Dublin: A Directory of Historic Locations*, Dublin: Dublin City Council, 2006.

Costello, Francis J., *Enduring the Most: The Life and Death of Terence MacSwiney*, Dingle: Brandon Press, 1995.

Craig, Maurice, *Dublin, 1660–1860*, Dublin: Allen Figgis, 1969.

Crozier, Frank P. (Brendan Clifford, ed.), *The Men I Killed* [1937], Belfast: Athol Books, 2002.

Cruise O'Brien, Conor (ed.), *The Shaping of Modern Ireland*, London: Routledge and Kegan Paul, 1960.

Dalton, Charles, *With the Dublin Brigade (1917–1921)*, London: Peter Davies, 1929.

Dublin's Fighting Story, 1913–1921: Told by the Men Who Made It, Tralee: Kerryman [c. 1948].

Dwyer, T. Ryle, *The Squad and the Intelligence Operations of Michael Collins*, Cork: Mercier Press, 2005.

Eagar, J. F., *The Inception and Early History of the Irish Bank Officials' Association*, Dublin: Robert T. White, 1920.

Ellmann, Richard, *James Joyce*, London: Oxford University Press, 1959.

Farrell, Brian, *The Founding of Dáil Éireann: Parliament and Nation-Building*, Dublin, Gill & Macmillan, 1971.

Farrell, Michael, *Northern Ireland: The Orange State*, London, Pluto Press, 1970.

Ferriter, Diarmaid, *The Transformation of Ireland, 1900–2000*, London: Profile Books, 2004.

Fingall, Elizabeth Mary Margaret Burke Plunkett, Countess of, *Seventy Years Young: Memories of Elizabeth, Countess of Fingall* (as told to Pamela Hinkson), London: Collins, 1937; reprinted Dublin: Lilliput Press, 1995.

Fitzpatrick, David, *Harry Boland's Irish Revolution*, Cork: Cork University Press, 2003.

Fitzpatrick, David (ed.), *Terror in Ireland, 1916–1923: Trinity History Workshop*, Dublin: Lilliput Press, 2012.

Foy, Michael T., *Michael Collins's Intelligence War: The Struggle between the British and the IRA, 1919–1921*, Stroud (Glos.): Sutton Publishing, 2006.

Gallagher, Frank, *Days of Fear* [1928], Cork: Mercier Press, 1967.

Gaughan, J. Anthony, *Thomas Johnson, 1872–1963: First Leader of the Labour Party in Dáil Éireann*, Dublin: Kingdom Books, 1980.

Geraghty, Tom, and Whitehead, Trevor, *The Dublin Fire Brigade: A History of the Brigade, the Fires and the Emergencies*, Dublin: Dublin City Council, 2004.

Gleeson, James Joseph, *Bloody Sunday*, London: Four Square Press, 1962.

Griffith, Kenneth, and O'Grady, Timothy E., *Curious Journey: An Oral History of Ireland's Unfinished Revolution*, London: Hutchinson, 1982.

Hall, F. G., *The Bank of Ireland, 1783–1946*, Dublin: Hodges Figgis, 1949.

Henderson, Frank (Michael Hopkinson, ed.), *Frank Henderson's Easter Rising: Recollections of a Dublin Volunteer*, Cork: Cork University Press, 1998.

Herlihy, Jim, *The Dublin Metropolitan Police: A Complete Alphabetical List of Officers and Men, 1836–1925*, Dublin: Four Courts Press, 2001.

Hittle, J. B. E., *Michael Collins and the Anglo-Irish War: Britain's Counterinsurgency Failure*, Dulles (Va.): Potomac Books, 2011.

Hogan, David [Frank Gallagher], *The Four Glorious Years*, Dublin: Irish Press, 1953.

Hopkinson, Michael, *The Irish War of Independence*, Dublin: Gill & Macmillan, 2002.

Irwin, Wilmot, *Betrayal in Ireland: An Eye-Witness Record of the Tragic and Terrible Years of Revolution and Civil War in Ireland, 1916–24*, Belfast: Northern Whig [1966].

Kautt, William H., *Ambushes and Armour: The Irish Rebellion, 1919–1921*, Dublin: Irish Academic Press, 2010.

Kearns, Kevin C., *Dublin Tenement Life: An Oral History*, Dublin: Gill & Macmillan, 1994.

Kee, Robert, *The Green Flag: A History of Irish Nationalism*, London: Weidenfeld and Nicholson, 1972.

Kenneally, Ian, *The Paper Wall: Newspapers and Propaganda in Ireland, 1919–1921*, Cork: Collins Press, 2008.

Kissane, Bill, *The Politics of the Irish Civil War*, Oxford University Press, 2005.

Kostick, Conor, *Revolution in Ireland, 1917–1923*, London: Pluto Press, 1996.

Labour Party, *Report of the Labour Commission to Ireland*, London: Labour Party [1921].

Laffan, Michael, *The Resurrection of Ireland: The Sinn Féin Party, 1916–1923*, Cambridge: Cambridge University Press, 1999.

Leeson, D. M., *The Black and Tans: British Police and Auxiliaries in the Irish War of Independence*, Oxford: Oxford University Press, 2011.

Luddy, Maria, *Prostitution and Irish Society, 1800–1940*, Cambridge: Cambridge University Press, 2007.

Luddy, Maria, *Women and Philanthropy in Nineteenth-Century Ireland*, Cambridge: Cambridge University Press, 1995.

Lyons, F. S. L., *Bank of Ireland, 1783–1983: Bicentenary Essays*, Dublin: Gill & Macmillan, 1983.

Lyons, F. S. L., *John Dillon: A Biography*, London: Routledge and Kegan Paul, 1968.

Lysaght, D. R. O'Connor, *The Making of Northern Ireland*, Dublin: Citizens' Committee [c. 1969].

Macardle, Dorothy, *The Irish Republic: A Documented Chronicle of the Anglo-Irish Conflict and the Partitioning of Ireland, with a Detailed Account of the Period 1916–1923*, Dublin: Irish Press, 1951.

McBride, Lawrence W., *The Greening of Dublin Castle: The Transformation of Bureaucratic and Judicial Personnel in Ireland, 1892–1922*, Washington: Catholic University of America Press, 1991.

McDowell, R. B., *Crisis and Decline: The Fate of Southern Unionists*, Dublin: Lilliput Press, 1997.

Mackay, James A., *Michael Collins: A Life*, Edinburgh: Mainstream, 1996.

McManus, Ruth, *Dublin, 1910–1940: Shaping the City and Suburbs*, Dublin: Four Courts Press, 2002.

Macready, Sir Nevil, *Annals of an Active Life*, London: Hutchinson [1924].

Maguire, Martin, *Servants to the Public: A History of the Local Government and Public Services Union, 1901–1990*, Dublin: Institute of Public Administration, 1998.

Mandle, W. F., *The Gaelic Athletic Association and Irish Nationalist Politics, 1884–1924*, Dublin: Gill & Macmillan, 1987.

Marreco, Anne, *The Rebel Countess: The Life and Times of Constance Markievicz*, London: Corgi Books, 1967.

Matthews, Ann, *Renegades: Irish Republican Women, 1900–1922*, Cork: Mercier Press, 2010.

Mee, Jeremiah (J. Anthony Gaughan, ed.), *Memoirs of Constable Jeremiah Mee*, Dublin: Anvil Books, 1975.

Midleton, William St John Fremantle Brodrick, Earl of, *Ireland—Dupe or Heroine*, London: William Heinemann [1932].

Mitchell, Arthur, *Labour in Irish Politics*, Dublin: Irish University Press, 1974.

Mitchell, Arthur, *Revolutionary Government in Ireland: Dáil Éireann, 1919–22*, Dublin: Gill & Macmillan, 1995.

Moran, May, *Executed for Ireland: The Patrick Moran Story*, Cork: Mercier Press, 2010.

Morrissey, Thomas J., *William J. Walsh, Archbishop of Dublin, 1841–1921: No Uncertain Voice*, Dublin: Four Courts Press, 2000.

Morrissey, Thomas J., *William Martin Murphy*, Dundalk: Dundalgan Press, for the Historical Association of Ireland, 1997.

Morrissey, Thomas J., *William O'Brien, 1881–1968: Socialist, Republican, Dáil Deputy, Editor and Trade Union Leader*, Dublin: Four Courts Press, 2007.

Mulholland, Marie, *The Politics and Relationships of Kathleen Lynn*, Dublin: Woodfield Press, 2002.

Murphy, Brian P., *The Origins and Organisation of British Propaganda in Ireland, 1920*, Cork: Aubane Historical Society, 2006.

Neligan, David, *The Spy in the Castle*, London: MacGibbon and Kee, 1968.

Ó Broin, Leon, *Just Like Yesterday: An Autobiography*, Dublin: Gill & Macmillan [c. 1986].

Ó Broin, Leon, *W. E. Wylie and the Irish Revolution, 1916–1921*, Dublin: Gill & Macmillan, 1989.

O'Brien, Joseph V., *Dear, Dirty Dublin: A City in Distress, 1899–1916*, Berkeley (Calif.): University of California Press, 1982.

O'Brien, William X. (as told to Edward MacLysaght), *Forth the Banners Go: Reminiscences of William O'Brien*, Dublin: Three Candles, 1969.

O'Connor, Batt (Brendan Clifford, ed.), *With Michael Collins in the Fight for Irish Independence*, Millstreet (Co. Cork): Aubane Historical Society, 2004.

O'Connor, Emmet, *A Labour History of Ireland, 1824–1960*, Dublin: Gill & Macmillan, 1992.

O'Donoghue, Florence, *No Other Law: The Story of Liam Lynch and the Irish Republican Army, 1916–1923*, Dublin: Irish Press [1954].

O'Donovan, Dónal, *No More Lonely Scaffolds: Kevin Barry and His Time*, Dublin: Glendale Press, 1989.

O'Halpin, Eunan, *The Decline of the Union: British Government in Ireland, 1982–1920*, Dublin: Gill & Macmillan, 1997.

Ó hÓgartaigh, Margaret, *Kathleen Lynn: Irishwoman, Patriot, Doctor*, Dublin: Irish Academic Press, 2006.

O'Malley, Ernie, *On Another Man's Wound*, London: Four Square Books, 1961.

Ó Móráin, Pádraig, *Irish Association of Directors of Nursing and Midwifery, 1902–2004*, Dublin: IADNM, 2004.

Parkinson, Alan F., *Belfast's Unholy War: The Troubles of the 1920s*, Dublin: Four Courts Press, 2004.

Perkins, Anne, *A Very British Strike: 3 May to 12 May 1926*, London: Pan Books, 2006.

Pinkman, John A. (Francis E. Maguire, ed.), *In the Legion of the Vanguard*, Cork: Mercier Press, 1998.

Rebel Cork's Fighting Story, 1916–21: Told by the Men Who Made It, Tralee: Kerryman, 1947.

Rigney, Peter, *Trains, Coal and Turf: Transport in Emergency Ireland*, Dublin: Irish Academic Press, 2010.

Robinson, Henry Augustus, *Memories, Wise and Otherwise*, London: Cassell, 1923.

Ryan, Annie, *Comrades: Inside the War of Independence*, Dublin: Liberties Press, 2007.

Ryan, Desmond, *Seán Treacy and the 3rd Tipperary Brigade*, Tralee: Anvil Books [c. 1945].

Ryan, Meda, *Michael Collins and the Women Who Spied for Ireland*, Cork: Mercier Press, 1996.

[Shaw, Henry], *New City Pictorial Directory, 1850 ...* Dublin: Henry Shaw, 1850 (reprinted as *The Dublin Pictorial Guide and Directory of 1850*, Belfast: Friar's Bush Press, 1988).

Sheehan, William, *A Hard Local War: The British Army and the Guerrilla War in Cork, 1919–1921*, Stroud (Glos.): Spellmount Press, 2011.

Sheehan, William, *Fighting for Dublin: The British Battle for Dublin, 1919–1921*, Cork: Collins Press, 2007.

Sheehan, William (ed.), *British Voices from the Irish War of Independence, 1918–1921: The Words of British Servicemen Who Were There*, Cork: Collins Press, 2005.

Smellie, John, *Shipbuilding and Repairing in Dublin, 1901–1923: A Record of Work Carried Out by the Dublin Dockyard Company, 1901–1923*, Glasgow: McCorquodale and Company, [1935].

Sturgis, Mark (Michael Hopkinson, ed.), *The Last Days of Dublin Castle: The Diaries of Mark Sturgis*, Dublin: Irish Academic Press, 1999.

Townshend, Charles, *The British Campaign in Ireland, 1919–1921: The Development of Political and Military Forces*, Oxford: Oxford University Press, 1975.

van Voris, Jacqueline, *Constance de Markievicz in the Cause of Ireland*, Amherst (Mass.): University of Massachusetts Press, 1967.

Walsh, Oonagh, *Anglican Women in Dublin: Philanthropy, Politics and Education in the Early Twentieth Century*, Dublin: UCD Press, 2005.

West, Trevor, *Horace Plunkett: Co-Operation and Politics: An Irish Biography*, Washington: Catholic University of America Press, 1986.

Whelan, Yvonne, *Reinventing Modern Dublin: Streetscape, Iconography and the Politics of Identity*, Dublin: UCD Press, 2003.

White, J. R., *Misfit: An Autobiography*, London: Jonathan Cape 1930.

Wolfe, Humbert, *Labour Supply and Regulation*, Oxford: Clarendon Press, 1923.

[Woodcock, Caroline], *Experiences of an Officer's Wife in Ireland* [1921], London and Dublin: Parkgate Publications (Tim Pat Coogan, ed.), 1994.

Yeates, Pádraig, *A City in Wartime: Dublin, 1914–1918*, Dublin: Gill & Macmillan, 2011.

Yeates, Pádraig, *Lockout: Dublin, 1913*, Dublin: Gill & Macmillan, 2000.

INDEX